Lua Getsinger

Herald of the Covenant

Lua Getsinger

Herald of the Covenant

by

Velda Piff Metalmann

George Ronald
Oxford

GEORGE RONALD, Publisher
46 High Street, Kidlington, Oxford OX5 2DN

British Library Cataloguing in Publication Data

*A catalogue record for this book is available
from the British Library*

ISBN 0-85398-416-6

Typeset by ComputerCraft, Knoxville, Tennessee, USA
Printed and bound in Great Britain by
Biddles Ltd, Guildford and King's Lynn

Contents

To Christoph

Preface

When the European Task Force for Women asked me to give a talk on Lua Getsinger at their second women's seminar in De Poort, Holland, I was amazed to discover how little we knew about this renowned believer and teacher of the Bahá'í Faith whose tireless travels from east to west in the United States, in Europe and in India attracted hundreds to the love of their Lord. Only nineteen years were left to her after her recognition of Bahá'u'lláh.

The Flame by William Sears and Robert Quigley, published by George Ronald, is a charming yet slender volume, but more of a book to promote the teachings of the Bahá'í Faith than to explain Lua Getsinger's life. The voluminous pages of *Star of the West*, the magazine published in America by the Bahá'ís for some decades starting in 1910, contained very little about Lua, even during the most active years of her service. For example, none of the speeches she gave in India were printed, though some speeches by Mrs. Stannard, her companion in that country, and Edward Getsinger were. "Why?" was my question.

"Why is it," I asked myself, "that so little is known of the one called 'Mother Teacher of the West' and 'Herald of the Covenant'? When so many Bahá'ís around the world name their daughters 'Lua' why do we know so little about her?"

An eloquent tribute to Lua Getsinger was written by that eminent believer, May Maxwell, a disciple of 'Abdu'l-Bahá, and the mother of the Hand of the Cause of God, Amatu'l-Bahá Rúḥíyyih Khánum.

"Lua has ascended to the Supreme Concourse" – those are the words I heard. For hours I have seen Lua, the woman, the child, all love and tenderness, dying far away – alone. Far from the land where she sowed the seed from the Atlantic to the Pacific – from the land where she arose like the dawning star heralding the light of Bahá'u'lláh in those days when the Occident lay frozen in the grasp of materialism – and far from all those who should have loved her and cherished her as a priceless gift from God . . .

Then I saw no longer the bruised and broken reed trodden and crushed to earth. I saw the victorious Lua, majestic in her death – the Lua who shall live through all ages – who shall shine from the horizon of eternity upon the world when all the veils which have hidden her today from mortal eyes have been burned away. As Kurat-ul-Ayn was the Trumpet of the Dawn in the Orient in the Day of Bahá'u'lláh, so Lua Aurora shall wave forever and ever the Banner of the Dawn in the Day of the Covenant. Even as her age and generation knew her not, seeing only her mortal frailties – so future ages and cycles will love her – adore her – venerate her blessed name – and strive to walk in the path of her utter servitude, severance, and sacrifice. The passion of Divine love that consumed her heart shall light the hearts of mankind forever and forever. (*The Bahá'í World,* vol. VIII, 1938-1940 [Wilmette, Illinois: Bahá'í Publishing Trust, 1942], pp. 642-643.)

"Why was she called 'the bruised and broken reed trodden and crushed to earth?'" "Why did she die alone 'far from all those who should have loved her'?" These questions burned in my mind to such an extent that I wrote to the Universal House of Justice asking for help. This came generously from the Archives Department at the World Centre in the form of many references. I found far more material than was needed for a twenty-minute talk at De Poort, but the questions kindled by my reading remained.

The World Centre Archives pointed me to the National Bahá'í Archives of the United States at Wilmette, Illinois, where I was told that there were no restrictions on Lua's correspondence. Through the kindness of Dr. Robert H. Stockman and Roger Dahl, the Getsingers' papers and many other personal papers were copied by the able Lewis

Walker and mailed to me in Denmark. I then typed all of Lua's correspondence and some of Edward's into my computer. Lewis Walker's prompt and helpful response to the many questions that arose during this work is greatly appreciated. The National Archives sent my queries on to Richard Hollinger who generously shared with me his unpublished paper about Lua and sent some information from his own research. I was alerted by my son, David Piff, who works at the Bahá'í World Centre, to the existence of letters from Lua to Elizabeth Nourse that were stored in the National Archives of the Bahá'ís of Hawaii. These were generously made available through the kindness of Gary Morrison, the secretary of the National Spiritual Assembly of the Bahá'ís of Hawaii, and of Ana Donato, chief of Archives, who had recognized the significance of the Nourse correspondence with Lua and notified the Bahá'í World Centre.

Many people deserve thanks for their assistance to this project. I would like to mention a few: Carina Bastlund for initial editing and encouragement; Catherine White, an American attorney residing in Denmark, for second editing and for researching the divorce laws in force in Washington DC in 1916; the members of the Writer's Group of the American Women's Club in Copenhagen for their encouragement; Shahla Piff and Siamak Zabihi for translation from Persian to English; Ingegerd Bischoff for translation from French; Herbert Goldhor for research into U.S. Census records; Anthony A. Lee for his helpful response to my questions; and Loni Diessner for her quick response to further questions. May Hofman's final editing has made the work a coherent whole and has made it possible to answer many of the questions that first agitated my mind about Lua's life.

Without the wholehearted support and assistance of my husband, Christoph Metelmann, this book would never have come into being. He checked the original copies of the letters against the transcribed copies, helped puzzle out difficult handwriting, gave unfailing support and encouragement on the entire project and unlimited help in every way.

This book does not claim to be a complete biography of Lua's life. It is mostly her own voice that speaks, fragmented by distance and time, as she wrote to her friends and relatives. A few letters written to Lua were also available and are included for flavor. All quotations are from personal papers held in Bahá'í National Archives unless otherwise indicated. These include the personal papers of Anna Albertson, John and Louise Bosch, Thornton Chase, Ella G. Cooper, Helen Goodall, Margaret Green, the Hannen Family, H. Emogene Hoagg, Leroy Ioas, Maude Lamson, Catherine Nourse, Agnes Parsons, Mary Rabb, Juliet Thompson, Louise R. Waite, Marie Watson, Albert Windust, and Frederick and Annetta Woodward, in addition to Edward Getsinger and Lua Getsinger – all in the Bahá'í National Archives of the United States. The Catherine Nourse papers, which include Lua's letters to Elizabeth Nourse, are found in the Bahá'í National Archives of Hawaii.

Tablets from 'Abdu'l-Bahá to Lua are quoted in the original English translations made by various Persian Bahá'ís in the early years of the twentieth century. It was these translations, however inadequate, that were familiar to Lua herself, and for most of the Tablets quoted no subsequent translations exist. The authorized translations of 'Abdu'l-Bahá's Writings made since the 1920s by Shoghi Effendi and for the Universal House of Justice have accustomed readers to a greater clarity of language and meaning than is afforded by these early, unauthorized translations. Where an authorized translation of a Tablet exists it is given in the endnotes.

In editing Lua's letters, I have tried to keep as close to the original spelling as possible, except for the name of 'Abdu'l-Bahá, where I have rendered the correct modern spelling in most instances, even though the name was often spelled in various different ways at the time when Lua lived. Standardized transliteration of Persian did not come into use in the Bahá'í community until the time of the beloved Guardian of the Cause, Shoghi Effendi. Similarly, I have preserved Lua's punctuation which in its use of dashes and underlining is characteristic of its time.

My questions at the beginning of this research lost all urgency as my acquaintance with Lua through her own letters increased. My growing insights into her character showed that chastity, purity, firmness in the Covenant and exemplary love of and obedience to 'Abdu'l-Bahá were demonstrated by a life-long service and devotion to the Cause. As I read, her progress on the path of service and sacrifice became apparent until at last she became a truly severed soul. Her relationship with 'Abdu'l-Bahá was the axis upon which her life turned. She depended upon Him for guidance in all matters, often waiting in one city for His permission to move to another. Her obedience to and love for the Master were the primary motivating forces of her life, and you will see that for yourself as you read her letters and see the stenographic records of a few of her talks. Her life bore witness to the truth of the words of 'Abdu'l-Bahá:

All who stand up in the Cause of God will be persecuted and misunderstood. It has always been so; it will always be so. Let neither enemy nor friend disturb your peace, destroy your happiness, prevent your accomplishment. Fix your soul upon God. Then persecution and slander will make you radiant . . .

Now praise be to God! Turn all your thoughts and devote all your powers to the Divine Covenant. Unless a servant in the Cause of God is subjected to all persecution he is not fit to spread the Heavenly Message of Glad Tidings. Follow 'Abdu'l-Bahá! Let nothing hinder or defeat you. God is your helper and God is invincible.

Thou must enter that country with a never-failing spirituality, a radiant faith, an eternal enthusiasm, an inextinguishable fire, a solid conviction, in order that thou mayest achieve those services for which I am sending thee. Let not thy heart be troubled. If thou goest away with this unchanging condition of invariability of inner state, thou shalt see the doors of confirmation open before thy face, thy life will be a crown of heavenly roses, and thou shall find thyself in the highest station of triumph.

Strive day and night to attain to this exalted state. Look at Me! Thou dost not know a thousandth part of the difficulties and seemingly unsurmountable passes that rise daily before my eyes. I do not heed them; I am walking in my chosen highway; I know the destination. Hundreds of storms and tempests may rage furiously around my head; hundreds of Titanics may sink to the bottom of the sea, the mad waves may rise to the roof of heaven; all these will not change my purpose, will not disturb me in the least; I will not look either to the right or to the left. I am looking ahead, far far. Peering through the impenetrable darkness of the night, the howling winds, the raging storms, I see the glorious Light beckoning me forward, forward. The balmy weather is coming, and the voyager shall land safely.

'Abdu'l-Bahá

I

Louisa Aurora Moore was born November 1, 1871 in Hume, New York, a small town located in northwestern New York State about 90 kilometers south of Lake Ontario. An average of half a meter of snow falls in the winters in Wyoming County, the part of the state where Ellen McBride Moore and Reuben D. Moore, her husband, brought up their ten children. Moore is listed as a farmer in the Wyoming County, New York, Directory for 1870-1871.[1]

Born in 1843, Ellen McBride was influenced by the millennial zeal of the mid-nineteenth century and she passed along to some of her children this passionate interest. Seeking answers to religious questions was part of their family life. Louisa, known affectionately as Lua, was the sixth child of the family and, like her brothers and sisters, was educated in the regular public school system of rural upper New York state.

In the early 1880s Lua went to Chicago to study dramatic art. She and her brother, William Moore, who was studying medicine, boarded at the suburban home of Chester Ira Thacher in La Grange. She may have worked as housekeeper in the Thacher home.[2] This large city gave her scope to develop her interest in religious subjects and she joined many groups seeking answers to the questions which had interested her and her mother. One of these groups was the Order of the Magi, a Masonic lodge which taught that the spirit of Christ was present on earth.

According to oral family history, Lua was present at the World Parliament of Religions held in Chicago in conjunction with the World's Fair.[3] Here, for the first time, on

1

September 23, 1893, Bahá'u'lláh, prophet-founder of the
Bahá'í Faith, was publicly mentioned by Henry H. Jessup,
a Christian clergyman of Beirut. He said, in part:

Just outside the fortress of 'Akká, on the Syrian coast, there died
a few months since, a famous Persian sage . . . named Bahá'u'lláh
– "The Glory of God" . . . [He] gave utterance to sentiments so
noble, so Christlike, that we repeat them as our closing words:

"That all nations should become one in faith and all men as
brothers; that the bond of affection and unity between the sons
of men should be strengthened; that diversity of religions should
cease, and differences of race be annulled. What harm is there
in this? Yet so it shall be. This fruitless strife, these ruinous wars
shall pass away, and the 'Most Great Peace' shall come . . . Let
not a man glory in this, that he loves his country; let him rather
glory in this, that he loves his kind."[4]

Whether or not Lua attended the World Parliament, she
must at least have read about it in the newspapers as there
was much publicity. Religion was held in such high interest
in those days that newspapers published sermons of popu-
lar ministers and priests.

At this time, it is probable that the only Bahá'í in that
city or indeed in all America was Anton Haddad. In 1892
he had left Egypt and settled in Chicago. There he was
joined in February 1894 by Ibrahim Kheiralla, who had
taught him the Bahá'í Faith in Cairo. Money became a
problem and Haddad returned to his family in Syria.[5] The
religious tenor of these days gave fertile ground for the
religious instruction classes which Kheiralla began soon
after his arrival. He developed a series of twelve lessons
teaching his own interpretation of the Bible and where the
coming of Bahá'u'lláh was gradually revealed. In the final
class, those attending heard for the first time the Greatest
Name, at which point most of them became Bahá'ís.
Kheiralla's classes were very successful and led to a rapid
growth of the Faith. There were two Bahá'ís in America in
1894, five by 1895 and twenty-eight in 1896. When Lua

joined the Chicago community on May 21, 1897, there were about sixty, and by June of that year over one hundred.[6]

A dream Lua had on October 17, 1896 seemed important enough for her to record it. She recounts:

I dreamed I was in an old one story wooden house – whose roof was somewhat sunken in and broken – My Father and Mother seemed to live in this house only I did not see them – and I was there to do the work – which ever seemed behind hand. I thought it was afternoon and I had not yet made the beds – which I set myself to do – and by the bed – which I thought my Father occupied I found a lamp burning very low – which I extinguished and on going about the room I found other lights burning – which I blew out also! Presently an old man came in who looked very much like Mr. Guile, and said "The King is here!"

"Is He?" I exclaimed – "Have you seen him?" "No," he answered. "But I think you can!" Upon hearing this I rushed from the house out into the road where at a <u>great</u> distance I beheld the King – though the King of what – or from what Nation I do not know! I only saw, dimly – him sitting upon a beautiful throne – surrounded by many people who seemed desirous of paying him honor and attention! I ran toward them – but as I approached a mist gathered before my eyes – and as I drew near the King it had completely shut him from view. However I knew I was before him and down through this misty vapor – he handed me a board it seemed – covered over with black velvet – upon which was set row after row of beautiful jewels – Pearls – diamonds – opals – emeralds – topaz and rubies – in fact – all kinds of gems – sparkled upon it! One magnificent ruby I noticed in particular and I thought I will put this in my ring – and then suddenly I felt that I must not do it – that I must bear them as they were arranged by the King! I hugged them to my heart – and went back to the old house where it seemed – in the meantime – quite a number had gathered – and I burst in saying "See what the King gave me!" They all crowded around to look – and as they gazed at the jewels some of them said "But these don't correspond with you – and your clothes – and this old house you live in", but I didn't mind their words, I was so happy over my possessions!

Although Lua was in Kheiralla's class, it is possible that Dr. Thacher or Madame Maartens had already introduced her to the Faith.[7] "Once she learned about the Bahá'í Faith, her zeal was so intense that she did not wait for Kheiralla's class to finish before she received the Greatest Name individually from Kheiralla on 21 May 1897. She may also have told her brother, Dr. William J. Moore, about the Bahá'ís; he graduated in the 18 June class."[8]

At the age of twenty-five, on May 26, 1897, Lua married Edward Christopher Getsinger, thirty-one (1866-1935), who was a professional lecturer and had a degree in homeopathic medicine. Edward was apparently not a Bahá'í at the time of their marriage, but after some months of careful study he abandoned his position as an atheist and received the Greatest Name from Kheiralla on October 26, 1897.

Lua soon introduced the Faith to her own family in Hume, New York. Her mother and four of her brothers and sisters became Bahá'ís.[9] Mrs. Moore soon became an able teacher of the Faith, corresponding with friends and "Truth Seekers". In one letter Mrs. Moore, having previously assigned the seeker to write by hand some "passages of sacred scripture", sends sixteen pages of explanation of the chapter the seeker had copied. The seeker is counselled not to let anyone who is not a believer see it as the explanation has been copied from the Master's approved works, "so we must be carefull and not cast the Childrens bread to the dogs for fear they may turn and rend us."

In the fall of 1897 Lua organized a Bahá'í class for friends and relatives in Ithaca, New York. Six of the nine in the class became Bahá'í[10] and in January, 1898, the class was visited by Kheiralla, who was loved and honored as the foremost Bahá'í teacher in the land.

The Bahá'ís did not know that he had told them an untruth. Kheiralla apparently thought his teaching would be more effective if he told his students that he had been in the actual presence of Bahá'u'lláh, and had been sent by Him to the United States to teach His cause. Anton Haddad knew of this falsehood but had been warned by Kheiralla never to mention it to the Bahá'ís. In fact, Kheiralla had but received a Tablet written to him by Bahá'u'lláh upon his declaration of belief.

In mid-December 1897, Anton Haddad returned from a visit to 'Abdu'l-Bahá. His radiant aspect and humble words very greatly impressed the Bahá'ís, who had their first opportunity to meet somebody directly from the presence of the Master. Isabella Brittingham[11] recalled the impact Haddad had upon her:

Dr. Kheiralla . . . then introduced Mr. Haddad, saying that he would confirm his (Dr. K.'s) Message. Anton Haddad, in very plain attire, but with that beautiful spirit in his face, brought from that Home of Light and Love ['Akká], spoke of his beautiful visit to our Master. He seemed so filled with that inhaled Spirit that he was at times touched with emotion. His talk was short . . . He spoke of the Master's Message of Love and of that Love between us all . . . and then he drew out of his pocket a little book, or piece of paper, and said he would read to us our Lord's own Words taken down from his lips. And then he read those Words – which constitute our *first* teachings from the Master, 'Abdu'l-Bahá, brought by the *first* returned pilgrim to America . . . They were the most beautiful Words I had ever heard. They completely crystallized the fact of the Message, in my soul, and *lifted* the Message out of and *above* the structure which Dr. K had built around it, in amplified series of teachings, etc. It was the Cup of Wine "which had no likeness" to my husband and myself . . . They produced so deep an effect upon me, at that blessed time, that certainly I *ate and drank* therefrom. "They were Spirit and they were life."

During Dr. and Mrs. Kheiralla's visit to Ithaca, other seekers were given the Greatest Name and on February 3, 1898 Lua wrote to a Mrs. Lawson:

I enclose a list of those who received the Greatest Name while Dr. Kheiralla was here also two letters which were written before he came. The work is progressing nicely here. I am rather lonesome since Mr. Getsinger went away still I do not mind it as I thought I would! This glorious truth fills up all voids, and takes away all sorrow. I enjoyed my visit with Dr. and Mrs. Kheiralla, and they did very good work here. I am so glad to hear of the advancement of the work in Chicago. Will you kindly remember me to all the believers!

In the spring of 1898 the Getsingers travelled to California to teach the Faith, and contacted Phoebe Hearst, the widow of Senator George Hearst and a noted philanthropist. They were led into the house by Robert Turner, Mrs. Hearst's butler, who was to be the first member of his race to become a believer in Baha'u'llah.[12] Mrs. Hearst's interest became so compelling that she added 'Akká to her itinerary on a journey she was planning to the Middle East, and invited the Getsingers to go along. Lua taught a Bahá'í class at the home of Mrs. Hearst.[13] Among the students was a niece of Mrs. Hearst, Anne Apperson, who shared the teachings with her friend Helen Hillyer. Helen and her friend, Ella Goodall [Cooper], both became believers. Ella in turn interested her mother, Helen S. Goodall, so keenly that Mrs. Goodall travelled to New York to find another teacher since Lua had left California before their lessons were completed. In New York the women studied Kheiralla's manuscript with Anton Haddad.[14] Mrs. Hearst also invited Ibrahim Kheiralla and his wife to accompany the party to 'Akká.

II

This first party of Western pilgrims sailed from New York City September 22, 1898, arriving in Paris on September 29 "after a very pleasant journey indeed". Lua kept a journal which is reproduced in part below. An inscription on the first page reads:

To the dear little messenger
that brought the
gladtidings
to me
with love and
gratitude
from
Helen of Troy
Sept. 13, 1898 San Francisco

. . . enjoyed my first trip across the "Briney Deep" much more than I anticipated. We were specially favored with fair weather and moonlight evenings. Our last dinner on board was very nice and we had a jolly time.

Sunday Oct 2
We visited the Tomb of Napoleon the Great also Eifel [sic] Tower. Then we had an extensive ride through Bois de Boulogne.

Oct. 3
Visited the Garden of The Tuileries. Marian [Mrs. Kheiralla], Aunty and myself had this bit of sightseeing together.

Sunday Oct. 9
Today we drove to Notre Dame and went inside. The sight made my blood boil and my heart to be kindled with fury. When will this deception and hypocrisy cease and God's creatures cease to be vultures that prey on poor suffering humanity?

Sunday Oct 29 [sic]
Edward, our Violet and I had a most delightful day driving through the "Bois". The Autumn tints make the wood most beautiful. We stayed until the night came on then rode back through the Champs Eleise [sic] and down by the brilliant Seine – I was most happy.

Tuesday, Nov. 1st 1898
My birthday!
    Twenty six years old today[15] and I feel so much younger and look it too. Still I am 26! Have had a perfectly lovely day riding with my husband – the very best and dearest man in the world. . . . A year ago today I was in Ithaca, N. Y. and today in Paris. I wonder where I shall be next year? Doing good, I hope wherever I am. My birthday presents were beautiful and best of all I had tea at 5 p.m. with my own "Queen Anne" . . . [this may have been Anne Apperson, a niece of Mrs. Hearst, with whom, according to the journal, Lua established a close friendship].

Thanksgiving Day Nov. 24, 1898
I have been very busy packing and getting ready to leave Paris today, but accepted an invitation from Mrs. Cropper[16] to eat Thanksgiving dinner with them at their Hotel Belmont. We spent a very pleasant evening together – during which I delivered to them the Glorious Message of the Coming of the Kingdom of God which they rec'd with great joy!

We leave for Haifa tomorrow and I am anxious for the morrow to come my heart yearns to be in the <u>land</u> of all <u>lands.</u>

Naples Italy 12/3/98
We have journeyed from France, stopping at Florence & Rome and now we are in sight of Mt. Vesuvius and about to set sail for Alexandria on the "Regina Margarheita"[sic] – every day brings

us nearer the Holy Place – although we have seen many interesting things the days pass much too slowly!

12/6/1898
Arrived at Alexandria this morning and was met at the steamer by Salim Effendi – who is a friend of Dr. K's and he was very kind to help us with our baggage etc. We transferred to the steamer "Achille" bound for Haifa and shortly before sailing Dr. Kheiralla's daughter Labiba came on board. We were very pleased to see her and she informed us that her eldest sister was in Haifa which pleased us very much also – as she speaks English and would be of great service to us in our meeting those whose every utterance is a precious gem.

Arrived at Haifa – Dec. 8, 1898 – and were met by several Persian Believers.

Permission for the pilgrimage must have been granted some time after October 10, 1898 when Lua wrote a petition from Paris to 'Abdu'l-Bahá with this request. The language of the petition may reflect the influence of Kheiralla but surely indicates that Lua felt she was writing to her Lord and needed the most elegant English in her command:

In God's Name –
To the Greatest Branch

My Lord, My Lord – from my heart I send Thee greetings and beg Thee to accept my life as sacrifice to Thy Will and wish. Oh my Lord, I praise God my Beloved that my supplication has been heard and I have been permitted to approach this near unto Thee – but oh Prince of the world my heart yearns for the exaltation of Thy presence and my eyes long to behold the glory of Thy beneficent face – therefore I am enabled to once more feel encouraged to come unto Thee as a child, pleading for consideration.
   I beg of Thee, oh best Beloved of the Father – that you will

specially bless my dear Teacher – who has guided me to the Blessed Tree of Life and who so kindly bears to Thee – oh Blessed one – this humble message – and oh Ruler of the House of David and King of the world – will you ask God the Mighty, the most High to cleanse me from mine iniquities and make my heart pure that I may be made worthy of completing the journey to The Holy City and kneeling before Thee to kiss the dust beneath Thy Holy Feet. Also I beg thee this blessed privilege be conferred upon my husband and the rest of our party who have thus far accompanied our Beloved Teacher. I salute Thee by the Name of Abha and humbly await Thy pleasure,

Thy unworthy Servant

Oct. 10th, 1898

The names on the list, in Lua's own hand, are:

Mrs. P. A. Hearts [sic]
Mrs. Henrietta M. Hoagg
Miss Helen A. Hillyer
Miss Anne D. Apperson
Mr. Anthony Caminetti
Mrs. Anthony Caminetti
Mrs. Maria F. Neely
Mrs. July B. Procht
Mrs. Mary A. Wilson
Mrs. Oraville Spreckles

Other records indicate that this pilgrimage group consisted of: Phoebe Hearst, Robert Turner (butler to Mrs. Hearst), Amalie M. Bachrodt (her maid), Agnes Lane (her niece), Julia Pearson (governess to Mrs. Hearst's niece), Lua and Edward Getsinger, Ibrahim and Marion Miller Kheiralla, Mrs. Thornburgh and her daughter, Mary Virginia Thornburgh-Cropper (who joined the group in Paris), May Ellis Bolles (who had become a believer through Lua's teaching in Paris[17] and joined the party), Anne Apperson (another niece of Mrs. Hearst), and Kheiralla's daughters – their grandmother may have come too. The pilgrims were

10

counted as fifteen and were divided into three groups because the arrival of such a large group of Westerners would have alarmed the authorities in ʻAkká. Helen Hillyer and Ella Goodall sailed together and brought the manuscript of Kheiralla's book, "Beha-ullah". It is probable that Helen and Ella are not counted among these first pilgrims.

From Paris Lua wrote to "My dear friend and Brother" (possibly Thornton Chase) describing her journey and comforting him that he was not among the pilgrim group.

I received your letter sent in care of Dr. Kheiralla and of course was very glad to hear from you but sorry that you felt so badly. I can realize though, what a great disappointment it was to you but to do justice to Dr. K. I do not think he was to be blamed – because he said he knew that you could not make the journey in two months – and as he was so very busy he did not think it necessary to answer your letter. He feels very sorry and wishes all of the Believers could go. The New York people felt equally as bad. We had a very pleasant journey all together – two days it was rough and rainy – and nearly all on board were sea-sick – but after that it was beautiful the evenings especially – as it was moonlight. We arrived yesterday all well and glad to get on land once more. The sea has its charms – but the land has more <u>by far</u>! I trust, dear brother that you will be faithful to the cause of God – and work on patiently as possible until this great and glorious privilege be given to you – as it surely will be – for God, our father never refuses those who beg of Him – and in His own good time rewards His faithful followers. I feel almost selfish when I think of the rest of you – who have been working in the cause so much longer than I have – still debarred from enjoying what your dear hearts most long for – and that the great blessing has been bestowed upon me. I <u>do not</u> and cannot feel that it is because I am more worthy of it – for I have done very little – but in my heart I have truly loved, and do love my God – and have had no <u>doubts</u> whatever. You know I asked in my letter last Spring that I might be the humble instrument of assisting Dr. K – financially to make the journey – and I feel this is the <u>direct</u> answer to my supplication – which God in His Infinite Mercy and wisdom saw fit to consider. I think it was answered more for

11

Dr. K's sake than <u>mine</u>. We are not going to Acca when Dr. K. goes – he goes ahead alone – and if he succeeds in getting an invitation for Mrs. K, Mr. G and myself we will follow later. I will surely write you from there and I am going to keep a diary – making a record of everything I see and hear. Now, my friend I sincerely hope you will weed out all <u>jealousy</u> and envy from your heart – and bear this great trial with patience and humility – praying to our bountiful and ever loving Father for the blessing to be bestowed upon you, and I am sure that it will be in time. One thing I want to speak about here – and I trust you will think about it carefully! I hear that many of the Believers in both New York and Chicago have <u>grave</u> <u>doubts</u> and that they talk them over together – this I believe to be entirely wrong – and it ought not to be allowed. If one has <u>a</u> <u>doubt</u> he should keep it <u>to</u> <u>himself</u> and pray to God for light and help because <u>talking</u> about it only sows seeds of distrust in the heart of some one else – and I am convinced that this is Satan's method of reaping a harvest! God alone can remove our doubts by giving us more knowledge and He <u>alone</u> is the one to go to. If we see faults in our <u>teacher</u> we do not mend them by criticism and harsh judgement – we only call the attention of others to them – and besides we should remember the words of our God and <u>practice</u> them: "deal not harshly – but pray!" also that kindness is "the lodestone of hearts and the food of the soul". Oh my brother – and all dear believers – stand firmly together – helping one another, and loving one another – thus showing to the world that we are in reality – <u>children</u> of God! My love is with you, and my prayers are <u>for</u> <u>you</u> <u>all</u>.

> May God bless you and comfort you
> With sincere affection
> I am your Sister in
> the glorious cause.
> Lua M. Getsinger
> Sept. 30, 1898

This first pilgrimage was not only an important historical event in the establishment of the Bahá'í Faith in the West. It transformed Lua Getsinger from a relatively care-free young woman, though loyal to her faith, into a passionate follower of 'Abdu'l-Bahá. He gave her a Persian name, "Liva" which means "Banner" in English, and Lua believed that He gave her, as well, a special mission to teach the Faith and granted her extraordinary powers to do so. From this period onward she devoted her life and energy to that end.

III

Kheiralla arrived in 'Akká on November 11, 1898, bearing the petition from the Getsingers. Permission was apparently granted, as the Getsingers arrived in the Holy Land on December 8, 1898. ". . . our first visit December 8, 1898 to March 23, 1899" is written in Lua's own hand in her journal. Lua was generous in writing about the inestimable privilege of her visit to the Master to the friends back home.

To the Assembly in Chicago
Greetings.

We reached Haifa Thursday, Dec. 8th, about 10:30 P.M. and were met by Dr. Kheiralla and two or three Babis [the Bahá'ís] welcomed us heartily and conducted us to a coffee house where we were served with refreshments. An old man was there waiting for us and he, as I was afterwards informed, is the uncle of the Greatest Branch, and was sent by the latter to welcome us. Never have I seen a face more full of love and kindness. He saluted us, and his countenance beamed with pleasure while he expressed himself as being so thankful upon our safe arrival. After drinking some tea, we went from this place to our hotel, several of the believers walking. The streets are very narrow and dark so a man, the hotel-keeper, walked ahead of us with a lantern to light the way. Our friends remained conversing with us at the hotel until after midnight, excepting the old gentleman, he did not accompany us, as it was late and he desired to leave early the next morning for Acca to report our arrival to the Greatest Branch – our Master!

We slept but little that night, our minds were occupied with the thoughts that perhaps tomorrow we shall see <u>Him</u>, and kiss the hem of the blessed garment of our Lord. We arose early the next morning, our hearts eagerly expectant, but all day no word came.

In the evening we were invited to the house of Housyn Effendi (one of the believers living in Acca), and upon our arrival he met us at the door, welcomed us, saying that he was the bearer of good news to us. He had received a letter from Abbas Effendi that day stating: "He would be pleased to welcome us on the morrow, and that His heart longed to see the first American pilgrims." We went back to our hotel after spending a most delightful evening, our host and hostess taking great pains to make us happy, showing us every kindness and hospitality; often remarking that we must not consider ourselves guests, for their house was ours, and everything they had at our disposal.

As you may imagine, sleep was out of the question that night, my husband and I were talking all the time, and congratulating ourselves upon our great blessings and good fortune, and counting the hours, which passed much too slowly, until the dawn of the morrow should come! We arose early, dressing ourselves with great care, feeling the best we had was not half good enough to wear upon this our first visit to the Holy City, and shortly after eight o'clock the carriage drove up and Dr. Kheiralla, his daughter, my husband and myself started for the place of all places, the New Jerusalem, the Holy Abode of the Most High and the Dwelling Place of our Gracious Lord.

It is about five miles from Haifa to Acca, – the road close to the sea – indeed in the sea, for the horses were walking in the water, and at times the waves dashed nearly to the top of the wheels. After riding about a quarter of an hour we could see the City in the distance; it was a beautiful morning and as we looked we could but think of the description in the Bible, "a city all of gold beside a crystal sea". It was bathed in a flood of golden sunshine and the sea splashing up against its walls sparkled with splendor! We gradually approached nearer and nearer until at last we passed "the shed which serves as a coffee house outside the wall", and entered the City by its "solitary gate", and drove straight to the house of Abbas Effendi. We entered the garden, ascended one flight of stairs, and were shown into a hall, or reception room, where we removed our wraps, and were welcomed by the uncle, who told us to pass into the next room. Dr. Kheiralla went ahead, and by the violent beating of my heart I knew we were soon to behold the Blessed Face of the Prince of the House of David, the King of the whole world. We reached the door and stopped – before us in the center of the room stood a man clad in a long raiment with a white turban upon His head, stretching one hand out toward us, while His face, which I cannot describe, was lighted by a rare sweet smile of joy and welcome! We stood thus for a moment unable to move – then my heart gave a great throb and scarcely knowing what I was doing I held out my arms, crying: "My Lord, my Lord!!!" and rushed to Him, kneeling at His Blessed Feet, sobbing like a child; in an instant my husband was beside me, crying as only men can cry! He put His dear hands upon our bowed heads and said, in a voice that seemed to our ears like a strain of sweet music, "Welcome, welcome, my dear children, you are welcome, arise and be of good cheer." Then He sat down upon a low divan and we sat on one side almost facing Him, Dr. Kheiralla and his daughter on the other side, and He began to talk to us. To my husband He said that "he should prosper in his scientific work, and God would bless him and enable him to do good in many directions. And as the vibrations of light emanating from the sun magnetize the earth, so should the word of God magnetize the hearts and draw them from the West to mingle in love with the hearts in the East." He remained with us but a few moments (as His time is so fully occupied) when He arose and again bidding us "welcome" went into another room, where He writes and meets those who come to Him for help and counsel.

We were then taken into another room where we met the Greatest Holy Leaf [Bahíyyih Khánum] and many other ladies. They welcomed us very graciously, the Holy Leaf taking Dr. Kheiralla's daughter and myself in her arms and kissing us very tenderly on both cheeks; then they made tea for us and showed us great kindness! We remained conversing with them until noon, then she took us by the hand and led us to the table, seating one on each side of her and serving us most bountifully with many varieties of food, which were very good indeed. After dinner we were served with coffee, the fragrance and flavor of which was most delicious. Then a servant brought us some sweet meats from the Greatest Branch, and such a generous supply that I am going to bring them home that you all may taste.

In the afternoon they read tablets aloud, and told us many interesting things connected with the early history of the Babis; so swiftly did the time pass that we were quite astonished when dinner was announced; they served a special meal for us, as they eat much later than we do, but so anxious was I to see my Lord again that I begged He would at least come into the room with us; this request was more than granted, for He came and sat at the table, seating me on His right and my husband at His left. I felt too happy to eat and sat with my eyes riveted upon His glorious face. He turned toward me and sweetly smiling, said; "The love of God burning in your heart is manifest upon your face and it gives us joy to look upon you." I then called His attention to St. Luke, 14:15: "Blessed is he who shall eat bread in the Kingdom of God." He thereupon took up the loaf and brake it and gave each one of us a piece of the same. I have kept mine, and am also going to bring it that you may see it. After the meal was over He left us and went out, as He had something to attend to, and did not return until about eleven o'clock, then he came into the room where we were sitting (all of us rising as He entered and bowing low before Him) and sat down and began talking to us in a low soft musical voice. My husband asked permission to sit nearer to Him, which He granted and sat him down at His right; I longed <u>intensely</u> to go nearer, but said nothing – after a moment He turned toward me, smiled, and waived His hand that I also might come; I sat down at His blessed feet, while He took my hand and looking down upon me tenderly as a loving father, He sat and conversed with us nearly half an hour, then He rose, bade us good night, blessing us, and we all retired. I couldn't sleep! My heart was too full! I was too infinitely happy. I could only live over and over again the precious moments I had spent in His presence and long to see Him once more.

I fell into a sweet sleep just as morn was breaking, after which I awoke feeling greatly refreshed, and arose dressing myself, impatient to be among my friends and the holy people, for I felt each moment with them to be a great blessing indeed, and every word falling from their lips to be a precious gem. Miss Kheiralla and I went to the apartment of the Greatest Leaf, who kissed us and enquired if we had rested well. Then a servant brought us some nice fruit and each a beautiful bouquet of flowers from the Greatest Branch, who had sent her to ask if we were well and comfortable.

During the day we were conducted to the special garden of

the Manifestation, the one (according to Dr. Kheiralla) as described in the prophecies thus: "The place of my throne is part on the water and part on the land, under a green tent that has neither ropes nor a center pole to sustain it." And it is <u>literally</u> so, for this garden is on a small island, a river on each side of it, and there are two places built, upon which the Manifestation used to sit, one in the east and one in the west of the garden, and these places are built in such a way that they are "part on the water and part on the land," then two large trees, one in each end of the garden, their branches meeting in the center, form the green tent most perfectly. In this most beautiful spot we sat down upon the seats before "His throne", and were served with tea by those who accompanied us thither, also the gardener brought us fruits and flowers from the "garden of our Glorious God", and they were delicious, both to taste and see. In one part of this place is a small cottage where the Manifestation used sometimes to stay, and we were permitted to enter this also, to go into the room which He always occupied, kneel before the chair upon which He sat, and to kiss the place upon which the soles of His feet rested! The spiritual atmosphere of this place was overwhelming; our tears fell like rain over our faces, and some of the believers with us cried aloud. Indeed, to enter this room is a great blessing. I have felt nearer to God since that day! On the chair was a wreath of flowers, and some beautiful cut roses placed there by the Greatest Branch, who commanded that they should be given to us (my husband, Dr. Kheiralla, his daughter and myself); also four large oranges, which were on the table opposite, as we left that most sacred place.

From here we were taken to the Tomb of the Manifestation, and you must excuse me if I do not enter into detail about this, I cannot find words to express myself, suffice it to say, that the Greatest Branch let me walk in His footsteps and led me by the hand into this sacred place, where I knelt down, and begged of God to cleanse my heart from all impurity and kindle within it the fire of His Love. I also remembered there the <u>Assembly</u> in Chicago and begged God's blessing to be showered upon you. I will try and tell you more when I see you, but I cannot <u>write</u> it. After this visit we walked in the garden and our Lord, with his own blessed hands, picked flowers and leaves, which He gave us to take to the faithful believers in America.

That night He sat us all at the table, and dismissed the servants, saying He would serve us Himself, and He did so. He did not sit at the table with us, but <u>waited</u> upon us! At the conclusion of the meal He said: "I have served you tonight that you may learn the lesson of ever serving your fellow creatures with love and kindness." He bade us good night and advised us all to rest early, so we went to bed and this night I had a long delicious sleep and rest!

The next morning He brought me a most beautiful bunch of white narcissus and allowed me to kiss His blessed hand as He gave them to me! He sat down and drank tea with us, then rose and bade us "adieu", as we were going back to Haifa that day and He had been called away. As we were quitting the City we saw Him standing by the Gate, and He smiled at us as we passed. Then we returned "by the road in the sea" to Haifa, our hearts both happy and sorrowful, happy because we had seen him and sorrowful because we were leaving Him.

Oh dear people, make firm your faith and belief, for truly He is our Lord. It seems to me that no one could doubt should He smile upon them, and no one could turn from Him should He seek to confirm them! But this He will not do, as God has declared that each must seek to confirm himself and gave to each of us the power of will for that purpose. I feel these words are very weak and inadequate, but I assure you no one could describe this place and tis foolish to try – to <u>know</u> each must see for himself, therefore pray God earnestly that the blessing of coming here may <u>soon</u> be bestowed. There is no other place in the world worth seeing, and surely no other King worthy of homage!

And now I send you all my love and pray God to bless you <u>all</u> <u>now</u> and <u>forever</u>! May your hearts all be united, and your souls become as <u>one</u> <u>soul</u> living in separate bodies. Thus you will resemble our Lord, and draw nearer unto God, the loving Father of us all!

Your loving sister and co-worker in the Cause,
LUA MOORE GETSINGER

Ibrahim Kheiralla and Muḥsin Effendi, 'Abdu'l-Bahá's son-in-law, were the only Bahá'ís in 'Akká who knew English so anslation was difficult.[18] Lua and Edward began to study Persian at the request of 'Abdu'l-Bahá and she established a close friendship with the daughters of the Master.

The Getsingers endeavored to learn all they could of the faith they had embraced and discarded any ideas previously held that did not conform to the Master's teaching. In this, they differed from their teacher, Dr. Kheiralla. It became apparent during their visit that Kheiralla did not translate the Master's words fully, avoiding teachings which differed from his own. Edward enjoyed the controversy caused by Kheiralla's stubborn refusal to abandon his own understanding where it contradicted that of 'Abdu'l-Bahá. Notes in Edward's hand, written much later, recount, "I always knew that Kheiralla was an imposter from the start in 1896. He knew that I did. There was for this reason no fellowship among us." At meals with the Master, Edward brought up the subject "for the benefit of Kheiralla" but instead of being corrected, Kheiralla clung to his own ideas. "The oftener we discussed it the madder he got," Edward wrote in his notes. 'Abdu'l-Bahá intervened and told everybody not to discuss controversial subjects with Kheiralla.

Lua wrote to Thornton Chase:

Acca, February 15, '99

My greetings of love to

My dear brother Thornton Chase

I suppose you have about concluded that you are not to receive a letter from me during my sojourn at the "Holy City" but this will, I trust annul such a conclusion and prove to the contrary – that I have not forgotten my promise to you. I have thought of you every day – and both Mr. Getsinger and myself have spoken of you to the "Greatest Branch" and have also remembered you at the Sacred Tomb. Truly – I feel like one in a dream, and now can scarcely collect my senses enough to write anything about this most wonderful and Holy Household. For the past two weeks I have been staying at Acca for the purpose of studying the Persian language – which Our Lord commanded both myself and husband to learn as soon as possible. One of His daughters is my teacher and though I have studied such a short time – I am now able to read easy words and know one prayer by heart. The atmosphere of the place is wondrous, knowledge and understanding seem to float in the air! I am simply be-numbed by the great privileges and blessings showered upon me daily, and so much so, that I feel myself to be a miserable worm of the dust, unable even to crawl. One can't imagine such love and kindness as they continually show – to be manifest upon this earth but it is true, and now I know that we Americans have only the semblance while they have the real thing. Oh dear brother try hard now to have the fire of God's love kindled in your heart – and strive earnestly to impress the necessity of it upon those around you. The Master continually tells us that without love we are nothing and can do nothing! Also that moralities are spiritual duties – and a tree to be a good tree – must bring forth only acceptable fruit! So I beg of you to "look well to yourself" and impress this also on the rest of the Believers. You will not I know be angry with me for alluding to the conversation you and I had – last spring – after the rest had gone – and let me tell you now that your thoughts at that time regarding your desires were not right – I have asked some questions bearing upon these matters and now I know!

The Great Branch told me that we must cut our hearts entirely from the world, and leave all material desires to those who cling to material things – then we would be acceptable to God and in a condition to receive the spiritual blessings.

When I left America I thought I knew a good deal – and felt that I was quite near the door of His bounty – but after seeing the Master and other members of the household, I am sure I know nothing – and as yet the sprinkles of His gifts have not descended! But I am praying for mercy – and hope I will succeed in becoming one of the chosen! Everything depends on one's own efforts, we must work our own way into the Kingdom – and tis no easy thing to do, while the world and its allurements surround us! But by the help of God – the most Merciful it can be done!

I know you are anxious to hear more about the Household, the Greatest Branch, the Holy Leaf & & but what can I write? I feel that there are no words in which to describe it, that one must

21

see for himself to <u>know</u>. Not that the house is so grand or its surroundings – <u>not at all</u> for everything – even their manners of dress – is simplicity itself – but there is a dignity and grandeur in <u>this simplicity</u> that is quite beyond description. The Face of the Master – is gloriously beautiful.– His eyes read one's very soul – still they are full of divine love – and fairly melt one's heart! His hair and beard are white, but soft and fine like silk. His features are finely chiseled and very classical – His forehead high and full – and His mouth supremely beautiful, while His hands are small and white like a woman. Now, I have tried to describe Him – but you see it is a feeble attempt, and I assure you it is inadequate in the extreme!

Dear brother of my heart – pray God earnestly that the blessing of coming here – to behold the Face of our Master may soon be bestowed upon you. I sent a long report of my first visit here – to Mr. James – last week – I trust he will receive it all right – and that the Believers will be glad to hear it. Dr. Kh. is well and of course sends his regards to you – though he is in Haifa at present. Mrs. Kheiralla will not return to America with the Doctor – but will go to England for a time – then return to Acca. The Gr. Br. invited her to stay here for one year – or longer if she wished. He has showed her great honors and called her the "white pearl of the Kingdom". Her health is much improved, and she is very happy. Dr. Kheiralla has translated some of his book into Arabic – but it is not yet decided when it can be published. We hope to unite all the believers in love and harmony – and this is the most necessary thing of all – and the first thing to be accomplished. Dr. K. is as changed as we all are – and has become less aggressive. We must all throw away our desires and weed out our imperfections then we will receive the full confirmation and in reality become children of God – simply taking the lessons and receiving the "Greatest Name" does not mean that we are confirmed, we must work for that great blessing – and without work we shall <u>never receive it</u>! And oh, it is worth all the effort we can make!

I enclose you a bunch of violets that came from the special garden of the Manifestation – and was given me by the Greatest Branch – after He smelt them and kissed them – so they are <u>trebly blessed</u>. Please give part of them to Mr. James – I would send another bunch if I could get them in the envelope for the

Master gives me some every morning – however, I will bring Mr. James a full bunch when I return, so keep these if you choose, or give him some as you like.

We all send you our love and the Greatest Branch sends you His greetings. I ask especially to be remembered to Mr. James, the father of the Believers and both Mr. G and myself send our love to all the Assembly – and a big share of the same to our dear brother Thornton Chase.

> Your loving sister and
> co-worker in the cause
> Lua M. Getsinger

I do not think we will reach America before May 1st. but perhaps last of April.

> God bless you all!

The enraptured Lua received her first Tablet from the hand of 'Abdu'l-Bahá dated January 18, 1899. She cherished the copy in the Master's own writing:

Forty-sixth year from the Year of Dawning.

—

HE IS GOD!

O thou shining and spiritual gem!

Glad-tidings to thee from the Generosity of thy Lord. Be happy on account of the Gift of thy GOD which shall soon surround thee. And thou art confirmed in the covenant.

> *(Signed)* 'Abdu'l-Bahá Abbas
> *(Translated by Anton Haddad)*

On March 5, 1899 Ella Goodall and Helen Hillyer arrived in 'Akká bringing the manuscript of Kheiralla's book, "Beha-ullah". This made it possible for the work to be corrected by the Master, but Kheiralla did not wish any changes. Doubts arose about the publication of the book. Ella Goodall wrote, "By the way, the book he has written has to be revised and so don't give anybody any of it until I see you for there are a few points not quite right and the

Greatest Branch has to see it all and correct it before it's published." To her mother she wrote, "Dr. K's book will not be published for some time yet so don't depend on that and I think it's better not to say anything about him, I mean don't mention him as a being a fine teacher. I will tell you why when I see you."[19]

After leaving the Holy Land Lua wrote again to friends describing their last hours in the presence of the Master:

Cairo, Egypt, April 4th, 1899.

As I have written an account of my first visit to the Holy Household, and sent to Mr. James, which undoubtedly you have read ere this, I thought perhaps you might be interested in hearing the description of my last visit there, though to me it was heartbreaking in the extreme.

On the afternoon of March 20th I said "Good bye" to Dr. and Mrs. Kheiralla, Nabiba and Labiba in Haifa (for they were to leave the next day for Port Said) and set out by myself for Acca, the gardener, Abdul Hasim [sic], who happened to be in Haifa, being my sole companion in the carriage, and he made the drive over very pleasant by telling me, in simple Persian, some of the tablets and words of the Manifestation.

When we reached the city, our Lord and Seyyed Yahya were standing near the gate, but we passed them without speaking or noticing them apparently for there were many of the Turkish soldiers standing about, – and went directly to the house, where I was most cordially welcomed by the "Greatest Leaf" and the daughters of our Master.

It was nearly dark, – so we went to the apartment of the Holy Leaf, where we had tea and then sat talking, waiting for the "King" to come. At last a servant announced that He was coming, so the two youngest daughters and myself ran out in the court to meet Him. I reached Him first and knelt down before Him, kissing the hem of His robe. He thereupon took my hand, and, saying in Persian "Daughter, welcome" helped me to my feet, and keeping my hand, walked with me into the house, where I sat down beside Him while He drank some tea, – and asked me

24

if I was "well, happy and content". To which I could only reply that to be in His presence was health, happiness and contentment itself. Then He said: "I am sending you back to America that you may work to gain a place beside me in the Eternal Kingdom."

Soon after this dinner was announced and our Master seated me beside Him, – then His wife [Munírih Khánum], the "Greatest Holy Leaf" and His daughters made up the rest of the party, while His sons-in-law waited upon us. This meal was served according to the Arabic fashion,– on a very low table, around which we sat on the floor, upon cushions. Once during the meal our Lord took a piece of bread, and putting on it some honey, handed it to me to eat, saying, as He did so: "Let all of your words be as sweetly flavored by kindness to all people – as this bread is flavored by honey." When I swallowed this mouthful from His blessed hand I truly felt a great spiritual blessing, – my heart was fairly melted by the power of love, and the tears fell like rain over my cheeks. The "Greatest Leaf" took her handkerchief, and, wiping my eyes, said: "You are blessed – be happy." Indeed I was happy – my tears were tears of joy! After the meal was over I poured the water on His hands while He washed His face (a custom in the Orient after eating); then He handed me the towel and I did likewise, – He saying, after I had finished: "Now you must go and wash from the faces of the people the clouds of ignorance, and from their hearts the love of this world – that they may receive the Spirit of Truth and shine as lamps in the Kingdom!"

He then went out to see some of the officials and I spent the evening with the "Greatest Leaf" and the daughters. We were chanting tablets and I was trying hard to tell them, in Persian, something about the Believers in America, and succeeded quite well for the little time I had studied the language, though sometimes we had a good laugh over my queer accent, especially on words containing the ' & '. They never tire of hearing about the work in America, and the four daughters are studying English very diligently so they can speak to the pilgrims as they come to Acca in the future! We retired about eleven o'clock, and I was very happy indeed!

Next morning very early the Babis in Acca began to assemble at the house of our Lord, the ladies going to the room of the

"Holy Leaf" and the men remaining down stairs. The occasion of this gathering was on account of March 21st being New Years Day, according to the Babis, so it was a feast day. Our Lord came into the room and gave to everybody some sweets from His hand, after which Rooha Khanum, one of His daughters, chanted a beautiful tablet. Then He arose, and, saying a few words of welcome, went to the room occupied by the men. There He gathered all of the children together and gave each of them a few coins, about ten or fifteen cents, which made them all delighted and very happy, of course, because He gave it to them. After drinking tea and visiting a little while, they all went away. Then we had lunch, and directly after prepared to make my last visit to the Tomb of the Manifestation. I went in a closed carriage with Rooha Khanum, and upon our arrival we went into a small room where we remained hidden until all of the others had made the visit with our Master and departed. Then He came and told us to come out, which we did, – the three of us then being in that Sacred Place alone! Immediately He led the way to the room where lies the Precious Casket which contained the Most Brilliant Jewel that ever shone upon this earth, – Bahá'u'lláh, – and there He lifted up His voice in supplication for me, – (worm of the dust that I am! Oh God, my heart burns like fire and my tears flow like rain when I think of it!) – asking that I should receive the confirmation of the Holy Spirit, and go forth to work in the Cause of God, guiding souls to the Kingdom! What this day was to me no one can ever know! My work, my words, my deeds must tell in the future whether or not He prayed for me in vain! I can only say I wanted to fall at His feet then and there, and give my heart, my soul and my life for the dear and sacred mouth that had spoken in my behalf! I then prayed for our teacher who was the means of giving us the Truth in America, for I felt that if I should live a thousand years I could never ask God enough to repay him for what he has done for me and for those I love in my own dear native land. I can never do it; God only can pay my deep debt of gratitude by answering my supplications for his welfare! As we turned away, my eyes lingered lovingly upon the Sacred Place, – and in my heart I could only feebly thank God for His great mercy and many blessings which I can never deserve, though I give my life for His sake by shedding my blood in His Cause, – which I pray may be my happy lot, – when His

26

Will in me is done!

It was dark when we reached the house of the Master in Acca, so we had dinner soon after. The Master was not present as He was obliged to go away on business directly after our return, to the house of one of the government officials. We had a pleasant evening in the apartment of the "Greatest Leaf", reading tablets, singing, visiting etc., – after which we retired.

Next morning, March 22nd, Mr. Getsinger came, and was welcomed by our Lord who kissed him tenderly on both cheeks and bade him sit beside Him while He wrote many tablets, occasionally smiling and speaking a few words to him, asking after his health, if he were happy etc., – though writing all the time. The great power of the Spirit is very apparent when he is thus occupied, and it is a blessing to be in His presence. All the day long He was very busy as many people came to Him, but in the evening He came into the room where His son-in-law, Mousin Effendi,[20] Mr. Getsinger and myself were sitting (we bowing before Him as He entered) and sat down upon the sofa, telling my husband to sit by His side, while He motioned me to my accustomed place at His feet. Then, putting one arm around him and laying Mr. Getsinger's head on His shoulder, at the same time gently stroking my head with His other hand, he began talking to us, His son-in-law interpreting what He said. "My children, – He began, – tomorrow you leave us, and while we would love to see you always, would always love to have you with us, it is better that you should go and work in the Cause of God, – for thereby He will open upon your faces the door of His gifts and shower upon you His blessings. Have no fears, – God is with you, and with all those who are striving to advance His Truth throughout your country. You must say to all the Believers in America that I love them and pray for them, and in turn I desire that they love and pray for each other, – ever seeking to be united together, living in harmony and concord, – for where division is – God is not. The law of His whole universe is unity, and discord must in no wise enter in among you. You must be kind to each other and act toward each other like true children of the Kingdom – thus you will all please me and please our Father Who art in Heaven." Oh, if you could have seen the expression of love and tenderness on His face as He uttered these words – it seemed that His whole great, noble soul was

27

pleading for the complete union, in every respect, of the Believers in America. Oh, I beg of all of you to love each other as He, our Lord, loves all of us. If you see faults in each other, overlook them quickly and forgive them – for His dear sake! He then sent His son-in-law for some bread and syrup, made from the juice of pomegranates, which he brought and placed before Him on a low table. Our Master took the bread and breaking it, dipped it into the syrup, and gave a piece to Mr. Getsinger, another to me, and took one Himself; then told us to eat it, – which we did, – it tasting most delicious, – after which he, smiling sweetly, said: "Now I send you out into the world to give to the hungry souls who are seeking to know their God – the 'Bread of Life' which is the Word of God, and to show them how sweet is the 'Water of Life' – which is faith in God."

Then He talked about our journey, inquiring most carefully how long it would take, and telling us, when we reached Cairo, that we should see Mirza Abdul[sic] Fazl and Abdul Karim, who would tell us some things we wished to know. (Mirza Abdul Fazl is, we find, a most learned man. He knows the Bible by heart and is a great Historian).[21] He then told us that He wished us to be in America in six weeks after we left Acca, so our stay in Cairo must be short. Arising and bidding us "good night", He went to sleep.

Thursday, March 23rd, our last day at the Holy Household, was a beautiful day. Early in the morning Rooha [Rúḥá] Khanum called me, and arising hastily, I went with her to the room of the "Greatest Leaf", where the Master was sitting. He bade me welcome as I entered, and I knelt before Him, kissing His hand, and then sat down at His feet beside the "Holy Leaf" and we drank tea together. As I looked at Him and thought "I must leave Him to-day" the tears came to my eyes and my heart was very heavy, though I tried hard to conceal my feelings. He noticed it and said: "Do not cry – be happy. I will go with you in spirit – the separation of the body is nothing – I will go with you." I dried my eyes and went with Him to the room where He writes, and with Rooha Khanum sat down while He began His work for the day. He took up Mr. Chase's picture which was on the divan beside Him,– also one of Mr. Clark and one of Mr. Struven (pupils of mine in Ithaca),– and looking at them, kissed first one and then another, then turned and said: "You must tell them that

I kissed their pictures and am glad to have them; that they are my sons and my heart longs to see them so I may kiss them."

Soon after He called Mr. Getsinger into the room and gave him a bottle containing juice of pomegranate; also to each of us a small bottle of the oil of roses. Shortly before noon He went out and we watched Him as he walked through the court for we wanted to see Him as much as possible. After a little time He returned and sat down to luncheon with us, one on each side of Him. We could scarcely swallow for we well knew it was our last meal with Him, and the thought of parting was breaking our hearts! As we left the table, a servant said: "The carriage is ready" – so then began the "Good byes" which were painful in the extreme, though everybody was trying to be brave, – but it was impossible – we all cried – and when we went to our Lord I was faint and sick. He came quickly from the room, and taking me by the hand, led me down one flight of stairs, and I pressed His hand to my lips, while He turned away and silently kissed Mr. Getsinger – then left us hastily. When I reached the court below it seemed that the sun grew dark for I realized I would not see Him again, and the pain of it was awful!

We rode in silence back to Haifa and very soon went on board the steamer. From the deck we watched Acca fade away out of sight, and then I knew that only my body was going away for I had left my heart there, – at His feet!

Please give my love to all the Believers, and tell them to all be firm in the faith for this is the Glorious Truth and will live forever and ever!

I am, yours faithfully in the Cause of God,
    Lua M. Getsinger

IV

The Getsingers left 'Akká on March 23, 1899, according to Lua's notes, arriving in New York City on May 20. They brought with them a photograph of 'Abdu'l-Bahá as a young man, a copy of the Kitáb-i-Aqdas in Arabic, a calligraphic rendering of the Greatest Name and a phonographic recording of the Master's voice. Anton Haddad began at once to translate the Kitáb-i-Aqdas and Howard MacNutt made arrangements for the photograph to be copied and sold.[22]

Kheiralla left 'Akká on March 21, 1899 and arrived in New York on May 1st bringing ambition and discord with him. His wife had gone to England, according to a letter written by Lua. Kheiralla was a troubled man, realizing that he could not remain the primary authority in the West and the chief Bahá'í teacher. Afraid that the Getsingers would expose his errors, he began to undermine their reputation in New York and told the Bahá'ís to expect the visit of unspiritual people. Most of the New York City Bahá'ís had never met the Getsingers before. When the Getsingers were told of Kheiralla's words about them, they prudently returned good words for bad and "praised Kheiralla to the sky". As a result, Kheiralla's insinuations, rather than undermining the Getsingers' influence in the community, came to undermine his own instead.[23]

Lua was hurt by Kheiralla's words against her, and wrote to a friend (probably Helen Hillyer) in California. The letter is undated but 1899 is written in parentheses at the top:

I will not tell you anything that is going on here – as I do not want to write any bad things. Dear Mrs. Hearst came home when we were in great trouble indeed and bestowed upon [us] her love in great abundance and stood by us like the true loyal soul she is . . . It is when one <u>stands for us</u> – when others upon whom we have relied <u>turn against us</u> – that we appreciate <u>that one's</u> friend-ship . . . Oh Helen dear . . . you do not understand how much Edward and I are <u>one</u> – consequently you do not know my <u>pain</u> when he is attacked in any way!

The letter includes passages where Lua expresses her love, "My darling Helen – I in spirit throw my arms about your dear neck and leave warm kisses upon your eyes cheeks and lips – and beg of God to bless you <u>now</u> and forever."[24]

Kheiralla had asked Anton Haddad to sign a letter to 'Abdu'l-Bahá requesting him to write to the richer Ameri-can believers and ask them to provide Kheiralla with financial support and a dowry for his daughter, who was about to be married. Kheiralla added that "I would also like the Master to authorize me to publish my book as a funda-mental basis of the Behai teachings in America. I also wish that Abbas Effendi would send me some tablets in which he praises me and my work, and commands the Believers to listen to what I say and obey me and not listen to other people who are only people of sedition and strife." Kheiralla told Haddad that he did not want the Bahá'ís to have the right to correspond with 'Abdu'l-Bahá.[25]

These changes in Kheiralla's attitude greatly troubled Anton Haddad and he confided in Phoebe Hearst who agreed that 'Abdu'l-Bahá must be informed of this. Mrs. Hearst enabled Anton Haddad to go at once to 'Akká to tell the Master what Kheiralla was saying. Haddad brought back a Tablet from 'Abdu'l-Bahá that did not support the idea of having "chiefs" in the Faith and described qualities Bahá'í teachers should have:

The guides and teachers who are in charge of this field must deny themselves, love all sincerely and practice chastity and purity, cut their hearts from the world, caring nothing for . . . any worldly thing. They must eliminate from their minds the word "Ego" or "I" and be servants of all, faithful and honest shepherds. . .

No reason is definitely known why 'Abdu'l-Bahá did not mail tablets directly to the American believers before 1899. Possibly the Master was protecting the Western believers from the machinations of the Covenant-breakers who were agitating and trying to separate the Bahá'ís after the passing of Bahá'u'lláh. The half-brothers of 'Abdu'l-Bahá, those "birds of night", had emissaries working hard in the East.[26] In the Eastern community there were many staunch and experienced believers able and ready to protect the Faith, while in the West, the new believers were more naive, vulnerable, and still inexperienced in coping with attacks on the Faith from within.

Friendships begun during the Getsingers' pilgrimage between Lua and the family of 'Abdu'l-Bahá were strengthened and renewed by her frequent visits over the years. This resulted in copious correspondence. June 9, 1899 is the date on a letter to Lua from Bahíyyih Khánum, the Greatest Holy Leaf, written in a beautiful hand with very flowery and inaccurate English. The letter mentions that the Holy Household was waiting to receive a picture of Miss Bolles from Paris but before the letter was mailed, the picture arrived. The writer wishes many spiritual gifts and bestowals upon Lua and tells her of the birth of "a beautiful baby daughter" to Díyá'íyyih Khánum, the eldest daughter of 'Abdu'l-Bahá.

A fourth of July picnic in 1899 held in La Grange, a Chicago suburb, attracted 300 believers. This was the last happy gathering of so many of the friends for a long time, as the wind of Kheiralla's defection blew them apart. In August that year Lua visited Chicago to talk of her pilgrimage. Kheiralla had spoken against the Getsingers so that some of the prominent believers had at first opposed her visit. Kheiralla was present at the meeting, as well, and she spoke highly of him, thus averting controversy.[27] 'Abdu'l-Bahá had given the Getsingers firm instructions to be kind to Kheiralla and they persevered in this attitude. This made a good impression on the Bahá'ís. Thornton Chase said of her: "Falsities were not to be endorsed but harmony was. God is with her (Lua) and will direct her, and she need not worry."

A letter from Lua to a Mrs. Bartlett dated August 18, 1899,[28] demonstrates these attitudes:

My dear Sisters:–
Your very welcome letter received this P.M. We also received one from the Doctor some few days ago, but have been much too busy to reply, although my husband has spoken many times of answering the letter and will, I believe, do so today. I thank God if I have been the means of doing any good, and if I am in any way worthy of being an example for others, I assure you it is not to my credit but it's all due to the mercy of God, and the small amount of the Holy Spirit that He has given unto me, for I am nothing and of myself can do nothing. Thus render unto God all the thanks and praise for what I seemingly accomplished.

Since my return to Detroit we have written a full report to Acca of my visit to Chicago, and we wrote who entertained me while I was in that City and for your household we have begged a blessing. Oh my dear, dear Sister, we have also been blessed greatly since then, for we have both felt the baptism of the Spirit, not fully, but as much as we could bear. We received a letter from Abdel Karim Effendi, begging us to pray for Dr. Kheiralla and we both have earnestly done so, and besides Mr. Getsinger wrote the Greatest Branch in his behalf, pleading that He should pray for him at the Tomb of the Blessed Perfection. Well, night before last, at about 9 P.M. we were sitting together in the twilight when suddenly we felt a powerful Presence in the room, which made me tremble and cry; though Mr. Getsinger was very white and calm, he was greatly affected.

We did not move for some time, then I became so weak I could not sit up and Mr. Getsinger helped me to the bed and we both lay down and the Blessed Presence still remained, though we did not see anything, and at the time I was very thankful for I know I could not have lived, my breath almost left me as it was and the tears were streaming over our faces.

It remained for about a half hour and we could not move or speak, then left us, but we did not sleep all night and we both felt our utter unworthiness to a degree that was painful.

We want to go home the first of the week so we can be as far away from the world as possible (in the woods on my mother's farm) that by fasting and prayer we may purge and purify our hearts until we are fit to receive the full baptism of the Spirit, and the Fire. We are not worthy of it, but God's mercy is great and great and we want to be the most faithful servants of our Master; thus we are bold enough to beg for the full Blessing. We are far from the world even now, but we want to overcome it to the degree that Jesus did, so we can say as did He: "The Prince of this world cometh and findeth nothing in me!"

In regard to your questions about Adam, etc., I told you what the <u>Master</u> <u>told</u> <u>us</u>. If Dr. K. says differently don't dispute with him or anybody, but pray. The Holy Spirit will answer your questions, then none can dispute you. If he has disputed what I told you, which came from the sacred lips of our Lord, I have nothing more to say and you must excuse me for not answering you, for I must not put myself in the attitude that would proclaim me "a stirrer of strife" for the Master commanded me to be a "Peace maker" and when I was troubled about some of the very questions, He read to me the 3rd chap. of 1st Cor. and I likewise tell you to read it and let it answer for the present. In time all will be known for the fire will reveal each man's work of what sort it is. Thus it will be with Dr. K's book. Wait. If it is the Truth it will <u>stand</u>, if not it will <u>fall</u> of itself. I would advise all of you now who are so hungry to stop all questions, all reading of books, except the words of Christ (Praise be to His every utterance) and <u>pray</u> without ceasing for the baptism of the Spirit: that is the most important thing, for then as the Master said "You will not need to ask questions of any man for the spirit will teach you."

In regard to the Manifestation having two wives at the same time: Dr. K. said before we went to Acca that this was <u>not</u> the case and I did not find out anything to the contrary while I was there. But if he says differently now, I won't dispute him for it makes no difference to us anyway. We must obey the laws and customs of our own country and undoubtedly that is what the Blessed Perfection did, but He wrote in the Kitab-el-Akdas that <u>one</u> wife was better, and the Greatest Branch has but one and He is our example. We are in <u>His time</u>, let us <u>look to Him</u> and find in Him the solution of all such problems!

I beg of you all each day to pray for Dr. Kheirella and be generous with his mistakes. He has done much for us and for this <u>alone</u> we should ever be grateful and pray God to <u>fully</u> open his eyes.

Please give my dear love to all the people I met at your house. I pray for you all. Oh children of God turn your faces and your hearts to Him who is <u>Abha</u>, the most Merciful, and know that He alone has power to give your hungry souls the bread and water of Life.

Please, Mrs. Bartlett, will you be kind and loving to poor Mrs. Dealy, I have received a letter from her that makes my heart ache! Remember what Jesus said, "Lovest thou me? Feed my sheep." All she needs is love, the food for the soul. If you love me at all, please I beg of you, be kind to her. Oh my God, my heart burns when I think of the state of Thy people; be with them, Oh God, make them know Thee and love Thee, then manifest this love one toward another.

I have sent Anna May's picture to Acca and supplicated a blessing for her. Give my greetings to good Dr. Bartlett. If God wishes we shall hope to see you again soon.

Love and kisses to Anna May.

God bless you all now and forever.

Your sister in the Spirit,

Lua Moore Getsinger

In these years, the Getsingers were apparently in agreement both in their love for 'Abdu'l-Bahá and to the degree of service they would each render the Bahá'í Faith. On February 23, 1900 Lua wrote from Detroit to Purley M. Blake of Cincinnati:

My dear Brother:

Your letter at hand and we have thought over the matter and have decided it will be best for me to go alone to Cincinnati, and simply read to the people there our <u>visit</u> to the Master and tell them the many interesting stories told us while there about the Holy People, from the time of the Bab until now making no mention whatever of the trouble which has arisen among the people. God knows my only desire is to tell the pure Truth to the people, – and from some words sent me from the Master – in a private tablet I feel this to be my greatest duty. I quote His words to you, but please show them to <u>no one</u> but Mr. Thompson.

"Say, Lua" (my given name) "Oh my Daughter – know that thou art a woman, whose words will have a great effect on the hearts of the people, and to whose words they will listen. Do not lose one single opportunity in this blessed time to talk to the people – be prepared on all occasions, and put forth all the efforts within thy power to deliver the message and do not look to thy comfort, or to what you shall eat or drink or wear – or to name, fame, renown, wealth, or even as to how you shall sleep, but look only to delivering the Truth with sincerity and true devotion sacrificing any and everything for the Cause! – And if you will do this – by God – you shall receive a confirmation – which you have never imagined – or conceived in your mind, and for this, I am the guarantee – and of it there is no doubt."

Of course – I cannot comprehend these words, and their vast meaning, until I have fulfilled the command – for at present I feel myself to be nothing and the most unworthy of all the Believers – but as my Lord has thus spoken to me I feel constrained to obey, and for that reason – I am going to Cincinnati alone. Mr. Getsinger also thinks this will be best for me – and for all concerned – and if this be agreeable to you – I shall be with you about next Friday or Sat. to stay over Sunday as you suggest.

Please let us hear from you.

With kindest regards and best wishes –

from all – I am yours faithfully

Lua M. Getsinger

Edward's loving devotion to the Master is evidenced by a poem he wrote on April 12, 1900:

To my Lord, my Spiritual Father;
The Greatest Branch;
The Beloved Son of God.

O kindly Light of el-Tor's Mount,
The glow is shed on foreign shore;
O Water sweet, of Life's great Fount,
From Acca's plain flows evermore.
Thy praise is sung in Psalm and rhyme,
Thy glory known in heaven and earth,
We seek Thee for Thy Love sublime,
Which vivifies from spiritual dearth.

O God Supreme! Thy Mercy's great,
Thy Bounty endless as the skies,
Thy Rule annuls a worldly fate
Of the soul that to Thy Bosom flies.
Extend Thine Hand, O Merciful,
Unto this one who seeks but Thee –
Thy Will to do – and be dutiful
To the charge which Thou has given me.

I humbly pray Thy tuneful Voice
May bid me to Thy Presence come,
Where my soul can in Thy Love rejoice,
And rest within my Father's Home.
My ear is list'ning, Father dear,
My heart, yearning for Thy embrace,
I am waiting Thy call to hear, –
And to look again on Thy Glorious Face.

I am standing on the mountain crest,
Watching for Thy beckoning hand,
That will bid me in Thy arms to rest –
And tread the shores of Acca's strand.
O bid me come – stay not the wing
That would fly me where my Father lives,
There at His feet as an offering
My heart I'll lay – my life I'll give.

unworthy servant,
E. C. Getsinger

37

The Getsingers made a second pilgrimage in the autumn of 1900. They remained in Haifa from September until January 1, 1901, then went to Port Said to study with Mírzá Abu'l-Faḍl, the foremost Bahá'í scholar of the period. They were in Port Said until March 1, when they returned to Haifa by permission of 'Abdu'l-Bahá. While in 'Akká they shared their experiences with the Chicago Bahá'ís:

Haifa, Syria, October 19, 1900.

My dear brothers and sisters in Chicago – Greetings:-
Once more, through the mercy and grace of God, my dear husband and myself have reached this blessed land; have been permitted to kneel at the Holy Feet of our revered Lord and Master, the Beloved Son of God, His Greatest Branch and Mystery; and our eyes have once more rested and feasted upon the Glory of His Face.

From this blessed land, surrounded by the sunshine of His Presence, do we send you our loving greetings, and in our hearts we humbly beg God to bless each and everyone of you, and facilitate the way that you may all come and see Him for yourselves. It is impossible to describe His Greatness, His Goodness, or His loving kindness to all the children of man, – be they Unitarian or Muhammadan, Jew or Gentile, – His heart is large enough for all, and the Cup of His Love is ever running over!

Oh my dear brother and sisters, listen to His words and be comforted. The same Holy Spirit, that spoke in Jesus Christ 1900 years ago, today speaks in Him, and through him doeth all good works. Every day of His life is a pure, holy and sanctified example for all the children of earth; to walk in His footsteps is not difficult if we can but succeed in cutting our hearts from the world, and turning our faces fully to God. Therefore, let not your hearts be troubled over anything – the most important thing is to pray without ceasing, and look not to the mistakes and faults of those around you, but each one must look to himself and purify his own heart that it may be a fit dwelling place for the Holy Spirit.

We have found since we are here this time that our dear Master (May my life be a ransom to the dust of His feet!) explained many things to Dr. Kheiralla during our first visit, which he (Dr. K) never translated to us, as the teachings of our Lord conflicted with his own ideas – thus he translated, if at all, everything that would substantiate his book. But, thank God, now everything will be made clear, for the Truth is like the light of the sun, – nothing can hide it.

Mrs. Kheiralla and Mirza Aseyd'ollah[29] are, I hope, by this time in New York and they are well prepared to give your hungry souls rich and delicious food. This teacher is one of the best and most trusted servants of our dear Lord, so you can rely upon his every utterance, and Mrs. Kheiralla is born of the Spirit and can show you the right way. Don't be excited or troubled over the question of re-incarnation, – all will be explained in the most satisfactory manner, – only be patient a little and pray much. Let unity prevail among you all; then the blessings of God will descend upon you in great abundance. What does it matter whether we were here on this earth before or not? We are here now, and it is our duty to make the most of each day as it passes, and to strive to attain a station near to God, not trouble our hearts and minds over questions which are not for our benefit! To turn our whole hearts to God, and beg that the fire of His love may be kindled therein is the most necessary and important thing to accomplish – after we have attained this, then all things will be made clear and we will all be at peace!

Our Lord has commanded my husband and myself to return to America for one year, and we leave here after one month, with Mr. Haddad and Mirza Abdel Fadhl, whose teachings and explanations of the Bible are authorized by our Lord, so we know they are <u>correct</u>!

May the love, peace and blessings of God be with you all, now and forever!

Your brother and sister,
Mr. and Mrs. Getsinger.

P. S. Our Lord will write a full explanation of re-incarnation that you may all know this matter as it is <u>exactly</u>. Until you get this, so no [do not] worry or let your faith in the Truth be disturbed at all! Mirza Abdel Fadhl can fully explain it to the satisfaction of each and every one.

Lua was in the Holy Land when on October 28, 1900, she wrote confidentially to "My dearest Brother", Mr. Blake. Her letter expresses a warm concern over the effect of the reincarnation issue:[30]

I beg of you to be strong and let not your faith be shaken at all, no matter what you may hear, for this is the Truth and our only hope in the world to come is in following it! Please give my love to Mr. Chase my "big brother" – I have never heard from him since I left Chicago but I love him the same as ever. Don't let this change in the teaching effect[sic] you, for we want to know the Truth as <u>God</u> teaches it, not as originated by man. I have heard from America that many people are shaken because they have heard Re-incarnation is not so – What does it matter whether we have ever been on this earth before or not. We are here now in the greatest period that has ever existed since the world began – let us make the most of it – and know that God doeth all things according to His Mercy and justice. Oh dear brother please try and comfort the people now – and show them that God's Way is best – we certainly want only the Truth! You are strong and you can I am sure stand this <u>test</u> – for it is a test of faith – and I pray God to make you a pillar of strength just now among all the people. Write to the believers all over and exhort them to be strong and stand firm. The Manifestation said – re-incarnation is not true – so accept it, and thank God that we know His way and let us follow Him.

We shall visit Cincinnati when we return and all things will be made plain to you. In your meetings read the Gospels and pray for the baptism of the Holy Spirit – and above all things <u>Love</u> each other. Go out of your way to be <u>kind</u> to each other! With much love I am your true sister.

Lua wrote many times to Ella Goodall Cooper. Their relationship was close enough that Ella could ask questions to which Lua would send answers from the infallible source of 'Abdu'l-Bahá. Even though she was with Him in person, the letter below reflects some misunderstanding of His station. 'Abdu'l-Bahá never claimed to be more than the servant of Bahá'u'lláh, emphasizing this point again and

40

again to the believers. Indeed, "servant of Bahá" is the meaning of the name He took. The Bahá'ís were dazzled by the perfections of the Master and saw qualities in Him so far beyond their own that even Lua, who was exceptionally well informed, wrote, ". . . the same <u>Holy Spirit</u> which spoke in Christ 1900 years ago speaks today in Abbas Effendi only in greater power and eloquency." This letter, written from Haifa March 23, 1901, attempts to answer some of Ella's questions:

My dear "Sitt Ella"
I was greatly surprised, as well as pleased to hear from you again, for I had concluded, as I had not heard from you in so long a time that my name had been stricken off the list of your correspondents – so your letter was a glad surprise. I remained in Haifa from Sept. until Jan. 1st. when we went to Port Said to study with Mirza Abul Fadhl. We were there until Mar. 1st when we returned to Haifa by permission of the dear Master – and just how long we are to be here now I do not know – for it is not yet settled when we are to return to America – if we return at all.
    Mirza Abul Fadhl and Mr. Haddad sail from Pt. Said Mar. 31st, I believe.
    You asked me to write you what I have learned since I arrived here, my dear, I would be obliged to write a book – for I have indeed learned a great deal – the Master gives lessons every morning from the Bible and every evening answers questions and explains everything for us most beautifully and satisfactorily – all of these teachings I have written, as well as all the teachings given us by Mirza Abul Fadhl during our stay in Port Said. And they are truly marvellous. – I suppose you know that reincarnation is <u>not</u> true & and that all of the teachings as first given in America are incorrect – except the historical facts of the coming of the Bab – the Manifestation – and our Lord Abbas Effendi. All the rest is wrong – i.e. the interpretations of the Bible &c. – You see, two of the daughters of the Master speak English very well now and in that way we have got to know the whole philosophy of the Truth as revealed in these great days – through Bahá'u-'lláh & and the <u>one</u> to whom He (Praise be to His Great Name) has delivered His Kingdoms. It is not nearly so difficult to

understand as the old teachings were – and it is very satisfying. All of the difficult questions the Master has explained Himself – and the interpretations of the Bible we obtained from Mirza Abul Fadhl – and we are more than sure that they are correct for we have varified [sic] them. I am so glad he is going to America, & I hope you will have an opportunity to see him. I will endeavor to answer your questions – "If God is Infinite and fills all space – how could He manifest Himself in a finite body?" by giving you the illustration regarding this same question which our Lord gave us. He likened the Infinite Essence – God – unto the material Sun. And the physical human body unto a mirror in which the Sun is reflected. If the Mirror is perfect the Sun will be reflected in it with such minute distinctness that it can say of itself "I am the Sun" the same as Christ said "I and the Father are one" – "I am in the Father & the Father is in me." Tho' the real sun does not leave the heavens – it is reflected with all its potential perfections in the mirror and the effect from the mirror is the same as from the heavens. We cannot look at the Sun in the mirror on account of its brilliance any more than you can look at it in the sky – and its two qualities heat and color are also reflected from the reflected Sun in the mirror! Christ was the most perfect Mirror of all the Prophets – because up to that time the people were not sufficiently developed to receive the full light of the Sun of the Truth – thus it had only been reflected according to their capacity to receive it. Browne[31] says in one of his articles in the Asiatic Journal – "We have seen that according to the Bab's teaching – all prophets are incarnations or manifestations of the Infinite Essence, the Primal Will. In this sense therefore they are all equal – but the same cannot be said of their revelations. For the human race is ever progressing & consequently, just as a child is taught more fully and instructed in more difficult subjects by its Master as its understanding ripens so also the Primal Will Infinite Essence, God – the Instructor of Mankind speaks in each successive manifestation with a fuller utterance. As children must be told things in a simple manner which they can easily understand, so with the human race in its earlier stages of development." Adam – instead of being the first man upon the earth was the first Prophet – of whom there is any account – and the light of the Sun of Truth was reflected in him in accordance with the ability of the people of his time to understand and comprehend it! Moses was a greater prophet than Adam for the people were more advanced – still how little spiritual teaching did Moses give – but <u>Christ</u> was a perfect reflection of the Divine Sun – and His teaching was all spiritual. But Beha'Ullah – was in comparison to Christ as the Sea is to a small pond – or we can say of Him that He is a Most perfect and exquisite Magnifying Glass which reflects all of the qualities of the Sun – its heat, light and power in such minute perfection and exaction – the effect is the same as tho' the real Sun had left the heavens & come down to dwell upon the earth. – And the reason for this great and perfect Manifestation is that since the time of Christ the world & its people have reached such a degree of perfection in education, development & and all material advancements – that nothing short of a perfect Manifestation of God – could satisfy their demand for knowledge & proof – and thus the Manifestation is called the "Blessed Perfection" – The Master said the "Holy Spirit" mentioned so often in the gospels can be likened unto the <u>rays</u> of the sun – and from this source all inspiration is received! I know now – that our Lord Abbas Effendi – is not in identity the Soul of Jesus Christ – for no soul is ever on this earth but once – but the same <u>Holy Spirit</u> which spoke in Christ 1900 years ago – speaks today in Abbas Effendi only in greater power and eloquence – and He is in reality <u>the Christ</u> of this day and generation – and we need never look for another – He is our only salvation in this world and in the worlds to come – for He is the Son of God – and all who turn their faces unto Him have indeed turned their faces unto the Father who hath bestowed upon Him every good and perfect gift – and whose spirit dwelleth in Him, and through Him doeth all holy and righteous works. I have been in His Holy Presence constantly for three months and never have I seen from Him anything save purity, holiness, godliness and absolute perfection. I see Him daily surrounded by difficulties and trials – such as no human being could endure – yet with it all He is patient, calm, and serene – people curse Him – and He blesses them – they seek to kill Him, and He smiles and prays God to forgive them! The only things that cause Him to be sad, is to see and know that those who call themselves believers – have no love in their hearts for one another – for they can only prove their love to God by manifesting it toward each other – still this fact seems to have crept into the minds of but a very few as yet, especially among the American believers – But he is very patient for we are but babes in the faith. In regards to the Manifestation having two wives – Remember that every Prophet has always obeyed the material laws of the Prophet preceding Him – but has established new laws for those who follow and come after Him. In the Katab el-Akdas the Book of Law – the Manifestation has said "That one wife is lawful" – tho' He had two – no one has the right to question as to why – for He was the establisher of the law, not the fulfiller of it. Our Lord now, is the living example of the fulfiller of all the laws – both spiritual and material. The Blessed Perfection did whatsoever He chose to do – for He was sinless and perfect – as is our Lord today – tho' in this respect they differ – inasmuch as One made the laws and the other puts them into effect! For example – suppose a king should forbid any of His subjects to enter a certain room in His palace – if they did so – they would be breaking His command and committing a sin – but that does not exclude the King from that room for the room belongs to Him – and He made the law for His subjects not for Himself.

Thus with the Blessed Perfection He was not subject to the laws He made to govern His creatures for He was perfect and above all constraints!

I could write on forever but must close. I shall be glad to hear from you and answer any questions I can for you at any time. Give my love to Helen when you see her and also my congratulations for her dear little baby!

> With affectionate regards
> I am faithfully yours in
> The Cause of God.
> Lua M. Getsinger

Mar. 23rd. 1901
Two years ago today you – Helen and I left here for America – do you remember?

Each time the Getsingers were in the presence of 'Abdu'l-Bahá, they listened carefully to his explanations and took abundant notes. Copies of Lua's notes, written in longhand, were widely distributed among the friends. Mrs. Helen

Goodall had many pages of these notes among her papers. They covered proofs of the Manifestation, interpretation of Bible subjects and Bahá'í stories such as that of Ṭáhirih. These notes are not dated but are thought to be of early origin, perhaps from 1900.

Edward's notes taken on their visit in 1900 comprise six typewritten pages and cover primarily interpretation of Bible verses, especially the prophecies about the coming of Bahá'u'lláh. The state of the soul after death was another topic of interest:

The soul or the energy which we possess is an abstract essence, separable from the material body as to its identity, or form, but in reality it is inseparable as to its actions or power. In every one of the worlds there must be a body suitable to the conditions on such a world. The spirit develops many qualities or degrees of bodies after death or decarnation, and progresses after demise from world to world, and refines the quality of the spiritual body from time to time without ever incarnating again in the flesh. Evil men will be in a state of torture out of which they must progress. The good men progress out of it in the flesh because of the torture they suffered while in the life here.

Ramona Allen Brown in her book *Memories of 'Abdu'l-Bahá* writes about her friendship with Lua Getsinger, who often visited Ramona's parents, the Allens.

Lua enjoyed being in our home with "her family" as she called us. I remember that she liked to sit in the corner of a room so that she could look into the face of each person while she spoke. Lua was a lovely portrait in her blue costume. She had pretty brown hair, ivory skin, naturally red lips, and blue eyes which were accentuated by a soft blue scarf falling from her hat across her shoulders. A celestial radiance seemed to surround her as she spoke with a simplicity and charm that attracted many people to the Faith.

Lua had at one time enjoyed wearing beautiful fashionable clothes. She told me that one day when she was in 'Akká, 'Abdu'l-Bahá sent for her and showed her a sketch He had drawn of simple wearing apparel. He instructed her to have garments made like those in the sketch and from that time on to wear them. One of Lua's outstanding virtues was her strict obedience to 'Abdu'l-Bahá's slightest wish; so she had the garments made. The dress was a lovely shade of dark royal blue – with a matching wrap, like anaba, for summer, and for winter a long coat of the same color trimmed with velvet collar and cuffs. From the sides and back of a small, round hat, of a matching blue, silky material, a full scarf fell to her waist. Later on she told me that the unusual blue costume had proved to be a safeguard to her during hazardous experiences in many countries as she traveled in service to the Faith.[32]

On which pilgrimage it was that 'Abdu'l-Bahá gave the sketch to Lua is unclear. It was to Ramona Brown that Lua gave a long pair of white kid gloves which she described as "the last of the finery".

V

Both Lua and Edward received numerous Tablets from 'Abdu'l-Bahá. Such Tablets were treasured by the one receiving, and then were many times copied and distributed to the friends, these copies making up much of the available Bahá'í literature of the period. Communications from the Master were often presented in a special form with the number "9" at the top of the page. The number nine signifies perfection and completion, being the last full integer. One Tablet to "Doctor Getsinger", as translated by Anton Haddad, 1900, follows:

> Beha Allah is on Him
> He is God

O thou whom I loved with all my heart, may God, my Lord, confirm thee, know that the greatest gift in this human world is to be prepared to show the Word of God i.e. to be overflow[ing] with its abundance, and the word of God is a fact comprising to all the Divine Perfections – Therefore O my beloved I ask God to make you a place where all sorts of perfection will appear, and embrace you with all care & surround you with all confirmation.

The traces of my love to you shall appear in such a degree more than you were hoping & wishing provided you will do according to my spiritual & merciful instruction – Be sure O my son that I have loved thee with all my heart.

Just as Lua was assured in her belief that the Master had given her a specific mission to teach the Cause, Edward believed that 'Abdu'l-Bahá had given him a special charge to develop a connection between science and religion. For this reason, he devoted his energy in other directions than earning a living. Money was often scarce and most of what they had for their travels came primarily from wealthy believers, among them Mrs. Helen Goodall and Mrs. Agnes Parsons. Others contributed, as well. The basis for Edward's belief in his assignment was formed by what he read between the lines in Tablets such as the one which follows upon which, in Edward's hand, is written this note: "Three tablets like this were received telling me to get out of business and into my research work. ECG."

To his honor Dr. Getsinger
(Upon him be Beha-ullah!)

He is God!

O thou who art directed to the Light of Guidance!
Verily, I read thy new letters & inhaled the breath of severance (from all save God) from the garden of its meanings, & my heart became thereby dilated.

Truly I say unto thee! Verily, the nostrils of 'Abdu'l-Bahá can only be perfumed by a fragrant odor emanated from an ideal severance from all else save God.

By the Life of God! If thou become endowed with all the virtues, they could not be compared as equal (to the virtue of) being separated, sanctified, & purified from all else save God. Verily, separation (from all else save God) is the light of "Baha", & severance from the worldly cares is the breaths of the Spirit of "Baha".

Verily, I beseech God to increase thy joy & fragrance, & to clothe thee with the embroidered garments of Sanctity, in the Paradise of Separation (from the world).

This is that by which thy face shall be illuminated in the Kingdom of El-Abha & whereby thine eye shall be consoled in the Assemblies of the Majestic One! This (i.e. severance from all else save God in all circumstances) is incumbent upon thee! Again this is incumbent upon thee under all circumstances!

Consider the disciples of Christ: Did they fly away into the Kingdom of Sanctity without the wings of entire severance (from all else save God)? Did they become plunged into the seas of

48

Oneness without (being on board) the Ark of severance (from all else save God). No! By the Lord, the Supreme!

Do thou beseech God to make thee as a sanctified light shining forth from the Horizon of Severance (from all else save God), so that thou may'st become like unto an Angel in the image of man, among people.

Know thou, verily, the supplications of 'Abdu'l-Bahá shall surely assist thee under all aspects & states; for I invoke God, every morn & even to make thee a sign of piety, a word of Guidance, & a humble & submissive servant unto the Threshold of Baha.

Upon thee be greeting & praise!
Abdul-Baha Abbas!

Translated in Washington, D.C. by A. K. Khan 28th Dec. 1901

September 7, 1901 is the date written in a corner of a Tablet from the Master to Edward translated by A.K.K. [Ali-Kuli Khan] in which he is counseled to be severed from the world, to turn unto the Supreme Kingdom, to be humble and submissive to the beloved of God, to love all mankind, and to show forth unison, harmony and leniency, to be kindled as a brilliant lamp, to become a sign of sanctity among creatures and a standard of the most great purity among all the nations of the earth. Edward is told that 'Abdu'l-Bahá never forgets him "even for a twinkling of an eye" and that He wishes for him what He wishes for Himself. In this Tablet he sends "greetings to the maid-servant of God, thy revered wife, announce to her the Grace of her Master and the Gift of her Ancient Lord. I beseech the Glorious Lord to enable her to serve in His extensive Vineyard, to make her fluent in praising Him among the maid-servants of the earth, to draw her by the magnet of His Love, with such attraction as may make her as a ball of fire ablaze with the heat of the Love of God. Upon her be greeting and praise!"

'Abdu'l-Bahá's loving concern is expressed in another Tablet to Edward, translated by Anton Haddad:

It is said that that heavenly gem your honourable wife is indisposed through the effects of catarrh, therefore give her my salutation and compliments and may God have her recovered and pleased through His Bounty and Benevolence.

We have sent you some fruits of the garden.

A.A.B

Lua was in the Holy Land many times, but the dates of her pilgrimages are not easy to find. It is clear that she visited the Holy Land at least eight times, and spent two long periods of time in the Master's household, once about 1902-3 and again in 1915. She seems to have spent very little time in America until 1905.

In the summer of 1901 Thomas Breakwell[33] became a Bahá'í. He had consumption and did not live very long after his declaration but he was loved exceedingly by 'Abdu'l-Bahá and his family. After his death, the Master wrote a moving poem about him which was translated by Dr. Yúnis <u>Kh</u>án with the help of Lua Getsinger, when she was again in 'Akká.[34] About 1902-3 Lua "came again on pilgrimage and stayed for more than a year, to teach English in the household of 'Abdu'l-Bahá".[35]

Howard Colby Ives in his book *Portals to Freedom* recounts a story Lua told about being asked by 'Abdu'l-Bahá to call upon a friend of his. Lua went gladly, happy to be asked to do a service for the Master, but she came back to 'Abdu'l-Bahá quickly and said that it was a terrible place, she had nearly fainted from the stench, there were filthy rooms, a degrading condition – surely He had not known. She said, "I fled lest I contact some terrible disease." 'Abdu'l-Bahá looked at her "sadly and sternly" and said, "'Dost thou desire to serve God, serve thy fellow man for in him dost thou see the image and likeness of God." He told her to "go back to this man's house. If it is filthy she should clean it; if this brother of yours is dirty, bathe him, if he is hungry, feed him. Do not return until this is done. Many times had He done this for him and cannot she serve him once?"[36]

For another account of incidents during one of Lua's pilgrimages: Shoghi Effendi, during his 16-month stay at Oxford (he had come in the spring of 1920) met with the Manchester Bahá'ís on Sunday, October 2, and after listening with much interest to the singing of hymns by the friends told them that, when Lua Getsinger made an extended pilgrimage, 'Abdu'l-Bahá would sometimes ask her to go out on the terrace of the house at Haifa in the cool, fragrant night and sing the hymn which always pleased him, "Nearer My God to Thee". Her voice would rise and fall clear as a nightingale to the joy of the Master. According to another account, "whenever she sang the famous hymn, 'Nearer my God to Thee', her gaze directed towards the Shrine of Bahá'u'lláh, it brought tears to the eyes of 'Abdu'l-Bahá."[37]

During the period when Lua spent over a year in the Holy Land teaching English to members of 'Abdu'l-Bahá's family, she took part in family and Bahá'í activities. On May 28, 1903, the night of the ascension of Bahá'u'lláh, she took part in the commemoration at His tomb with Bahíyyih Khánum, the Greatest Holy Leaf. She described this experience vividly in a letter to Hippolyte Dreyfus. The letter is undated but written in Lua's own hand.

Allaho'Abha

My dear _____
Your several letters have arrived and I regret to say that it has been impossible for me to reply sooner. I am now, indeed very busy! Beside teaching the Holy Leaves – I am teaching M. Badi Ullah [Mírzá Badí'u'lláh, half-brother of 'Abdu'l-Bahá] – M. Mousire [sic], M. Younass K. [Yúnis Khán-i-Afrúkhtih] and M. Aristoe [Arasṭú Khán] English every evening which with my own lessons takes nearly every moment of my time. But, I have not for a single hour forgotten you – nor have I failed to mention you both in the Holy and Sacred Presence of our Master (rouhi fedah) and at the Blessed Tomb! I spent the night of May 28th (The night of the ascension of the Blessed Perfection) there with

the Greatest Holy Leaf, and the other members of the Household
– It was a wonderful night and one which I shall never forget.
There was no moon – but the blue sky was thickly studded with
brilliant stars, whose soft mellow light was even more beautiful
than silver moonlight could possibly have been. The warm balmy
air was laden with the rich perfume of roses and jasmine, while
the lights, gleaming from the small villages away on the distant
mountain side seemed like funereal tapers dimly burning over
the silent dead! During the whole long night, we were walking
in the garden around the Holy Tomb or under the pines not far
away chanting tablets and lifting up our voices in supplication
unto God!

Then – oh my dear – I remembered you, and begged God in
His great and infinite Mercy to bless and keep you under the
great pavilion of His Protection and tender Love! The Greatest
Holy Leaf and I lighted all of the Lamps and candles surrounding the sarcophagus – and just as the first streaks of dawn began
to appear, and dye the east with crimson and gold – we all
repaired to the Holy Tomb – and kneeling before the Holy
Threshold lifted up our hearts and souls unto Him who is the
Creator of Heaven and earth – who manifested Himself in the
Glorious Physical Temple of Bahá'u'lláh, established His Kingdom upon this earth, abdicated His Throne in favor of His
dearest and Eldest Son, and departed unto His Placeless Kingdom, in the unknown and mysterious realms of the hereafter!
At that moment I realized, as I never had before, what that
departure meant to the inhabitants of the world and also what
it meant to the angels in heaven! By the tears which fell like rain
over our faces – and the sobs which shook our frames as saplings
pines are shaken by a tempest, I knew what was the condition of
the people from whose midst He had departed eleven years ago
that morning – and from the Glory of the eastern horizon, whose
light was not yet sufficient to drown that of the morning stars –
still set like jewels in the sky – I knew what was the joy of the
saints and heavenly host as He had appeared among them,
making Heaven more beautiful by the Beauty of His Face – and
filling all space with music from the melody of His Voice, until
those "morning stars sang together" songs of praise and joy! Yea,
verily all the earth mourned at that time but the heavens rejoiced
in welcoming him their own divine "Sun of El Abha" whose

radiance has been veiled by a "material cloud" but which now burst forth once more in its full splendor & complete Glory in the ethereal realms of never-ending Light and Love! Slowly the sun crept above the Mountain top – flashing its long arrows of gold over valley, hillock, and plain and kissing the crest of the waves of the sea in the distance – causing night to fold its shadowy mantle and steal like an Arab over the desert – leaving the sorrowing world, in the warm embrace of another new born day! Thus again dear – I remembered you and asked God to let that day be the dawn of a new peace, a new power and a new & fuller hope within your whole heart! Thus you see, though you did not receive my letter you have had something better from me, my tenderest thoughts and most sincere prayers! Our Beloved Lord just this moment came into my room and asked what I was doing. I replied I am writing to our brother Mr. Dreyfus – have you a message to send him? Yes, He answered, come with me, I will give it to you. I went to His room and He gave me the enclosed tablet for you which He had just written – and which being enclosed, makes my letter its humble servant, and worthy of sending to you! I hope I may ever have such beautiful messages to send you, and that God will ever thus bountifully bless & remember you! Your box of things as well as the two bath tubs – have arrived and been distributed! All were pleased with your remembrances and send you thanks for the same. I was very sorry to hear of poor Sibyl's death[38] – and went at once to our Lord to beg His pardon and forgiveness for her! He said "I pray God to forgive & accept her in His Kingdom!" May her family be comforted by the love and Mercy of God and may her mother and Marion soon realize the truth which she did not accept! I was also pained to hear of Dr. Dreyfus Brasac's death! What a pity he should be taken when so many were looking to him for life and health!

Dr. Yúnis Khán-i-Afrúkhtih spent the years from 1900 to 1909 in the Holy Land serving as 'Abdu'l-Bahá's secretary and interpreter with exemplary devotion.[39] Lua was present for long intervals during Yúnis Khán's service and they formed a close friendship, promising to pray for each other. In a letter written October 9, 1901 to her from

'Akká, he writes that he has prayed for her and wishes, "May God help you to be firm and steadfast in your humbleness, submissiveness and evanescence in the Glorious Cause."

Also mentioned in Lua's letter to Hippolyte Dreyfus is Dr. Arasṭú Khán, who was also serving the Master at this time.[40] An undated letter written from Batum to Lua by Arasṭú Khán expresses the thought ". . . I know that our hearts beat in sympathy with each other, & and we are one in devotion, submissiveness & love to our Beloved Lord & Master," 'Abdu'l-Bahá. The day the letter was written was the second day after Arasṭú Khán's arrival in Batum and he mentions a believer named A. Sheik Ahmad, Eff., "who is a very very lovely & spiritual gentleman". Arasṭú Khán asks Lua to write to him and not to forget him in her prayers and in the Holy Presence and in the Holy Tomb.

The date on one letter from Yúnis Khán to Lua has been corrected so that the last number is indistinct. This letter, probably dated November 14, 1902, reminds Lua of their reciprocal promise to pray for each other; he is happy that a pure angel of God is praying for him, "a poor sinner who am unworthy to be remembered by the chosen beloved of God".

9
Allaho Abha!

To

My dear and spiritual sister who is flying upon the air of the Holy Will of the Merciful God and looking down upon the people of the world who "are contented with their earthly nests, standing aloof from the Eternal Abode."

Sess Lua (upon her be El-Ebha)

Dear Sister,

Here is a holy tablet from our divine Lord addressed to Djenabe Esmollah El Mehdi who is working at Ashkabad. I found it good for you who may chant in the meetings, so I translated for you and ask you to receive it with my hearty good wishes for your successfulness in your blessed Mission and your high intentions.

I remember our reciprocal promise to pray for each other and am very happy to see that a pure angel of God prays for me, a poor sinner who am unworthy to be remembered by the chosen beloved of God.

I hope I will soon translate the Holy Prayer you gave me.

May God help me to serve the faithful servants of my Lord, such as you are, pray God preserve you and bless you more and more is the sincere prayer of your faithful brother in the Faith!

> M. Youness Khan
> Acca 14th Nov. 1902

He kept a record of his experiences and recounted some stories of her in his memoirs.[41] Describing the difficult conditions in 'Akká at the time owing to the imprisonment of 'Abdu'l-Bahá and the insidious attempts of the Covenant-breakers to influence the Bahá'ís, he says that Lua was among the few pilgrims allowed to come. Apparently she was willing to adapt to the restrictions it was necessary to impose. She stayed for over a year and, "wearing simple attire, which the Christians of Akka generally wear, was counted among the companions and rendered services worthy of mention".

Lua's intense feeling for the Faith and her longing to serve it affected everybody. She worked tirelessly teaching English, helping with correspondence and translation. She longed to give her life for the Faith and, Yúnis Khán recounts with some humour, enlisted everyone in her attempts to persuade 'Abdu'l-Bahá to grant that she might become a martyr. She would prostrate herself at the Master's feet and beg him tearfully to allow her to go to Persia and proclaim the Faith as Táhirih had done; but 'Abdu'l-Bahá did not agree. However, Lua did not give up. Sometimes she would pray all night for martyrdom, searching out special prayers of the Báb. Once the 1903 martyrdoms began in Yazd and Isfahan she could not control her tearful longing. The intensity of her emotion so affected the

Bahá'ís that she soon had them praying for her too. Yúnis Khán wryly confesses that he and his friend Araṣṭú Khán, both of them young men serving as secretaries to the Master, were among those who agreed to pray that 'Abdu'l-Bahá would allow her to become a martyr. They even agreed to get up at dawn and recite the two well-known prayers of the Báb: "Say, God sufficeth all things. . ." and "Is there any Remover of difficulties. . ." "to the number of Qadir" i.e. 314 times!

Still Lua was not satisfied. She managed to persuade Yúnis Khán and Ḥájí Mírzá Ḥaydar-'Alí, an aged and eminent believer, to approach 'Abdu'l-Bahá on her behalf and plead her cause. This they did not once, but several times.

The gist of the Master's reply was that martyrdom was a high station which Bahá'u'lláh conferred on whomever he chose. The physical fact of being killed was not the point, for there were those who had not been killed but were counted as martyrs, and also those who had been killed but who had not attained the station of a martyr. The essence of martyrdom was service, and she had, thanks be to God, arisen to serve. She should be assured that he would pray for her to attain that station,

Yúnis Khán says that as soon as they told Lua what the Master had said, she would ask them to go back and plead for her one more time! At last, he says, the loving counsels of 'Abdu'l-Bahá took effect and she resigned herself to the will of God, attained the station of martyrdom and became "annihilated in God".

Yúnis Khán also links Lua's fervor, which he describes as her "state of attraction", to the great effect her speech and manner had on others, particularly those who were unfamiliar with the Faith, and even on those who were its enemies. Lua, he says, was often sent to talk to these people, himself acting as interpreter. In each interview, he recounts, her faith was so vibrant that it affected her hearers physically: they would tremble, burst into tears and prostrate themselves.

He tells of one such interview, which took place when a Covenant-breaker from Bombay, a man named Mírzá Ḥusayn-'Alíy-i-Jahrumí, came to the Holy Land ostensibly to ask forgiveness. He was apparently one of those who were trying to minimize the importance of the activities of Mírzá Muḥammad-'Alí, half-brother of 'Abdu'l-Bahá and Arch-breaker of Bahá'u'lláh's Covenant. Jahrumí came to 'Akká with the idea, so he said, of judging for himself who was right, Muḥammad-'Alí or 'Abdu'l-Bahá! In fact he was one of the chief promoters of the Arch Covenant-breaker in India. The Master asked Yúnis Khán to meet with him, and then Ḥájí Mírzá Ḥaydar-'Alí. Yúnis Khán found him insincere, and uninterested in truth, but Jahrumí insisted on seeing 'Abdu'l-Bahá who granted him an interview.

When Lua heard of this, she asked the Master if she could meet with Jahrumí once. Yúnis Khán reminds us that at this time none of the believers were permitted to exchange a single word with the Covenant-breakers, but the Master allowed Lua to meet Jahrumí, with Yúnis Khán as interpreter.

Lua entered the room in blazing indignation. On finding Jahrumí evasive, she asked without warning, "Is Mírzá Muḥammad-'Alí a Bahá'í or not?"

Jahrumí replied that he was a close relative of Bahá'u'lláh and it was necessary to preserve his eminent position in the Faith. To this Lua answered, "I am not asking about his family relationship or his eminent position: I want to know whether he believes in the Blessed Beauty or not."

"Who is more a believer than he?" said Jahrumí.

"Then why doesn't his belief have any effect?" Lua asked. "Christ tells us that we should know a tree by its fruit. Where are the signs of his belief? How many has he taught the Faith to so far? What kind of belief is this, that its fragrance has not been perceived by anyone? I am an ignorant American woman, but since I heard this call I have taught the Faith to more than fifty people. There are thousands of women in America better than I – their faith and certitude has perfumed the world. What has Mírzá Muḥammad-'Alí done so far except to try to deceive the American believers? A Bahá'í should be fair. Is this the result of faith? Is this his fruit – that he should be the cause of confusion among the believers? Is this his eminent station in the Cause? Does such a person expect the believers to turn to him?"

Such was Lua's determination that Jahrumí gave up and asked permission to leave. "I must say a prayer", said Lua, and she began to recite a short prayer in Persian with much emotion. Jahrumí left the room deflated and weeping, "such a going", writes Yúnis Khán, "that he is still on his way."

Yúnis Khán was profoundly touched by the change he perceived in Lua as her long visit drew to a close and she came to say goodbye. For him this was an unforgettable, indescribable experience. Her face was so radiant and spiritual that she seemed to him like an angel. "I marvelled at her bearing, and wondered what kind of face this was, that I had never before seen in a human body."

Next day, when Lua had gone, the Master asked him if he had noticed the state she was in at the time of her departure. Yúnis Khán said yes, he had, and had been lost in wonderment. The Master said, "Alas, she will not stay in that condition, it is impossible to stay in that condition. See where we find such souls, see how we educate them!"

VI

In the autumn of 1902, Lua was in France with Mariam Haney[42] (the mother of the Hand of the Cause, Paul Haney) at the request of 'Abdu'l-Bahá, preparing a petition to present to the Sháh of Persia. Photographs taken at the time show Mariam's austere and refined appearance to be a perfect balance for the beautiful and somewhat dashing Lua who had not, as yet, adopted the costume that 'Abdu'l-Bahá would design for her. The petition is dated September 1902 and was written and signed by Lua, translated into French by Hippolyte Dreyfus, and presented personally to His Majesty the Sháh by Lua, accompanied by Dreyfus, at the Elysée Palace Hotel in Paris, in the name of the Bahá'ís in Paris.

The petition asked three favors: First, the privilege of an audience; second, the protection of the Bahá'ís in Persia; and third (undoubtedly Lua's own idea), that His Majesty the Sháh would permit 'Abdu'l-Bahá to "go only to Haifa and Mt. Carmel as He was wont to do, that He may again inhale a few breaths of God's pure air and I beg His Majesty to grant me this favor for the sake of the love I bear My Lord which burns like a consuming fire within my heart. If His Majesty, the Sháh, will but ask the Sultan of Turkey to give my Master, 'Abdu'l-Bahá, the permission to go outside the gate of Acca once more, I swear by the one God . . . that I will render unto His Majesty, the Sháh, my allegiance, my prayers, my gratitude, my devotion and my life."

A second petition to the Sháh was made a year after the first, and was signed by Lua as well as Hippolyte Dreyfus, Edith Sanderson and other believers in Paris. It was translated into French and sent with the Persian translation of the same by M. Yúnis Khán, direct to Teheran. It was occasioned by the fresh persecutions in Yazd, Isfahan and other places. In it the touching stories of the martyrdom of Varqá,[43] his eleven-year-old son, and his maternal uncle are recounted.

In December 1903 Lua wrote again to the Sháh expressing "sincere and humble thanks for your Majesty's prompt action in establishing order and justice in Yazd and Isphahan, for punishing the transgressors and assuring the safety and happiness of the beloved of God!" She implored fervent blessings from God upon the Sháh and says that "the angels of the Supreme Concourse will glorify and praise your Majesty for this just action, the brilliancy of which outshines the most lustrous gem in your Majesty's Crown; and those innocent souls who have so recently ascended on the wings of faith and steadfastness to the Kingdom of the All-Knowing, the Almighty God, will plead before the Door of His Mercy for your Majesty's protection under the Awning of His Pardon and Compassion!" This letter was signed by Lua and several of the Paris believers, including "Monsieur Hippolyte Dreyfus, M. and Mme. Winterburn [Americans whom Lua would meet later in Tropico, California], M. and Mme. Lucien Dreyfus [parents of Hippolyte], M. and Mme Meyer-May, and Mlle. Edith Sanderson".

Lua's presentation of two petitions to the Sháh of Persia is a remarkable achievement and one for which 'Abdu'l-Bahá carefully prepared her. It was the Master Himself who selected Mrs. Haney as Lua's travelling companion. Mrs. Haney wrote of her experiences with Lua in an article published in *Star of the West*.[44] The article is titled, "On Behalf of the Oppressed":

. . . The recent serious troubles, not only in Tehran, but also in other cities in Persia where the Bahá'ís have been more or less persecuted, brings also vividly to mind the picture of an American woman, Mrs. Lua Moore Getsinger, and her dramatic and tragic appeal to a former Shah of Persia when he was in Paris in 1902. Mrs. Getsinger was well known in America, for she was the first woman Bahá'í teacher in this country, and to her belongs the distinction of being the spiritual guide of many of the old and staunch believers. She traveled extensively as a Bahá'í teacher and made several pilgrimages to Aqá. Her irresistible charm, her remarkable gifts as a teacher, her forceful character and unique personality with the great and added charm of the spirit, this together with the fruit of her confirmed and distinguished services, placed her in the class of the world's greatest Bahá'í teachers. She passed away in Cairo, Egypt, several years ago, but her spiritual children not only in this country, but around the world, know that she is ever LIVING. The writer of this account accompanied Mrs. Getsinger to Paris, and was with her during those weeks preceding her presentation to the Shah. The close association makes it possible to recall now her intense longing to intercede in behalf of those sincere and faithful servants of God so persecuted in far-off Persia, how her prayers ascended daily and even hourly to the Court of the Divine King that the heart of the Shah might be softened and that he might listen to her appeal, how she faithfully labored to formulate her petition in such a way as to touch the heart of the former Ruler of Persia. Truly here is a picture worth preserving for future generations, for among the world's great women there are none who should come nearer receiving honor and distinction than those who in truth share the suffering and sorrows of their fellow human beings, and who offer the sacrifice of their own life that others may live.

Two petitions reached His Majesty, the Shah, one presented in person by Mrs. Getsinger on behalf of the Bahá'ís in Paris, at the Elysée Palace Hotel where the Shah and his entourage were staying in September, 1902. She was accompanied by M. Hippolyte Dreyfus, a French Bahá'í.

The scene in the Elysée Palace Hotel when Mrs. Getsinger presented her petition was graphically described in a letter to her friends. It was not an easy matter to personally render this service. His Royal Highness the Grand Vizier promised that everything would be done to grant her petition, and added, "Be at ease and know that His Majesty loves and protects all of his subjects." But Mrs. Getsinger was not to be put off in this way, she insisted that she wished to hear these words from the Shah's own lips. Thus it was that in the grand reception hall of the Elysée Palace Hotel where the entire suite of one hundred and fifty Persians were awaiting His Majesty, this one American woman, the only woman in this large group of men, stepped forward and handed to His Majesty the petition she had faithfully written. His Majesty then and there promised that all should be done that had been requested, and that was within his power, and bade Mrs. Getsinger be at ease. After this scene he left the hotel with the Grand Vizier, stepped into his waiting carriage and drove away with the petition in his hand.

The following is a copy of that part of her petition which deals specifically with the subject of the persecutions:

"We humbly supplicate His Majesty, the Shah, to extend his gracious protection over our brothers in the Faith of Bahá'u'lláh, and save their lives from the hands of those whose object it is (or thus it seems to us) to contribute only to that which brings discord and inharmony among the people of the Nations, instead of that which conduces to the unity and happiness of all mankind. When we hear, as we have recently, that our brothers in faith, loyal subjects of His Majesty, the Shah, have suffered martyrdom in the path of Bahá'u'lláh whose exalted words, unequaled doctrines and evident wisdom have caused us not only to accept and realize that His Holiness, Muhammad, was a true Prophet of God, and that His Holy Book, the Koran, is the undisputed word of God (for such is the excellency of the knowledge of Bahá'u'lláh that after 1,300 years of persecution of the Christians by the followers of Muhammad, those same Christians now accept, honor and glorify His name), but also have filled our hearts with a love the like of which we have never before experienced for the land which gave Bahá'u'lláh His birth, and over which now ruleth the "King of Kings", His Majesty, the Shah of Persia.

"In the exalted teachings of Bahá'u'lláh we have found the remedy for our sick hearts, also the healing for the nations, inasmuch as He has taught us in the unity and singleness of God, to realize that all nations are as one nation, and all the people of the world are His children – therefore, our brothers, sisters and friends.

"Thus, Your Highness, when we hear in this enlightened century that the Mullas, who claim they are teaching the Truth revealed through the Prophet of God, Muhammad – are spilling the innocent blood of their own countrymen whose only offense is that they have turned toward Bahá'u'lláh whose high and holy words have caused the people all over the world to recognize and accept him as the Manifestation of God – our souls tremble, our minds are agitated and our hearts burn and break! For that precious "Sun of Truth" arose in your midst, and thus we naturally turn our eyes toward your country as the Supreme Horizon from which the Light has shined which shall illuminate and enlighten the whole world; and now that we find its brilliant path again stained with the blood of those who but worship its Beauty, we have but one recourse, the mercy and justice of His Majesty, the Shah.

"And of you – oh Your Highness, his Grand Vizier, it has been said that you are the most intelligent man in all Persia, and as such I beg you for one moment but contemplate the teachings of Bahá'u'lláh, who has emphatically and irrefutably commanded the Bahá'ís in Persia and every other country, to bear allegiance and prove loyal to their governments and governmental laws, declaring such allegiance and loyalty to be the corner stone of His Holy Laws and mighty legislation – the like of which has never been produced by any one of the Prophets of God in the past days and ages – then answer me if the protection of those who embrace such doctrines is liable to benefit or not the country wherein they are protected? And if the whole world at large is likely to gain or lose by the diffusion of such teachings?

"Let us look carefully at the commands of Bahá'u'lláh and 'Abdu'l-Bahá, who have arisen and offered themselves as a sacrifice in the way of removing discords and bloodshed from among nations and unifying the people of the world – that we make not a record for future history like that made in the past. So at the present time as long as the Mullas have the power to stretch out the hands of oppression toward your people, it deprives you of the opportunity to emancipate them, and give them freedom of thought that they may manifest to you their greatest loyalty and devotion, because, it soon becomes impossible for any people to live in harmony and loyalty except they are commanded by their religion to bear allegiance to the head of their government; thus

63

in this instance the protection of the people who are followers of Bahá'u'lláh becomes the protection of your government as well, inasmuch as every Bahá'í will die sooner than disobey one of His holy commands.

"Thus we humbly supplicate that His Majesty, the Shah, extend his protection over these people who according to the dictates of their faith in God are his most loyal subjects and faithful friends."

The second petition by Mrs. Getsinger, personally, was presented through the usual official channels, and a copy of it follows:

"O Great King!

"Having been graciously granted an audience with your Imperial Majesty while the City of Paris was enlightened by your presence, we do not approach you as strangers, but rather as those whose hearts have been filled with secure hopes, having implicitly trusted in the promises of your Majesty to extend your kind protection over our brothers and co-religionists in Persia, and upon your Majesty's assurance that all would be done with your 'power and duty' to grant our petition!

"Thus, oh King of Persia! knowing that your power is mighty, we once more beg your gracious attention!

"We, as well as the whole civilized world, have been shocked over the news of the recent martyrdoms of the Bahá'ís in Yezd, Isphahan and other places in Persia; and believing it far from what you consider your 'duty' to allow such cruelty, persecution and bloodshed – in the Name of the One God (and there is but One) we entreat you to arise in your supreme might and justice, and abolish such atrocious murder and fanaticism from out your country, that the pages of its future history be not blotted by so black a stain, and that all the people of the world may commend your Majesty for righteousness of action, instead of pointing at you and your government the fingers of censure and scorn!

"Oh Great King! Know you, that, through the holy and heavenly teachings of Bahá'u'lláh the Bahá'ís all over the world are looking toward Persia with loving hearts and willing hands to assist her Ruler, your Imperial Majesty, with their prayers, their devotion, their love and allegiance – because from that 'Land of the Sun' arose the Most Mighty Sun of Truth, the 'Sun of Reality' Whose penetrating rays have dispelled the dark night of spiritual ignorance and unbelief, causing the dawn of a new Day, a new Era, a new Dispensation to enlighten the faces, brighten the eyes, dilate the breasts and rejoice the hearts of the denizens of the entire universe. And be assured that this Light will never be extinguished, even should you permit the blood of the Bahá'ís to run in rivers throughout your land, for it is evident that the blood of the Persian Bahá'ís is but the oil which has fed and will feed the flame in the Lamp of the Cause of Bahá'u'lláh . . .

"For over half a century now your Rulers, statesmen and Mullas have been trying to quench this Light by deluging It with the innocent blood of the beloved of God! and what result have you?

"Instead of quenching It, they have caused It to burn so brightly that not only Persia, but every country in the world, is more or less enlightened by Its incomparable radiance!

"If the Divines and Mullas would but glance over the history of their own religion so nobly founded and established by Muhammad, they would soon see that the shedding of blood is not a means of annulling, but rather the cause of promulgating every religious movement which has appeared on the part of God since time began! For in such instances, blood becomes the cement, adhering together the hearts upon which the Cause of God is founded and His Mighty Edifice is raised! Should all of the people of the world conspire together, could they prevent or even deter for one hour the material sun from rising and diffusing its rays? No, by the Truth of God. Then how much more difficult and impossible is it to stop the shining forth of the Spiritual Sun when God the Almighty ordains It to appear upon the horizon of humanity?

"The Mullas of Persia are supposed by the people of the world to be men of intelligence and learning; but when we see them killing their own countrymen, thinking thereby to arrest the Will and Cause of God, even the children of the peasants in France denounce them, not only as being ignorant men, but uncivilized and barbarous! For, what else can be said when they suddenly cause a Bahá'í to be seized, dragged through the streets to the market place, and there, with a meat axe, chop off his flesh; then bleeding, fainting – but never denying His Lord – cause him to stand and walk before his tormentors?

"His little son, eleven years old, is also attacked by his school fellows, and upon refusing to curse Bahá'u'lláh, is stabbed to death with small pen knives in the presence of his teacher, who refuses him protection!

"His maternal uncle is also killed; after which the bodies of the father, son and uncle are bound together and dragged through the streets!

"The poor wife, and mother of that noble boy (whose faith and constancy is an unparalleled example for the whole earth!) – desiring only to weep for her dead, throws herself upon their mangled corpses, and in consequence is beaten into insensibility, by the inhuman beasts into whose horrid claws these poor victims had fallen!

"Oh Great King! Can such deeds, which cause all hearts to burn and break, be the result of intelligence on the part of your Clergy? And is it justice on the part of your Majesty to allow such heinous crimes to go unpunished?

"Your Majesty is informed that Bahá'u'lláh has commanded all of His followers to be submissive, and never by word or deed, be the means of disturbance or trouble; thus they stand like sheep before the slaughter, without offering the least resistance – in faithful compliance to His Holy commands, thereby proving their loyalty to their king, as well as standing like rocks for their faith in God!

"Oh your Majesty! Do you not perceive that in allowing such sincere and steadfast people to be killed, you are depriving yourself of your most faithful and loyal subjects, leaving your Imperial Majesty surrounded by those whose thirst for blood may one day demand your own?

"We humbly beg God to enable you to arise for the protection of those who truly love and obey their King!

"God ever strengthens those who stand for right and justice, thus your Imperial Majesty needs no other Helper, though our love, devotion and prayers are with and for you!"

For several years following the presentation of these petitions, there was a remarkable cessation of persecutions. Gradually as the birth of the new cycle is fully explained and understood, as the new ideals fill the hearts of humanity and are translated into the world of action, the darkness of all "superstitious fancies will be annihilated," for mistakes and trials and difficulties appear through "limited interpretations".

VII

A Tablet from 'Abdu'l-Bahá confirms Lua's actions with praise for "that which thou has accomplished in Paris".

9

Through Ali-Kuli-Khan (Upon him be Beha'Ullah!)
New York
To the maid-servant of God Lua (Upon her be Beha'Ullah!)

He is God

O thou who art attracted towards God!

Verily, I invoke God with all my heart, that He may make thee a sign of Severance, a banner of attraction, a lamp of Sanctity; so that thou may'st be severed from all the grades (or concerns) of the earthly world & be adorned with the fullest Gifts of the Kingdom; until no voice may be heard from thee except "O Beha-El-Abha" & no quality may be known in thee except sacrifice in all conditions in the Path of God; that thou may'st sacrifice thy spirit for the Spirit of God, thy good pleasure to the Good Pleasure of God, thy desire to the Desire of God & thy will to the Will of God; & that all may testify that "this is no other than a severed, detached, sanctified & purified maid-servant in the Threshold of Beha." Truly, I say unto thee! This is a station the lights of which shine & beam forth in the Kingdom of God, & the morn of which dawns upon all regions forevermore! All else save this is no other than confused dreams, imaginations & superstitions "which fatten not (i.e. impart no benefit), neither shall they satisfy one of any truth."

O maid-servant of God! I was informed of that which thou has accomplished in Paris & the people of Sanctity are therefore praising thee. Verily, I will not forget this, & beg of God to increase thy faith, assurance, firmness, steadfastness, love & attraction.

O maid-servant of God! It is incumbent upon thee to follow thy dear husband, his Honor the excellent Doctor. Do thou not depart from his good pleasure, & act not except in that which he judges (bids or decides). Inasmuch as his good pleasure is a desirable matter before 'Abdu'l-Bahá. It is required of the wife to manage affairs in a manner desired by her noble husband. <u>This is that which is commanded by God in the Books & Tablets!</u> Do thou by no means depart from (or disobey) his wish, & do not act except in that which he wishes & approves of.

Upon thee be greetings & praise!

(sig) Abdul-Beha Abbas

Both Lua and Edward were recipients of many Tablets from 'Abdu'l-Bahá. Some are dated while others are not. On the top of the page of the translation of the Tablet quoted above is written "Lua 1903" and in Edward's hand, "No original present – was taken by Lua". He noted further that the Tablet is "backed" by 'Abdu'l-Bahá's own hand. The Tablet, which praises Lua's work in Paris in presenting the first petition to the S͟háh, and also counsels her to be obedient to Edward, may indicate that their unity was fraying. It could be that Edward, who was a professional lecturer before he married Lua, now found it galling to be bested in this field by his own wife. The Tablet is similar to many others written by 'Abdu'l-Bahá to women who are having difficulties in their marriage relationships. The Master always counselled unhappy mates, male or female, to be loving and kind to their partners and to try to please them. The translation quoted above, rendered by Ali-Kuli Khan, is dated December 9, 1902 from Washington, DC, and is clearer than the copy bearing Edward's note.

Lua was again in the Holy Land when she received the following Tablet from the Master to prepare her for the work she was soon to do in Paris in presenting the second petition to the S͟háh of Persia.

To the maid-servant of GOD, Lua
Haifa, Syria, Nov. 17, 1903.

HE IS GOD!

O thou maid-servant of the Protector, the Everlasting GOD!

To-day with an enlightened heart, a divine spirit, a heavenly attraction, a Christlike detachment and a celestial sanctification, thou must be occupied in diffusing the Breaths of God that the Word of God may affect the reality of all things. Because the Word of God is like a glass cup, and the attraction, sanctification and detachment of its speaker as the ruby wine therein! The Cup devoid of Wine produces no intoxication, and the body without spirit produces no fruit! On this journey I hope thou mayst obtain this spiritual gift, and unfurl in Paris a Flag of the Remembrance of God, bring joy to the souls and inflame the hearts.

Open thy mouth in teaching in the Cause of GOD, giving the explanations of its meaning and reality. Man was created to diffuse the Breaths of GOD and for no other purpose; because whatsoever one sees in this contingent world has no lasting result except this great Gift. Therefore, hasten to Paris, and during the days and nights obtain the inspirations, giving the greetings thereof to the maid-servants.

(signed) Abdul-Baha Abbas
(Translated by Monever Khanum and L.M.G.)

The fact that the above Tablet was translated by Munavvar Khánum, ('Abdu'l-Bahá's youngest daughter) and Lua indicates that both of them had made much progress in language. Lua was becoming fluent in Persian and Munavvar Khánum in English.

A constant stream of guidance flowed from the Master to Lua:

To the honorable Mrs. Getsinger:-

HE IS GOD!

Oh thou, that spiritual gem and supplication who pleads to the merciful Kingdom! Clad thyself with the clothes of sanctity.

Ornament thy head with the crown of humility and submissiveness to the Omnipotence of thy God. Be humble and submit thyself to the directions of the Most Merciful. Be an example to all women who are drawn by the Spirit of Sanctification and Integrity, and be a good model of the heavenly characteristics, through the Spirit of Confirmation.

These make thou thine aim; the mentioning of Bahá thy work; the thinking of Bahá and place before thine eyes the Lights of Bahá. Thus thou shalt be enable to spread the fragrance of the Holiness of thy God, the Supreme.

Give my salutations and praise to all my heavenly daughters in those far away places.

Abbas – Abdul-Beha

Prayers were revealed for Lua by the Master. Her notes and letters indicate that she took the supplications in the prayers to be God's special word to her, considering each with seriousness and reverence. Often the prayers seem to have prophetic meaning; a prayer revealed by 'Abdu'l-Bahá for Lua on March 28, 1905 seems to foreshadow wandering and loneliness for her. Years later, as she was about to leave Egypt for a teaching mission in India, Lua sent a copy of it to a friend in America. She wrote, "I am enclosing a copy of a prayer revealed for me – when I was sent to do some work in Paris nine years ago! Please read it in the Friday meeting on my behalf – I think it covers all the ground!" The translation given here is the one Lua knew and used, although a new authorized translation exists.[45]

Upon her be Bahá'u'lláh

O GOD! Thou testifiest and Thou knowest in my heart and soul there is no desire except to attain Thy pleasure and assistance and to be strengthened to render unto Thee my devotion and servitude and to sacrifice my soul in Thy path. Thou witnesseth and Thou knowest that these are my only desires.

For the sake of Thy love will I leave everything and wander in deserts and over the mountains crying out the Appearance of Thy Kingdom and proclaiming unto every ear the tidings of Thy Call.

71

O GOD! Assist this helpless one. With a burning heart and tearful eyes I am supplicating at Thy Threshold saying "O GOD! I am prepared to meet all calamities in Thy way and desire every trouble for Thy sake, with all my heart and soul, but keep me, O GOD, in the hour of tests. Thou knowest that I have left everything and am freed from every thought and occupation save Thy Mention and Praise, and that I ask for nothing save a strength and power which shall enable me to devote my life, my mind, my heart, my soul and my spirit unto Thee, O GOD! O LORD of all the worlds!"

(signed) 'Abdu'l-Bahá Abbas

A portion of a Tablet from the Master to Lua expresses His happiness that she had endured tribulation. In a future letter, Lua would refer to having "nervous prostration", hoping never to have it again; the exact time of her illness is not known. Perhaps this Tablet was sent to her at such a time of trouble. Since we do not know what problem Lua is dealing with, 'Abdu'l-Bahá's words may be said to be applied generally when one has problems. The portion is quoted below:

The more difficulties one sees in this world the more perfect one becomes. The more you plough and dig in the ground the more fertile it becomes. The more you cut the branches of a tree, the higher and stronger it grows. The more you put the gold in the fire, the purer it becomes. The more you sharpen the steel by grinding, the better it cuts. Therefore, the more sorrows one sees, the more perfect one becomes. That is why in all times the prophets of GOD have had tribulations and difficulties to withstand. The more often the captain of a ship is in the tempest and difficult sailing, the greater his knowledge becomes. Therefore, I am happy that you have had great tribulations and difficulties; – of this I am very happy – that you have had many sorrows. Strange it is that I love you and still I am happy that you have sorrows!

Lua was in the Holy Land, in 'Akká, when she wrote to Juliet Thompson on August 26, 1903. Juliet was a fellow-

Bahá'í, an artist, who lived in New York City. She was a friend for whom Lua always had a special regard, mentioning her in letters to others and expressing fervent love.

Allaho Abha!

My dearest Juliet, Your two dear letters have reached me and I rejoiced indeed to hear from you! Yes, God is most Merciful to me to let me remain so long near our Beloved Lord though I am not at all worthy of His blessings – and am, I am sure, chosen to be the recipient of the same in order that you and all the others may be encouraged, and assured that soon you will be allowed the joy of seeing His Face. For if I the poorest of His servants am so blessed what cannot you expect? When thy little portrait arrives dear I will do all you say regarding same, and will again as I have already done – beg our Lord to bless you in your work! Dear little Girlie, do not be grieved if you do not just have all you desire of <u>material</u> things – because they are fleeting and soon vanish into the obscurity from whence they came – but to attain spiritually is the real riches which will benefit you now and throughout eternity – ! I have such evidence and proof of that in the Life of the Master – which is one of complete self-abnegation and denial – yet how rich He is in power and spirit – so much so that all of us are beggars at His Door – Oh my dear – how my eyes have been opened, since my last visit here! I see this world and all therein as only a passing shadow of the everlasting world beyond, where there are <u>no shadows</u> and no change, – but eternal understanding and spiritual knowledge in the Presence of God, our dear Father, who will bestow upon each according to his deserts and capacity to receive! Dear Juliet I know now, how fruitless is the strife here – if we be striving for material things or if our hearts contain one mortal hope! At last all must be put aside, and we must turn only to God the <u>Knower</u> of all things – and face death alone! Thus I now find life to be only the school wherein we learn how to die bravely and well for the sake of God.

I shall certainly ever pray God to bless and prosper you in your work – and I am sure that your work is His work for you, because you are using the talent He has given you: only my darling sister use it all for Him – for His Glory – for His praise. Thank you so much for writing about my beloved husband. I hope you will see him soon after receiving this letter and give him my love and fondest prayers. I am longing to see his dear face again and am only content without him by being here in our dear Master's Presence, where I can daily supplicate at the Fountain of God's Mercy – for his ultimate success and prosperity. I am glad you have come to know what a real treasure Ali-Kuli Khan is – and I am happy to know you are friends! He here is greatly loved by all the people here as well as my humble self! Give him my sincere and faithful regards. I have written him four letters but I suppose he is too busy to reply. I beg you remember me to your dear Mother and brother and to you, my dearest Juliet I send my sincere and earnest love! Write me again soon,

Ever your devoted friend Lua

I am sure Alice is an angel of God's vineyard and may she be the source of Life to many.

P. S. The Master (Praise be to His Holy Name) is now very sad and depressed over the fate of the Believers in Persia – who are being killed so mercilessly by the Moh. clergy – and the Shah has not power over it! For the religion rules the State. Though thank God we have recently heard that he (the Shah) is doing all in His power to right the matter, and the killing has ceased! Please dearie write me about my husband and tell me if he is well and happy? And do give him my message! The daughters of our Lord, who are studying English with me, send their love and all are unanimous in saying they would love to see you, for I have told them about you! Write again soon

to your loving
Lua M. Getsinger

Although Edward was not in the presence of 'Abdu'l-Bahá, he was always within the circle of His love and care for his spiritual development. A Tablet to Edward from the Master translated by Ali-Kuli Khan on October 27, 1903 follows:

9

To Mr. Getsinger (Upon him be Baha'Ullah!)
New York

HE IS GOD!

Your last letter was received and I was informed of all its contents. You had written concerning the beloved of God and the slight difference of opinions. You must know this, that the principle of the Divine Foundation is love, unison, oneness and the purity of intention. When love is attained the mystery of truth will then become manifest. No one should adhere to different titles: one title (or station) is enough, and it is "'Abdu'l-Bahá". All must agree in this word, until the difference of opinions may be entirely removed from their midst. But that which is essential to the acknowledgement of this Word (i.e. 'Abdu'l-Bahá) is attraction, the Love of God, service to the Cause of God, diffusing the Word of God, severance from all else save God, affinity, union, oneness, humility, meekness, nothingness and servitude to the beloved of God. If one does not become characterized with these attributes, he has not acknowledged the title (or station) of 'Abdu'l-Bahá. Because 'Abdu'l-Bahá is the Banner of the Love of God, the Lamp of the Knowledge of God, the Herald of the Kingdom of God, the Commander of the hosts of Peace and Reconciliation, and the Orb of Union and Harmony amongst all the nations of the world. Consequently, every one in whose heart the love of 'Abdu'l-Bahá has irradiated, must act in this manner; and when persons walk and move in this path, all difference shall be removed.

O dear one! This Dispensation of the Beauty of Abha is the time of deeds, not words. The purpose is not words, but deeds! All the beloved of God must be characterized with the heavenly attributes, and appear in such conduct that the brilliance of Mercifulness may pervade all regions. Every person who is strengthened in these heavenly virtues, is my partner and associate in the service of the Holy Threshold.

O dear one! All nations await two manifestations, and these two Manifestations signify the Blessed Beauty (i.e. Bahá'u'lláh) and His Holiness the Báb. Words are different, but the purpose is one. One has called Him "Mahdi" and another hath called Him "Christ". One hath named the Blessed Beauty (i.e. Bahá'u-'lláh) the "Lord of Hosts" and another hath called Him the "Heavenly Father".

Briefly: you should adhere to that which hath issued from My Pen and Tongue. It is just as thou hast written: When (people) recognize the Beauty of Abha and arise in His Teachings, they have recognized all the Prophets and have arisen in Their Teachings; but if they do not recognize Him (Bahá'u'lláh) and acknowledge all the Prophets, it will impart no fruit, nay, they will fall in manifest loss. Consider that in the Day of Christ, whosoever acknowledged Christ, is a believer in all the Prophets and Messengers, and whosoever denied Christ, was deprived of all (of them).

Consequently, you should know the Blessed Beauty (Bahá'u-'lláh) and call in His Name, and promote His Teachings. All have sought Light from that Sun and are illumined with that Light. Consider if the sun casts rays upon a thousand mirrors, the brilliance of these mirrors is received from the same (one) sun; and when thou knowest the Sun, thou has known all the mirrors, for they are all under its shadow (i.e. subordinate to the sun).

O dear one! This is a time that thou mayst heave with the billow of the Love of God, like unto the sea, and be aflame with the Light of the Knowledge of God and illumine the world.

I was very much rejoiced with thee, for that thou art thinking concerning the union and harmony among the beloved ones.

O dear one! Consider how in Persia, the friends of God are sacrificing their lives in the field of sacrifice, and drink the Cup of Martyrdom with the utmost thirst! They sacrifice property, family and home, with all joy, in the way of the Beauty of Abha and boil like unto a sea at the time of martyrdom and raise the outcry "Ya Baha-ul Abha!" These souls are the faithful friends of 'Abdu'l-Bahá!

And I hope that the beloved of America will also sacrifice their reality, body and soul, like unto these souls.

This is the essence of the subject! If a man attains to this station, he will become the light of the two worlds and an eternal life to human kind

(Signed) EE Abdul-Baha Abbas

Edward wrote to 'Abdu'l-Bahá asking questions to be answered by His infallible interpretation. These questions show that the Bible was, indeed, important to the teaching of the early American Bahá'ís. In November of 1903 Edward wrote:

The Blessed Perfection mentioned something that the River Jordan and the Great Sea have or would come together or be united. Did He mean by that statement He, the Blessed Perfection was the Christ returned himself, and that He was the Father also?

Also, the Branch mentioned in Daniel and in Isaiah and in the Prophets who 'was to be from the Ancient Root of David and Jesse': was the Blessed Perfection the appearance of that Branch? Is the Blessed Perfection both the God and The Lamb, or is He only the one, and another is meant by the 'Lamb'?

Many of the Tablets from 'Abdu'l-Bahá received by the Getsingers are not dated, such as the following to Edward in which the Master again describes His station:

He is God!

Oh my dear friend
The letter thou has written is received and contents noted. Thou knowest how kind is 'Abdu'l-Bahá to thee! I supplicate the merciful Lord, that thou mayst become the sign of benedictions and the receptacle of the providence of the Beauty – El Abha! Regarding the questions you have asked know ye that now their answer will produce confusion among the friends and will end in strife & discord causing sadness in the hearts – therefore we do not pen the replies. Only I say the mention of 'Abdu'l-Bahá must not be the origin of inharmony among the Beloved of God because my desire is to be the means of concord, harmony and union among all mankind, inhabitants of the Earth, and all this depends upon all the Believers saying the same as is revealed from my Pen and not surpassing one word! My mention must be 'Abdu'l-Bahá and that is all! Beside this no word has been written by my pen nor uttered by my tongue! The Friends must be

77

content with this Name. Whosoever asks you what is my station say "'Abdu'l-Bahá"! and no more! No matter how much you may be urged to speak – you must say – "We are commanded to obey and acknowledge what He says! Therefore His Station is 'Abdu'l-Bahá!"

Oh my dear, how much I would like to answer your questions but wisdom does not permit.

Upon thee be greetings & praise
   (signed) ain ain
   'Abdu'l-Bahá Abbas

Regarding Mrs. Jackson[46] – deal courteously with her and never speak any words which will cause her to be angry or sad!
   [signed again] ain ain

On February 4, 1904, Edward had a dream that he considered significant. He wrote, "I sent a copy of this to ['Abdu'l-Bahá] and he said it was a true vision, and he had sent Jesus to me to comfort me. (I was very lonesome and discouraged.) The dream follows."

A dream. February fourth after Four A. M.

I had arisen at about four oclock in the morning and said my tablets and prayers, and then again retired to bed waiting for daylight, when I again fell asleep and had the following dream:

It seems that myself and Lua were about retired for the night, we were in one large room, her bed in one end and mine in the other, but I could plainly see onto her bed. As I looked to her bed I did not see her there, but for just a second I saw one appear in her place, a figure with an oriental head dress, and as the lady disappeared I seemed to think that it was Mary Magdalene. At once Lua was there again. And as I again looked toward her bed I saw a large figure approach me smiling.

At once I recognized it to be that of Jesus, although he did not look anything like the painted pictures of Him in existence. I looked closely at him and noticed how different he appeared than the people believed him to look. I did not see any halo or glory around him, but just as he was in flesh and blood 1900 years ago. At this I marveled. As He came toward me I recognized Him at once and cried out to Him, "O Jesus, forgive me for my sins and my weaknesses. You know how earnestly I am trying to advance toward the Kingdom, and how slow is my progress. You know my heart and sincerity." He put His arms around me just as my Master in Acca had done several times and said, "It is all right, be at peace. It is all right." Then he said, "You know 'Abdu'l-Bahá, do you not?" I said, Of course I do, "Well," he said, "He and I are one." I said, "I have always known that" (Meaning from the time of knowing the message). As I looked at him more I marveled at his coming to me in such a material looking body, and I asked "How is it that you can come to me like this". He said, "You have been developed so that now your organism (body) is such that I can come to you any time like this that I wish": This I hardly could believe and marveled. Then he again vanished. It was prophetic of my body or soul would become such.

Then in the dream it seems I arose in the morning and went to Dr. Moore, Lua's brother, and told him and her the dream, and described the appearance of Jesus as I had seen him and what he said to me. Then it seems I went about my business in the dream, and at the night of that day I again went to sleep in the same room and bed, but as before, I was not yet asleep when the appearance of Jesus came again to me, smiling, and said: "Last night you did not believe that I could come when I wanted to you, so you see it is true": and smiling He again vanished, and in the dream I went to sleep.

The dream was ended, having fallen asleep at about four, I awoke again at six oclock.

This was the appearance of Jesus. As I had never believed that Jesus looked in life as the artists have painted him, yet I had no idea at all as to how he really looked. But here he seemed to be a tall person, about six feet tall, large bones, strong build, large hands, large face and features, prominent cheek bones, eyes were dark but not very large. He had deep black hair which came to his shoulder, but not as long as the Master's – *rhouhi fedah*. He had a small beard, which was thin and curled close to the cheek and chin and seems had never been cut or shaved, and was a man who was about 30 years old of the Hebrew race. His mouth was large, lips thin. He impressed me with being a man of courage. His nose was not like that of a Jew at all, but more like a nose as would be on a Russian face. It was straight and broad, but the end of it was slightly flat and looked as if it was a little turned-up at the end, but this was not true, only in appearance, as the flat appearance made it seem so only. He was kindness and gentleness and love.

It must be understood that in this dream it appeared to me that I was in bed not asleep, and a vision of Jesus appeared. Then in the dream I went to sleep, awoke up the next day, and told Dr. Moore (who is not in the city), about the dream or vision, then in this same dream I went to bed again, and Jesus appeared again in a vision, yet all this in reality occurred within a space of less than two hours in reality. So that in the two hours, two nights and one day elapsed and two visions of Jesus were had.

In early February 1904, Lua, in Paris, wrote in her journal:

I wrote to Eugenie the former Empress of France asking to take her a message from the Master which is very important for her – but like her husband Napoleon III she refuses and thus – a crown of glory is denied her head. God in His Mercy desired to re-establish her and solace her broken heart – but today (Feb. 9th) she refuses to hear even the message and thus once again the fate of France is sealed! When I received her reply I felt very strange for I realize that in my weak and feeble hands repose the future of this Great Nation (or rather the positive knowledge of its future!) Oh Empress Eugenie – soon the dust of the earth shall reclaim your body and your soul shall soar to the Supreme Judgement seat of God and there and then you will know what has passed away from you! May God help you and keep you in the hour of your humiliation.

Lua cabled the Master, "Eugenie refused to see me shall I write her your message". On February 17th she "received this morning from Acca the following telegram sent to Madame Jackson: "Dites Lua d'abandonner cette dame"! [lit. "Tell Lua to abandon that lady"] Thus there is no more to be done. – And now poor woman undoubtedly she will share the fate of her husband having refused the Mercy of 'Abdu'l-Bahá whose heart is indeed full of compassion for her."

On April 27, 1904, Lua and Mrs. Jackson took notes of the "Words of 'Abdu'l-Bahá in Acca". The notes are titled, "Mercy and Justice":

Madame Jackson asked: "Why, from among all the people of the world, have we attained the blessing of knowing and coming here?"

'Abdu'l-Bahá replied: "God possesses the attributes of both justice and mercy. Justice demands that bounty be given to all equally, while mercy gives bounty without regard to merits or deserts, upon whomsoever God wishes. For example, you (Madame Jackson) show great kindness to Sigurd (Russell) and treat him as though he were your son, while in reality he is no relation to you, and this is because you love him, and thus God, because He loves His people chooses some to receive His mercy only, instead of His Justice. Jesus said, "By justice all are called but by mercy a few are especially chosen. To the latter you belong, and for this reason you are here with us, – the others who have been called are still far away.

"Caiphas was the most learned man of his time and knew the Bible by heart yet he was deprived of knowing Christ because he was only called, while Mary Magdalene, who was ignorant and knew nothing, was chosen and accepted him.

"If all the creatures of God were dealt with in the same way there would be no mercy, for, indeed, this attribute is manifest where justice is withheld, besides the order of all things throughout the universe would be disturbed. For instance, if all were rich there would be no opportunity for the appearance of mercy, and on the other hand, if all were poor the blessing of riches would not be known or appreciated.

"If all men were birds instead of human beings, there would be no minds to comprehend the mercy of God. So there must be different conditions and stations that the mercy of God may be appreciated and known". . .

VIII

During Lua's extended visits to 'Akká a warm friendship developed between Lua and two of 'Abdu'l-Bahá's daughters, Rúḥá Khánum and Munavvar Khánum. They had given her lessons in Persian, while she had given lessons in English to the Holy Family and others. Numerous letters exist, mostly undated, from both of them to Lua. Pet names were used and honorific titles of affection such as "darling mother Lua", "dear dear Mama Luni" "most affectionate mother Lua," and others.

An undated, sorrowful letter from these daughters of 'Abdu'l-Bahá was written after a long and happy visit of Lua to the Holy Family. The letter is spotted, apparently with tears, which the girls describe as "running over our cheeks". The girls felt the whole house and everything in it mourned for the sad parting of the friends.

Our dear Mama Luni
We are writing you these few lines with our tears running over our cheeks. Dear Lua we never thought your going will affect us so badly. You cannot know how the house & everything therein look to us, they are all mourning for your painful parting, we really now realize what my Father meant when He wrote to Dr. that our house is the house of sorrow & mourning – because it is really so now. It is three o clock now, mother is in bed & so are all, but my Father has not come yet, we are sitting in your sorrowful room & at your crying table, writing this letter only to feel as if we are speaking with you as we used to do every night like now, but you do not know how painful is to do & to be so. Shortly I will tell you we cannot express our feelings in words. After you went deary my Father went to bed & was I am <u>sure</u> [underlined 3 times] thinking about his only pleasure (you) so my mother

said. Then after an hour He came to the other room to take tea, while doing so He said "Really Lua is spiritual & entirely detached from this world & everything therein, & if she will stay in this condition she will do many great services in this Cause & she will be assisted & helped wherever she will be", then He turned to us & said "Did your Lua go, never mind do not be sorry, I will bring her for you again, she is really in a good state." My mother said that the reason He said you must leave from our house & my Aunt & sister must come to tell you goodbye here, was that He wanted to see you alone & to tell you good-bye well as He liked. Because He thought this house is more quiet than the other house & many people won't be here, but see at last He could not do as He liked. Because so many people come here & it was like the other house. So this was the reason He said "you must leave from here". Dear He has just come home & came straight way to your room to us & said "Oh Lua where are you now, I am sure you are very sad for her parting, because she was such a good friend" but we cannot tell you how He pronounced the word "Lua". We have to stop writing to you as He called us to go to Him & we will tell you what He will say about you in the next letter.

Dear do not cry, take care of your health & remember His words & kindness. Write us as soon as you can & <u>please</u> believe what we said about your beloved, because by Him we swear every word is true. With tearful eyes & broken hearts & bitter tears we kiss you good-night.

Yours forever
Juni & Rooha

Excuse me for this bad writing we could not help our tears,

Monever

Please mother take care of your health & do not be sad in the steamer. I thought this time I will not cry for your going as every time, because this time you went entirely submitted to the will of God & our Lord promised us that you will work for Him in all your life but believe me since you left we could not stop our tears, and we both do not know how we shall spend tonight without you do pray for us . . .

Lua mother where are you now, why did you leave your poor R[úḥá] and we cannot be patient without you.

Rúḥá Khánum often expresses her regret that Lua has left
'Akká and commiserates with her loneliness and lack of a
permanent home. A special friendship between the two
seems indicated by the openness and confidence of the
letters. One letter was written at one of the times that Lua
had left 'Akká for Paris, probably about May 1904 after her
visit with Madame Jackson in April. "I was very glad to
know that you are going to Paris with Maddam[sic], because
as long as you are in Paris, there is a hope in my heart, that
you will come again to Acca, and I will see your beautiful
face in this world. My sister and myself are staying in the
house with Laura [Barney] and Miss Rosenberg, but our
Lord and my mother are in the other house where my aunt
stays, and every day or every other day our Lord comes and
sees us here. . ."[47] Rúḥá Khánum commissions Lua to buy
a corset for her sister Ḍíyá'íyyih Khánum, describing the
kind wanted and giving measurements. (Ethel Rosenberg
was another Western Bahá'í sometimes charged with these
delicate missions.) Lua is cautioned not to buy an expensive
corset and is told to use the money from the sale of some
shawls to cover the expense. This letter is full of love and,
as in so many of Rúḥá Khánum's letters, fervent avowals of
never-ending friendship and accounts of crying into her
pillow at night from worry over Lua's troubled state, though
we are not told what those troubles are. Lua's picture had
come and the Greatest Holy Leaf, Bahíyyih Khánum, has
hung it in her room: "and every morning our Lord takes
His tea in that room so you see as if you are still with us
every morning, taking tea with us," Rúḥá Khánum says that
it was as if Lua herself was there as they gathered in that
room to drink tea together in the mornings.

August 5, 1904 is the date of a letter written from 'Akká
by Munavvar Khánum, who signs herself "Junie" and
addresses Lua as "Lunei". She writes that 'Abdu'l-Bahá has
come outside the walls of 'Akká and visited the Holy Tomb.
This letter indicates that Lua has recently left Paris to
return to America.

84

August 5, 1904

Dear and sweet Lunei

Because of my unlimited love for you and the desire to have you with us this day in order to share our happiness I took pen and ink to write you a few lines, even though I am so busy.

Is it not lovely to think that our dear Lord has at last come outside the walls of Acca to the Holy Tomb for this is just the thing I am coming to tell you of.

O it was enough to make us cry for very joy to see Him go out and have some fresh air! It was such a surprise for us all and I am sure for you also.

O dear Lunei I wish I knew where you are now. I had been thinking of you all this time and wondering how you are getting on. I have no rest these days; even in the night I lie awake thinking of you and when at last I go to sleep it is to dream of you and to wonder what has become of you! But now and again when I feel quite restless this thought will come just as a balm soothing a wound, that the more trouble you have the nearer you are to God and that it was only through these troubles that you were so detached from all the enjoyment of this world. Oh what comfort this thought gives me & will remove all my restlessness about you.

Dear Lunie I always keep in mind that we know each other and that I will never change towards you, but remain faithful and true to the end. Remember the sweet words you told me, and be assured I am always ready to help & sympathize whenever you are in need of either. And that I shall always try to keep my promise to you. My Father is feeling much better these days, my mother and sisters are staying in Haifa where they have taken a very nice house in the German colony. The children are also there for their holidays. Only my Aunt, Rooha, & myself are in Acca.

Miss B & Miss R are still here; they are studying Persian very diligently. Please do yourself try to learn Persian because I am sure you will you will learn it very soon & it will be very good for you.

And now dear please write and tell me about yourself as quick as possible and explain in detail everything concerning you. You cannot imagine how sad I felt when I heard that you were starting for America it did give me such a pang only I hope that it has turned out for good as many times things do turn out so. At all events I am sure that you will accept anything and try to bear your sufferings for the sake of your B. Above all never for one single second entertain the thought that you are being forgotten, even for a moment by your B because nobody can ever take your place. Now dear once more I would ask you to write very soon and accept much love from us all especially from your loving & faithful

Junie

P. S.

I received the letters you sent me and thank you very much for them. I can never do anything to repay for all that you have done to me and the motherly tenderness you have shown towards me!! . . .

Another undated letter from Rúḥá Khánum, probably written not long afterwards, expresses warm regards and extends the comfort that Lua should always know she has a friend who is interested in all she does, who will love her even if all others forsake her, that her name is more precious to her than any other and that Lua is first in her heart. Rúḥá Khánum commiserates with Lua at having to return to America when she didn't want to and asks Lua to write and "tell me how you have done with your husband". She hopes everything will be good for Lua in America and that "you will not be in trouble any more".

Allaho Abha

Most affectionate mother Lua
I could scarcely read your letter because of the tears that would come down on my cheeks. Oh dear to think that you have gone to America so far away and against your wish too! My sympathy went out towards you in full waves, and my heart yearned to hold you and give you loving and comforting words. You must always remember dear, that you are not alone in this world, but that you have a friend ever ready to help and comfort – to whom the sound of your name is more precious than any other sound, and who is willing to give her whole heart to you. Never doubt for

86

one moment that you occupy the first seat in my heart, and be sure that no one can take your place, for you are a part of my heart already! Darling, I would entreat you to remember these words when you are despondent, and to know that there is an ear ever ready to sympathize with all your doing and concerns. I wonder where you are now, in Paris still or in America. I have heard nothing of you or from you, and I have sent to the father of HabibAllah asking him to send me some information concerning you.

O dear you cannot fathom my deep love for you and realize half my anxiety in behalf of you. You only break my heart in saying you have no friend in this world, for if all should forsake you I will not do so, but will love you more and more.

Miss Barney & Miss Rosenberg are still with us, Miss Barney is trying to learn Persian. Oh dear how I wish you were with us these days to share our joy in the news which my sister told you of in her letter. I know how glad you would feel to see our Lord go out of the city, how I wish you could be here to enjoy ourselves together as before and meet with our Lord in Haifa! I hope this joy will be given us again, as there is nothing impossible in the sight of God.

Meanwhile try to comfort yourself and do not be sad – remember the beautiful words you heard when you were here which is the only comfort left to my heart when I think of your trials and afflictions. Though dear I know that it is a great sacrifice on your part to remain in this world where you have never drank out of the cups of happiness,

My aunt, my mother, and sisters send you their best love & greetings, telling you that they always think of you and all hope that one day will come that you may come once more to Acca. My sister Jia Khanum [Ḍíyá'íyyih K͟hánum] did not yet receive the corset, and the shawls we heard nothing about, did you leave them in Paris I wonder with whom, or take them with you to America? Please tell me in your letter what you have done with them. I wish you would sell them with whatever price you can get for them, and if it is impossible for you to sell them, I wish you would send them back, my sister is very sorry to trouble you. I hope you will not forget to write us about that. Please write me & tell me how you have done with your husband, I hope everything it will be good for you in America, so that you will not be in trouble any more, Do write me & tell about everything as soon as you can.

Your little pet Ruhi always speaks of you, he liked your photo very much, and was very happy to have it. I do not know with what address send your letter that it will reach you safely, will you tell me in your letter dear? It is all right if I send them in the address of Miss Bals?

With warmest love I send my letter thank you very much for the copies you sent me. Your ever affectionate friend Rooha

The correspondence between Lua and Rúḥá Khánum apparently did not run entirely smoothly, as Rúḥá Khánum wrote a long, unhappy letter to Lua complaining that Lua had forgotten her, misunderstood her, changed her heart toward her. She reminds Lua that in the past Lua had written on a nearly weekly basis, long letters full of love and now months have gone by without reply. Rúḥá's letter was written at a sad time in the lives of 'Abdu'l-Bahá's family when they well could have used the support of warm friends. This was when the Master was under investigation (probably by the Sultan's Commission of Enquiry in 1904, or else in 1905[48]), confined to the city and could not visit the Holy Tomb. His wife Munírih Khánum was not well and could not remain in 'Akká; many of the believers had been advised to leave for Egypt, for their own safety. Rúḥá wrote that the Master was happy to have difficulties in the path of God but the family could not help feeling sad to see him confined.

. . . Now dear Lua if you want to know about our condition in Acca. It is more than three months that our Lord is in great trouble from the government, He is again confined in the City of Acca, one day they say they are going to exile Him to Sudan and the other day they say something else nobody knows what they are going to do, one of the natives who was a believer since our Lord came to Acca, is put in the prison and is severely punished for leaving his own religion and becoming Bahai. Oh dear Lua; it is so difficult for us to see our Lord in such trouble

He never had such a difficult time in Acca before even the people of Acca who were friends to Him now getting great enemies, everyone is trying to hurt Him, and those few who remain friends the governor sent them away from Acca so now our Lord is in the middle of great difficulty without any friends or anybody who can help Him, though we all know that nobody can help Him or do anything except God, but still we cannot help but feel sad when we see Him in such difficulties, but all the time He is telling us that we must be very happy whenever we see Him in trouble because He says "I came to this world to give spiritual life to the people of the world and this cannot be until I will be in trouble and affliction, therefore this trouble which is caused for giving the Truth and the spiritual teaching to the people by which they gain the eternal life is a great joy to me and I can never called it trouble, it is a great happiness to me whenever I have some difficulties in this Cause and it is the desire of my heart by which my happiness will be completed is to shed my blood in the Path of God." But as we look we see the world needs our Lord very much and there is nobody yet who can really serve in this Cause after our Lord departs this world and see everything is unfinished in this Cause, therefore we cannot help but be sad when we see Him in danger. He sent many of the believers who had their home in Acca to Egypt that if anything will happen to Him they will be out of the trouble, our Lord thinks about the happiness and comfort of everybody except Himself, Now Oh Lua dearie we all are so sad these day to see all our friends going away leaving us alone in the middle of great difficulties and surrounded with the enemies, Oh Lua darling, I wish you would be with us these days it would be such a comfort to us to have you with us these day. I am sure you could not help but crying all the time if you see your Lord in such difficulties all alone.

Now my dear I think when you read this letter you will be tired, because it is getting very long, therefore I think I must end it now, though still there is many things in my heart that I wanted to tell you, Oh Lua I wish I had two wings and fly away to you where I will have a long conversation with you and tell you all that which is in my heart, then perhaps I can prove to you that I am the same Rooha. Now Lua dear I again write you in the end of my letter and ask you, please let us forget all the past and begin our friendship again from beginning. Oh Lua please try to make your heart all right with Rooha and try to love her a little, believe me there is nothing in my heart for you except love and devotion. Please try to write me from now after as usual, indeed dear your letter means great deal to me, I was sure that you have realized that before. I am so glad to hear that you are living with dear Mrs. Cole,[49] indeed she is a most sincere and faithful friend, I am so happy to hear that you are a great friends, I hope sometimes you will both come to Acca. I am so anxious to see her once more in Acca in the Presence of our Lord. We all felt so sad to hear about her severe illness, and now we are very happy to hear that she recovered and got over her illness. Oh dear Helen I love her with all my heart and can never forget all that she has done for us, please give her my warmest love and devotion and tell her I will be so glad to hear from her. I hope she received my last letter, I am going to write her again. My aunt, my mother and all my sisters send you their best love and kind remembrance to you and to dear Mrs. Cole, and they all hope that one day will come that you both will come again to the Holy Land in order that we will have the pleasure of seeing your dear faces again. My mother is still not well she has to be all the time out of Acca because the climate is not good for her, and that is not possible for her therefore she is all the time ill, my sister Zya Khanum [Ḍíyá'íyyih Khánum] got a baby little girl and the child of my other sister is very ill, dear Lua if you want to know the true, we all are not feeling very well and we all are very sad to see our Lord is confined in Acca in such a bad climate and is not free to go anywhere, oh Lua pray for us that we all come out of these land and come to a free land where our Lord will have a little freedom in the rest of His life, we feel so sad to see everybody in this world is free except our Lord.

My best love to all the believers as well as to your dear self. Hoping to hear from you very soon.

'I remain ever your devoted friend
Rooha. . .

Munavvar Khánum wrote a long letter to Lua describing their feelings when 'Abdu'l-Bahá was taken to the governor for questioning. The guards were rude and searched Him for letters. He was forbidden to write to foreigners and a guard was set at his door to watch day and night. Munavvar said that for three months nobody came to see them and nobody spoke to them on the street for fear of being arrested. The conditions were improved at the time of the writing of the letter.

My darling Lua
With a heart full of love and happiness I received your dear letter this week. I could hardly believe that it was a letter from you, you, whom I hope will not think of us as rarely as you write us. It reached me very late, first because I think it was delayed on the way some where & afterwards because I was not home when it reached there for I was ill & sent to the country for five weeks to have a change. When I felt better, I came back home where I found your letter waiting for me. Being your letter of course it could not be left unopened until I could come back so it was soon opened by Him.

When I came back He gave it to me and said "read it well to me again" He answered you and I am enclosing it I hope you will receive it soon and will at once do accordingly. Dear Lua, I think I need not tell you how happy I feel to think that I am going to see you again & look into your dear and lovely eyes, for, you must have know it by this time and realized our Love for you. But your dear letter which I read over & over makes me doubt this a little, for it is not yet exactly like those of old, but I am sure when we will meet, which I hope is getting near, everything will be clear to you and you will know that you were a little mistaken in what you thought at this last long separation. I am sure that you will be again my dear old Lua and in every way come back to us all.

Dear Lua the circumstances have been very bad here lately. I think it has never been as hard as this time. For three months we have not seen anybody of the people of Acca neither friends nor enemies. No one from the natives could dare to look at us or speak to us for, if they would do so they would be at once taken to the house of government and tried, they told them that they must not do it again for they will be punished for it. Few Arab believers were imprisoned for five months, a soldier was put at our door to watch day & night, we could hardly send off our post, all our letters from every where were kept in Port Said and Haifa for they would be taken by the government, twice our Lord was taken to the government where He was searched well all over to see if He has got any letter in his pocket and after searching Him very rudely the governor told Him that He is not allowed to see or to write to any foreigner. You can imagine dearie, what was our state when He was taken to the government. We thought perhaps we were never to see Him again on this earth for the circumstances were so hard that one could think they would do anything to Him, send Him where we could not know or separate Him from us for ever; but thank be to God that they had not done so and after few hours which seemed to us like years, He was given back to us by the Mercy of God only for I am sure God, who was looking at us then, only could realize what and how we felt and seeing how much the world is in need of Him and therefore changed the events. The thing was, Lua dear, that we feared separation from Him, for we only wished to be with Him, be it on earth or in heaven, be it in paradise or hell we did not care but to live without Him was the thing we could not think of and beyond what we could endure, otherwise seeing Him persecuted, suffering and even killed, knowing these are His greatest desires & happiness and realizing that these are like life-giving dew for the Tree of the Cause, would not make us the least bit sad or troubled; for, day and night during these few months He was telling us that He is waiting for the day in which He will be able to offer His life as a sacrifice for the Cause. But oh Lua, dear Lua, I cannot put in words what we felt when all at once in the afternoon while sitting together and taking tea with Him, He was sent for and taken hastily from our midst and then we looking at Him from the window until He disappeared and saying "here He is gone from us and perhaps forever": no no I could not tell you what we felt, but I am sure you can realize it if nobody in this world could. I think I better stop writing you these things and making your dear & tender heart so sad, for thank God the troubles are nearly all removed now and instead of the sad things I told you, I think I have good news to give you and make you as happy. That is that our Lord yesterday had a nice walk in the country of Acca outside the city where he could breathe nice fresh air and He will be soon going to the Tomb. Dear Lua do not mention to anybody this news for the governer who was the cause of it thinks that it is wiser & safer that it not be known for few months & therefore we are trying to keep it a secret.

All this time of trouble my mother and Yeah K [Ḍíyá'íyyih Khánum] were in Egypt, but now they are all back. Is it not sad deary that my mother's health does not permit her to stay in Acca, she has to stay almost always away. Our family is smaller than the time you were with us, for mother and Rooha are nearly all the time in Haifa. Shogy & Roohi are also in Haifa for their school.

How is our dear brother Dr. Getsinger I wonder if He received my letter in which I enclosed a long tablet to him? Please give him our best love & greetings.

I am sure my bad & awful English will cause you a great trouble to read it for, it is so long since I have not worked at it as my broken health does not let me do so & therefore I am entirely forgetting it.

Here all send you their best love. Especially my sister & Yeah K.

> I remain yours affectionately
> Monever

Lua had other correspondents in the Holy Land besides the Holy Family. Ḥájí Siyyid Muḥammad Taqí Manshadí, one of those responsible for sending and receiving the Master's correspondence, writes to her from Haifa on June 20, 1904 calling her "my dear mother" several times in the letter and signing himself "your faithful son". Lua was still in Paris at the date of writing.

My dear mother,

Your beautiful favor, dated May 25 including a letter, were received; as I was in Acca, your letter was translated and presented to the Holy Presence of our Beloved Master. Through His mercy He read it, and commanded me to write to you "Have assurance, have assurance, have assurance", this exalted word, three times were repeated, and also many other words of blessings were uttered in your behalf, which, I cannot remember now to put them down in English words, but I believe you have heard them in the spirit.

Indeed I must be very proud of having such a dear, kind and faithful mother who serves the Cause with all sincerity and devotion, and earnest to direct the people to this Glorious Kingdom. . .

Another correspondent from 'Akká was "Cohar [probably Gawhar] Bayome" who wrote:

Akka July 27, 1904
He is El Abha!

To my dear and spiritual sister
Lua Getsinger (may the Glory of God be upon her).
Dear Sister,
The first thing I like to write you in the beginning of my letter and I am sure it will gladden your heart exceedingly, is the news of the good health and spiritual happiness of our dear Lord the reflections of which happiness enlightens the hearts of those who are sincerely devoted to Him.

The exalted Holy Leaf and the Holy Household are well and send you their love and greetings.

I remember you always, specially in the Holy Tomb as well as in the Holy Presence of our Heavenly Master and ask Him to strengthen you more and more.

I shall never forget, as long as I live, those happy days I spent with you in the Holy Land and beg of God to speed the day I shall see you again.

We must boast [praise] and glorify God for being learned in this sacred and greatest Day for which all the Prophets and Saints have foretold.

I hope and pray God to support you, with His invisible Hosts, to perform great works in the Holy Cause of God.

I thank you for your kindness and acknowledge the receipt of your letter and the money you had sent to Port-side [Port Said] – the price of the ring.

All the believers are well and send you their love and greetings. Please give My regards to all the believers in your city.

And believe me
Yours very sincerely
Cohar Bayome

Yúnis Khán, her long-time correspondent, also wrote:

Allaho Abha
Akka 9th October, 1904

Dear Spiritual Sister in the Servitude,
I have received several letters from you to which I have not been privileged to answer, but I am very happy to tell you that I have tried to perform the services you have required from me by presenting the translations of your letters, with their enclosures, to our Merciful Lord, and by praying for you in the Sacred Tomb, as I had promised you. As I have always done what is the desire of your pure heart. I hope you will be kind enough to forgive my long long silence in writing to you, and you will continue to write to me as ever. I trust my hearty prayers for you will be answered and I shall have the pleasure of seeing you once more in the Holy Threshold of our Divine Lord.

I have had letters from dear Mirza Arastoo in which he remembers you with loving Behai'e greetings. He sends you a pair of Persian Melekee – cotton shoes – with two silk handerkerchiefs that I am forwarding you through our dear brother Manshadi.

May God help you to be firm and steadfast in your humbleness, submissiveness and evanescence in the Glorious Cause, is the sincere prayer of your unworthy brother

M. Youness K
Allaha Abha to all!

Lua also corresponded in French with Mrs. Ridwania Yazdi. We do not know what sad event has taken place for which Lua needs comfort but the loving heart of Mrs. Yazdi responded on February 9, 1905 with warm support.[50]

My very dear Sister,
It is with a heart filled with sorrow and grief that I am writing to you. Oh my dear Lua I do not know how to express the pain we felt in learning the sad news which has broken your poor heart. But what can you do, my dear, unfortunately one cannot fight one's destiny, finally our life on this planet is a vale of tears, and

unfortunately that is but too true.

I assure you that not a day passes without thinking of your loving, sweet and good person. I can never forget our last evening at sea where we were alone until after midnight.

How can I stop thinking of our last evening at Port Said when the tears poured down your lovely cheeks as a rose in spring. You know already, my friend, that you occupy a large place in my heart.

Our splendid and loving Master – *rouhi feda* – is enjoying good health, and the Holy Family remembers you always. You are always missed in our meetings, but what can we do, we can only hope to see you one day again amongst us.

My mother, my husband, my brother are in good health and send you their best regards. My best regards for all the believers who are with you, first of all to your husband, Négar and Toufic give you many kisses and think often of you.

Receive dear Sister two thousand hugs from your little sister who loves you so and will never forget you.

R. Yazdi

Mrs. Yazdi wrote again to Lua on September 22, 1905, at a period when 'Abdu'l-Bahá was once again in great danger. False accusations against Him made by his half-brothers, the Covenant-breakers, caused the Turkish government to send an inspector to question 'Abdu'l-Bahá.

To my dear sister Lua!

I have received with much joy and pleasure your nice letter of which the first part was written by Mrs. Caule [Helen Ellis Cole] whom I love so much and would have liked to see more, but up till now taking care of little Toufic has taken almost all my time, so I only got to see her very few times. I do remember very well the times we were together in Caiffa [Haifa]. They were only too short.

I do regret not having been able to answer before but you will understand when you learn about what has happened.

I was in Acre when your dear letter was transmitted and you know already that an Inspector has arrived and it is total madness. In the newspapers one could read, "Preparations made to exile Abbas Effendi and his followers." But where – nobody knew – a lot of other not very nice things. They permitted no one to leave Acre. You can imagine, dear friend, our sorrow and grief for our dear and beloved Master – *rouhi feda*. Thanks to God, things go better now – but not really good.

But our magnificent and dear Master asked the believers to leave Acre. That is for those who are capable of leaving, several families have already left for Cairo.

Dear Lua – I have given your message to our great Master – *rouhi feda*. He said that He will never forget you and He sends His blessings. He has also written a Tablet for you that will come with a letter from Miss Rúḥá Khánum. The Holy Family sends all their affection and regards. Also to our sister Mrs. Cole. The more time passes, the stronger grows our friendship, because it is based on a solid foundation. We are always thinking of you and particularly when we are together we miss you, dear Lua, and are hoping that once again you will be with us. Munavvar Khánum has asked me to write her very sincere regards. My parents, my husband and my brother send their most affectionate regards.

Négar and Toufic send their sweet kisses. Please, dear Sister, present all my most affectionate regards to the believers, in particular to those I know, and also to your husband.

Excuse my dear Sister, if my letter is not very well written, it is a long time since I studied French.

In hoping to receive your news now and then which is so dear to us, I hug you very tenderly and with all my heart.

Your sister who will never forget you.

R. Yazdi

IX

On her return to America Lua and Edward appear to have lived for some time with Helen Ellis Cole in New York, before settling in Washington DC. Lua immediately began to teach and to visit other Bahá'í communities. One talk she gave on service during April 1905 in Washington is just as vivid today as it was then:

None of us are sufficiently single-minded! We wish to serve in the Cause of God, but we particularly wish to do it in our own way after our own fashion, and when it suits our convenience, and that is just what God won't have. Once engaging in His Service, we must work in accordance with His Way, after His fashion, and when it shall please Him.

In His Vineyard there are many kinds of labor to be performed, but each are equally necessary. The servants are assigned tasks which correspond to their capacity to serve, – as seen in the parable of the talents. To one the power of speech is given; to another money is given; yet to another the ability to attract people and interest them; and still to another a comfortable home, wherein strangers can be housed and the hungry fed! Now let us see how all these, when working together in harmony, can please the Lord of the Vineyard! The one who has the ability to attract the people, can do so and hand them over to the one who has power to teach; that one can deliver the Message of Truth, and hand them over to the one who has the home – if they be in need – and the householder can turn for help unto the servant who has the money, who, in obedience unto the Command "Distribute the money that I gave thee upon my poor, that thou mayest distribute in heaven from the Treasure of Exaltation" – may hand unto the Lord of the Vineyard a new servant, attracted, enkindled, instructed, fed, clothed and equipped for His service.

And what a joy for the servants who have made such a good

use of their talents; in such a case each one receives the "Well done! Enter thou into the joys of thy Lord!" On the other hand, suppose they should hide their several talents in the earth. The first one should say – I cannot teach – therefore I shall attract friends unto <u>myself</u>! The second, I have no house to teach in, therefore I shall not deliver this Message, I but use my power in teaching something which will benefit <u>myself</u>. The third, – this house is only large enough for my own use. I am not going to let strangers and poor people come in for I have no money to clothe and feed them, I will use it for my own family and be comfortable <u>myself</u>! The fourth, this money is mine, God did not give it to me, I earned it myself, or my husband did, and I am not going to part with it for the benefit of others lest some day I shall come to want <u>myself</u>! Now what have they done? Each one has taken the spade of "myself"– and digging in the earth of his own selfish desires, accused his Lord of being "a hard man, reaping where He has not sown." When the truth is, He (the Lord) has sown His Talents among them, and they have failed to do the reaping; and truly in the end that which was given, shall be taken from them; or rather they shall be taken away from what was given them; for in the end they shall die, and their talents which they buried in the earth of "selfishness" shall remain in the earth, but <u>they shall be taken away</u>!

One day we shall all know that, verily, we are beggars – every one of us – at the Door of God's Bounty, and all we have now, or ever will have is only what He has given us, – whether it be power to attract, the gift of speech, a comfortable home, or money – they are but His Talents, which He has distributed according to our "several abilities", and the account of which we will one day be called upon to render to the Lord of the servants! Therefore, "O Son of Man! Distribute <u>My</u> <u>Possessions</u> among My poor, that in heaven thou mayest receive from boundless treasures of glory and from the stores of eternal bliss."

In working in the Cause of God, we underrate the enormous power of His Holy Spirit and the tremendous hold it has upon us after once we are brought in contact with It! Therefore, it behooves us to become <u>actually</u> good – not merely approximately so – or the Fire of the Spirit which has descended from Heaven to touch us, will burn to ashes! Let us remember too, that after contact with the Fire, the least atom of the old leaven of selfishness or unwillingness to utilize our talents will slowly leaven the whole lump of our lives, eventually rendering them unfit even to be counted as the unleavened bread of sincerity and truth in the material world, to say nothing of the spiritual existence.

Like the ore when thrown into the fire – we must surrender ourselves to the flame – taking on its attributes and characteristics, that the dross of clay may be burned away, and the pure gold of the spirit shine forth and be manifest within us. In Divine service only those complain of ingratitude who in trying to surrender to the Fire of the Holy Spirit – hold something back! When we declare we have sacrificed ourselves for others, for the sake of the Cause of God, and have received nothing in return (not even the joy of having done good) be sure that after the manner of Ananias and Sapphira, we have kept back part of the price! For when we give in the right spirit – be it a penny or the all we possess – we get <u>back</u> our mete as we have measured always, and generally it is pressed down and running over! For in giving all, we get all, and this is the Divine Law! When we are really ready to give up <u>all</u> for God, to seek His Will and serve Him absolutely in singleness of heart, with not the faintest thought of serving ourselves or our own interests at the same time, then we will strike a chord in the hearts of our fellow creatures which no wiles of the world, the flesh, or the devil can succeed in putting to silence! Then the Divine Surrender in us will call for the Divine Surrender in others, and by our good deeds (the proper use of our talents) will we stand before God and the world as sincere and accepted servants in His Holy Vineyard – His Glorious Cause – receiving His commendation of "Well done good and faithful servants, enter thou into the joys of thy Lord".

In the late Autumn of 1905 Lua travelled from New York to Boston to give a series of classes. She was a challenging teacher who urged her students to seek the truth for themselves. She taught that there is no middle position in relation to Bahá'u'lláh; one should either recognize His station as Manifestation of God for this day or denounce Him as an imposter. Harlan Ober and Alfred Lunt were among her students in the Boston group:

Before Harlan had recognized the station of Bahá'u'lláh, he gradually decided that His Revelation had either the power to unite mankind or to mislead it. Aware of his confusion, Mrs. Getsinger said to Harlan: "You must discover the reality of this Faith and, if it is true, you must accept it, but if it is false, you must denounce." She urged him to pray. This he had not done formally for a number of years, and, because of his recent interest in Hinduism, had lately turned to the practice of what he described as "concentration." Harlan promised her to say a prayer if she could find one for him that was "sufficiently universal" so that he could say it without feeling that he was engaged in "self-hypnosis". . .

One day in the spring of 1906, taking with him the prayer Lua had chosen for him, the Bible, the *Kitáb-i-Íqán*, the *Hidden Words* and a scholarly explanation of Biblical prophecy . . . Harlan went . . . to Boston and booked a room for himself in the Commonwealth Hotel for a week. Cutting himself off from his family and friends, he spent this time in study and prayer . . . He subsequently stated:

"Through the mercy and bounty of God, doors opened, knowledge replaced uncertainty and ignorance, and I became conscious of the mystery of Unity . . . My whole being was quickened . . . When I went out into the streets and through the Boston Common and the Boston Public Gardens, I looked upon every soul . . . with a new love. I saw in the blossoming of the magnolias the clear evidence of the return of spirit as outlined in the writings of Bahá'u'lláh in the Íqán."[51]

In the files are copies of speeches and lessons apparently given by Lua which show how much she depended upon the Bible for authority in teaching. She used Bible stories to illustrate her themes. An eleven-page paper entitled "The Practice of Prayer" has several points: 1. Begin to ask; 2. Be instant in asking; 3. Keep on asking; 4. Ask in all things; 5. Ask and ye shall know God; 6. Ask and your joy shall be full; 7. Ask, because there is a giving by God which comes only by our asking.

Lua looked to 'Abdu'l-Bahá for guidance in things both great and small. Often she was the center to whom Tablets from the Master were sent with messages for others. Communications such as the one below, with meaning for Edward and the Cole family as well as for herself, were often received.

To the attracted maid-servant of GOD, Mrs. Getsinger (Lua) New York
   (Upon her be Bahá'u'lláh EL ABHA!)

HE IS GOD!

O thou attracted leaf!
Your letter was received, and the news of the ascension of the heavenly leaf, the merciful maid-servant of GOD Mrs. Cole was a cause of great sadness and regret, for she was indeed firm and sincere, patient and expressive. When she came to this Blessed Spot, she spent some days in chanting the Verses of Oneness with great submissiveness and a spirit of communion. During that period she did no other work except praising GOD, and entertained no hope save for the Divine Mercy and Bounty. Then she returned to those regions in the utmost spirit and fragrance, and good news was always received from her. In Green Acre she made a great effort and strove to assist the friends. She did not fail to do what she could, until she soared – like unto the birds – to the Horizon of Eternal Glory!

Be not sorrowful and grieve not! Although she was bereft of a mortal life, yet she became an inmate of the Sanctuary of the Lord and found the Life Eternal. She passed beyond the drop and joined the ocean. She was set free from the cage and soared to the Illimitable Realm; she bid the world of darkness farewell, and hastened to the Illumined Space. Therefore, forgiveness and pardon should be sought for her in all spirit and fragrance, so that she may attain a new blessing every moment in the Eternal Kingdom, and that the Lights of Meeting may illumine her in the Assembly of Light to the degree of attaining Divine Radiance. Upon thee be greeting and praise!

Convey the longing greetings of this Longing One to his honor, the doctor, and say to him that he is always in Mind and present in the meeting of the Merciful. I ask GOD to increase his faith, certainty, knowledge and firmness.

Upon thee be greeting and praise.

(signed) Abdul-Baha Abbas

Translated by Ameen Ullah Fareed. Chicago, May 23, 1906

On an earlier Tablet from 'Abdu'l-Bahá to Lua quoted on p. 69 of this book, Edward had made a note indicating that Lua's obedience to her husband was "backed" by the Master Himself. No such emphasis is found in another Tablet written to him counselling him to "show forth kind treatment and respect" for his wife. The Tablet is dated July 25, 1906 and follows in the translation made at the time.

9

Announce in my behalf respectful greeting to the attracted maid-servant of God Mrs. Lua Getsinger. Truly I say, she is the Center of the Love of God; and engaged in diffusing the Fragrances. You must show forth kind treatment and respect for her from all directions.

Upon thee be greeting and praise!

(signed) 'Abdu'l-Bahá Abbas

July 25, 1906.

'Abdu'l-Bahá decided, in the winter of 1906, that the time had come for some American Bahá'ís to visit India so that they could teach the Cause there and show its people that Bahá'í communities existed in the West. For such an important mission, 'Abdu'l-Bahá relied upon the advice of Mírzá Abu'l-Faḍl who suggested Hooper Harris. The Master then revealed a Tablet in which He requested the community to send Mr. Harris and a suitable companion on an extended trip to India. The community chose Dr. William Moore, Lua's brother, to accompany Mr. Harris. Shortly afterward, Dr. Moore died of yellow fever. A letter from Rúḥá Khánum shows the tender concern felt for Lua under the circumstance of her brother's death. It also shows much improvement in English, though her command of it is not yet perfect.

My darling mother Lua

Just now our Lord came in and gave me your letter which you wrote to him, and asked me to read it at once to Him which I did.

Oh dear I can hardly express in word how we all felt when we read of the death of our dear spiritual brother Dr. Moore. At first when our Lord heard he was very quiet and looked very sad, after a little time, He began to speak, He said many beautiful things of him, He said we must not be sad over his death, because there is a great wisdom for his departure, though he was a very sincere worker in this Cause, and really his whole desire was to spread the teachings of Abha amongst the people, and during these years that he was a believer he never did anything to displease me. Though my dear Lua it was a great consolation for us to hear our Lord speak such beautiful things of him, but still dear heart it was a great grief and sorrow for all of us, indeed it was just as if one of our dear own family departed from this world. We all know that he is very happy now in the Kingdom of Abha where his spirit always been desiring to fly away and leave the cage of his miserable body, where he can get the everlasting happiness and life. Really dear heart we must not feel sad for his death, because we know how tired he was from this world, where is nothing but trouble and afflictions, but still his family and friends will miss him very much, I am sure he had no enemy, and everyone who met him spoke many beautiful things of him. That day our Lord was speaking of him again, he said Really Dr. Moore did not die, because the sincere servants of Abha never die because they have got everlasting life. Oh dear friend try to comfort your poor broken heart with these words from our Lord, I cannot think of your condition and your grief over the loss of your dear brother, I know how much you loved him, be sure dear we all shared with your grief, because if he was your physical brother he was our spiritual brother too, and beside that he was such a sincere believer and worker for the Cause of Abha. I am sure he could do great work in this Cause, it is so sad that he departed from this world at this time when we see there is no worker for the harvest of God, but very few, and this few is getting less and less.

This morning our Lord called me, and gave me two tablets to send them to you, which I enclose, one is for your husband Dr.

Getsinger, and one for your poor mother and sister. He wrote one for you last week and gave it to Miss Barney to send it to you, I hope you have received it soon. I am sure these Tablets will be a great consolation for you and your mother, and sister, it is just like a balm for your poor wounded hearts.

My dear aunt and mother and sisters all join me in sending much love and warm greetings, to you and to Dr., they all say that they never forget to pray for your dear brother in the Holy Tomb, and they also ask God to give you the power of enduring all the afflictions and troubles which come to you in this life, and they all say that they shared with you in your grief over the loss of your dear brother.

Dear you cannot know how we all felt yesterday, when Mr. Sprague left for India, We so much thought of your brother, and the work he would do if he would go to India to teach. As you know it was our Lord's desire to send him there, but now I am sure if he did not go to India with his body, I am sure in spirit he is with Mr. Sprague.

Hoping to hear from you soon dear friend, even you may not like to write me but I hope I will hear from you through others. I am ever your faithful & devoted friend Rooha

(I wrote this letter with great haste, as I want to catch the mail, therefore I wrote it very badly, I hope you will be able to read it.)

Lua asked Harlan Ober to take her dead brother's place as travelling companion to Hooper Harris, and when his parents would not agree to help him go to such a dangerous place as India, Mrs. Getsinger borrowed a sum of money from Mr. Hervey Lunt, Alfred Lunt's father, for the purpose. How she proposed repaying the sum is unknown, as she had no fixed income and was often supported in her travels by donations from wealthy believers. However, the New York Bahá'ís had raised a sum of money. In the letter above it appears that Rúḥá Khánum has confused Harlan Ober with Sidney Sprague, who was the first Western Bahá'í to visit India, in 1904.[52]

An undated letter in Lua's handwriting, apparently a translation of a letter from a Persian writer in the Holy Land, may have been a letter of condolence at the death of her brother William. Lua is addressed in the flowery and pious language that Westerners often find excessive:

He is God! To the Rose of garden of faithfulness, and the Verdant Leaf in the Orchard of Love and faithfulness the maidservant of God Sister Lua: I send you Behai greetings and peace which proceed from the heart and soul and which refreshes the spirit with the delicate zephyr of immortality . . . I adjure you by the Greatest Name that these humble ones wish always the well-being, prosperity and general salvation of the whole world; love much more for the believers who are the chosen ones of God . . . In fact the great affliction that has fallen upon you from the direction of fate is very difficult to bear. . .

Lua was working nearly full time lecturing for the Faith. On September 5, 1907 she wrote from Pine Hill, New York, to Juliet Thompson sending messages recently received from 'Abdu'l-Bahá. "I am glad to be the humble instrument of these messages to you dear Julie! I trust you have had a nice vacation and that you are rested and well . . . and do be in Washington on the 24th inst. if possible."

"About 1907-8" is written in the corner of a letter from Munavvar Khánum to Edward. Lua was apparently teaching in Canada at the time, for Munavvar Khánum wrote, "We were so happy to hear of Lua's work for the Cause in Canada and we would much like to hear about it."

By early 1908 she was once more on her way to the Holy Land, this time with Stanwood Cobb, who accompanied her on pilgrimage in February of that year.[53] September found her in Geneva, so it is possible that she stayed in the Holy Land and in Europe for the intervening six months, probably carrying out what would nowadays be called "external relations work".

As we have seen, 'Abdu'l-Bahá had sent Lua to Paris in 1902 and 1903 to write and present petitions to the S͟háh; in early 1904 she was writing to the Empress Eugenie; and two letters from an official at the Persian Legation in Washington in the Spring of 1906 (one dated April 24th, the other May 12th), show that both Lua and Edward were keeping in touch with the Persian authorities. In early September 1908 she writes that it will be unnecessary for her to attend a Congress in Paris because another American Bahá'í will be able to go instead, but that she has had to wait in Geneva, Switzerland, in order to see the Persian Consul from Port Said.

In the meantime Edward, in America, was much occupied with his proposal for a national Bahá'í organization.[54] He submitted an eleven-page document to the Master outlining his ideas and received a Tablet dated July 8, 1908, from the Master responding to Edward's "long report" which "notwithstanding the great hindrances" was "perused with utmost care". In this Tablet, 'Abdu'l-Bahá writes that this was not the time for the formation of a National Assembly as the Cause had not been strengthened and spread sufficiently in America. The time would come for the organization of the National Assembly but "today teaching the truth is the most necessary object. This is the real foundation."

A letter from Lua in September 1908 to Elizabeth Nourse of Atlantic City is the first indication we have of a friendship which was to continue for the rest of her life. It was to Mrs. Nourse that Lua revealed her most intimate thoughts and her spontaneous joy in life, as well as her brilliant powers of description. Elizabeth Nourse came from a family with strong Presbyterian connections and of social standing. Her mother, Kate Smith, had a significant dream before her early death, that two great souls were on earth. She told Elizabeth to watch for them. After her mother's death, Elizabeth had to leave school to run the household in Washington – which with a large house, many servants and a social position to keep up, was a heavy burden for a young girl. She did look for the great souls, but without much effort, and was active in the Church. One day, while shopping for antiques, she heard a baby crying and went to see what was wrong. The mother said that the baby was sick and that a "nice lady" had given her the Greatest Name to hang over the crib to make the baby well. The lady was Lua. Elizabeth immediately felt assured that the Greatest Name was right. She was very excited and called on Lua. An undated note among Lua's papers reads:

Mrs Nourse –
Lately accepted the message and sent a letter of supplication through me in care of Rooha Khanum.
   I beg that she be accepted and that a blessing will descend upon herself, children and husband.

Mrs. Nourse received a Tablet from 'Abdu'l-Bahá which according to Lua's notes read:

You are accepted in the Kingdom of God, be assured. I ask God that you will attain your desire and that you will travel much in this world which will ultimately be the Cause of your travelling in the Kingdom! Show great kindness to your husband and children on my behalf and give to them the Heavenly Tidings.

Elizabeth Nourse's uncle was Minister of her church, and spoke against her from the pulpit. She lost her social position as a result of becoming a Bahá'í. Her husband, however, supported her in the Faith, although he never became a Bahá'í himself. Lua and Elizabeth Nourse became the best of friends, and Lua would stay with her for months at a time, while her children, particularly her son Phil, were great favourites of Lua, as the correspondence shows.[55] "Menita", as Lua called her, was the only Westerner to whom Lua seems to have mentioned unhappiness in her marriage before 1915.

Grand Hotel du Parc   Sept.1st.1908
    et du Chateau
Monnetier-s/-Saleve

My very dear Menita

I had so hoped to be with you today and how many miles I am from you! I have been detained for ten days in order to see the Persian Consul from Port Said who did not arrive until Friday the 28th. – I expect to leave for Paris in the morning and as soon as I can attend to some matters there I leave for London and hope now to be able to sail the 10th. I am trying not to stay for the Congress – for I find another American Representative of the Faith will be present so it is not necessary for me and I do so want to go home. I shall surely stop on my way to Washington to see you. Your letter of the 19th reached me today only – how glad I was to hear from you and how many times I have read it over! I am so thankful that Dr. Stearns spent some time with you and am so happy to know it did him good. I was afraid when I left W– he would be ill. I miss his father and dear "Little Mother" – so much – in fact I am quite as homesick to see them as I am to see the members of my own family! I have been for the past ten days in the most wonderful place – the old Chateau of which – I sent you last week a picture – is a most interesting castle – high up on the Mt. and fairly teeming with ghostly towers and strange stairways – dungeons etc.! There are but a few people here and at night we sit around a big grate fire and recount weird tales – it seems impossible to do otherwise – for the wind howling around the house and sobbing through the pines is so suggestive that we all fall under the spell! This afternoon we went to the very top of the Grand-Saleve and watched the sun set on Mt. Blanc and Mt. St. Croix! It was wonderful beyond all words to describe! I stood on a high peak – utterly oblivious of everybody and everything save the Grandeur of the scene. The city and Lake of Geneva were ten thousand ft. below us – bathed in a Glory of Golden Light – while the wonderful sky above was by an invisible hand painted in all the pastelle shades of purple, crimson and gold! The entire chain of peaks crowning Mt. Blanc – rearing their snow covered heads against the matchless blue of the sky – caught the different shades of light and in turn reflected each change of color – with such supreme beauty and splendor that I found myself silently weeping perfectly enraptured unable to move or speak. It was freezing cold; – the air was blowing straight from the snow fields and carried frost and ice in its wings – but I didn't feel it until the sun sank out of sight and some one called my attention to the new moon – shining like a silver sickle over my left shoulder! I made my wish of course – and then the deep purple shadows crept so swiftly over us – that I shivered with the cold and realized night was come! It took us more than an hour, by train, to descend and we were glad to find dinner and a nice warm fire waiting for us. I am afraid I have taken a little cold for I have been sneezing – but I guess a hot bath and sleep will make me all right for my journey to Paris tomorrow. When I start for Paris I shall feel I am on the way home! I have accomplished my work thus far all right – and do not expect any difficulties to arise now to hinder my homeward progress!

But, oh the trackless waste of ocean that I must cross before I reach your little "nestie" and those I love at home! I shall be impatient from this moment on – til I see the Light House off Sandy Hook – and discern the shores of my native land in the distance. – Then I shall be more impatient!

I hope you will someday visit this spot. You will feel – I am sure – that life means more than it ever did before after viewing the world from this altitude. I am better, oh so much better and broader in mind, heart, and soul!

My love to you and all in your household. My dear spiritual child.

Good night from your "Spiritual Mother"
Lua Moore Getsinger

I'll telegraph you from New York. You'll find this full of mistakes for a lady has been singing and playing marvellously well – while I've been writing and I couldn't help listening somewhat! –

Correspondence between Lua and the daughters of 'Abdu'l-Bahá continued, as 'Abdu'l-Bahá sent advice to Lua.

Sep 22d 1908
Dearest Lua

... Now let me stop tiring and boring you with myself and begin to tell you what our Lord wants me to write you from Him in regard to the letter Mohamed Ali[56] wrote to Mrs. J. He said that what you suggested about her answering him and asking him to send her the writing of Bahá'u'lláh. It is not wise to do this now, and that if she will again say anything about it you try to change her mind from ever communicating with Mohamad Ali or asking him to send her any Tablet which are not at all from Bahá'u'lláh and if they are they are changed by Mohemed Ali's hand so much that you cannot at all trust or be sure of them. And you know how the poor Mrs. Jackson is always influenced both in the right way and the wrong way. So we must protect her against Mohamed Ali's tricks.

Dear Lua please will you let me know if you ever received the long Tablet in which also was the permission for you to come to Acca? It was in one of my letters to you and the letter was registered. I cannot believe that it did not reach you.

Much love from all and all to you dear Lua and from me who shall never forget you

Monever (poor old Junie)

Enclosed you will find a Tablet for you from our Lord.

The fervor of Lua's friendships is well disclosed in the following rather mysterious letter which Lua wrote to Louise Stapfer (later Bosch) in November of 1908. Louise had been engaged to be married to Lua's brother Dr. William Moore, but he had died before the marriage could take place. Lua considered Louise ("Lysa") one of her special "five" souls for whom she would gladly sacrifice her life: the others were Mariam Haney, Mary Lucas, May Maxwell and Juliet Thompson. She referred to these five in correspondence from time to time.[57]

Why this letter was written is unknown nor do we know whether or not Louise received it, but the letter is preserved in Lua's files. One wonders if this were written at the time when Lua suffered from the "nervous prostration," mentioned in a later letter.

Nov. 20, 1908

My beloved Lysa

If your eyes ever behold these pages it will be after my spirit has fled into the world beyond – for I am writing this to tell you something my lips could not say to you in life. Always, I have loved you Lysa – and never have I been able to do for you the things I have desired, to make your life more easy! This has been the pleasure of my child, my "May Violet" – Still Lysa you belong to me, and are mine in a wonderful way! I am buying you for the Kingdom of God and paying for you with my soul! – Or, at least – I am going to offer it and by the time you read this – it will either have been accepted through God's great mercy – or rejected because of my unworthiness! You are one of <u>five</u> – for whom I seek salvation – redemption and forgiveness from God! – I am going to beg and supplicate Him, to accept my soul as a sacrifice for all of you – and no matter what you may have done, or not done – during all the days of your lives here – I seek to bear the burden and responsibility of the same throughout eternity – and even though hell be my portion – I shall rejoice, if only <u>you</u> <u>five</u> gain the glory and grandeur of His Kingdom, and His Presence! Oh my dear Lysa – I do hope you will be happy the rest of your days upon this earth, and that you will have peace and plenty from now on. Often have I thought about you & wished so earnestly to assist you, but never have I been allowed and <u>this</u> has been hard for me! But if only I am now permitted to render you this everlasting favor I shall cease to regret and be more than happy! Please do not forget me, and know that throughout all time I shall not forget you! We have had some good times together, and we certainly have known life – and seen it sometimes, from the same view point! You will attain the meeting with "Danny" and I never may, so to you I entrust the task of telling him of my love for him! Never once in all the years – did it waver but grew stronger daily – and so will it be throughout all time to come! He has already attained the "Supreme Horizon" and I have no hope that my eyes shall ever behold it – but yours will dear, and this thought gives me joy – for indeed you are worthy of it! I shall draw very near to you in spirit as you read these poor words – the last you will ever read from my pen – and I shall see you, and touch your hair (the hair we have all so much admired!)

Please dear Lysa – overlook all my faults and short comings – and know I suffered by them, more than you, or <u>anyone</u> else ever did! "Unto me was much given; and so much was expected of me" that I failed for lack of power – to <u>make</u> <u>good</u>. And oh, only God knows how it hurt – and how I suffered for it! The agony of my soul has been terrible at times, and I have cried out for death! And now my cries are heard! The soul belongs to God – and once it turns to Him – He never lets it turn away! Nay "He refines it as silver is refined – and tries it, as gold is tried!" There was always war between my body & my soul, – dear – until the conflict wearied the angels who watched over it – and I made a final struggle – and have sacrificed them both! One by one, the things of earthly joy were all swept away until I had only my soul to give – and I have done so gladly – oh so gladly to yield that up too – and sacrifice it – <u>completely</u> for your dear sakes! Oh that it may be deemed worthy of acceptance. Goodby now – <u>my Lysa</u> – may the dear good God protect & keep you, and grant unto you, all your heart desires – "Till the glorious Day dawns and earth's shadows flee away!"

I greet thee, with the salutation
    <u>Allaho'Abha</u>
From your loving, but unworthy
    <u>Lua</u>

By early 1909 Lua seems to have recovered, and was busy making plans as usual. Agnes Parsons was to become a regular correspondent and confidant who loved and supported Lua throughout many years.[58] At the time Lua wrote this note Mrs. Parsons had only recently heard of the Bahá'í Faith and was not yet a confirmed believer. The note indicates that Mrs. Parsons had wished for Lua to meet one of her friends who was interested in the Cause; Lua's charm of person and fascinating way of speaking, as well as her passion for friendship, endeared her to many.

151 E. 36th St.
New York City

My dear Mrs. Parsons
Juliet told me of your intended visit to New York! I am so sorry but do not think I can wait until March 2nd. I should so love to

113

meet anyone you have interested in the Cause so near my heart.
I have a message for you from 'Abdu'l-Bahá and He has sent you
what you requested. I am very anxious to see you indeed! If you
can come sooner please do! Or, if you wish me to see your friend
can you not send me a letter of introduction to him and I will go
to see him?

> Yours very Sincerely
> Lua Moore-Getsinger
> February 16th, 1909

Another Tablet to Lua from 'Abdu'l-Bahá follows asking
her to be kind to a Persian Bahá'í, probably Ahmad Sohrab,
who was in the United States. The translator is unnamed
in the copy.

9

To
The Maid-Servant of God – who is favored and attracted by the
Fragrances of God and enkindled by the Fire of the Love of
God –

> Lua M. Getsinger
> Upon her be Bahá'u'lláh

Oh thou who art attracted by the Fragrances of God!
Exercise thou infinite love and kindness on my behalf to thy
beloved (spiritual) son, his honor Mirza Ahmad and say – Oh
thou spiritual youth! Thank thou God that thou art confirmed
in the translation of the Tablets of 'Abdu'l-Bahá and hast
crowned thy head with this Glorious Diadem. Although, now in
appearance the greatness of this mighty and exalted station is
not manifest and evident, yet in the Kingdom of Abha it is the
hope and the aspiration of the approximate Angels and 'ere long
it will become apparent and establish that this thy Station has
been greater than the sovereignty of the whole world. Therefore
thank thou God for that which He hath bestowed upon thee and
specialized thee by this great Bounty, Glorious favor and Manifest Outpouring!

Verily He electeth whomsoever He desireth to perform that
which He willeth.

(signed) Abdul Baha Abbas

The original of this tablet was written by the Master's own hand and dated March 17, 1909.

By the end of the year, however, as Lua prepared to leave for the Holy Land once more, she received bad news which she immediately shared with Elizabeth Nourse:

My dearest Heart "Child"
Your letter came this morning and finds me in the deepest depths. My baby-brother had a relapse Sunday night and there is little, if any hope of his recovery. He was taken to the hospital this morning and I have laid him upon the Altar of God's Holy Will. He has suffered such agony that will be a release to his spirit which is now imprisoned in a cage of pain. He is such a beautiful soul heaven will gain what we lose! This may be the end of my woes for 1909 – I do not know – only I know I love God and praise His Holy Name. It is at such times that I realize how much I love Him and what He means to me. I shall be obliged to store our things for we cannot go on – but it is all right – God knows best. My trials are not greater than others. Mrs. True's husband was brought home dead to her last Monday – and five believers have been killed for the Faith recently in the East – near Ishkabod where the temple is. Their wives and children were driven out of house and home and their property all confiscated! Yet they do not deny the Faith or murmur one complaint! So, I think I can endure what ever comes upon me.

In regard to your going to Acca now, or any other time, you must do as you think and feel. I do not wish to influence you at all, I only thought it would be so well for you physically and spiritually to see 'Abdu'l-Bahá. I know it would be a sacrifice on your part to go, but Menita we have to pay to enter that Presence, and whenever you go – you, like all others must pay the price! He, our Lord is the "Pearl of Greatest Price" to all human souls – and to receive a touch of His Spirit means more than you even dimly suspect at the present time! I love you more than you can know – and always shall throughout all the worlds to come. As you love your "Kittens" – I love you – only more – and some day you will see how and why. So my darling child – I leave you to the Guidance of God's Holy Spirit and you will see the "Light on the Path".

Has Mr. Nourse done anything about the patent? I did not know Dr. G. wrote you. Do not feel that you must do anything! – I am sure God will assist us in the right time. Dr. G. does not know which way to turn and his faith must be tried to the utmost the same as that of others. He suffers – but through it he will learn as I have, and as others have, and as others will – That "to be hopeless from all else save God" is the only thing in this world, that ensures one moment of rest, peace, or assurance. I know God will try us all in the fire until He can see the reflection of His Face in each soul then He will remove us, and send upon us the cooling showers of His Mercy, Divine Love and <u>Heavenly</u> Blessings.

If He takes my darling brother, it will mean that He loves more and better than I do or can and because He has need of him in a better, fairer world than this. Praise be to His Holy Name – and in all humility I say "May His Holy Will be done!"

Much love to the Kittens from Aunt "Luda". And don't forget to remember me to Anisa with loving and best wishes. Kind remembrances to Mr. Nourse. and heart full of tender love to you one of my "youngest ones".

Your own

"Little Mother"

Dec. 15, 1909 Lua

Louisa ('Lua') Moore with two of her younger brothers

Edward C. Getsinger as a young man

Lua Getsinger, an early portrait

May Bolles Maxwell, who established the first Bahá'í community in Europe. Lua Getsinger introduced her to the Bahá'í teachings in Paris in 1898. May Maxwell was one of Lua's five 'special souls'

Edward and Lua in the early years
of their marriage

The first Western pilgrims. Ibrahim Kheiralla is in the middle of the front row, with Lua next to him, second from right

Western pilgrims in 'Akká, early 1901. Standing, left to right: Charles Mason Remey, Sigurd Russell, Edward Getsinger, Laura Barney. Seated: Ethel Rosenberg, Madame Jackson (in whose house in Paris Lua often stayed), Shoghi Effendi, unknown (possibly Helen Ellis Cole), Lua Getsinger, unknown (possibly Emogene Hoagg)

'Abdu'l-Bahá
'The Face of the Master is gloriously beautiful. His eyes read one's very soul – still they are full of divine love – and fairly melt one's heart!' (From a letter written by Lua Getsinger from 'Akká, 1898)

Lua Getsinger and Mariam Haney in Paris, 1902, when Lua
presented a petition to the <u>Sh</u>áh of Persia pleading the cause of
the persecuted Bahá'ís in that country

Lua, a portrait taken in Paris. As a young woman Lua loved dressing up in fashionable clothes; later she gave them all away in obedience to 'Abdu'l-Bahá's preference for simple dress

Lua, a studio portrait taken in the blue costume she had made for the numerous occasions when she was required to speak in public

With 'Abdu'l-Bahá in New York, 1912. Lua standing on left; Edward, back row, right

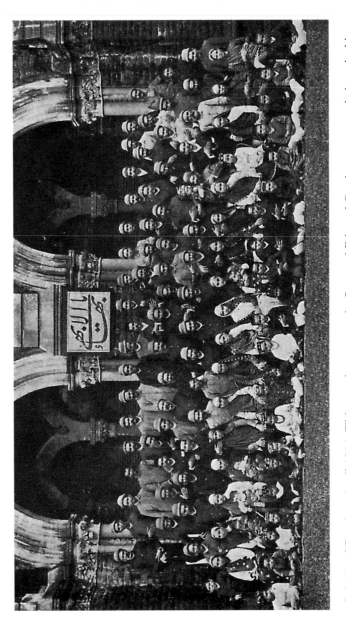

Bahá'ís of Bombay, April 1914. This was the community Lua and Edward Getsinger met on their arrival in India in late 1913

X

A report in *Bahai News* (the magazine that would shortly become *Star of the West*) reads: "Mrs. Getsinger, who has completed another visit to Acca, is expected to return about the 10th of March. Dr. Fareed is returning with her."[59] Dr. Ameen'Ullah Fareed had studied medicine in the United States. He did much translating during this period and was admired for his brilliant skills. He was welcomed as the son of Mírzá Asadu'lláh-i-Iṣfáhaní, one of the teachers sent by 'Abdu'l-Bahá to America in 1901 to clarify the issues raised by the defection of Kheiralla; he was also a member of the family of 'Abdu'l-Bahá, the nephew of Munírih Khánum, 'Abdu'l-Bahá's wife. Fareed's disloyalty to the Covenant and illicit solicitation of funds from the believers was quite obviously not known to Lua, nor to the American believers in general at this period nor for some time to come.

As the next issue of *Bahai News* told its readers, "Mrs. Getsinger and Dr. Fareed arrived in New York from Acca, bringing with them the merciful glad-tidings of the love of 'Abdu'l-Bahá to the beloved of God in America, and giving several talks in the New York Assembly. Dr. Fareed brought with him a general Tablet from the presence of 'Abdu'l-Bahá to the American believers, embodying the same precious admonitions to build the stable foundations of unity upon which the structure of the sacred Mashrek-el-Azkar could be erected. . ."[60]

Lua and Dr. Fareed attended a meeting in Washington shortly after they arrived, with Joseph and Pauline Hannen and Edward and Carrie Kinney one Friday evening on March 25th.[61] "We were rejoiced to welcome our beloved sister, Lua Getsinger, returning from the Holy City", said the report. "A telegram announced her coming, together with Mr. and Mrs. Kinney and Dr. Ameen Ullah Fareed. These dear friends were tendered a reception at the home of Mr. and Mrs. Ripley Saturday evening, attended and addressed the Sunday School, received the friends Sunday evening, and on Monday morning the Kinneys returned to New York, taking the sincere love of the Washington friends with them. Mrs. Getsinger and Dr. Fareed have been kept exceedingly busy attending group meetings during the week, and a large audience attended the regular meeting Friday April 1, at which both spoke effectively on Unity." On March 27th they were among a group which visited the grave of Mrs. Amalie Knobloch and read "the Visiting Tablet revealed by 'Abdu'l-Bahá".[62]

Lua was working very hard for the Faith. Edward and Lua spoke in Boston on June 12, and Lua spoke at a Unity Feast in Washington on June 24, with Faraju'lláh Khán, Fareed, Mason Remey and Carl "Nategh" Hannen, the young son of Joseph and Pauline Hannen who had just returned from school in Stuttgart.[63]

By August Lua and Edward were together in Washington. Lua wrote to Louise Stapfer (later Bosch) in New York, about their beloved May Maxwell's expected baby. (The baby had been born two days earlier, although Lua did not know it yet.) May Bolles Maxwell had become a believer on the Getsingers' first visit to Paris on their way to pilgrimage in 1898, and was greatly beloved to Louise as well. The expected child is now the Hand of the Cause, Amatu'l-Bahá Rúhíyyih Khánum. May Bolles Maxwell was one of Lua's loyal friends whose love never wavered and whose tribute to Lua is quoted in this book.

> 314 E. Capitol St.
> Wash. D. C.

My dear Lysa
Your long looked for letter was indeed very welcome! I have so often wondered why I have never heard from you! Yes, I was in

118

Acca last Winter and it is true that the Master now lives in Haifa – Acca is no longer a prison! They were all well and enquired after you! Have you heard from May recently? I saw her in New York in June and she was expecting to be confined in July and very happy over the prospect of having a baby. She looked so well and, as I have never seen her before! I have not heard anything since and am so anxious to know about her if you have any news please let me know! My dear Lysa there is a great reason why you love me so – and feel as you do when you mention me! 'Abdu'l-Bahá knows and so do I! In this world you may never know, but dear – if you die before I do just know that when I come to you everything will be right – and if I go first when you come, just ask for Lua and then you shall understand. I love you dear "Lysa of the Lillies" with all my heart and you are always with me – you – May – Mary and Marian are the stars of my existence with one other whose name you do not know now – but you five together are a glorious collection of souls & you are mine. Now and always – God only knows how much I love you! Dear the love for 'Abdu'l-Bahá will come as you go on and obey the commands of Bahá'u'lláh – for His words are creative and have the power to give life even – to say nothing of love, and faith. Aunt Charlotte Colt passed on [to] the heavenly Kingdom last Friday – dear old angel soul she was! Oh Lysa, what a joy to leave this dark and gloomy sphere! May my release soon come! I am so weary of clay! I am going to see my mother next week for a few days! But answer here I will receive it. I do not live in Worcester – Elwyn & Ursie and Hebe live there. Elwyn married Ursula Sherman! Edward is with me in Washington for the present – I dont know where we will live in the future. I gave all of my furnature [sic] to Elwyn & Hebe so I have nothing but my love for God and "My Five" left of this world's goods.

Write me again soon
Always your devoted
and tender
Lua
August. 10th, 1910

Another of Lua's correspondents was Mírzá Asadu'lláh-i-Iṣfáhaní, who had been sent to America by 'Abdu'l-Bahá in 1901. The flattery of Lua and exaggerated piety expressed by Mírzá Asadu'lláh might well have dazzled her, for the writer was a man famous for his previous exemplary service to the Cause. He did not, however, remain "the servant of the Covenant" but followed his son out of the Cause in years to come.

Dec. 2. 1910

Haifa, Syrie

Spiritual Sister

If God wishes you will ever be occupied with the diffusion of the fragrances of God, the promulgation of the Cause of God, the resuscitation of souls and the service of the friends of God. His Holiness The Lord of Mankind 'Abdu'l-Bahá, may the spirit of the world be a sacrifice unto Him, has said in one of the Holy Tablets – "Service to the Beloved of God – is service rendered the Beauty of Abha." This sublime station has He first chosen, thus night and day is he restless for ameliora[ting] the conditions of the Beloved of God. He passes all His time and spends all of His strength in Service just as that revered one (yourself) has witnessed. Now I hope through the Bounty and favor of God that all His Servants may be clad with his precious garment.

Praise be to God that loved and revered one – from the inception of her acceptance of the Cause of God has been confirmed in such great services. In all His letters Dr. Fareed gives the accounts of your zeal attraction constancy in the Service of the Cause of God and loving and tender assistance to His loved ones.

This unworthy Servant has asked often assistance and help for you at the Holy Threshold and will do so always – hoping that you will be enabled to accomplish worthy services in the Days of God! Your letter which was eloquent regarding your firmness, steadfastness & evanescence in the Presence of the Center of the Covenant (may our lives be a Sacrifice for Him) was duly received & I was informed of its contents. You have asked for the meaning of your vision. Know you that this is one of the true visions and it means that the confirmation of the Ancient Beauty and the aids of the Center of the Covenant will assist you in a great Service which will be most acceptable and praiseworthy in the sight of God – and which will make the blessed heart most happy.

120

This Servant will implore and supplicate at the Holy Tomb and at the Sacred Garden of the Báb for special assistance in order that the utmost desires of your heart may be realized and the Cause of God may be rendered victorious.

Verily He helpeth whomsoever He wisheth in whatsoever He desireth – and verily He is the Giver the Precious the Generous. Please convey greetings and sincere regards of this servant to His Honor Dr. G. Upon him be Bahá'u'lláh.

His honor Dr. Fareed is most overcome with your loves and services to the point of being ashamed.

We are likewise most grateful and apologize for your loving services to his Honor Mirza Farage Ullah Khan.

Both this Servant and Dr. Fareed's mother implore God's confirmation and a thousand fold blessing and reward in your behalf. God has said "He who does a good deed (for another) verily in truth he has done it for himself."

Truly the results and fruits of every good deed return to the donor and doer.

The harvest belongs to the sower. Blessed you are for every tongue mentions you and many hearts remember you with love. Dr. Fareed's mother and sister join me in these greetings.
(Signed) The Servant of the Covenant
Mirza Assad'ullah

The American believers began to have hope that 'Abdu'l-Bahá would visit them now that He had been released from prison. Lua was among those who strongly wished for this journey to take place and it was to her that the Master wrote about the requisite condition for His coming – absolute unity among the Friends.

TO THE MEMBERS OF THE ASSEMBLIES OF BAHÁ'ÍS IN AMERICA
To the beloved ones and the maid-servants of the Merciful!

HE IS GOD!

O ye dear friends and maid-servants of God!
Your epistle was received [a letter sent by the Washington DC

Assembly on behalf of the Assemblies of America, supplicating 'Abdu'l-Bahá to visit that country]. You have expressed joy and happiness because of the trip of 'Abdu'l-Bahá from the center of prison (Acca) to the land of the divine Joseph (Egypt). There are divine wisdoms in this journey! I am hopeful that it will be productive of results.

Now – praise be to God! – some time is passed with the utmost of spirit and fragrance in this country, and we are occupied with the service of the Cause of God and servitude to the Holy Threshold.

When the service which is our (present) purpose is realized for the Kingdom of God, perhaps we shall journey to other parts.

If the beloved of God in all America strive for unity and harmony, attain perfect love and accord, and act according to the divine teachings and the precepts of the Blessed Perfection, this will prove a magnet attracting 'Abdu'l-Bahá, so that, perchance, he may journey to America.

But, until the light of oneness, unity and love shine forth from the lamp of America, and the beloved act in accordance with the divine teachings and precepts of the Blessed Perfection, and all the believers in America become united and harmonious, my coming to America will be hindered – nay, impossible.

Therefore, strive ye that ye may become the embodied teachings of the Blessed Perfection, confirmed in the divine precepts, resurrected in holiness and purity, severance, humility and meekness, set aglow with the fire of divine love; and loosen your tongues with the praises and commendations of the Heavenly Kingdom.

Thus may the great attainment be realized.

Upon ye be Bahá'u'lláh-El-Abha!

'Abdu'l-Bahá Abbas

Translated by Dr. Ameen U. Fareed, December 8, 1910. Note – it is the wish of 'Abdu'l-Bahá that this Tablet be read in all Assemblies.

The Master sent Lua the following Tablet, also translated by Dr. Fareed.

O thou dear maid-servant of God! Your epistle was received [this refers to the letter from the Washington, DC Bahá'í community requesting the presence of 'Abdu'l-Bahá] and the desire and request of the beloved ones and the maid-servants of the Merciful became known.

The conditions requisite for the coming of 'Abdu'l-Bahá to those regions have just been written for the friends and maid-servants of the Lord – through you. I am hopeful that these conditions will be carried out, perchance at some time a trip to those regions may be taken; but if these conditions be not realized, this will hinder a trip to those parts.

Convey most reverend ABHA greetings with the utmost longing to his honor the Doctor [Getsinger].[64]

In early 1911 'Abdu'l-Bahá cabled instructions for Lua and Dr. Amin Fareed to "conquer California". This journey and Lua's friendship with Fareed were to bring her immense joy, according to the letters from California, as well as great pain in the future. She was later to remark that she had been "bitterly deceived". The teaching work which they did together was a gratifying experience, as such work always is. Every Bahá'í teacher has felt the heady excitement that a warm response to the message of Bahá'u'lláh brings, and Lua's letters from California express her ecstasy in this experience. Their teaching successes were widely publicized in various issues of *Star of the West* current at the time. But travelling with a man other than her husband, even at the instruction of 'Abdu'l-Bahá, eventually caused defamation of Lua's character. This was, of course, exacerbated after Fareed's defection, some of the Bahá'ís believing that she had reached the extremity of being disloyal to the Covenant.

Even at such a momentous time, Lua on the eve of her departure took the trouble to go shopping for some henna for her friend Agnes Parsons, and to send full instructions for its use:

Chicago, Ills.,
March 10th, 1911

Dear Mrs. Parsons:

The other day I wrote you from Field's and in a few hours later I received your letter of February 25th from Dublin.

After investigation yesterday, I found at last the one place in Chicago where the real vegetable henna was in existence. It is a Syrian store and the quantity I am sending you is all the store contained of henna. He is going to have some more from Beirut and when you finish this, we will get you more. The amount contained in the package I have sent you is sufficient for five (5) times. Therefore, divide it into that number (5). Possibly you may need twice (2) as much the first time as you will in the future. Take two portions this time on this account.

Directions for the Use of henna:-

The amount indicated is moistened with warm water and kneaded until it obtains the consistence of dough. It must then be left six hours in warm air, after which it is ready for use. It is good to leave it over night.

The Way to Use it:-

Wash the hair well two (2) days before the use of henna. Do not wash the hair just before use. Mix the henna "dough" (which has been made six to ten hours before) with sufficient hot water to make it like a paste. Then begin with the roots of the hair (the scalp) and rub henna in and cover all your hair with the paste as you fold the hair and do it up on the head. Be very <u>generous</u> with it the first time. Leave it on for sometime (from 1/2 - 1 hour) In a few minutes (if your mixture has been done correctly) it will somewhat dry and hold the hair in position on the head.

The length of time depends upon the taste of the person in regard to shade of color – the longer the darker till it becomes black. I suggest that after 30 minutes, you examine the hair (part of it) by washing that part to see the color. Now when the desired shade is realized the hair is washed with hot water till it is clean and clear. The color lasts a month or more. In fact it lasts a very long time except that the ends (roots) of the growing hair next to the scalp will show the gray first. This agent (henna) is said to be absolutely harmless. In fact in the Orient, it is considered as a great tonic to the hair roots. I can not give a personal testimony. Mrs. Cochran's Address 514 W. 114th St. New York City.

May you be successful with the "henna".

Your devoted
and loving
Lua
We leave today for Cal.- -

Thirteen years after the Getsingers had first taken the message of Bahá'u'lláh to California, Lua was back in obedience to 'Abdu'l-Bahá's instruction to "conquer" that State. The first two weeks of the journey were spent with the friends in Chicago en route to the Pacific Coast.[65] After an exhausting journey lasting a week, they arrived to be greeted almost immediately by the tragic news of the death of Lua's younger brother Elwyn. "My heart almost broke when I first heard the news," she wrote to Agnes Parsons, "but fortunately the people began to arrive soon after, and I was obliged to go out and meet, and speak to them of God 'who wipes away all tears from our eyes' – and crush down my heartache that they might be comforted by the utterances of the Holy Spirit! It was wonderful the way God assisted me <u>then</u> and has enabled me since to go smiling and forgetting that my last brother has gone and I was not allowed the comfort of even seeing him. But, it is all right – for He doeth all things well! His Love robs 'death of all its sting' and the Grave of anything like 'Victory'."

Her letter to Elizabeth Nourse, though still courageous, was not quite so gallant; one page of the letter is missing:

Hotel Argonaut
San Francisco
March 27, 1911

My dearest Menita
We reached Los Angeles after many wrecks and washouts on the road. We were one week from Chicago to Los Angeles so you may imagine how tired and worn out we were. We had tourist tickets and after a few days the car became very dirty and the sight of lunch boxes and baskets became sickening! . . .
. . . So dear, "I was obliged to crush back the tears – it would have been sweet to shed – and Smile, so others might have joy instead!" – Which, by the help of God and My Mariam, I was able to do in such wise that no one knew I had a heartache. But, sometimes – I just feel I <u>must</u> see my brother again – my <u>last</u> brother and the baby of the family. He was a beautiful believer

125

and ready, if ever a soul was – to go into the other world and I
should rejoice – but I miss him and shall miss him all the
years!. . .

I am thinking so much of you these past few days and longing
for you so. Those big tears that used to wet your bosom, will
occasionally roll down my cheeks in spite of my self!

Well, God's Will be done! He wanted my brother and took
him – and I must bow my head in submission to His divine
decree!

We found our mission here to consist of a much needed work
among those who have heard the Message. For there has been
false doctrines and teachings given which threaten to corrupt the
Truth and destroy the Cause! We have gotten hold of the situation and the clearing up process has already begun! It is a case
of the people being ignorant rather than wishing to do any harm.
There have been notices in the papers some good and some bad;
but we are just telling it all simply and plainly and the Spirit is
doing the rest. I do hope you will see Edward if you go to Wash.
and if possible my little Sister. Poor girl. She I know feels very
badly over the loss of the brother she tried so hard to keep here!
We have been here in San F. only two days – and I do not know
just how long we are to be here – but I wish you would write me
in care of the Haney's Los Angeles. I got your dear letter there
and it was a sweet help to me. Oh, I wish I were in Phil's little
Nestie tonight – with you sitting by me for a wee while! I long to
feel your arms about me and to hear you say "My dear!" Dr.
Fareed is tired and weary too – but he is very kind and thoughtful and has tried so hard to help me bear this one more trial in
His Path! He sends you greetings and love and so often speaks
of you all! Poor Dr. G. it is very hard for him and my heart aches
for him too! But, I have to leave him to God – and just go on
talking and teaching – believing all will come out right in the
end! God is watching over all of us – and in time will straighten
all affairs!

I do not know when we are to return, as yet. The Master has
not said how long we must remain here – but I suppose until we
carefully remove the tares – and teach them the right way. I shall
write you from every place so you will know where your "little
Mother" is – and how goes it with her! Tell Phil to love me hard
– and send me a kiss every night by the Evening Star.

And now dear heart, with ever so much love, and deep appreciation for you – Kind remembrances to "Gayne" and Brownie – Best Wishes to all the "Kiddies" –
   I am your devoted
   "Little Mother"
   Lua

Lua and Fareed had a busy schedule, speaking sometimes twice a day to various organizations in San Diego, La Jolla, Point Loma and even on the battleship *California*. A Bahá'í on that ship, Mr. Mack, held Bahá'í meetings in his cabin. In Tijuana, Mexico they gave medical assistance to the wounded. Fareed was appointed surgeon and Lua acted as nurse. Hundreds heard the Message.

In her letter to Mrs. Parsons, Lua shared her excitement in the teaching work she and Fareed were doing in California. The tender relationship between Agnes Parsons and Lua is evident from Lua's use of the pet name "Noor" in writing to her. This is a derivation from a Persian word meaning "light", now usually spelled "Núr". Persian names were often bestowed upon the friends by 'Abdu'l-Bahá.

Los Angeles, Cal.
April 17, 1911

My dearest Noor,
I have truly been occupied day and night since coming to the Coast but I had thought to write you long ere this, and Dr. Fareed has also hoped – to tell you something of our mission here before now – but we have moved rapidly and talked so much, writing has seemed out of the question. However, I now wish to tell you the reason of our being sent here principally is the fact that the teachings of Bahá'u'lláh are not being rightly presented by some enthusiastic, good souls, who desire to spread the Cause without having been properly prepared to do so. Also that some articles have been written, which are false and the publication of which had to be stopped! The people on the Coast seem ready and hungry for the Truth and it is most important, that it should be correctly given especially when the Cause is new in so many cities! Thus we are working as hard as possible!

The next day after our arrival I had the very sad news of my brother's death – the one whom I left so ill when we went to Acca – a year ago! He took cold and the old conditions returned; but this time it was painless and he just quietly smiled, and slept away! My heart almost broke when I first heard the news – but fortunately the people began to arrive soon after, and I was obliged to go out and meet, and speak to them of God "who wipes away all tears from our eyes" – and crush down my heartache that they might be comforted by the utterances of the Holy Spirit! It was wonderful the way God assisted me <u>then</u> and has enabled me since to go on – smiling and forgetting that my last brother has gone – and I was not allowed the comfort of even seeing him. But, it is all right – for He doeth all things well! His Love robs "death of all its sting" and the Grave of anything like "Victory".

I have one more dear one waiting to welcome me to the shore of the "Morning Land" when I shall be allowed to go. And I am glad my little brother was ready and glad to obey the summons! He was laid away – on the first anniversary of his wedding day – and his wife has written me such a beautiful helpful letter about it all – showing how God has also enabled her "to suffer and be strong".

I do not know how much longer we shall be here – for 'Abdu'l-Bahá has not yet written us to go back East. Tomorrow we are invited to Point Loma to visit Mr. and Mrs. Lyman J. Gage who have become interested in the Revelation. Besides Point Loma is a great Theosophical Center and we may be able to establish a new Assembly there!

We have been to San Francisco – Oakland; Berkeley, Alameda, and Fruitvale and other little suburban places about the Bay teaching and talking on the Cause. Dr. Fareed has been asked to give a course of lectures on other topics – and is planning to do so in interest of his hospital. Mrs. Goodall and her daughter Mrs. Cooper were very kind to us while there and made it very pleasant as well as easy to get about for they have a very fine Automobile which was at our disposal and this saved a great deal of nervous strain in making our way among people in unfamiliar places. We did not see Mrs. Hearst as she says she does not want to hear any more about the subject!

By the way dear – did you receive the henna we sent from

Chicago and have you tried it? I hope it has proved entirely satisfactory to you.

Do let me hear from you when you can. I wish I were in Wash. now to visit with you. My husband writes that you look well and will remain there until warm weather.

With much love from
Your devoted

2022 Tobermann St.   Lua
c/o Mrs. Haney
    Los Angeles, Cal.

Since Mrs. Parsons was a close and much-loved friend, Lua kept her informed of all they were doing and it was Mrs. Parson's generosity which financed much of the journey. Lua's letter expresses her longing for her husband as well as an artless admiration for Fareed's work, both as a physician and as a Bahá'í.

Tropico, May 12

My dearest Noor,

Enclosed find your lovely tablet and copies of two – to Dr. Fareed! You should rejoice dear heart (and of course you will, as you always do) over the hopeful promises of the Beloved One. We wrote Him from Chicago of your assistance also since we have been here, for you have been the "means" of the Guidance of all we have thus far been able to guide upon this journey! Through you we have been able to carry the Message freely "without money or price" to the people and to be independent from all else save His Bounty through the instrumentality of your dear hand. Blessed you are dear Noor, for thus you prove yourself a "trustworthy steward – inasmuch as you have been faithful in small things – ye shall be made ruler over great ones!"

We are doing so many kinds of work. Translating – teaching – lecturing and healing the sick spiritually – i.e. through spiritual power! You know Dr. Fareed had just completed his course at Johns Hopkins when we were commanded to come here. And, tho' unable to open an office he is practicing – but from the standpoint of Spirit, as of course he has no medical license in the State of Cal! But his medical knowledge enables him to make

129

right diagnosis – and dictate proper diet – Then he chants the healing tablets, – and wonderful results have followed in several cases! Which have helped us with the C. S. people! When we can give them what they have, and <u>more</u> they do not hesitate to come into the Bahá'í Movement. This morning we arose at 6:00 o'clock and went to the home of a poor afflicted woman (who has three small children, one a babe of six weeks) – suffering from tubercular trouble – to chant the healing tablets and give her necessary sanitary instructions! She was so grateful and hopeful and so was her husband that I feel sure the healing is accomplished! Some, he has only seen <u>once</u> and they recover. All of this work Dr. does freely and cheerfully! This morning while walking to the new patient he said – "Perhaps it is for this purpose that I have spent all of these years in study. For who knows – I may yet be used as the Instrument for God's healing power and be called to minister unto multitudes!! – And it may be so! For, he is so willing to give up <u>his</u> plans, and desires and do exactly as the Master commands! He is expecting great results from our journey here and we want you to pray that we will not fail or disappoint Him! We are planning a Spiritual Campaign – and we need the help of all the Friends. Wonderful ways are opening up before us and great souls are becoming interested! I am stopping at present with some old friends whom I taught years ago in Paris. Mr. Winterburn is Chief of the Art Department in the Los Angeles Polytechnique School – and Mrs. Winterburn is a great authority on History and Rhetoric, having written text books on both! She is helping us with a new edition of the Arabic and Persian Hidden Words which we hope to get out in a separate volume – containing the English and Arabic & Persian! Thus it will be a wonderful help for the Friends in the East, who are studying English. We hope this translation will be the "St. James Version". We are translating a most marvellous new book written by Mirza Asadullah – Dr. F's father, also, which will be a great help for advanced Bahá'ís. It is a very clear explanation of intricate spiritual problems. – Thus you see how occupied we are! Sometimes we have three meetings in one day at different places. We are both very well and happy in the service! If my husband were here I would not desire anything more. There is a Prof. Laskin here who has become a Bahá'í – greatly interested in Astronomy and other sciences – whom I wish Dr. Getsinger could meet.

130

Prof. L. – has read Dr. G's articles years ago and wishes very much to investigate his new sun ring theory! But this is as God wishes and I must be patient! I am writing my husband to communicate with him. We did not receive the program for the Congress in London! I wonder if it could have become lost – or did you not send it? If you have not sent it – never mind – for we do not need it! – Please remember me to Mr. Parsons – Royal and Jeffrey Boy – and for your own dear self. Noor of the Kingdom – accept my grateful love and tender devotion. Do write us when you can – and please pray for us – <u>daily</u>! We do so long to succeed that the heart of the Master may be gladdened by the news of the <u>spiritual</u> conquest of California – –

Your loving,

<u>Lua</u>

P. S. Dr. Fareed suggests that you do not mention our translating work at present to anyone: for it might create feeling. And it will be time enough when we have completed it. We will send you copies for criticism soon we hope.

On the same day Lua wrote to Elizabeth Nourse:

Tropico, Cal.
May 12 1911

My dear Menita:–

Enclosed you will find copies of the last instructions from 'Abdu'l-Bahá, which necessitates our planning a campaign for the Spiritual Conquest of California! We thought we were about through and ready to start East but it seems not! So we are going to set about it and work with might and main! Some wonderful openings are being made, and we are making ready for the fight(?)[sic]. If Dr. G. were here now, he could be a most valuable help as there are scientific people interested whom he could handle well. We are both well and working hard as anything. Sometimes, we have three meetings in a day! We were entertained in San Diego at the home of Mr. and Mrs. Lyman J. Gage. Mrs. Gage became a Bahá'í and wrote the Master a letter of acceptance! And Mr. G. is most deeply interested! We are at present out here with some old friends of mine whom I taught in Paris years ago. Mr. Winterburn is at present Chief of the Art department in the Polytechnique School at Los Angeles and Mrs. W. is an authority on History and Rhetoric having written text books on both subjects. So you see we are in the right atmosphere for good Bahá'í Service and surrounded by competent helpers!

Mr. and Mrs. Haney are too, ever ready to assist us – so we have great hopes for success – but dear we want you to pray for us. Tell Phil to pray for Aunt Lua, each night that "she may be successful, send 'Abdu'l-Bahá the good news of victory and soon get home to Phil." I am sleeping out of doors every night now under the roses and stars in a swinging bed! And I feel so well and fine. My cheeks stick out like "Mister-Mind Your Mother's" and are getting a <u>high</u> <u>color</u> of both red and brown!

I found a lovely little girl in Point Loma who writes me letters ever since. I enclose one for Phil to hear. Tell Catharine she need not be jealous of "Smiles" – for her little son – is true to his "Little Mother!" Oh, I long for you all, so much, at times – I just would like to fly to you and after loving, hugging, and kissing you all good and hard – fly back again "to do battle for the Lord!" I am sure I'd be a better soldier if I could just do that, now and then! How long did Dr. G stay and did you enjoy him? And was he happy? I do hope so!

Please do write us whenever you can find a minute. And just call on the Lord long and loud in our behalf now!

With tenderest love and longingest thoughts I am as ever

Your devoted
"Little Mother"
Lua

Loving greetings to my dear "Little Mother" Katharine, to her father and mother and to her brothers (my uncles!)
From
Dr. Fareed

The triumphant tour of California continued and Lua's ecstatic letters to Mrs. Parsons show her whole-hearted enthusiasm.

San Diego, Cal. June 10th, 1911

My dear Noor.

We are here, and after Mrs. Goodall and Cooper leave us, we are invited to be the guests of Mr. Gage who is deeply interested in the movement. The reporters found out our names in the hotel registry, and came to interview us because the name Goodall is famous all over Ca. and of course Mrs. G. arriving with an Auto party created a sensation! They called for her, and she referred them to Dr. F. The first reporter was so impressed that he said – "Really I am not competent as a writer to do this credit – I will send you another man". And he did so! The other man wrote the enclosed article. Both reporters were deeply impressed and the last one said "Well, the world needs this and I certainly wish you success!" Then he asked if he might report any public lectures that we might give. We are all lunching with the Gages today and are going to decide upon a plan of procedure for San Diego. Mr. Gage knows everybody, and is anxious to help us spread our Message. Thus God assists those who arise for the service. Our "spiritual conquest" has begun – and we are very happy – all of us!

Mrs. Goodall is perfectly fearless and says if others have sacrificed life she can well afford to sacrifice social position, if necessary. She is a beautiful soul and a wonderful Bahai. Had Mrs. Hearst[66] been like her – the Cause here would have <u>two</u> marvellous pillars.– There is so much to do that I cannot write more this morning. Will write often and keep you informed of the progress we make.

> With much love, and
> longing to see you
>> I am as ever
>> Your devoted
>>> Lua

As before, she wrote a more informal note to Elizabeth Nourse (on the letterhead of the U.S. Grant Hotel advertising itself as "European Plan" and "Absolutely fire proof").

San Diego, Cal.
June 10th.

My dearest Menita,
We have arrived in San Diego, quite a party of us. Mrs. Goodall
brought us all down in her motor, and we have begun the
"spiritual conquest" of San Diego. The name Goodall is so well
know in Cal. that in a little while after our arrival the reporters
were after us. Mrs. G. referred them to Dr. Fareed, and the
enclosed is the result. She (Mrs. G.) is a fearless Bahá'í. She says
she can well afford to sacrifice social position, when other women
have sacrificed <u>life</u>! So, – she just goes ahead and is a beautiful
Bahá'í. I am very busy this A. M. and therefore cannot write
any more. Will write again very soon. I am <u>down</u> among the
"wealthy" – and indeed I am <u>rich</u> – richer than they know.
   We all send you much love. Kisses
   for the Kiddies – Especially "Kaptain Kido" Phil –
      Your loving
      <u>Lua</u>

Lua kept in touch with other of her friends while touring
California. On June 25, 1911 she wrote to "My dear Eleanor", probably Ella Cooper. In this letter Lua expresses her
conviction that Fareed is rendering great service to the
Cause at a cost of much self-sacrifice on his part.

                    Hotel Cabrillo
                    James A. Wilson, Prop.
                    La Jolla, California

                    <u>Tuesday!</u>

My dear Eleanor,
We came out to La Jolla yesterday and last night Dr. Fareed
spoke to one hundred and twelve people (Mr. Adams counted
them) and interested them so deeply that they all asked us to stay
& tell them more.
   The people here are so thoughtful and seem to not only have
time, but to <u>take</u> <u>time</u>, <u>to</u> <u>think</u>!

We have taken two rooms here for the present until we can arrange matters! We rented the hall and will continue to do so once a week both here and in San Diego, as long as the people are interested!

Just as Mr. Adams predicted there is tremendous interest aroused and we only need to stand firmly – to meet and vanquish the opposing "arrayed army of the world!" Dr. Fareed had an invitation to attend the A.M.A. Convention in Los Angeles but he would not go – saying "as the general of this spiritual conquest – he could not desert his forces or yield an inch of ground!" Thus he is standing by his command and sacrificing his great desire to see and meet all of these M.D.s and hear their interesting discourses! But, the servants of God must be so – His Cause and His Work must <u>ever</u> <u>be</u> <u>first</u>! The great secret of the power of Jesus Christ and 'Abdu'l-Bahá – lies in <u>self-renunciation</u>! Tell the people there who were <u>upset</u> about my dream – that we are only beginning to learn how to lay down the arms of <u>self</u> and take up the weapons of God – which are "non-resistance" and "love"!

We will let you know "<u>how goes it</u>" – from time to time. We wish you were here! My how much we and you would enjoy ourselves!! My love to your Mother and your own dear "smiling directorship"!

> Your loving friend
> and fellow servant
> I. H. N.
> Lua

June 25, 1911

The visit to the battleship *California*, the "Flag Ship of the fleet", is described in Lua's letter to Mrs. Parsons written from San Diego. Lua gives a vivid account of her experiences observing a battle. This letter shows Lua's meticulous obedience to 'Abdu'l-Bahá, as she could not accept funds from anyone except Mrs. Goodall, whom He had, apparently, directed to pay the expenses for this part of her journey.

135

[U. S. Grant Hotel stationery]
San Diego, Cal. June 29, 1911

My dear Noor,

We have been quite successful thus far, and began our "spiritual Conquest" on board the Battleship "California"– the Flag Ship of the fleet which until last Sunday was in San Diego Harbor. The enclosed article appeared in the paper – and one of the Junior officers on board the "California" had heard of me in Washington thus he came to the hotel and called! After which he invited us on board the ship and introduced [us] to the officers – who asked about the Movement etc. Mrs. Gage invited them all to her home the following Sunday afternoon with some other people from town and we had a very interesting afternoon given over to spiritual thought entirely! In turn we were invited on board the S.S. [California] again to lunch and again we waged our warfare of Peace with <u>their</u> <u>guns</u> frowning upon us! Some of the officers were present in town at the public meeting last Saturday night (250 people were present)! – We were invited to La Jolla last Monday by Austin Adams – the Writer who was formerly – an Episcopalian Clergyman in New York – but now a Socialist of great force!

We had another large meeting in a public hall – and many are apparently interested. Tomorrow I am to speak to all of the ladies in the parlors of the largest hotel here in La Jolla – and by the way this is a very beautiful resort – (all thoughtful people too!) with none of the usual distraction of a sea side Summer resort. Thus we are working away! Oh, I am forgetting to tell you how we stopped the war! Mrs. Gage's mother is Pres. of the Red Cross in San Diego, and the day of the <u>last</u> battle on the frontier,[67] she asked us to go with her, and help. We did so – and on the way over – to the border Dr. Fareed said "We must end the war today by declaring peace in the Name of God!" And strangely enough – the battle was quickly over – The rebels surrendered to the U. S. troops – and the <u>war</u> ended. We helped dress the wounds of two men who were wounded (one very badly) and fortunate enough to get over the line! But all of the others – over sixty – were shot – and remained unburied for days! It was terrible – some of them were Americans too – It was an awful thing – just that little bit of real war! – Men actually shooting and killing each other while we stood on the ridge of a hill and watched them. Hundreds of people went in automobiles to see the spectacle – and it was a glimpse of <u>hell</u>! It was all over in a few hours – and the hill side was strewn with wounded wretched bleeding men who were disarmed and shot like dogs and left to lie in the sun! – The Red Cross sent men – under the Red Cross flag – over to beg for them but they would not give them up – remarking "We will <u>care</u> for all the wounded." And thus they cared for them – poor fellows! – I am having wonderful experiences – and such as make me a better advocate of Peace – as you may readily judge! Sometimes I wonder that God is <u>so</u> patient! –

Do write us when you can and we will let you know "How goes it" from time to time.

> With much love
> in His Name
> Your devoted
> Lua

We have heard recently that 'Abdu'l-Bahá – is in Paris – enroute to London!
P. S. I am waiting here to hear from Mrs. Goodall whom the Master (as you know) told to pay my expenses. I cannot accept assistance from anyone else until I hear from her. And if possible communicate with the Beloved. I have cabled her but so far (after one week) no reply – Have sent her the photographic tablet also.

> Yours as ever
> devotedly
> Lua

During this period, the Getsingers were serving the same Cause in different places. *Bahá'í News* of December 12, 1911 mentions that Dr. Edward Getsinger lectured on August 1, 1911 at the Oriental University in Washington, DC and at the "Fete Day", November 26, on the East Coast.

In the letter to Mrs. Parsons shown below, Lua mentions, underlining her words four times, that they <u>know</u> that the Spirit as manifested in the Bahá'í Reformation heals both bodies and souls. Her conviction that Fareed is a great healer is apparent. An interesting sidelight is Lua's statement that helping to build the Temple (the Bahá'í House of Worship in Wilmette, Illinois) which was the major concern of the American Bahá'ís at this time, is not the task set for her by the Master. That mission is given to Mrs. True (Mrs. Corinne True, Hand of the Cause of God, 1861-1961) and others. Lua could only continue to speak of the Temple, asking others to contribute to it.

U. S. Grant Hotel San Diego, Cal. Aug. <u>11th</u>

My beloved Noor

Yours of July 25 – and Aug. 1st received for which I thank you with all my heart! You were dear to ask 'Abdu'l-Bahá to allow us the privilege of coming to you. We have had no other instructions since we received the last one to make the Conquest of California which we are doing to the best of our ability and capacity day by day.

I have never been more busy! Oh, how hungry the world is for God! – and poor world of sick humanity it does not know its physician or remedy!

I have fully demonstrated what 'Abdu'l-Bahá has meant – all of these years of patient instruction – regarding "severance of all else save God"! – for I have been forced to learn at last the lesson! Service with <u>self</u> entirely eliminated – sacrifice with <u>pure love</u> as an altar and Faith supreme, based upon a practical working <u>knowledge</u> <u>of</u> God – constitutes the Severance taught by Bahá'u'lláh and enforced by 'Abdu'l-Bahá! I note all you say about the Temple and I agree with you – but dear Noor <u>this</u> is not the task set me by the Master! Thus I cannot enter into it. Mrs. True and some others must answer those points for that is their mission and labor.

In regard to the Temple I have only been commanded to <u>speak</u> about it and urge others to give for it, which I have done, and will continue to do. – Of course a <u>Temple</u> not more land is the thing desired. Perhaps if 'Abdu'l-Bahá comes to America <u>He</u> will solve the problem! We have had no word as to when, or to what city He will come! We will telegraph you as soon as we hear anything <u>definitely</u>. In regard to Royall we will assuredly pray earnestly! I wish I had the time now to go into detail of my work and the great service of Dr. Fareed. We <u>know</u> that the Spirit as manifested in the Bahá'í Reformation – can, and does heal bodies as well as souls for we have proven it! – Oh, we will have so much to tell you dearheart – We will need a whole week just to talk to you – our beloved spiritual "confidante" and friend! What a power there is in unity – You are always with us helping us in our labors. – I have often thought of you and felt the help! "The doors of the Kingdom are opened" upon the faces of those who are united! If you hear from Juliet won't you please tell us the news?

> With all loving Greetings
> from us both
>> In His Name
>> Your loving and devoted
>>> Lua

We leave here for Los Angeles Tuesday a.m.
Address until further notice
#2020 Toberman St.
c/o Mrs. C. F. Haney

At this period in Lua's life when she was joyously travelling in California promoting the Faith, her handwriting changed, becoming quite loose and flowing, much larger than before. It was in such a hand that she wrote to Agnes Parsons on September 1, 1911 telling that 'Abdu'l-Bahá was pleased with the new translation of the *Hidden Words*. She felt that a great wave of interest in the Cause was sweeping over the country. She enclosed yet another newspaper article. Fareed, posing as a man of independent means, was really dependent upon 'Abdu'l-Bahá for his support. This fact was not known by Lua.

Los Angeles
Sept. 1st, 1911

Dearest Noor,
Next Sunday Dr. Fareed is to speak in the Unitarian Church in Pasadena – and I am to speak in Los Angeles at Walker Theater where we both spoke last Sunday. A great wave of interest is

sweeping over the Country up and down this Coast just as 'Abdu'l-Bahá said it would – and He now wills that thus far it is only a beginning – He is greatly pleased with the last translation of the Hidden Words! And says the publication thereof in English, Arabic, and Persian is a most useful matter! If it could only be bound in Oxford what a lovely little Hand Book of God it would make and what a means for union of East and West.

Enclosed please find copy of an article which came out! The six million dollars refers to the believers of Russia and Baku who have been the largest contributors to the Temple there. And Dr. Fareed's being a man of independent means – comes from the fact that he told the reporter that we were not allowed to teach for money, and each teacher must be independent of the people unto whom he went to deliver the Message of Truth. Great interest is being manifest on all sides – Have you heard from Juliet since she left for Paris? Was it not too bad that so many were disappointed in not seeing the Beloved in London. The Christian CommonWealth and The Magazine of Current Literature for September contain splendid articles–

> Write us when you can
> > With devotion and love
> > > Your
> > > > Lua

1317 Jackson St. Oakland
c/o Mrs. N. S. Goodall will always
reach me. She forwards everything.

Very few letters to Lua from Juliet Thompson are available but those we can read show a deep and abiding friendship between the two. By this time, the American believers were becoming confident that the beloved Master was coming to their country. Some of the American friends, of whom Juliet was one, were able to travel to Switzerland to meet 'Abdu'l-Bahá there.

> 48 W. 10th St. New York
> Oct. 4th.11

My beloved own Lua:
If only this could be a talk instead of a letter. Mrs. Parsons wrote me she had sent you my last letter to her; so you know, dear that

I have been waiting to get your address to write to you direct. I had not a moment to write you as I wished while I was in Europe but kept hoping for the time. As soon as I returned I wrote to Mrs. Parsons for your address. She told me to send care of Mariam Haney – now Kate Ives gives a later direction. Kate also has told me the wonderful news of the great spread of the Cause through you and Dr. Fareed in California. Oh Lua! How blessed you are – to be such an instrument of His will – to be chosen to prepare the way in all the Western Coast for His Coming. For that He is coming I know – as of course you know too, and coming to California. What instructions you have received I do not know. Nor am I sure that either you or I have any right to say this, but He has told me that when the believers are united He will not only come to America, but pass through America, and He mentioned California. Still, I am sure I am not telling you news, for both you and Dr. Fareed know this.

Lua, what a work I had. You know by now that He sent for me to come to Him. I wanted to write you before I left – not only to share the news with you – but to ask you to write to dear mama, reconciling her to my going, as only you could do. But, my dear, I was rushed off so suddenly – I had only two days to prepare, after the difficulties cleared away, and I knew I was going. Less than a week, indeed, between the receipt of my Tablet and my sailing with Silvia. We were moving just at that time to this address – and I did not have the moment.

I went, as you also know, thinking to meet Him in London at the Races Congress, assured by Mr. Spiller that He would be there. Imagine my despair when I found He was not there, that his coming to Europe was uncertain, and in any case, He would not be there for a month. I cabled, and received the reply to "Wait". That was all, just that one word. I waited part of the time at dear Miss Rosenberg's. Mrs. Stannard was staying there too. Laura and Hippolyte came to London. Hippolyte for the Congress, then later with Laura. I saw so many of the believers, from everywhere, among them dear, beautiful Marie Hopper.

Then, Lua darling, came the cable calling me to Thonon. Oh Lua, if I could only have shared with you those marvelous days at Thonon, – on the Lake of Geneva, the Alps all around us. What a wonderful setting it was for our King! Have you ever been there? It seems like a bit of the etherial world, the mountains, the lake are always veiled in mist. It is like a <u>vision</u>, its beauty is so immaterial. Laura and Hippolyte were there and the five Persians who were with the Master. <u>Dear</u> Mirza Assadullah. Can you not imagine the joy of seeing him with the Master? It was so precious to see <u>him</u>, so like those days in Haifa and in Acca. But Laura and Hippolyte were the only European or American believers there beside myself, for two days. Those days were unspeakably dear. We were always in His Presence. They were His days of rest. We drove with Him, walked with Him, sailed with Him on the lake, (which is very like the Sea of Galilee I think), followed in a little group . . . Can you imagine what that was like, Lua? or what it brought home to me? Lua, I have seen in the <u>Master</u>, Bahá'u'lláh, – the Two inseparable – the Father in the Son, – the Eternal sun in the Mirror, – the Ever-returning Spirit.

Never have I seen such Power and Glory as I saw the last time in the Master. Whether the Sun of the West is shining more powerfully as it climbs to the Zenith; whether this is the strength of the noon-day Sun, – or whether some veils have fallen from my eyes, I could see more clearly; – or whether <u>both</u> are true, I am not wise enough to say. But, as I said, I have never seen Him so powerful or so radiant.

Every eye turned to follow Him as He passed among the people with His great Majesty. He never was unheeded, even though in Switzerland, unrevealed.

One precious day we spent with Edith Sanderson. That was the first day of my visit. On the third Annie Boyland had come over from Lausanne. (I went on the Fifth). In Vevey your name was mentioned, Darling. We were sitting at the table. The Master, Mrs. Sanderson, Mirza Assadullah, Tammadun-ul-Molk,[68] Edith and myself, when dear Mrs. Sanderson asked me, "Have you heard from Lua lately, Juliet?" He caught your name. "Ah! Lua!" He said in an indescribable tone of love. "I love Lua", Mrs. Sanderson went on to say. "So does my mother", I replied, "as of course you know I do. My mother just adores her." "So do I" said Mrs. Sanderson. . .

By November, 1911 Lua and Fareed were back in the San Francisco area, speaking nearly every day, Lua mostly among the women. At a meeting of the Jewish Women's

Council Lua spoke to 600 members and their friends (elsewhere it is reported that 900 heard the Message at this meeting). The platform was arranged like a Persian harem with a tea party performed with Persian, Turkish and Jewish ladies. The subject was "Bahá'í Influence and Effect on the Lives of Women in the Orient". Fareed came in garbed as a Persian sheik and addressed them.

Lua gave a course of addresses on the deeper meanings of the Faith at Professor Giffens' studio. Earnest seekers heard the first three of the *Seven Valleys*, probably with the new translation which they had recently prepared.

In a *Star of the West* article, Helen S. Goodall reported the travellers had given the Message to 5000 people in southern California.

In early December Lua wrote to Elizabeth Nourse:

Bellevue Hotel
Geary and Taylor Sts.
San Francisco,

My Beloved Menita
The Yule-Tide is nearly here again and how far away I seem from you and it! The roses are blooming, the birds singing, and the sun shining all around us here which seems more like May-time than December! Yet there is at times a little sharpness in the air! It is almost a year since I saw you – the New Year makes it so completely! Oh, how I wish I might see you for just a little while – I am weary dear, and long for you.

There is so much my heart wishes to tell you which cannot be transmitted across the miles! We are more and more busy each day. Stanford University has opened its doors to the Bahá'í Movement and we are to go there for the first time tonight! The Editor of one of the newspapers has taken up the subject with great earnestness and seriousness – and thus another city in Cal. has opened its doors to the Light of the Kingdom! It is wonderful, but the spirit which is to accomplish all things in this day – is doing its Mighty work!

The three very beautiful "nighties" have arrived just in time to keep me from going in quest of some for I was near "nightieless". They are just a perfect fit – and I like them so much! You are a dear good Menita to send them to me.

In regard to the white dress – I sent it to my sister-in-law and she writes that it fits her all right and will send me enough for it to buy material for a new one. So you see dear heart, it has turned out that you help me, after all to get the much needed new dress and I appreciate it all the more because you made a sacrifice to do it! What a beloved, blessed, spiritual child you are – and how proud I am to be your "Little Mother".

I was greatly pleased to hear of Phil in school! Let him dance and sing all he wants to. I know his prayers help me and I just do hope he will not forget one single time to remember me!

Tell him I am always looking for "his smiles across the sea" and for his kisses from the star! They help me live each day and make the night more restful! He is such a good Phil, I love him "heaps and heaps" and all "the other chilun" too! But, I can't help it if Phil comes just a wee bit first for he and I were born that way!

We may go back to Southern California for a time as they seem to need us there – but it will not be before Jan. 29th as we are engaged up to that time here, – and in near by places. Dr. Fareed is speaking so wonderfully well – and is meeting men of such insight and education! Our great cause is spreading and growing marvellously. Well dear it is almost time to go to Palo Alto – so must close – Do write me soon again – and tell the Kiddies to watch out long about Christmas time for the Brownies especially "Mister-Mind-Your-Mother" and "Mister don't tease your sister". They are sure to be there.

With much love to all, and kindest wishes to C. D. and all the Nourses –

I am as ever
Your own
"Little Mother"
Lua

Dr. Fareed joins in all loving wishes for the Christmas and New Year.

On Sunday evening, December 17th, Lua gave a talk at the California Club Hall in San Francisco, on the subject "The

Word of God". Introducing her, Dr. Fareed said:

We thought of combining two talks tonight, but inasmuch as both of the talks are rather lengthy, and inasmuch as the one Mrs. Getsinger is to give you is profound and requires your closest attention, we have decided to postpone the one on social and economic considerations of the Bahá'í Movement, or the Bahá'í consideration of economics and sociology, to a later period, and tonight you are to listen to an exposition of the great Word of God as taught by 'Abdu'l-Bahá. This talk which Mrs. Getsinger will present is, in substance, the fundamental teaching of the Bahá'í Reform, the great Bahá'í light on this most interesting and absorbing subject. . .

Lua's talk was "stenographically reported" and is available to us today, together with a few of the many talks she gave at this time. Three of the talks given in California may be read in their entirety in the Appendix. Reading them today, we can understand what 'Abdu'l-Bahá meant when He wrote to her in 1900:

Oh my Daughter – know that thou art a woman, whose words will have a great effect on the hearts of the people, and to whose words they will listen. Do not lose one single opportunity in this blessed time to talk to the people – be prepared on all occasions, and put forth all the efforts within thy power to deliver the message and do not look to thy comfort, or to what you shall eat or drink or wear – or to name, fame, renown, wealth, or even as to how you shall sleep, but look only to delivering the Truth with sincerity and true devotion sacrificing any and everything for the Cause! – And if you will do this – by God – you shall receive a confirmation – which you have never imagined – or conceived in your mind, and for this, I am the guarantee – and of it there is no doubt.[69]

By late December, Fareed was summarily summoned by 'Abdu'l-Bahá to return to the Holy Land. He was in Chicago on the 24th of that month on his way back. Lua remained in California and spoke on December 31, 1911 to the Oakland Chamber of Commerce. She lectured at the Oakland Club, a women's group, the Short Story Club, Saturday morning Club, and at the Mill Valley Club House where all residents were invited. She went to San Quentin prison to investigate prison conditions and spoke with the prisoners, recommending two for parole. She spoke to the Federation of Women's Clubs, continued her series of lectures at the California Club, which Hyde Dunn[70] attended, and spoke on Monday evenings at the homes of the friends for twenty to fifty people.[71]

On a Tuesday afternoon, January 9, 1912, Lua spoke at the Bellevue Hotel in San Francisco, telling those gathered there that no one had taken Jesus' place, but Bahá'u'lláh had come in the station of the Father. She said that though this claim might seem strange, we need have no fear of it, for whatever is _not_ of God will die of itself and whatever is of God will prove itself and live. She mentioned that all the signs prophesied for these days had now appeared. The Tablet of Bahá'u'lláh to Pope Pius IX was read by Thornton Chase, following which Mr. Chase spoke about the meaning to the world today of the Bahá'í movement.

The following Tuesday, January 16th, Lua spoke about the plan of God for this day, and the part each human being has to play in bringing it about.

. . . we must all recognize the fact that God is one God, one Father, one Creator of us all, and that we are all now here, living in one home, members of one family, brothers and sisters.

We do not realize this. Very few people on earth realize this great truth, this great fact. If we did, we would have peace. We would not be _talking_ about it so much. We would _have_ it. It would be an established fact. It would just _be_. The sun does not have to declare itself over and over as a shining luminous body. It _is_. And could humanity come into the understanding that God is one, that this earth, this whole planet, is a home for His creatures, and that we are all _now_ members of His family, brothers and sisters, why peace would _be_. It is just a lack of realization on our part . . .

146

. . . Every one of us is part of that great plan, and the plan will not be perfect until it is worked out to the perfection of all its parts.

I have something to do in that great plan. The work that I have to do is there to be done. If I fail to recognize the point, or the fact, that that work is there for me to do, the opportunity will be given me to do it, until it is absolutely proven to the great Mind of God that I am not going to do it, that out of my little individual egotism and conceit I think I can get along without performing my part of the work that is necessary in His great plan, and then another servant willing to do my work does it, and the plan goes on, irrespective and regardless of me. It does not make a bit of difference.

The great plan, in the end, will be worked out, only just that little part designed for me is delayed a little while, but in the great plan of God time is not taken into consideration very much, for before the great Eye and Mind of God a thousand years is just as the twinkling of an eye, and the work is done. There is all eternity before me to regret having missed the opportunity to do my part of the plan.

What is my part? To so prepare my own heart and soul, through the knowledge of the Word of God, as to make myself an entity, an individual stone, in the great temple of His truth that constitutes His kingdom on earth to-day. His kingdom "on earth as it is in heaven" will be a spiritual kingdom. In heaven it is a spiritual kingdom, to be sure. On earth it will also be a spiritual kingdom. . .

But how patient is God! Oh, how patient is God! All these years He gives us to do just a few little things. First of all, to turn to Him, the Great Helper, the Giver of Knowledge, the Giver of Love, the Giver of Faith, the Giver of all good Gifts, and just realize that He is the Helper, and Giver and Bestower of whatever we may need, or want, or desire, for the full completion and working out of His will.

How foolish an architect and builder would be if he called together all the people to build a house and did not supply them with materials. No matter how perfect his plan would be, if he did not have the material to carry out the minutest detail of his plan, it would be incomplete, it would not be finished. So, as we are parts of the great plan of God, we have only to turn to Him

147

and get all the material necessary to build His great plan to its utmost perfection.

The only question is: "Do we want to? Do we <u>want</u> to?"

The question is not: "Does He want us to?"

It is: "Do <u>we</u> <u>want</u> to do it?" This question is for each one to answer to himself.

The Bahá'í teacher to-day can only tell the good news – the "glad tidings" as they call it in the East – that the Great Architect has appeared, the Father has come, the Prince of Peace is here, the plan is all made out perfect, ready for the builders, and invite you all to come and take your place according to your ability and talent and capacity, and work under His direction and guidance for the completion and fulfillment of His kingdom.

As the time of 'Abdu'l-Bahá's arrival in New York drew near, Lua's eyes were turned wistfully towards the East coast – so far away.

Bellevue Hotel Geary and Taylor Sts.
San Francisco , April 11th, 1912

My beloved Noor,

Only think – 'Abdu'l-Bahá will be with you by the time this letter reaches you – and you will once more see Him face to face. Mrs. Pinchot wrote me a few days ago of her desire to meet Him and said you had promised a private interview for her. I am so happy. I trust Mr. Gifford P. will also see Him privately. Tell Dr. Fareed to arrange it.

Mrs. Goodall and her daughter Mrs. Cooper leave here Saturday for Washington to attend the Convention. I have no permission to leave Cal. yet so – I remain. My heart as you may imagine is many miles from here – yet I am happy to go on spreading the Message for every day some new ones hear it.

Please dear, do remember me in His Presence – and beg for me – His blessing and through Him a great outpouring of His Spirit with an abundance of God's Mercy. Mrs. Goodall and I went to Napa yesterday a small town not far from San Francisco – where I delivered the Message to quite a number of new people – who were so pleased that they have asked me to come again which I shall do very soon probably. How I would love to be there with you now. He will be in your home! How blessed you are! But you deserve it and have earned it. I wrote Dr. Jung yesterday to be sure and see the Master – Please call her up dear – for she was so kind to me – and you remember 'Abdu'l-Bahá sent her a Message by me. I know you will be very busy but I wish I could have just a word from you.

Maybe after the convention is over you can spare me a few moments!

I wish for you and yours every blessing and heavenly gift! I am sure the Giver of all God has chosen you for his favors.

With love
In His Name
Your devoted
   Lua

XI

And now came the most wonderful time of all to the American Bahá'ís. At last 'Abdu'l-Bahá was in their land, arriving in New York on April 11, 1912, not to depart until December 5, 1912. The eight months of that historic and world-changing visit were charged with wonder for his followers. Lua, given permission to come to New York, was with Him as much as possible and Edward was part of His entourage. Lua and Juliet Thompson were united in their love for the Master and comforted each other when not in His presence. Among the retinue of 'Abdu'l-Bahá was Ameen Fareed, often serving as interpreter.

Edward was engaged every day from seven in the morning until eleven at night in attending upon 'Abdu'l-Bahá and making arrangements for Him. The Master refused to be bound by a schedule, saying that the spirit "arranged to send the contingencies". That Edward was pleased to be of service in this delicate but challenging assignment is shown in his letter to Mrs. Parsons written April 15, 1912.

Hotel Ansonia
Broadway, 73 to 74th street
New York City
Apr.15, 1912

Monday 4 p.m.
Dear Mrs. Parsons:
Just time to write a hurried line. 'Abdu'l-Bahá has made appointments for Thursday all day, and it looks now as if he starts for Wash. on Friday. In the party is 'Abdu'l-Bahá, Dr. Fareed, Mirza Mahmood, and Seyed Assadulla (not Dr. Fareeds father) and myself. Two or three of the party were sent back from Naples,

and hence I have been placed in charge of many details. Mirza Mahmood and Seyed will occupy a room together, separate beds if possible and the Dr. and myself will also room together, separate beds.

Mirza Ahmed goes to Wash. Wednesday I think and will go to his own quarters and come to 1704 when he chooses. I also have my own quarters, and will be ready to go there if he so wishes upon arrival, but there is so much (underlined twice) detail to look after continually that I am simply in the rush from 7 to 11 each day.

Now one important thing: –
We have tried to have 'Abdu'l-Bahá say that he would for certain be your guest, but without avail. He said "I cannot be bound to any place or arrangement before the day arrives. The spirit arranges to sent the contingencies." I said "then if you might want an apt. by yourself, it is best I write to have one found. He said "very well, but do not engage it, if I like it when I see it, I will choose it, if not, then I don't want it". This was Friday, and that so stands at this writing. He said, "If I should go to the hotel or apt., I will spend my time at Mrs. Parsons, but have my quarters at my own apt."

I hardly think you can get the reception date, unless you go ahead and when the moment comes, ask him to lend his presence. I have found, through the friends, an apt. on Harvard and 14th Str. of which I have not yet informed him. This is not far from you, and he will thus decide.

Just now Mirza Ali Khuli Khan has sent a letter to be handed to Him personally, and I dont know its contents as yet. I wrote the Turkish Ambassador before I left, leaving the presentation in abeyance, pending His arrival. 'Abdu'l-Bahá said "that if my presentation to the Press includes also my declaration of citizenship of any country, then I will decline, as I am a citizen of the world."

So this decides the matter for Mr. McVeagh and you can quote the above words to him in order to ease his mind on that score.

New York has given 'Abdu'l-Bahá a most dignified and praiseful reception. Sunday morning service in Church of Ascension 10 St & 5th Rev. Percy S. Grant. He was given the Bishop's chair to sit in and the church was crowded to standing room. Next day 7 of the greatest dailies reported His words in most elegant terms. Ella Wheeler Wilcox today in NY Journal give a great laudation to Him in a three column article. The great men of the city are beseeching for interviews. The bishop of the Episcopal Diocese of NY comes at 5 today. Mr. Carnegie asks for him at his home, as he apologized not being able to come to Him on acct. of throat trouble. Over 70 people were here from 9 to 3, and He speaks to 50, and I am writing in His absence.

I am just stating facts as they are so you can be prepared. Very truly yours in Abha E.C. Getsinger

2nd Edition
    Monday 7 p.m.
Dear Mrs. Parsons: 'Abdu'l-Bahá has just made appointments covering all day Friday. So our hope is Sat. for Wash.
        E.C.G.

The Mother Temple of the West was dedicated in Wilmette, Illinois on May 1, 1912, in conjunction with the National Convention of the Bahá'ís. Lua Getsinger turned the first spadeful of earth at the request of 'Abdu'l-Bahá.

There were snags in carrying out the dedication ceremony. The golden trowel given to the Master to dig a hole for the dedication stone wasn't strong enough to break through the ground. An ax, borrowed from someone across the street, was handed to 'Abdu'l-Bahá, who swung it powerfully, again and again, until He broke into the earth below. Finally, a shovel was produced by a young man who had borrowed it from a work crew near the village center. When the shovel was handed to the Master, Corinne True reportedly suggested to Him to have women participate in the ceremony. 'Abdu'l-Bahá called on Lua Getsinger to come forward. It required a second urging by the Master to draw Lua to Him. Mrs. True was the second one to dig up a shovelful of earth. Following her, representatives from different races and nationalities took their turn with the shovel. After placing the stone in the hole, the Master pushed the earth around it and declared, "The Temple is already built."[72]

Lua's name is listed in *Star of the West* along with many others as a guest at the Convention in Chicago in late April,[73] and a photograph of the Master with the friends in Cleveland, Ohio, on May 6th shows Lua to be present.

Lua and Juliet Thompson had permission to be always with the Master and on May 11, 1912, May Maxwell, Carrie Kinney, Kate Ives, Grace Robarts, Juliet and Lua worked together to prepare the apartment for 'Abdu'l-Bahá. For the first time Lua, May and Juliet, the friends who loved the Master and each other so dearly, were together in His presence. On May 15, Lua telephoned Juliet from 'Abdu'l-Bahá's apartment saying she could come up now if she wished.

'Abdu'l-Bahá spoke at the Church of the Divine Paternity on Sunday, May 19, 1912. Juliet Thompson described this meeting in her diary.[74] "This was unbearably beautiful . . . Oh the look of His that day! . . . I wept through the whole service. At the end of the pew in front of me sat Lua, her eyes fixed on the Master, rapt, adoring, her beauty immeasurably heightened by that recognition, that adoration."

The greatest pleasure of Lua and Juliet was to be in the presence of the Master. On May 22, 1912 Juliet wept in Lua's arms because for two days 'Abdu'l-Bahá had not even looked at her. 'Abdu'l-Bahá sent for her and she and Lua were with Him together. On that day He told them their eyes were "rivers of tears".[75]

"From this moment," cried Lua, "Juliet and I dedicate our lives to Thee and we beg to at last die in Thy Path – to drink the cup of martyrdom. Oh, it would be so good for the Cause if two Americans could do this! Take hold of His coat, Julie, and beseech." I touched the hem of His garment. "Say yes," implored Lua. "Oh Julie, beg Him to say yes." But in Thonon (Switzerland) I had told the Master I would not ask for that cup again but would wait till God found me ready for it.

"I accept the dedication of your lives now. The rest will be decided later." And it was clear what He meant. How we must amuse him!

A letter from Lua to Agnes Parsons at the end of May demonstrates her appreciation of Mrs. Parsons' generosity and also her unquestioning obedience to 'Abdu'l-Bahá. Interestingly, this letter shows that Lua was already prepared by 'Abdu'l-Bahá to go to California ahead of Him.

May 25, 1912

My dear Noor,

How disappointed I was not to be able to see you. 'Abdu'l-Bahá wished me to go on to New York so I could not stop off in Washington. I rec'd your lovely long letter and was most pleased to hear from you – regarding the Master's visit. I too, wish I could see you and talk with you. I want to thank you for sending half of my expenses to Mrs. Goodall – it was just like Noor to think so lovingly of me.

The Master told me also how you had spoken to Him regarding me – and your desire to always help me. I appreciate this love on your part dear – and I feel all unworthy of it. You have always been very loving and kind to this maid servant, and I ask God to ever bless more and more abundantly you and yours. We are waiting for the Beloved to come from Boston. I did not go this time with Him. I may go very soon to the Coast in advance of Him. It is not definitely decided. I shall be very sorry not to see you and dear Mrs. Pinchot before going so far away again – but I am a "Bugler" in the vast army of God and try always to obey orders willingly and cheerfully.

With deep love and gratitude
Your loving and devoted
Lua

On June 2, 1912 Lua and Juliet were in a front pew at Dr. Grant's Forum enjoying the Master's presence and spoken message. 'Abdu'l-Bahá saw the Bahá'ís every day and spoke in public almost every day. He spoke on June 8 in New York City, and twice on June 9,[76] in Philadelphia, Pennsylvania. On June 11 He spoke at the home of Mr. and Mrs. Edward B. Kinney, 780 West End Avenue, New York, and twice at 309 West Seventy-eighth Street, New York. He spoke again at that address on June 12.

Despite her busy schedule, Lua found time to write a note to Elizabeth Nourse:

> 309 W. 78th St.
> New York – Tuesday
>
> My own Menita.
>
> Such a busy day – but I must drop you just a line to say that we all reached home safely – the Master very tired but content with his visit to Philadelphia. After you had gone – He asked for you and said I wanted to bid her "goodbye" – I told him your train time came while He was sleeping and you did not wish to disturb him – so it was all right. Oh dearest child of my soul – I have not seen half enough of you – it was only a little glimpse. Dr. Fareed and Mr. McNutt went to Wash. D. C. this A. M. to stay until Friday. Dr. F. wished me to remember him to you and sends much love to his "Little Mother". Do please have Mr. Nourse furnish us with all the proofs possible of A. E. Davis – I want to save those poor people on the coast from his clutches.
>
> I haven't another moment – must run and wash dishes, etc. etc. Mrs. Hinkle Smith comes this P. M. for her first lesson. She is going to stay right here for a week – & will come to me every day. Then I shall send her to you! I want you to write 'Abdu'l-Bahá and ask Him to guide you in the service of God from now on. You know we talked of this. The Master told me if Mrs. Boyle would do only as He [underlined three times in the copy] said everything would be right for her – and I want everything right for you through His Words. – Oceans of Love to my own Phil.
>
> Your devoted but unworthy
> "Little Mother" Lua

Teaching meetings were held in different locations in the city and Lua was often the speaker. The stenographic notes of her talk on June 13, 1912, when 'Abdu'l-Bahá was travelling, may be found in the Appendix. Lua answered such questions as "Why turn toward the East for prayer?" Her answer: for unity. (She may not have been aware at that time that the Qiblih for this day is the place where the earthly remains of Bahá'u'lláh lie, regardless of which direction one must turn to face it.)

"How can any human being let love take possession of the heart?" She answered that the most important fact for each human being is to determine whether Bahá'u'lláh is the Manifestation of God for this day. She went on to say that there is no middle ground in the matter. Bahá'u'lláh is either the Manifestation of God, the Christ returned, the Holy Spirit of God, the Father made manifest, the Prince of Peace or He is not. He is not a good man who has come to reform the world. She gave proof of the efficacy of Bahá'u'lláh's word and explained that He had come to remove religious, patriotic, racial and national prejudices. She used her own experiences to illustrate this point, recounting an occasion when seventy pilgrims were gathered at the table of 'Abdu'l-Bahá. She said that these pilgrims in themselves showed that such prejudices had been abolished by them gathering in this a manner. Lua said that the answer to this basic question can be obtained by prayer; through prayer and study of the Holy Writings, one obtains knowledge and it is only through knowledge that we have faith.

Joseph Hannen was instructed to arrange a meeting in Baltimore for 'Abdu'l-Bahá for the following day, June 14. Lua would undoubtedly have wished to be with him, but that day found her giving another long talk in New York City, explaining Christian doctrine in relation to the Bahá'í Faith and giving the message of the coming of the Báb and Bahá'u'lláh (see Appendix). Lua wrote a letter from New York City to Mrs. Parsons discussing the June 14th meeting and urging the importance of making arrangements for meetings to be held in Washington, DC. Lua, Howard MacNutt and Dr. Fareed were departing on the day the letter was written [undated] for Philadelphia. The Master wished the meetings in Washington to be very large.

* * *

In the morning of June 19, 1912 'Abdu'l-Bahá publicly clarified His station as Center of the Covenant. This proclamation was made to about 125 people gathered in His house on West 78th Street. What He said on that occasion does not appear in *The Promulgation of Universal Peace*, but was recorded and later published in *Star of the West*.[77] This was a special day in Lua's life, for it was on that same day that 'Abdu'l-Bahá named her "Herald of the Covenant".

She and Juliet Thompson were together with the Master in New York. Lua was able to speak some Persian by this time but not enough to understand the import of the mission laid upon her by 'Abdu'l-Bahá. Juliet describes the scene in her diary.

The Beloved Master's portrait is finished. He sat for me six times, but I really did it in the three half hours he had promised me; for the sixth time, when He posed in His own room on the top floor, I didn't put on a single stroke. I was looking at the portrait wondering what I could find to do, when He suddenly rose from his chair and said: "It is finished." The fifth time He sat, Miss Souley-Campbell came in with a drawing she had done from a photograph to ask if He would sign it for her and if she might add a few touches from life. This meant that He had to change His pose, so of course I couldn't paint that day. And the fourth time (the nineteenth of June) – who could have painted then?

I had just begun to work, Lua in the room sitting on a couch nearby, when the Master smiled at me; then turning to Lua said in Persian: "This makes me sleepy. What shall I do?"

"Tell the Master, Lua, that if He would like to take a nap, I can work while He sleeps."

But I found that I could not. What I saw then was too sacred, too formidable. He sat still as a statue, His eyes closed, infinite peace on that chiseled face, a God-like calm and grandeur in His erect head.

Suddenly, with a great flash like lightning He opened His eyes and the room seemed to rock like a ship in a storm with the Power released. The Master was blazing. "The veils of glory," "the thousand veils," had shriveled away in that Flame and we were exposed to the Glory itself.

Lua and I sat shaking and sobbing.

Then he spoke to Lua. I caught the words, *"Munádiy-i-Ahd."* (Herald of the Covenant).

Lua started forward, her hand to her breast.

"Man?" [I?] she exclaimed.

"Call one of the Persians. You must understand this."

Never shall I forget that moment, the flashing eyes of 'Abdu'l-Bahá, the reverberations of His Voice, the Power that still rocked the room. God of lightning and thunder! I thought.

"I appoint you, Lua, the Herald of the Covenant. And I AM THE COVENANT, appointed by Bahá'u'lláh. And no one can refute His Word. This is the Testament of Bahá'u'lláh. You will find it in the Holy Book of Aqdas. Go forth and proclaim, 'THIS IS THE COVENANT OF GOD in your midst.'"

A great joy had lifted Lua up. Her eyes were full of light. She looked like a winged angel. "Oh recreate me," she cried, "that I may do this work for Thee!"

By now I was sobbing uncontrollably.

"Julie too," said Lua, not even in such a moment forgetful of me, "wants to be recreated."

But the Master had shrouded Himself with His veils again, the "thousand veils." He sat before us now in His dear humanity: very, very human, very simple.

"Don't cry, Juliet," He said. "This is no time for tears. Through tears you cannot see to paint."

I tried hard to hold back my tears and to work, but painting that day was at an end for me.[78]

Juliet said that it "nearly killed" Lua to be left behind when the Master left for Montclair. Being with 'Abdu'l-Bahá was the highest pleasure in her life and in the lives of many of the believers. Numerous stories are told of the magic of His presence, how He knew their innermost wishes, often granting them without the wishes being voiced. But Lua, regardless of her wishes, was not invited to New Jersey and involved Juliet in her misbehavior. Juliet tells the story in her diary.

On June 21, the Master left for Montclair to stay nine days. I was with Him all day till He went. I had lunched with Him nearly

158

every day that week. Lua, Mrs. Hinkle-Smith, Valíyu'lláh <u>Kh</u>án, and I bade Him good-bye on the steps of His house.

It had nearly killed Lua not to be taken to Montclair with Him. Two days later she said to me: "Let's go to see Him, Julie."

"How can we, Lua? He didn't invite us," I answered. "He bade us good-bye for nine days."

"Oh but <u>you</u> have an excuse, those proofs of Mrs. Kasebier's pictures. You really <u>should</u> show them to Him, Julie."

And she whirled Georgie Ralston and me off to Montclair with her.

We were punished of course, and our first punishment was that lunch was unusually late (so that instead of arriving after, as we had planned, we arrived just in time for it). And this was <u>agonizing</u>, for there weren't enough seats at the table, and the Master wouldn't sit down to eat. One of us had to occupy <u>His</u> chair, while he Himself waited on us, carrying all the courses around and around that table. I couldn't get over my mortification.

At the end He came in with the fruit, a glass bowl full of golden peaches. Without turning His head – His face was set straight before Him – He sent a piercing glance from the corner of His eye toward Lua and me. Such a majestic, stern glance, like a sword thrust.

After lunch, and this was our second punishment, He banished the three of us – Georgie, Lua and me – leading us to a small back porch and abandoning us there. But before very long He returned and asked us to take a walk with Him.[79]

It was in Englewood, New Jersey on June 29th, according to Juliet's *Diary*,[80] that 'Abdu'l-Bahá told Lua she must go once again to California. Juliet recounts an amusing story that before accepting the Master's wishes, Lua tried to change His mind by deliberately walking in poison ivy. However, as we have seen, by May 25th Lua was already aware of 'Abdu'l-Bahá's intention to send her to California in advance of His arrival, "a 'Bugler' in the vast army of God".

Lua . . . went off alone, an exceedingly naughty purpose in her mind. The Master had just told her that she must leave very soon for California. So now she deliberately walked in poison ivy, walked back and forth and back and forth till her feet were thoroughly poisoned. "Now, Julie," she said (when the deed was done) "He *can't* send me to California.". . .

That night our Beloved Lord returned to New York. The next morning early I flew up to see Him, but he sent me at once to Lua, who was staying with Georgie Ralston in a hotel nearby.

She was in bed, her feet terribly swollen from the poison ivy.

"<u>Look</u> at me, Julie," she said. "<u>Look</u> at my feet. Oh, please go right back to the Master and tell Him about them and say: "How can Lua travel now?"

I did it, returned to the Master's house, found Him in His room and put Lua's question to Him. He laughed, then crossed the room to a table on which stood a bowl of fruit, and, selecting an apple and a pomegranate, gave them to me.

"Take these to Lua," He said. "Tell her to eat them and she will be cured. Spend the day with her, Juliet."

Oh precious Lua – strange mixture of disobedience and obedience – and all from love! I shall never forget her, seizing first the apple, then the pomegranate and gravely chewing them all the way through till not even a pomegranate seed was left: thoroughly eating her cure, which was certain to send her to California.

In the late afternoon we were happily surprised by a visit from the Master Himself. He drew back the sheet and looked at Lua's feet, which by that time were beautifully slim. Then He burst out laughing.

"See," He said, "I have cured Lua with an apple and a pomegranate."

But Lua revolted again. There was one more thing she could try, and she tried it. The Master had asked me to paint her portrait and I had already had one sitting. The following day, at the Master's house, she drew me aside.

"Please, Julie, do something else for me. Go to the Master, now, and say, "You commanded me to paint Lua. If she is in California and I here, how can I do it? The portrait is begun; how can I finish it?"

Again the Master burst out laughing, for this of course was too transparent.

"In a year," He said, "Lua will join Me in Egypt. She will stay in New York a few days on her way to Me and you can paint her then, Juliet."

So poor Lua had to go to California. There was no way out for her.

On July 3, 1912, Lua wrote to Mrs. Parsons that she went "willingly to uphold the Covenant", showing no sign of the reluctance that Juliet reported. A more customary attitude exhibited by Lua was the sincere eagerness to follow the commands of 'Abdu'l-Bahá shown in this letter.

300 W. 78th St. July 3, 1912

My dearest Noor.

In reply to your letters – I must briefly state – that first I am expecting to leave for Cal. again next Sat. at the command of the Beloved.

2<u>nd</u> Yesterday He told me to write you to let Royall return to Dr. Ring.

3<u>rd</u> This morning He told me to write you that it is not yet known whether He can go to you or not . Perhaps He may come. Now He has work to do. Twice He said – "Perhaps I may go to her". His going to Cal. at all is now doubtful!

I am commanded to return there and teach the Cause! It is very difficult to leave the Beloved – Yet, I do gladly and willingly to uphold the standard of "the Center of the Covenant!" – Please pray for me dear, that I may ever be the slave of the Word of 'Abdu'l-Bahá and execute <u>His</u> Will! How I wish I could see you for a little visit but this is impossible now – in heart and spirit I am always with you – but to see your dear noble face now and then is like finding an oasis in the desert!–

I love you and send you my tenderest devotion! I thank you for all of your kindness to

Your unworthy but
loving friend
Lua

July 3rd. 1912

P. S. The feast was very wonderful!

July 11, 1912 is the probable date that Lua left for California at the request of 'Abdu'l-Bahá. By July 19 she was busily at work giving lectures, carrying out 'Abdu'l-Bahá's instructions to "go forth and proclaim, 'This is the Covenant of God in your midst.'" With characteristic modesty, she refused to claim any special "mission" for herself: "I do not want you to be under the impression that I come to you today as a special messenger from Him . . . I am not sent especially to the friends, my work is what it always has been – just a bugler in the army of the Lord."

402 Lick Building, San Francisco, California
Friday, 3 P.M., July 19, 1912

— oOo —

Mrs. Lua M. Getsinger, having just returned from New York, and being asked to address the meeting, said:

I want to read to you a prayer. It is called the Prayer for Illumination:

"I ask Thee, O my God – by Thy Power, Might and Dominion, which have encompassed all who are in Thy heaven and earth – to point out to Thy servants Thy straight pathway, that they may acknowledge Thy Oneness and Singleness with a certainty that shall not be clouded by the imaginations of doubters, nor veiled by the conjectures of straying wanderers.

"Oh God, illumine the eyes and the hearts of Thy servants with the light of Thy Knowledge, that they may know of this, the Highest Station and Glorious Horizon, that they may not be withheld by false voices from beholding the effulgence of the light of Thy Oneness, nor prevented from turning unto the horizon of Renunciation." (*Hidden Words,* page 74.)[81]

I want to call your attention just now to the postal card which you have sent out announcing this meeting, because I received one, and from it I gathered the information that I was coming to you with a message.

I have a beautiful message for you, but it is a message that 'Abdu'l-Bahá spoke in New York on the 19th of June, and He spoke it for the entire inhabitants of America, as well as of the world, but I do not want you to be under the impression that I come to you to-day as a special messenger from Him.

Though I am back in California at the command of 'Abdu'l-Bahá, I am not sent especially to the friends, my work is what it always has been – just a bugler in the army of the Lord. I am here to-day because God is very good to me, but not with a message that 'Abdu'l-Bahá spoke just for the believers which I have been sent to deliver.

It became evident in New York some time ago that the attention of the people must be called to the Covenant of God, and up to this time 'Abdu'l-Bahá had never made any mention of Himself save that of 'Abdu'l-Bahá.

Some time ago some people went to Acca as pilgrims to visit that glorious spot while 'Abdu'l-Bahá was still a prisoner, and they asked Him regarding His station, saying:

"Some say you are Christ; some say you are this; some say you are that."

'Abdu'l-Bahá answered by saying:

"Christ and Lord and Master are all rays of light emanating from the Sun, but 'Abdu'l-Bahá is a dome covering all these perfections."

'Abdu'l-Bahá, as you know, means the "Servant of Baha," and just the day before we left New York 'Abdu'l-Bahá, in speaking of Himself, said:

"In the threshold of Bahá'u'lláh I am pure evanescence. I am 'Abdu'l-Bahá."

And then, turning to one person, He said:

"Nineteen hundred years ago Jesus Christ turned to Peter and said, "Whom do you think that I am?" And what did Peter answer?

And the one addressed said:

"'Thou art Christ, the Son of the living God.'"

And again turning to the one, 'Abdu'l-Bahá said:

"Whom do you say I am?"

And the one addressed replied:

"I say you are what Bahá'u'lláh declared you to be: the Greatest Branch extended from the Ancient Root, the Center of the Covenant of God, the Mystery of God, and the Word of God manifest in the flesh among us to-day."

And He answered:

"I am the Center of the Covenant of God."

163

On the 19th of June, 'Abdu'l-Bahá made this proclamation of being the Center of the Covenant of God to about one hundred and twenty-five people who were gathered in His house on West 78th St.

Those present will never forget that day, I am sure. Though He spoke the message very quietly and impressively, it went forth with such a power that I am sure the whole city of New York was affected by it, and I know, without any doubt, that every person present that day was touched with a spirit which in itself was recreative. But before reading to you the message which He spoke that day I want to speak to you a little bit about the Covenant of God and what it means.

God made a covenant with Abraham, which He promised was to be an everlasting covenant, and the covenant which He made with Abraham was fulfilled, as far as Abraham was concerned, with Moses.

When Moses came, He covenanted with the people, and His covenant was fulfilled with the appearance of Jesus Christ.

When Jesus came He also covenanted with the people, and His covenant was fulfilled in the appearance of . . . Bahá'u'lláh, who was the greatest Manifestation of God the earth has ever known, of whom we have any record whatsoever, for in the appearance of Bahá'u'lláh the Sun shone forth in all of its splendor, might and glory, while in previous Manifestations it did not shine forth in all its power, might, splendor and glory, for this reason, that the people of the world were not spiritually prepared to see it in its greatest light.

Before Bahá'u'lláh departed from this earth, He covenanted with the people and brought forth His covenant, before the eyes of all the world, in the person and presence of His Son, the Greatest Branch, 'Abdu'l-Bahá.

In all religious history the world has never had a parallel of this great Day, because this is the Day of God. In previous times, the people have waited long years to see the covenant of God fulfilled. How many hundreds of years elapsed between Abraham and Moses, between Moses and Jesus, between Jesus and Mohammed!

But in this Day we have the Covenant of Mohammed – the Báb; His Covenant – the Manifestation of God, Bahá'u'lláh; and His Covenant – 'Abdu'l-Bahá; all present on the earth at one and the same time, each manifesting forth the light as it was given Him to manifest it in His time and in His day.

Now I want to read to you the Words of 'Abdu'l-Bahá. This was uttered just before He departed from New York for Montclair, where He spent ten days. He said:

"To-morrow I wish to go to Montclair. To-day is the last day in which we gather together with you to say farewell to you. Therefore, I wish to expound for you an important question, and that question concerns the Covenant.

"In former cycles no distinct Covenant has been made in writing by the Supreme Pen; no distinct personage had been appointed to be the Standard differentiating falsehood from truth, so that whatsoever He was to say was to stand as Truth and that which He repudiated was to be known as falsehood. At most, His Holiness Jesus Christ gave only an intimation, a symbol, and that was but an indication of the solidity of Peter's faith. When He mentioned his faith, His Holiness said, 'Thou art Peter (which means rock) and upon this rock will I build my church.' This was a sanction of Peter's faith; it was not indicative of his being the Expounder of the Book, but was a confirmation of Peter's faith.

"But in this dispensation of the Blessed Beauty, among its distinction is that He did not leave people in perplexity. He entered into a Covenant and Testament with the people. He appointed a Center of the Covenant. He wrote with His own pen and revealed it in the Kitab-el-Akdas, the Book of Laws, the Book of the Covenant, appointing Him ('Abdu'l-Bahá) the Expounder of the Book. You must ask Him regarding the meanings of the texts of the verses. Whatsoever He says is correct. And outside of this, in numerous Tablets He (Bahá'u'lláh) has explicitly recorded it, with clear, sufficient, valid and forceful statements. In the Tablet of the Branch He explicitly states, 'Whatsoever the Branch says is right, or correct; and every person must obey the Branch with his life, with his heart, with his tongue. Without His will, not a word shall any one utter.' This is an explicit text of the Blessed Beauty. So there is no rescue left for anybody. No soul shall, of himself, speak anything. Whatsoever His ('Abdu'l-Bahá's) tongue utters, whatsoever His pen records, that is correct, according to the explicit text of Bahá'u'lláh in the Tablet of the Branch.

"His Holiness Abraham covenanted with regard to Moses. His

Holiness Moses was the Promised One of Abraham, and He covenanted with regard to His Holiness Christ, saying that Christ was the Promised One. His Holiness Christ covenanted with regard to His Holiness 'The Paraclete,' which means His Holiness Mohammed. His Holiness Mohammed covenanted as regards the Báb, whom He called 'My Promised One.' His Holiness the Báb, in all His books, in all His epistles, explicitly covenanted with regard to the Blessed Beauty, Bahá'u'lláh – that Bahá'u'lláh was the Promised One of His Holiness the Báb. His Holiness Bahá'u'lláh covenanted, not that I am the Promised One, but that 'Abdu'l-Bahá is the Expounder of the Book and the Center of His Covenant, and that the Promised One of Bahá'u'lláh will appear after one thousand or thousands of years. This is the Covenant which Bahá'u'lláh took. If a person shall deviate, he is not acceptable at the Threshold of Bahá'u'lláh. In case of difference, 'Abdu'l-Bahá must be consulted. They must revolve around His good pleasure. After 'Abdu'l-Bahá, whenever the Universal House of Justice is organized, it will ward off differences.

"Now I pray for you that God may aid you, may confirm you, may appoint you for His service, that He may suffer you to be as radiant candles, that He may accept you in His Kingdom, that He may make you the cause of the spread of the Light of Bahá'u'lláh in these countries, and that the teachings of Bahá'u'lláh may be spread broadcast.

"I pray for you, and I am pleased with all of you, each one, one by one and I pray that God may aid and confirm you. From Montclair I will come back to you. New York is specialized, because I go away and I come back to it. The friends in New York must appreciate this. At present, farewell to you!"[82]

In speaking one other time, regarding the Covenant of God, 'Abdu'l-Bahá said:

"The Cause in America is not at present established, grounded and well founded, because it is in the state of formation, and the people in America must realize what the Center of the Covenant is, and for what great heavenly wisdom the Center of the Covenant was left among them."

You know it was prophesied in this great Day of God the Sun should rise in the West. Do you realize that with the coming of 'Abdu'l-Bahá to America the glorious Sun of Truth has actually risen above the Western Horizon?

166

'Abdu'l-Bahá to-day is like a great window through which the effulgent Sun of glory, of heavenly light, eternal understanding and truth, is flooding America, is flooding all the Western world, as well as the Eastern world.

People often say, "Do you worship 'Abdu'l-Bahá?"

No, we do not worship 'Abdu'l-Bahá, humanly speaking, for if one turns to the window to behold the light of the Sun he does not turn because the window is a window, but because it is a channel through which he not only beholds the light of the Sun but the Sun itself.

'Abdu'l-Bahá does not want any worship for himself. He wants the people to realize that Bahá'u'lláh was the Great Physician who appeared to remedy all of the ills of the world, and the remedies which Bahá'u'lláh has left to be administered to sin-sick humanity by 'Abdu'l-Bahá are His heavenly teachings, His holy utterances, – and His divine guidance through this world of darkness and ignorance to His heavenly Kingdom of light and knowledge.

'Abdu'l-Bahá is the <u>way</u> now to that Kingdom, and in His way, and after Him, we must walk. This is a very, very important matter, and now all of the believers must try to realize the great importance of turning to the Center of the Covenant.

I want to tell you a story that was told us in New York by a young Persian who has lately arrived from Persia.

You have heard, I suppose, of the wonderful story of Mirza Vargha [Varqá] and his young son Rouh'Ullah [Rúḥu'lláh]. This young man is a son of this heavenly soul who testified to the glory of God – by sacrificing his life in the path of 'Abdu'l-Bahá. He said one day before his martyrdom his father told this wonderful story.

Mirza Vargha was once in the presence of Bahá'u'lláh, when Bahá'u'lláh arose and began to walk back and forth in the room, and turning to him said:

"Oh Mirza Vargha, all the Manifestations of God are endowed with an ethereal spirit and power which takes effect in everything. When They walk, the earth is no longer the same as before They walked. When They turn and speak, everything becomes affected because of this ethereal power They possess. Jesus Christ possessed this ethereal power to such an extent that the people called Him a perfect man. But He said Jesus Christ could not bear to associate with fools, and this is not a sign of absolute perfection."

And just stop to think a minute, how it is recorded in the Gospels that Jesus would talk to the multitude, and be among them for a little, and then suddenly disappear from the midst of them and go apart with His disciples, who possessed a little spiritual capacity and understanding, and to them He would explain the spiritual significances of His utterances. Why? Because the people of His day had not the capacity to admit of any explanations.

But Bahá'u'lláh said:

"Look at 'Abdu'l-Bahá, how He associates with everybody, until His patience is marvelled at. What will the effect in the world be when He arises!"

And at that time Mirza Vargha supplicated to sacrifice his life in the way of 'Abdu'l-Bahá.

And of 'Abdu'l-Bahá what can any one of us say, only what Bahá'u'lláh Himself has said: "He is the Branch extended from the Ancient Root of the Tree of Life. He is the Center of the Covenant of God, and he who turns to Him has turned to Me;" says Bahá'u'lláh; "he who turns away from Him has turned away from Me; he who sees His face has seen My Face; he who hears His Word has heard My Word. He is the Mystery of God, and verily He is the Word of God."

And He has been left to us that we might all turn to Him, because how ignorant we are spiritually, how like veritable little children we are in the understanding of spiritual things. And though the Word of God has been spoken to-day through Bahá'u'lláh, the Greatest Manifestation, the Father, in such clear, lucid utterances, devoid of parables, divested of similes, yet we do not understand. Our ears are still too full of the din of the world to hear the clear voice of the Spirit of God unless it is expounded to us and interpreted for us. And that no one should be left in perplexity, and that his Word should become absolutely clear as the sun at midday, God, in His great mercy, left unto us His Son to be the Expounder of all the Holy Books – the Center of His Covenant, the Rainbow of Promise, spanning the sky of human existence – to Whom we must all turn, for this reason: that without a Center there is no circumference. We are all dots on the great circle of the circumference of God, and without the

Center upon which every eye must be fastened, there will be no circumference whatsoever.

Just think of a wheel for a moment. Suppose a spoke becomes detached from the hub, the very momentum of the wheel will cast it out as it goes around. So to-day no one must feel he has anything, or can do anything, or say anything, unless he has turned toward the Center of the Covenant of God, and is confirmed by the power of the Spirit of God that is radiating through that Center to-day. And there can be no greater blessing than this: that we realize that this great opportunity is ours and that it is here in America.

Whether 'Abdu'l-Bahá comes to California or not, the great object for every one is to realize who is the Center of the Covenant, and if you realize that 'Abdu'l-Bahá is the Center of the Covenant, blessed are you for having realized and believed without having seen.

You know, to some, the physical body is a great test. It comes between the seeker and the Sun, for, to realize Truth, it must be apprehended by spirit, and in spirit there are no obstacles. To realize Truth, one simply has to turn to the Word of God and obey It.

We all accept Bahá'u'lláh as the Great Manifestation of God, and all we have to do is to take His Words, and know what He has said regarding all subjects, and especially regarding the Center of His Covenant, and then turn to that Covenant in absolute obedience. And obedience constitutes the first step in the realm of spiritual attainment.

Now I am not going to talk to you any more, because Mrs. Ralston is here, and she has come from New York also, where she has been basking in the sun of the Center of the Covenant of God, and she is a Californian and a San Franciscan, and I know you all want to hear her.

— o0o —

Following a few remarks by Mrs. Ralston, Mrs. Getsinger said:

There are few Assemblies that 'Abdu'l-Bahá has passed by, and when you think that from California went forth the first people to see 'Abdu'l-Bahá it means a great deal. It means that you are

His sheep whom He can trust. You are in the fold. You do not need just the special personal care and attention of the Shepherd, but His spiritual attention is always with you, and I say blessed are you for being so firm and so faithful without having seen.

When I left Him, He said:

"Now is not the time for weeping. Now is not the time for tears. <u>Now</u> is the time for rising to serve and to spread the glad tidings of the Kingdom of God."

So now all of you get up and serve. Go and work. It is the time now. The best way to <u>learn</u> this Cause is to <u>serve</u> this Cause. The best way to learn to teach the Cause of God is to open your mouth and teach it.

XII

When Lua left New York, she was not certain that 'Abdu'l-Bahá would come to California. For a while it looked as though He might not. Lua described the disappointment of the Bahá'ís in a letter to Agnes Parsons.

Bellevue Hotel Geary and Taylor Sts.
San Francisco, July 30th

My dearest Noor.
I am sure I need not tell you how glad I was to receive your letter or how thankful I am for its enclosure. May my work in the Cause prove my gratitude. I have not been well since my return to Cal. and hence have thus far accomplished very little. I was extremely tired before I went East – because for a year and three months I had been constantly going about teaching, nursing, helping in any Bahai way I could whoever needed me. And after Dr. Fareed left in Dec. for the Orient my work was doubled. But when I saw 'Abdu'l-Bahá, in my enthusiasm and delight – I <u>forgot it</u> and under new impetus I went on, and now nature seems to have rebelled. I have no strength at all – any exertion seems almost too much for me. The Doctor says I am on the verge of a collapse – and having had nervous prostration once – You can imagine how I shrink from it.

But I am trusting in the Words of 'Abdu'l-Bahá to make me strong and well – hoping the confirmations of the Holy Spirit through the Center of the Covenant will enable me to arise and serve in the Cause better than I have ever done. It was very difficult for me to leave 'Abdu'l-Bahá – for His Face spells <u>home</u> and all that is worth while in this <u>material</u> world to me. It was a great joy to be with Him and serve, and I did so hope I could accept your kind invitation to visit you while He was with you – but He decreed otherwise and sent me back here as far from you

171

all as I can be!

But dearest Noor – if my loss has resulted in your gain – then I am glad to have lost – I suppose I need my portion for discipline and in some wise way – that which I do not clearly see and understand is best for me! I am poor comfort to the people here who were expecting to see Him waiting anxiously and longing for His coming. I have taught them that He alone can bestow upon them the heavenly knowledge and the blessing of the "King's touch!" A week ago Friday I got out of bed to go the meeting – and that day His Message came that He was called to the Orient and could not come to the Coast. Never, so long as I live – shall I forget their faces, their bowed heads and the silence – broken by one bitter stifled sob of a poor woman who was there on crutches. Two days afterwards in meekness and submission they as an assembly wrote a short little letter to 'Abdu'l-Bahá acknowledging His decree in loving acceptation. A day or two later I rec'd a letter from one who was present saying – "The Friday afternoon meeting is a thing of the past & now we all know that what we had hoped for, longed for and lived for will not be – and that only the people with money to pay their way to Him – will be able to see or experience the Light of God, which you taught us, attends 'Abdu'l-Bahá – and we must go on in the same old weary human way! The divine Presence that can obliterate and destroy the human way – will not shine upon us! We must still remain in this "far country" of human darkness unable to see or reach our Home, where rest is – for rest is Divine Love personified – to bring us satisfaction &c" – It is all very heart breaking! – The writer of the letter came one day to see me – and I tried to comfort her but she said – "You have talked to me so long now about 'Abdu'l-Bahá and if I cannot see Him to be touched by the Holy Spirit which you say He manifests – and which you say has given you your light – of what use it is to me – to hear you talk." And she left me weeping bitterly. Oh dear Noor – I write you this that you may tell the people to appreciate the blessing of His Presence, for through the Perfect Wisdom of His Great and Wondrous Soul the Light of God The Sun of Reality – does surely shine. If they do not see it, it is because the effulgence blinds them! The people of San Francisco have had a great affliction – the earthquake laid waste so many homes while the fire consumed the ruins, and destroyed others. Death faced them on every hand. Rich and poor laid down side by side upon the ground with only God's blue sky for their shelter – and together in silence accepted the blow! People tell me how great crowds would be assembled in the parks – in the ferry building – and on the hillsides – all silent! faces white & set – heads bowed – but silent! –

And the silence which followed the announcement that the Beloved was not coming to San Francisco – was like that which they manifested when the other great blow fell!

And just as they all arose after a while – and set to work to rebuild their city – so the believers got up – subdued – quiet – sad – and went out one after another to their homes, their children, their different occupations – to do the best they can, stumbling along life's weary way – without the Glorious Light of His Divine Presence to make the Pathway clear, luminous and bright. No words of mine can prove effective – because I have taught them to look to Him – to wait for Him – to know Him only as the One whose reply can clarify, purify, and make the road of all lives straight! –

I supplicate Him, through you dear friend – in whose home He is the Heavenly Guest – to pray for the Friends – in this "Golden State" by the "Golden Gate" – through which the light of every setting sun – transforms the city – into a fairy land of beauty above an ambient sea – but leaves their hearts unenlightened, unvisited, and untouched! – Present to Him my humble greetings accompanied by my sincere wishes that He is enjoying beautiful Dublin – and finding productive soil in the hearts of the people! And with remembrances to all members of His party –

Love for your dear self
   I am as ever
   Your devoted
     Lua

Say sometimes a little prayer for me!

The hope that 'Abdu'l-Bahá would nevertheless come to California began to animate the Bahá'ís. Lua's letter to a fellow believer (possibly Mrs. Hurlburt) on August 5, 1912 expresses this hope:

Bellevue Hotel
Geary and Taylor Sts.
San Francisco, Aug. 5, 1912

My dear Bahá'í friend

So many thanks for the lovely peaches you sent me – how delicious they are, but no more so than a night-letter from Dublin with a message from 'Abdu'l-Bahá saying if all the assemblies unite in Cal. it may be the means of attracting Him here after all. You and I will just keep on thinking that He <u>is</u> <u>coming</u> and we will pray God to send Him to us. Oh, how I hope He will come! He is the <u>Light</u> that illumines the hearts of men and women today. Read Isa. Chapters 44 & 42. Give my tender love to my dear Mrs. Thompson she is very good and kind to think of me so lovingly.

May the peace of God abide with you and may the great desire of your heart soon be realized. My kind remembrances to Mr. Hurlburt.

Greetings and love
In His Name
Yours very sincerely
Lua Moore-Getsinger

The news that 'Abdu'l-Bahá was definitely coming cheered Lua's heart after a "low"; but her loneliness and longing for those she loved is apparent in this letter to Elizabeth Nourse.

Sept.13.1912

My beloved Menita: –

I am ashamed of myself for not writing you before but dear ever since my return from the East, until ten days ago I have not been well at all – I had quite a serious time. I became extremely nervous and wept "buckets of tears" all alone by myself. I was too weak to write or even <u>think</u> straight! So I did nothing and kept on doing it for some weeks. About two weeks ago I began working in earnest and am now much better. I think the positive knowledge of the Master's coming has made me much better. Oh, I shall be so glad to see Him again! And how I do wish you and Mr. N. and the dear kiddies could be here too. If only my

Phil could be here with me, not then only but all the time! Why could I not have him, Menita – You have two besides Phil and then if – you missed him too awful much you could have another one! Tell my own dear little faithful supplicator – to look at the brightest star every night – and ask God to make Aunt Lua independent from all else save Him! You may have to explain what independent means – but that is what I want him to pray. I am wearing my blue stockings now – and they are very beautiful and I just do hope they will never wear out. Say to Phil also – that every night I see one big bright star right up above my head – and I look at it until it twinkles right down on me – then I say – Hello! Bright Star – please twinkle on Phil tonight, and tell him I love him still "in the same old sweet way". – And please dear Star go to him when he falls asleep and tell him a nice story, as you guide him through dreamland! – –

Oh my Menita, I sometimes feel very far away – yet – when I ask what am I far away from – I hardly know – for the only thing worth while is here as well as everywhere else! I go to Sacramento the Capital City of Cal. tomorrow to speak twice on the Message during Sunday. Then return for two talks in Berkeley on Monday and Monday evening. My dear if I have to stay here all winter won't you and your family come here for the Winter months? Could it be possible? You could rent a furnished cottage very inexpensively – and it would do you all good – just to change for a time. Do think about it dear and let me know. It made me think you would not want to go back if once you came here! Do write me again real soon and give my love to everybody in your little "Nestie" especially Phil.

Your "little Mother"
Lua

By the time 'Abdu'l-Bahá arrived in California on October 1, 1912 Lua had made many arrangements for him. Her heart was overflowing with joy at being with him again and filled with gratitude for His vitalizing words to the students and seekers with whom she had been working. 'Abdu'l-Bahá visited Stanford University and his speech was reported in the press. As usual, she shared her enthusiasm with Mrs. Parsons.

Stanford University
Palo Alto, Cal.

My dearest Agnes

We have had a most wonderful day with 'Abdu'l-Bahá here. This morning He spoke to fifteen hundred students – introduced by Dr. Jordan. His subject was international peace and such splendid attention was paid Him! Not a murmur not a distracting move – during the hour and fifteen minutes that he addressed them. When He finished they cheered and cheered until he arose – and then the <u>whole</u> <u>audience</u> rose – and the students gave the college yell! It was perfectly splendid. Dr. Jordan and Dr. Reed (Unitarian Minister in whose church He speaks tonight) entertained the whole party. And tonight we dine with Mrs. Merriman (one of my pupils) and several Professors & other important men are to be here. Oh, my dear Noor – how wonderful it all is! How much more than a <u>thousand</u> times I am repaid for all the work I have done here the last year and a half! – And so far He has only been to three cities. There is Los Angeles, San Diego, Sacramento and Berkeley yet to visit. How God assists us when we rise to serve Him. And to think dearest, you have a share in this service – for you are assisting in my expenses. – 'Abdu'l-Bahá spoke to me so beautifully of you last evening. I am so proud of you and your attainments! May God ever bless you and yours, more and more abundantly. We heard the story of "Her Holiness the Cow" Sunday night – and we are laughing yet!

Must stop now – Will send you word whenever I get the opportunity –
Your devoted
Lua

'Abdu'l-Bahá occasionally used His healing powers and after His remark to Lua that He would cure Mr. Parsons, Agnes's husband, she wrote to Mrs. Parsons urging her to make arrangements for her husband to be seen by the Master.

Bellevue Hotel Geary and Taylor Sts.
San Francisco, Oct. 25

My dearest Noor –
Just a line to tell you we are leaving for Sacramento – and that is the beginning of the Master's return East. Yesterday I read to Him your letter – and He said "If I could <u>see</u> Mr. Parsons – I would cure him". I am writing this immediately that you may make any arrangements you can – so Mr. Parsons can have this great blessing. He ('Abdu'l-Bahá) is going to Wash. from Chicago – Dearest try to have this meeting between Mr. P. and the Master brought about. I have no more time but will write you very soon. I am to return to San Francisco for a while –

> Your devoted and
> loving
> Lua

The next day she wrote again reporting the wonders of the Master's visit. She used hotel stationery from the Hotel Sacramento (which advertised itself as the "only absolute fire-proof hotel in Sacramento"):

Hotel Sacramento
Sacramento, California Oct. 26

My dearest Noor
We came here yesterday with the Beloved Master and He has watered my garden in this city with such a power as to produce in a single day and night the most wonderful flowers and fruit. I came here some weeks ago and gave three talks – The first Sacramento had heard – but today the city is aglow with the Light and love of God! How wonderful is our Master! Surely He is the Heavenly Window through which the Sun of Reality and Truth is shining! Oh, if the people would only turn to this Window of the Covenant and behold the radiant Light which alone can dispel all darkness! I am to leave California before long and have permission to go to Washington for a few days. I hope you will be there for I so want to see you again. From Washington I go on a journey which I cannot <u>write</u> about just now – but which I will tell you when we meet. Dearest do have Mr. Parsons see the Master and be <u>healed</u> by Him. He healed Dr. Allen of Berkeley

177

by a telegram – and he was much more ill than is Mr. Parsons. Oh Noor dear 'Abdu'l-Bahá is the <u>Great</u> <u>Physician</u> – Seek Him while yet He is near, so your dear husband shall be freed from those <u>physical</u> difficulties which hamper the progress of His Spirit. It is <u>possible</u> for the Beloved has told me so! I will write you often and let you know all of my movements. The Master was speaking of you to me last night – and said – "Mrs. Parsons – is steadfast, firm and sincere. Her heart is very pure and all of her intentions are good." I thanked Him for the love you have for me – for I consider it one of God's good gifts to one of His humblest servants. Yesterday the Master told me to leave Cal when he left America – if this changes I will let you know.– You may see Him very soon now for I think He will be in Wash. after ten days. With much love

As ever

Your devoted

Lua

I return to San Francisco today after He leaves.

Lua felt that the visit of 'Abdu'l-Bahá to California had changed the Golden State to a diamond one. Her response to His galvanizing presence was a desire to become as nothing in the path of His good pleasure. A letter to Agnes Parsons describes her longing.

Bellevue Hotel

San Francisco Nov. 5<u>th</u>

My beloved Noor,

Your nice long letter just arrived and I have read it with joy – and thanksgiving. Probably by the time this reaches you you will be in the Presence of the Beloved Master again – and I so sincerely hope good Mr. Parsons will have received the blessing of "the King's touch" which shall free him from "every defect and weakness" and purify him from all illness and disease!

Oh, what a blessed privilege to be thus favored by the "Center of the Covenant" from whose Face is radiating the light of the eternal Sun of Truth – from whose eyes the glances of the Merciful One rest upon us – and whose words are vibrant with a power

178

to confer life upon weak suffering humanity. – I pray that Mr. Parsons will be receptive and that within his heart the all consuming fire of love and faith may be forever enkindled!

What a blessing was 'Abdu'l-Bahá to this Golden State of Cal! All the work we had done previous to His coming, was but a plowing of the ground, a harrowing, and preparation for the sowing of the seeds of the wonderful words of God – ever falling in divine abundance from the doorway of heaven – His beautiful mouth! His pure and holy thought – became crystallized jewels of speech – scattered so profusely as to transform Cal – from the Golden to the Diamond State – leaving every searching heart therein studded with precious gems. We all feel now as though we were awakening from some wonderful dream in which a Messenger from the Most High Heaven had appeared, and for a little time gently walked and talked with us! And we are loath to waken, we all would dream again! But we are happy that the resplendent vision still continues to haunt our shores and Washington is to be the next place of visitation!

I would dearly love to be there with you – and I may be before very long as I have permission to visit my sister when I go East. Since the Beloved came to us – a new and marvelous bird has alighted upon the tree of my heart singing a song so strangely sweet, as to intoxicate my soul! For the past few days I have been physically ill in bed – but my spirit under the spell of the Magic songster has soared aloft freed from the fetters of all desires save one, and that to see once more His Face – to hear once more His voice – and become as naught in the path of His Good Pleasure. Severed from all else save Him, freed from every mention save His Name – and sacrifici[n]g in the Highway of His Praise – that all America may know ('ere it be too late –) her shores have been visited by the King!

I shall be interested in the new picture and will write you regarding it.

I humbly supplicate at the Holy Court of Bahá'u'lláh – that the heavenly gift of 'Abdu'l-Bahá may be fully appreciated in the City of Washington, the Capital city of America – also, that upon you and yours may descend the choicest blessings through the "Center of His Covenant."

Remembrances to Mr. Parsons and Jeffrey Boy. Begging you

to remember me in the Light of the Face of our Beloved –
    I am your devoted
        Lua

Rarely did Lua complain of her life, but disappointment in the delayed return to the East, for which she longed, and perhaps fatigue from overwork, influenced her letter to Mrs. Parsons written in December. It may also have been difficult to face being alone and far from husband and family during the holidays.

                              Bellevue Hotel
                              San Francisco, Dec. 18
My dearest Noor
Many thanks for your letter and enclosure. I was to leave on Dec. 5th for the East, but it was changed and I am to be here yet a little while. I am working day and night; so many new ones are coming. Mrs. Wise whom you met in Washington has returned like a brilliant lamp, to enlighten the city of Berkeley. She has opened her beautiful home to anybody and everybody and I am teaching there, beside being at Dr. Allen's home one day and evening of each week. I am so happy that you and my beautiful Mariane [sic] Haney[83] went to see the Beloved off on the steamer. I was so pleased and interested with your description of it all! How glad I am that you know my "Angel" – I am sure you will enjoy each other very much – for she is just <u>pure</u> spirit. I did so want to go East to Washington and Baltimore to see my husband and sister that I was homesick for days and I fear I was not a very good soldier for a time. However I did not become a deserter – though I was terribly tempted. It is almost two years since I came here and while "the world is my country" I feel more at home in some places than others. I am not to be here so very much longer that I know, and I will let you know when I leave for the East. I think it will be about Jan. 5th – If I should start earlier will let you know. Do write me about Mr. Parson's health now. Are you going to Europe this year? I have something very interesting to tell you when I see you, regarding the Orient and I hope you are going there this Winter. Do you ever see Mrs. Pinchot? Give

her my love when you see her again. And now with all loving best wishes to you for a Happy New Year and delightful "Yule Tide"
I am as ever
Your loving and devoted
Lua

A few months later in Evanston, Illinois Lua planned to undergo an operation by "command" of the Master. The surgery mentioned below in her letter to Mrs. Parsons may have frightened her, but her trust in the wisdom of the Master was complete.

My dear Noor,
I want to take this opportunity to thank you for all of your many kindnesses to me. I appreciate all you have done for me and beg God to bless you and yours always. I have not felt well some time dear, in fact have not felt quite myself since I was ill in New York last summer. I go to the hospital tomorrow and shall undergo a minor operation. Probably, I shall come out of it all right, but in case I should not I just want you to know that I go with full trust and confidence loving the Beloved Master with all my heart. My peace is all made and should the call come – I shall go gladly! May all joy and many blessings attend you and your efforts to serve the Cause! May you at all times under all conditions, be the recipient of the Good pleasure of 'Abdu'l-Bahá, favored with a power such as will enable you to endure all tests, and withstand all trials. Dr. E. H. Pratt of 32 N. State (Chicago) St. is to operate. He is a devoted Lover of 'Abdu'l-Bahá and does this for me simply because he has known me for twenty years and because I am the Master's servant.

He is a great surgeon and I would rather be in his care than anyone I know. I have been visiting at his home in Evanston Ill. for the past three weeks. Last month I went to Champaign, Ill. to speak in the Unitarian Church. The University of Illinois is at Urbana only a mile away – and the audience was largely made up of Professors and students. The pastor of the church is a Harvard man (Rev. Mr. Vail) and a Bahá'í. It was a very enjoyable meeting and in spite of not feeling at all well – I talked for an hour and we had an hour and a half of discussion. I am invited to go again if possible. Great interest is being manifest everywhere it seems to me. Mrs. Pratt went with me and was surprised at the interest of the students. Mr. Vail has been giving a series of sermons on the subject so they were well prepared.–

Again thanking you dearest friend – and with fond remembrances, I am always

Yours lovingly
In His Name
Lua

Evanston, Ill.
April 1, 1913

I communicated with the Master and He cabled me to submit to the operation! So whatever is the outcome it is according to His divine Command.

L.M.G

On May 5, 1913 Lua wrote to Agnes Parsons from Evanston where she was staying with Dr. Pratt who had performed the surgery mentioned above. She said Dr. Pratt was very skilled as a surgeon and full of the love of God and of 'Abdu'l-Bahá and recommended that Mrs. Parsons seek Pratt's advice for "Jeffrey Boy". Apparently Mrs. Parsons had queried about "two viewpoints" and Lua answered that she had kept Mrs. Parsons turned to the only viewpoint worth having – that of 'Abdu'l-Bahá Himself. Lua said she knew of many things "that are distressing – but why dwell upon them – they all come from error and ignorance and will soon be dispelled by the Light of the Covenant." Another reason why Lua had kept disquieting issues from Mrs. Parsons was that they had hurt her so much that she did not want Mrs. Parsons to suffer too, as long as she could help it. She went on to say that some things are better left unsaid and untold. "We have the Beloved and nothing else matters!"

Evanston, Ill.
May 5, 1913

My dear Noor

I have waited to answer your letter thinking the promised picture would come (as you wrote you had sent it) that I could thank you for both at the same time. But so far the picture has not put in its appearance. Did you send it to the hospital? Your dear letter was forwarded from there as I had left just a day or two before it came. I do hope the picture is not lost. Dr. Bagdadi has returned bringing us all news of the Convention. Yesterday he came out to Dr. Pratt's home, where I am still staying – and told us all about it. He told me, too, dear about his visit with you and that you were contemplating having some orificial surgery for Jeffrey Boy. – I do wish Dr. Pratt could do the operating for he is the greatest orificial surgeon in America, if not in the world. I am sending you under separate cover the Journal of the Am. Association of Orificial Surgeons – containing a lecture given by Dr. Pratt the last week in April before a large clinic which he held here in Chicago – He operated for four days lecturing all the time, and had some most remarkable cases all of which are recovering splendidly. He knows so much of the spiritual law, and applies it so wonderfully! I put Jeffrey's case before him as Dr. B. had told it to me and he said "I would not circumcise a child and remove tonsils at the same time. With a dilation of the rectum after the circumcision, I hardly think it would be necessary to remove them at all. I have had cases of children where that trouble all vanished after the other work was done! Dr. Pratt is a great soul full of the love of God, and 'Abdu'l-Bahá – Very sympathetic and a lover of children – especially boys – for he lost his little son when he was about Jeffrey's age – through an accident on the street cars. –

He operated upon me dear so skillfully and successfully – at the command of 'Abdu'l-Bahá and he will not accept one penny for it – because I am the Master's servant. His knowledge of the sympathetic nervous system is very great – in fact he is the greatest authority in the subject that we have in America. He has been a professor in Medical Colleges for twenty-seven years, and has invented nearly all of the instruments that he uses. – I couldn't help writing you about him dear for I know you want the best that can be procured for Jeffrey. And I have such faith

183

in Dr. Pratt for I saw him operate several times before I went to the hospital under his hands – and it was wonderful. And the results most wonderful. – I feel like another being – all the nervousness from which I suffered, has disappeared. I trust you will not think me presumptuous – but so many Mothers bring their children to him I felt I must let you know about this skill. – Write him if you want to know more. – Or, if I can serve you in any way let me know.

Dearest, regarding the two viewpoints – I kept you turned to the one viewpoint worth contemplating – 'Abdu'l-Bahá – Himself! Do you not remember how very anxious I was that you should go to Him – for I knew after you met Him – the other things would take care of themselves. Just always look to Him and obey His commands – then nothing will annoy or disturb you! I know and knew, of many things that are distressing – but why dwell upon them – they all come from error and ignorance – and will soon be dispelled by the Light of the Covenant. Another reason why I kept them from you was because they had so hurt me – that I did not want you to suffer from them as long as I could help it – Oh Noor dear, I loved you then as now, very much indeed! Some things better be left unsaid and untold anyway! We have the Beloved and nothing else matters! You remember when I wrote to you last summer to help me – it was to be only during my stay in California therefore I did not write you for I thought you understood.

This letter seems very disjointed – for I have been interrupted several times. How I wish I might talk with you! I may be able to now before long –

I wish for you and yours, every good thing – 'Abdu'l-Bahá is greatly pleased with you and this is the greatest blessing of all –

Ever your devoted
Lua

#722 Hinman Ave.
Evanston, Ill
c/o Dr. E. H. Pratt

XIII

Lua had hinted in her letters that she would soon embark on a project which could not, as yet, be mentioned. It is probable that 'Abdu'l-Bahá told her of it when they were together in California. In early July 1913 she left America – for the last time, although she could not know this.

Lua wrote a short note to Elizabeth Nourse on her departure.

Norddeutscher Lloyd, Bremen
Dampfer July 5th

Dear Noursee
I recd all of your letters – Thank you I am sailing now away to the Beloved. My deep love to the Master Doctor Lady Lottie and all – Thank God I leave with nothing but love in my heart for <u>anybody</u>
Ever your loving and
grateful Lua

<u>Allaho'Abha</u>
Keep your face toward the "Center of the Covenant". <u>Always</u> no matter what happens.

A letter dated July 10, 1913, from Lua to a friend in Washington, Margaret Duncan Green, was written from aboard the German ship, the *Prinzess Irene*. Lua thanks her again and again for writing to her and writes that she regretted not having been able to see her friends in Washington. She exhorts this friend to love and serve the Covenant.

July 13, 1913
Norddeutscher Lloyd, Bremen
Dampfer Prinzess Irene

Sailing away-away!

My dear spiritual Friend and Sister

What a happy surprise was your letter! Thank you again and again for thinking of me enough to write such a beautiful missive. It has meant much and I have read it several times. My stay in Washington was very short of necessity and I deeply regretted the inability of seeing many of the dear believers whom I love. Mrs. Woodward and Miss, Mr and Mrs. Hannen, Claudia Coles, Mrs DeLangrel and oh so many in fact <u>all</u> of the faithful servants of 'Abdu'l-Bahá including you, dear Mother, I would have loved to see again for perhaps, I shall never pass that way any more – I am going so far away this time! But distance makes no difference in the hearts of those who love each other for the sake of 'Abdu'l-Bahá the Mighty Center of the Covenant. Absence and distance, time and space shall have no effect on the Love of God burning in the soul of His Friends save to increase it! Sometimes I think it is better not to meet formally so often for personalities are apt to engender jealousy while Service in the Cause buys its own reward in the reward of bond which ties together the hearts and souls of those who serve and love for the <u>sake</u> of God alone! When I hear now of any service rendered by any servant, my soul rejoices and I pray that yet greater things may they accomplish for the Glory of the Cause and God – for are we not all members of one family? Hath not one God created us all? and is not that <u>one</u> God our <u>Father?</u> Thus when His Love burns in the heart, the good works and Service of anyone of His children cause, or should cause the hearts of all to be happy and feel spiritually proud. Are not all leaves upon one Branch? Is it possible that especially beautiful leaf or leaves could mar its beauty? Or cause the others to suffer by comparison? 'Tis the Branch whose Beauty and Perfection in its entirety we adore and not the <u>leaves</u> who cling to it. Oh, let us all forsake the thoughts of self and be glad if we are <u>just</u> <u>leaves</u> – tho insignificant upon the Branch of the Great Tree of Life. For verily our Life and sustenance are from the Branch and <u>It</u> is powerful to make glorious and beautiful even the most insignificant – should it become the good pleasure of the Branch to do so! The Branch alone knows the capacity and possibilities of each Leaf. Jesus said, "Let those who think they stand take heed but they fall!" May we all stand side by side, shoulder to shoulder, like true and tried soldiers in His service loving each other, being glad for all the good things that come from the Hand of His Mercy to each soul, praying for the weak and rejoicing in the strong!

May God bless you in all of your efforts and enable you to ever be the recipient of the Good pleasure of the Glorious Center of the Covenant and may the sacred seal of His "Well done" crown many successes in His service!

With thanks and all best wishes from your unworthy and humble teacher

In His Name
Lua Moore Getsinger

To her much-loved Phil Nourse she wrote:

Sailing farther way
Every Day!

Norddeutscher Lloyd, Bremen
Dampfer "Prinzess Irene"

Oh My own Phil.

I look at the moon each night, and also that very bright star not far away, and wonder if you are looking at them too thinking of your lone Aunt Lua – so far, very far out at sea? – I have not been one bit ill – I have slept and slept and twice I dreamed of you! I thought you were treating my arm – and saying "Kemow Kimow daro mare" – "Now Aunt Lua get up, you are well and have slept long enough!" I sat up quick to find I had indeed slept long for it was high noon and very hot in my cabin. – So I took a nice cold bath and went on the deck to wander about and dream of you and the good times we all had together so very recently! I can hardly believe I am so far from you now – and just last week I was with you. An old Brownie by the name of "Move-on Joe" has got behind me and I 'spect – I'll have to move on – move on all the time till I see you again – and even old "Move-on-Joe" don't know <u>when</u> <u>that</u> <u>will</u> <u>be</u>. How I wish he would get behind you and move you on across the sea straight to me! Would we have good times together though! – Of course we'd send a wireless to Mother every day so she'd always know at night just where in the wide world to find us, and then she wouldn't miss you so much you see! If you were only just a little older I would just gobble you up and off we'd go on a trip around the world. You hurry up now – be a good boy– "Mind your teacher and your parents fond and dear" and when I come sailing home across the seas again – I'll never leave on another journey without you. – You must be a soldier in the army of 'Abdu'l-Bahá as well as a Doctor remember that – and you shall go off to the war with me sometime just's sure's you're born! Last night, I am certain I saw your face in the moon and your right eye winking at me! I was up on the top-deck all alone talking to you across the silver path – and all of a sudden I looked up and right in the middle of the moon you peeped out – winked your eye – and then on the night breeze I heard you say "Good night Aunt Lua – I love you all the way along!" Oh dear me, I was so happy I just laughed out loud – all alone by myself – for all the rest of the people were dancing on the deck below – all save the wireless operator who was in his cabin just near by – and he came out all of a sudden – and looked up at his wires, etc. – and then said – "Are you stealing my messages?" – I said, "No sir – not unless your sweetheart lives in the moon too!" And then he laughed and said – "Sometimes I'd feel better if she did!"

Well, Phil boy I must go now its dinner time – and so I'll just send my love to Mother and everybody – especially Mr. and Miss Tompkins and for this time say farewell.

From
Your truly own
Aunt <u>Lua</u>

July 12th 1913

On July 23, 1913, Lua arrived at Port Said, Egypt where the Master was staying. Edward came soon after.[84] 'Abdu'l-Bahá said that a man must go along and Lua asked Him to send her husband with her. The great new task: Lua was to go to India.

Lua was now summoned to new heights of service. 'Abdu'l-Bahá's words to her at Ramleh were published in

Star of the West[85] and can be accepted as a goal for all those who would serve their Lord.

Thou must be firm and unshakable in thy purpose, and never, never let any outward circumstances worry thee. I am sending thee to India to accomplish certain definite results. Thou must enter that country with a never-failing spirituality, a radiant faith, an eternal enthusiasm, an inextinguishable fire, a solid conviction, in order that thou mayest achieve those services for which I am sending thee. Let not thy heart be troubled. If thou goest away with this unchanging condition of invariability of inner state, thou shalt see the doors of confirmation open before thy face, thy life will be a crown of heavenly roses, and thou shall find thyself in the highest station of triumph.

Strive day and night to attain to this exalted state. Look at Me! Thou dost not know a thousandth part of the difficulties and seemingly unsurmountable passes that rise daily before my eyes. I do not heed them; I am walking in my chosen highway; I know the destination. Hundreds of storms and tempests may rage furiously around my head; hundreds of Titanics may sink to the bottom of the sea, the mad waves may rise to the roof of heaven; all these will not change my purpose, will not disturb me in the least; I will not look either to the right or to the left. I am looking ahead, far far. Peering through the impenetrable darkness of the night, the howling winds, the raging storms, I see the glorious Light beckoning me forward, forward. The balmy weather is coming, and the voyager shall land safely.

Kurat-el-Ayn [Ṭáhirih] had attained to this supreme state. When they brought her the terrible news of the martyrdom of the Bahá'ís, she did not waver; it did not make any difference to her; she also had chosen her path, she knew her goal, and when they imparted to her the news of her impending death, no one could see any trace of sorrow in her face; she was rather happier.

Although she never cared for dress, that day she wore her best white silk dress and jewelry and perfumed herself with the most fragrant attar of roses. She hailed the chamber of death as a happy bride entering the nuptial bower of the bridegroom.

To this lofty summit of unchanging purpose thou must attain; like Kurat-el-Ayn, nothing must shake thy firm faith.

Lua was always happy in the presence of the Master and on September 15, 1913 she wrote from Ramleh to Ella Cooper announcing her new mission to India. Lua asked the friends in California to pray for her that she could attain the spiritual condition necessary to carry out the duty given her by the Master.

Ramleh, Egypt
Sept. 15, 1913

My dear spiritual Elinor

I have been so busy since my arrival in the Master's house that I haven't had a moment for anything. I am studying Persian, memorizing a prayer (monajat) daily beside listening to spiritual instructions regarding my work in the new far away field of India! The Master sent for Isabel Frazer and Edward G– to accompany me. He said a man must be with us and I begged not to be sent with anyone but my husband again. I don't know how Edward will endure the extreme heat of that country – but he has to go with me, and I am very happy. Isobel F arrives today and we have not yet heard when Edward will reach here. The Master's household at present consists of His sister Bahaya Khanum, His eldest daughter Zeah Kh. her two sons, Shogie and Hausein, Mariam, the eldest daughter of Rouha Kh. and your humble sister-servant.

It is nearly two months that I am here, and so happy – that the time, when I was not so is but a dimly remembered dream! Hardly a day passes that the Beloved does not mention the names of your kind spiritual mother – Mrs. Ralston, and your own dear good self! Praising all of you, and commending your firmness, steadfastness and services. And every time I hear Him, it causes my heart to rejoice and I supplicate Him to increase His Heavenly Favors and Kindnesses upon each of you until your services in the Cause will become so great and acceptable that humanity will never cease remembering them! He the Beloved, has verified my thoughts regarding the services of your Mother; for one day He said "She is my heavenly daughter upon whom I can always depend – she has served and is serving with ever increasing steadfastness and firmness. She is very dear and acceptable for she is a kind spiritual mother for the Believers in California and elsewhere." He speaks still with great pleasure of His visit to California and said He found conditions there

190

better than any other place in America. This made me very happy and I am sure it will be a cause of rejoicing to you and all the friends.

Increase your endeavors in that field till you will bring forth a good harvest and perhaps He will come again to reap the same. He was greatly pleased with Mrs. Bell's letter – which I translated with the assistance of Zeah Kh. Please give her my Bahá'í greetings. I trust more letters containing such good news will reach Him soon and often! We are going to India before the Master (if He goes?) – He told me the other day that there was a special work in India which I must do and He is in a great hurry that our departure shall be soon. So – probably we will sail about the middle of Oct.! He said also to do this work, I must be in a state of <u>complete</u> <u>severance</u> from all else save God! So, dear Ella, I entreat you, your good mother, Georgie, and all of the Believers in California to pray for me that I may attain this spiritual state and render this service for the sake of the Beloved. One day while talking about the work in India I said, I fear I have not the spiritual ability to attain this condition which insures the accomplishment of this great work. He replied – If you could not attain it I would not have called you from America – but you must pray and strive with all heart and soul! For myself, believe me Ella, I do not care – but I do not want to disappoint Him. I desire to do this work according to His Holy Will. Thus I beg all of you to assist me with your prayers for His blessed sake. He has done so much for America and the Americans – pray that this one poor unworthy American may do something acceptable by way of proving our appreciation. I say <u>our</u> – because your Mother is given the privilege by the Beloved of assisting in this matter – materially! I am enclosing a copy of a prayer revealed for me – when I was sent to do some work in Paris nine years ago![86] Please read it in the Friday meeting on my behalf – I think it covers all the ground! In closing, please remember me to all the Friends, the Allen's especially and my good "Angel" Miss Haste. Mrs. Nourse will send you some stones belonging to Mirza Moneer – if you are pleased with any of them and want them for $1.00 each – take them sending money to him. If there are more than you wish return the rest to her. I've not yet found the beads to my satisfaction to send you – but Mirza Moneer selected some & will send for your approval. The Ezelies[87] have arrived in New

York I heard from the Master. But you have all necessary instructions – a long tablet was sent to Ali Kuli Khan. Also I am sure you have heard of Mr. Mac Nutt's pardon and forgiveness. He wrote one of the most beautiful supplications to the Master I have ever read. And I pled for him with all my heart! He said he did not realize that anything he had said could be so misunderstood but if so he was very sorry! – The Master has granted him permission to come with Mrs. M – and will state the time, in another tablet. How merciful, pitiful and forgiving is 'Abdu'l-Bahá – our Teacher, Father and Heavenly Friend! If a soul is possessed of His care – it needs nothing else in this or any other world. I have written this in a great hurry – but hope you can make it out. Please give especial to the <u>whole</u> Theodore Cooper family – as well as the other Coopers.

> Very lovingly and
> Sincerely
>> Your sister-server
>> in the Cause of God
>> Lua

I am sure you will be pleased with my selection of Isabel Frazer – for she will write for the "Star of the West" during the whole journey.[88] If you care to write me address:
c/o Ahmad Yazdi
It is needless to add that I am well, fat and happier than I ever imagined mortal could be!

> L. M. G.

Lua's letter to Juliet from Ramleh conveys her joyful excitement at her new assignment.

Ramleh Sept. 20, 1913

My dearest Juliet,
We are so happy over the arrival of Isabel and here we are together in the Master's house. Edward G. arrives in a few days and then we go to India. We are having most marvelous and wonderful experiences here with the Beloved as you may imagine receiving spiritual instructions and teachings relative to our new work. Oh Julie how I wish you were going with us! Tell May when you write her that the Beloved Master and I often speak of her and her assistance to the Friends. He loves her and is so pleased

192

with her. The Haneys also are often the subject of conversation. He <u>depends</u> upon Mrs. Parsons and loves her greatly. How happy it makes me to hear Him speak so lovingly and tenderly of those whom I have been privileged to teach. Julie darling leave <u>all</u> for His dear sake and become His <u>devotee</u>. –

Just this moment I went to His Holy Presence and mentioned your name. He said "Write her that you mentioned her name and I said, Send my best love to my dear daughter Juliet and because of her work for the Cause and her firmness in the Covenant I am very pleased with her!" Dearest I wish you could have seen His blessed Face as he spoke these words – You would never weep or feel sad again – over anything or anybody. My tenderest love to y[our] Mother and for you my heart's best wishes. The Master often says "Juliet is Lua's daughter". – So see dear what a wonderful tie there is between you and Him and me!

      Your own Lua
  My tender greetings for all the friends

After visiting the Master in Ramleh, the Getsingers went to 'Akká to visit the Holy Shrines. On their return to Egypt, Lua wrote a postcard to Agnes Parsons on November 7, 1913 saying "The Beloved comes here tomorrow after which I soon sail away, to further service I hope, in the Glorious Cause. I have just returned from a visit to Haifa and Acca – where you were often remembered. I missed you!" (An earlier postcard to Mrs. Parsons stamped "Napoli" and apparently written from the ship mentions that it was "so lovely here, not too warm and with cool breezes and such marvellous moon light nights" that Lua did not want to retire that night at all.)

Lua wrote to Annetta Woodward ("Natekeh")[89] of Washington on November 8, 1913, on stationery from the Grand Hotel in Port Said, Egypt. The letter explains that no matter how much Lua had wanted to "send him [Fred] the money he asked for," she couldn't. Lua asks that her friend will earnestly pray for her that she can attain that state of "unchangingableness" to which 'Abdu'l-Bahá had summoned her. She thanked her friend for criticism which had helped her on the path of detachment.

Port Said Nov. 8th 1913

My beloved spiritual Sister

Dearest "Natekeh":

Your most beautiful letter is in my hand through the kindness of Mrs. Hoagg. Oh how thankful I am to have it just as I am expecting to go away into a greater service! Truly <u>Love</u> brings a rich harvest! Mrs. Haney will tell you that not once has my love wavered for <u>you</u> dear. I have loved and prayed for you all the time and feel that your dear letter is but one more evidence that God hears and answers prayer. Oh my dear Natekeh – can you imagine, what I felt away thousands of miles from you when I rec'd dear Fred's letters. Only God knows how I desired, and still desire to send him the money he asked for – for I was sure it would be a <u>test</u> to him – but I <u>couldn't</u>. I wrote him the truth about it but I shall yet send it – I am sure God will grant me that great privilege and blessing for the sake of my dear little "God-child" if <u>for</u> <u>no</u> <u>other</u> <u>reason</u>! I want to be the means of proving to Fred that there are some Bahá'ís who honestly intend to fulfill their promises, and keep their word. Oh my dear ones – when I remember the many days we spent together in loving confidence and trust, the many hours we read together the Blessed Words of Bahá'u'lláh and 'Abdu'l-Bahá – in your home, I cannot thank God enough for knowing you and now with your letter before me, I am overcome. Know this that you do not love me more than I love you and if you have suffered so have I. You ask what you can do for me? Only this – <u>pray</u> – pray with all your soul that God in His Mercy will enable me to be the means of quickening Fred's spirit again – and that I may walk upon the path of Severance and Sacrifice in fulfillment of the desires of 'Abdu'l-Bahá as expressed in the tablet you have read. I have found out beyond <u>any</u> <u>doubt</u> that to depend upon any help or power save God is worse than <u>foolish</u>! Since I first entered the Cause sixteen years ago – my instructions from the Master have ever been the same. "Go and teach: Speak the glad tidings – and be <u>severed</u> <u>from</u> <u>all</u> <u>save</u> <u>God</u>." How I have suffered to learn that these <u>words</u> are the <u>real</u> and <u>only</u> <u>measure</u> <u>of</u> <u>my</u> <u>capacity</u> <u>as</u> <u>a</u> <u>Servant</u> <u>in</u> <u>His</u>

Vineyard. God in His Mercy has denied me everything on a material plane until at last, I have learned the lesson. Do not feel badly over anything you may have said against me, for you helped me, by so doing to become more detached! I loved you, and depended upon your faithfulness too much – so when I heard things it hurt – but it helped me spiritually more than you can ever realize! So dear I thank you for helping me to learn my lesson of detachment! We love each other better now than ever before – for the personal element is entirely out of it, and we love each other now for the sake of God and the Beloved "Center of the Covenant" which is, as it should be of course! Be thankful that you have realized that all is mortal save "His Face" and that you have looked upon that "Face"! Read daily for one month – the "Tablet of the Branch" – that you may have a deeper spiritual understanding of 'Abdu'l-Bahá – the Center of the Covenant and remember those are the words and testimony of Bahá'u'lláh. How merciful and good is God to me! To allow me this long time in the Holy Presence of the Master who has taught and prepared me, for the service upon which He now sends me! Oh that I may faithfully perform His Wishes – Oh that I may be strengthened to walk in His Way – sacrificing everything for His sake! Pray dearest sister that I may attain the state – the "inner-state" of unchangingableness to which He calls me! This means that, at all times I must be entirely selfless! Nothing must hurt or disturb me, – (for as long as one is or can be hurt by the saying or doings of the creatures – he is still enveloped by a veil of Self) – No outward circumstances must have any effect upon me – even should all rise up and hate me – I must go on forward – upon the "chosen highway" radiant and spiritually happy, welcoming every hardship "and desiring every trouble for His Sake with all my heart and Soul" – To do this, I need spiritual assistance and confirmations to descend constantly and successively upon me! So I ask you, as you have begged to do something for me – to pray that I may not fail – but fulfill the wishes of the Beloved – and that I may be permitted to give the full testimony of faith in Bahá'u'lláh and His Glorious Branch "the Center of His Covenant".

Thank you for sending the pictures of Unis. I have rec'd one through Mrs. Haney also! They shall go with me everywhere! If

I had a picture of myself I would surely send it immediately! But I have none! If possible I will have some taken before sailing! I am sending a rosary – blessed by the Master specially for her which I want you to teach her to use daily, for my sake. Dear little girl, I hope she will one day be proud of her "God Mother"! Ask her to pray for me too that God will enable me to do the will and wish of the Master! My beloved Sister, let nothing ever disturb your peace again. Turn from all save <u>your</u> instructions from the Beloved Lord – and begging of God His assistance and confirmation, go ahead to <u>fulfill</u> them! In regards to Charlie – rest assured I will supplicate again for him before I leave the Master's Presence. Oh how I wish he would pray for himself a little. You know the soul <u>receives</u> by <u>asking</u> and this is one of the laws of God – and each soul must <u>ask</u> <u>for</u> <u>itself</u> as well as asking for others. I am so sorry for him; you know my dear I have always desired his good. I shall supplicate for Fred too as you have requested. The Master is well and busy as ever. He is still weak from the long journeys and hard work. I have just returned to Egypt from the Holy Land Haifa and Acca where I visited the Holy Family also the Holy Tombs of the Báb and Bahá'u'lláh. If we never meet again in this world it does not matter – so long as we love and are united in spirit. See Mrs. Haney whenever you can, she is a pure radiant spirit and will help you much I am sure! I send my sincere Bahá'í greetings to all the Friends especially the Hoppers. I have not heard from them since I left America though I sent a cable and wrote them. May the blessings of God be poured out upon the Bahá'ís in Washington! I shall write Unis soon.

Thanking you again for your letter and begging God's blessing upon you & yours –
I am as ever your devoted friend and Sister

      Lua

P. S. I can desire no greater blessing than to sacrifice myself for the Friends in America and if I am but for this purpose as you state – Know dear that I shall rejoice and be happy – though I am all unworthy of such a blessing and privilege I should be glad to die if they would live as real Bahá'ís should! L.M.G.

On November 13, 1913 Edward wrote to Joseph Hannen[90]

from Port Said saying that 'Abdu'l-Bahá had *called* him to go to India.

Grand Hotel de la Poste
Port Said le Nov. 13/13

Dear Bro Joseph:-
Been neglecting you, but as you know here the time slips away, unawares and you fail to know that a month has elapsed.

Well, we, Lua and I, were in the Holy City nearly three weeks, and in the Holy Tomb I remembered as many of the friends as I could recall, about 25-30 and the assembly as a whole.

We expected to go to Bombay on Oct 6 but could get no accommodations everything full, and then Mrs. Fraser had to return to U.S. so the plans had to be changed for time being and we did not know whether we were going or not for a time. But 'Abdu'l-Bahá never lets go of an idea. We are now going to Bombay on the first steamer that we can get accommodations on, sailing on 18 or 20th Nov. with party Zoroastrian believers from Bombay who came to make the visit.

The Master is here in Port Said and Ahmed alone came with him. Am quite certain that He will not again go back to Haifa for a long time to come. It looks as if he was setting the example "to leave family and all and go out and teach" – Of course the Holy family feel upset about his not coming and they prepared his room and everything, are keeping watermelons, pomgranutes/ etc. for him – but alas!

The Master is quite well, but some days when sudden change of temperature he gets very weak. This happened yesterday.

I had the blessing to rub his blessed feet and limbs for an hour and he soon got stronger, so he could speak to us.

I know it is hardly any use of my saying much in detail, but a word to the wise is sufficient, all the friends in America are under great tests, and it behooves one and all to endeavor with all their might to <u>live</u> the Bahá'í faith. To serve, to efface self. To stop backbiting, to "get together and maintain the brotherhood". Since He left U. S. the "rooting out" period has begun, and many strong trees are being uprooted. No one is safe, and the storms will rage fiercer as next few years elapse.

I have heard him say "only those worthy and severed will endure those storms".

He has written of these before. Also, would it not be a good idea if the friends in their homes had a book of prayers on the dining table and read a prayer or Hidden Word each meal for 2-3 minutes, espec. where there are children. This dont take long, and it begins a practice in vogue when we were children. Set this agoing, when I was in the Holy City, the Masters grand-children, several of the little boys, 4-6 yrs old, who could not yet read, had memorized long tablets, several of them, and in the evenings 2-3 times a week when meetings were held in the basement room of this house, these little chaps would chant without hesitancy great long tablets in unison with the larger boys who could read. I marveled at this and it interested me immensely and I thought how our little friends at home found it difficult to memorize them. Little Hussein, about 5 yrs. old could sing, "Tell the Wondrous Story" in English, after 2 lessons, yet he knew not what it meant. Mrs. Waite's songs are translated and being sung by the Persians here, and in Berrout [sic] College by the students, who have a glee club there.

Beware of the Ezeles [Azalís] and NyC had several cablegrams and tablets from 'Abdu'l-Bahá concerning these. He said "I tell them to beware and then they go right and receive them with open arms. They dont do what I tell them to do."

I suppose we are too much concerned about our petty affairs, so that when the crucial time comes we have forgotten the great commands.

The India work is important. Some special work to be done first. And its publicity might interfere so we say nothing. Many rumors may float around at home, but nothing is known save with us. It was the last thing I expected – to be called here to go to India, but as 'Abdu'l-Bahá said, "Many are asking to go here and many asking to be sent there, but I have <u>called</u> you to go to India for me."

When I sail, will send you brief cable "Bombay" and you please convey to Barutz family and friends. Our address will be c/o Ardeshians's father. Give my love and greetings to all the friends.

By the way, . . . when a question comes up regarding meetings feasts, explanations, it was said by 'Abdu'l-Bahá in my presence that the written word or tablet must be taken as guidance, and not the spoken word, for "have I not said on the steamer in NY that they will say he said so and so, but pay only attention to the

Tablets written with my signature and seal" He said . . . – so it is with all matters, those who claim authority for this and for that he said "have they a Tablet to that effect?" All tests my dear Joseph strewn right and left. It is more important now that the friends individually get the true Bahá'í confirmation and regeneration than it is to teach. For only those who are severed will be told to teach or sent forth to work. The example must be set by the teachers: We must know a Bahá'í by his acts and deeds, not by the name of his faith. Let him who is without sin cast the first stone – can well be remembered, and see if we cant see some good quality in each to mention. To be severed from personality and feel that no one opposes us personally, but oppose the <u>spirit</u> we <u>claim</u> to serve. And let that spirit do the defending, to sacrifice all our personal aims and personal plans, personal gratifications, to prefer the other brother & sister to ourselves. etc. In fact so much is written by His hand of what we ought do, then why my feeble efforts – will they do any good?

For a time I thought I might be sent to Stuttgart to wait, while India plans were being reshaped, but instead went to Acca, Haifa, We Americans have not learned the ABC of sacrifice yet. The Persians and oriental Believers know the alphabet backwards about sacrifice & My! My! the stories of sacrifice I hear and have seen – Americans as a rule, wont even sacrifice a little pride, a little vanity, a little money, a little honorary position for each the other – all, it seems, want to be top notchers, to <u>command</u> instead of to <u>serve</u> . . .

Enough of this Joseph – but I realize how precious is the time we are losing, precious days going to waste and no headway being made in severance. Again, my love and greetings to all and I remember many of you always in far off lands,

Yours within His service

E. C. Getsinger

XIV

'Abdu'l-Bahá returned to Haifa on December 5, 1913 and the Getsingers arrived in Bombay shortly thereafter, beginning vigorous teaching work. Lua shared her first impressions of India with Elizabeth Nourse:

> Forbes Street
> Bombay, India
> c/o J. Khodadad
> Dec. 26th

My dearly loved Menita: – Your Christmas Card came yesterday and I was so pleased with it. I was secretly thinking quite a bit of "the dear old U. S. A." – for Christmas in India is very different than anything I have ever seen. The sun's rays pouring down like mid summer – streets filled with half naked men and women – strange noises filling the air, and the Believers coming bringing fruits and New England cakes & English plum pudding! A strange mixture indeed!

Well, so much more to make up my life's funny experiences! I was thinking of you all – and longing for the frost and snow! Oh how I would like some real cold weather – with a sound of sleigh-bells ringing in the freezing air! I have not been well since my arrival here – the long journeys, change of climates and spiritual emotions have all told upon my physical body which was not over strong anyway! I am feeling better now however and hope to soon be occupied in great work for the Beloved 'Abdu'l-Bahá. – Oh my dear – how India needs His divine Presence! His mere Presence could do much toward awakening this people who are by nature simple and religious. I wish America would send Him to India as Persia sent Him to America! In what better way could America show her gratitude! Can you not arise in this matter and do something? I know Mrs. Stannard[91] has written you and several others and I do hope that it can be done. Mind you 'Abdu'l-Bahá has not told us to do this – but He told Mrs. Stannard if you desire this for the Cause – perhaps God will accept it! Oh Menita – if you will write to others who have means and start such a fund – I am sure others would contribute. Sixteen thousand dollars were raised to bring Him to America which He did not accept. Now would it not be beautiful if such an amount or even less – could be raised to send Him here to these people who need Him even worse than we did? If $5000.00 – could be raised it would be sufficient to start with and money could be sent afterwards! I cannot tell you how strongly I feel regarding this matter. I am here as His "Herald" telling the people of Him – His Greatness – His Glory and most of all His Power to confer Spiritual Life – but they <u>need</u> Him! And I am making them feel their need more and more every word I utter! Oh Menita – arise and send Him to India if possible it will be a great blessing for America and every Believer who helps. Poor Persia sacrificed everything that we might have Him with us. Now I hope America will pass on the blessing to India and India may send Him to China & Japan who knows? Write Mrs. Maxwell 716 Pine Ave. Montreal Canada and Mrs. Parsons Dublin New Hampshire. I wish the women of America would do this thing for the Cause and sake of humanity! Of course, He will go to India for it is prophesied in the Hindu Scriptures that He will come and be in Delhi but how grand for <u>America</u> to send Him – See the union it makes – Each country giving the Center of the Covenant to another country! Don't let Persia do this alone especially as she cannot have Him in Persia on account of the Persecution it would bring! Since I left America two Bahá'ís have been killed – on their way back from a visit to 'Abdu'l-Bahá! . . .

The Theistic Conference of 1913 was held in Karachi, India, between December 25-29. Mrs. J. Stannard, the Getsingers' companion in India, represented "the Bahá'í Movement". In a letter, Lua mentioned that she was ill and could not take part. Mrs. Stannard's speech at the conference is recorded in *Star of the West*, along with a report of the Getsingers' activities in early 1914.[92]

In Bombay the Getsingers discovered that teaching material written from a Christian point of view was useless.

This change of approach must have been difficult for them because the only religion they knew anything about was Christianity. Edward wrote to Joseph Hannen from Bombay requesting literature from the standpoint of "Universal Peace, Brotherhood and Universal Principles". He mentioned in a postscript that few of the friends spoke any English but of "such matters of current interest we will find a translator". It was difficult for the Getsingers to find translators who understood what they were talking about.

Edward also takes up the idea suggested by Lua to Elizabeth Nourse, that the American believers might raise money to make it possible for 'Abdu'l-Bahá to visit India.

Bombay, India
Jan 9/14

9

Dear Joseph:
The mail for steamer is about to close and must get this off. We are O.K. and work slowly proceeding.

Please send me about 5 copies of each of those Persian Am. newspaper advance sheets which were intended for the press during A.B. visit in U. S. Just such as I can use for press here and mail by parcels post or newspaper post. Also a copy of ahemeds [sic] diary,[93] as it will do great good here to be read at meetings. Esp. those from date of Oct. 15 – to date, as they can be sent around from here.

Mr. Vakil[94] gets on occasionally. He is a fine Bahá'í.

My greetings to the friends. Any leaflets that can be used here gladly received – "Unity", Sprague's book or the like. But from Christian standpoint but little literature is of use – more from Universal Peace, Brotherhood and Universal Principles are required.

I told Barutz family I would cable you when I left Port Said. So I did on Nov. 3 or 4.
Hannen, Wash.
Bombay
Getsinger
Did you get it? As Barutz dont mention your telling them.

'Abdu'l-Bahá has said that if the Am. Bahá'ís want to send funds for his journey to India, they will be accepted. But better not send dribblets to him in Acca. Have the amount collected in one sum, a list of names and amt. made and sent in one Draft on Port Said Bank. Dont fail in this, or else the small amounts reaching Acca will cause him great trouble. He dont want to take a nickel from India friends, for India journey, but they sent funds for U.S. journey. Now he wont take from them, but will from us, – so that we thus serve each other instead ourselves. In this there great wisdom. It is hoped He will come to US again via Japan and San Fr. thence NYC to Acca, and I am afraid when he once enters again, he will never leave it after. I must close. Warmest greetings to the friends in Wash.

> Yours in His Service
> E. C. Getsinger

Bombay. 9/13

Dear Bro. Joseph:
I forgot to write our address in my previous letter. It is
> c/o Bahá'í Assembly
> 29 Forbes Str. Fort
> Bombay

There are so few among the friends that understand English at all, that it is of little use to send them (assembly) anything in English, but such matters of current interest we will find a translator. We have diff. in getting translator who can grasp your intent – not mere words – and then there are Hindus, Guzerati Parsees, Persian believers all together, one not fully understanding the other, but sit in brotherly love together.

The friends want to be remembered to Mason Remey and Howard Struven.

> Yours in His Service
> E.C. Getsinger

On January 13, 1914, Lua wrote to Juliet Thompson from Bombay that Julie could not know what it meant to her "to get letters from those who <u>really</u> love me". She said the work in India was "pioneer" work which meant that it was hard. Lua mentioned that 'Abdu'l-Bahá's love was a cool stream in the desert of her life.

Bombay January 13

My beloved Julie,

What ages since I had heard from you until your dear letter came the other day! Oh dearest friend you cannot know what it means to me now to get letters from those who <u>really</u> love me. The work here in India is pioneer work therefore hard! But my path never has been an easy one! What you read between the lines of the Master's Words to me is but too true. Nevertheless I am walking on the "chosen highway" and I hope I shall not falter no matter what obstacles I encounter. It was terrible at first to leave the shelter of the Master's Presence – but He is with me – His Love is a cool stream in the desert of my life!

He has called me to still loftier heights and as usual the tests and trials are to be met and dealt with. Sometimes it is very hard but my eyes are fixed upon the goal! Glad you and the dear Kinneys are united. I prayed so for them, as I saw their faces the last – as the ship left the dock when I sailed away last July!

Oh do love each other. Love is the <u>greatest</u> thing in the world! Remember me most kindly to them and tell them my love for them is the same – it was tested – but remained firm and is purer for the trial they gave it! I prayed for your dear Mother and for you too dearest – You should soon have better work. I supplicated for you and the Master said "I desire all things good for Juliet" – Keep in constant touch with Him dear – He is the gateway to all good – and through Him only can any soul <u>attain</u> anything. Oh when the people once realize Him as He is – all things will change! Unity will be the natural environment of the Believers – And the time when it was not will be only a bad dream soon forgotten!

Mrs. Stannard has done some splendid work at a conference in Karachi. I could not attend it for I was not well enough. I nearly had typhoid fever as I was not very well when I left for India – and I am just feeling a little like myself once more! The intense heat at this season of the year proved too much for me. However – it is passing, I am stronger and go to Surat tomorrow to begin my active work. Do pray for me Julie darling that I may truly be "<u>Monadi Ahd</u>" you understand! – How I wish Isabel

Fraser were here! She is so needed! Send her my love and say I am hoping yet she will come! It is time to storm India! Glad to hear that Mr. MacNutt comes to meetings again. Give them both my love! How I supplicated for them at the Holy Feet of the Beloved. – Dearest please write me often if only a word. Love to your Mother and all the Believers. May God bless each and every one of them.

Edward is here with me. Sends greetings.

Your own "Mother"

Lua

Oh Julie truly our love for each other has for its origin the "Heart of the World" 'Abdu'l-Bahá!

The Getsingers were engaged almost every day in giving talks about the Bahá'í Faith. On January 22, 1914, Lua spoke in Surat at the Theosophical Hall. Her subject was "Purity and Divinity". On January 24, her subject was "The Bahá'í Movement, Its Rise and Progress". She spoke for an hour in the Pratana Manlir Hall.

Edward also had speaking engagements. He spoke on January 28, but the subject of his talk is not known. It is apparent from their letters that the Getsingers believed they had reason to hope that 'Abdu'l-Bahá would travel to India and that their work was but a preparation for His coming. Lua expresses this theme in a letter to Agnes Parsons.

#29 Forbes St.

Bombay, India

My beloved "Noor"

I suppose you have heard from 'Abdu'l-Bahá long ere this about a new name and probably you have rec'd. it but I do not know it – so I still address you by the one which I had learned long ago to love and associate with you. For in The Cause of God you are "Light!"

I do trust you are very well, strong and happy. Please let me hear from you and through you about Royall. I did not know until recently that you had not returned to Washington for the Winter. I am sure Dublin is much better for you after your being in the hospital. And how is dear little Jeffrey Boy?

The climate of India, especially Bombay, is very trying. I have not been well since I came but am going ahead just the same working for the Cause. Mrs. Stannard of London is here and for the present we are working together. I enclose clipping of our first public lecture.

We are preparing the way for the Master – we hope. And oh, how India needs His Holy Presence! Here the people are prepared through their own great Masters and Teachers to meet and accept the Master-Teacher of the 20th Century! His mere appearance will accomplish in one day what speaking and lecturing a whole year will not do! How eager they are, and what yearning they manifest. There are a great number of highly enlightened people among the Hindoos – college men – also among the Parsees! – They left off thinking long ago – where the people of the West have but recently begun! I find them simple and most wonderfully ready through their own resources and researches for the "Great World Teacher" whose appearance they are expecting. May they soon realize their expectations, in the "Center of the Covenant".

I am called now so must close. With tender love and devotion – I am as ever

In the Service of 'Abdu'l-Bahá
Your devoted
Lua

Jan. 29, 1914

I was greatly interested in Winston Churchill's article – "The Modern Quest for a Religion" which appeared in Christmas number of "The Century". It seems to me the tide of human thought and search is turning in the right direction at last.

Please get in touch with him if possible and let him know that a great Personality has come just when the world so needs one, to fulfill all the great Personality of 1900 years ago promised. I feel sure you are the one to bring this to Winston Churchill's attention. Get in touch with him . . .

Lua was busy in the early part of February, speaking on February 1, 1914, on "The Universal Aspect of the Bahá'í

Movement". She spoke again on February 4 on "Individual Spiritual Progress" and on February 6 her subject was "The Messengers of God". On February 8 she visited the Ideal Seminary for boys, distributed prizes to the students and spoke on "Service as an Act of Worship".

The letter that Lua wrote to Louise Bosch (Louise Stapfer, who had married John D. Bosch in January 1914) on February 7, 1914, from Bombay expressed Lua's knowledge of "all the things" said about her in America. Lua wrote that she had done nothing to hurt the people who spoke against her and that if she were to return they would be the first to come forward to praise her. She said she had gone through fires "to learn the <u>reality</u> of praise and blame – and the reality is <u>nothingness</u>! One word from the Lips of Truth – (the sweet mouth of 'Abdu'l-Bahá) is worth more than the praise of all the people in the world! . . . My refuge is 'Abdu'l-Bahá! My strength is 'Abdu'l-Bahá! My stronghold is 'Abdu'l-Bahá! Who can prevail against me while I am faithful to Him – trying my best to do His Will?" Lua expressed the thought that the people should rejoice over a sinner forgiven by the Master rather than soiling their tongues by reiterating sins. "Oh, Lysa – when will the people begin to <u>practice</u> the teachings?"

> #29 Forbes Street
> Bombay India
> Feb. 7th. 1914

My beloved Lysa

Your letter reached me yesterday and I hasten to reply for I have longed to hear from you! Your letter does not surprise me – for well I know <u>all the things</u> said about me in America, but this is not the first time and probably it will not be the last. All I can say is "God bless those who hate me!" I have done them no harm! I was the first person to ever mention the Cause on the Pacific Coast, and recently I worked very hard there again! The Cause is spreading – it doesn't matter what is said about those who spread it! Ask anyone who speaks against me – "What did she ever do to you?" – and you will see they are silent. Should I return to California the very ones who now speak against me – would come forward to love me and praise me. As happened last summer in New York. Juliet was with me and saw it all! Oh Lysa, my dear one – I have passed through many fires to learn the <u>reality</u> of praise and <u>blame</u> – and the reality is <u>nothingness</u>! One word from the Lips of Truth (the sweet mouth of 'Abdu'l-Bahá) is worth more than the praise of all the people in the world! I do not deserve His loyal love and mercy – but He has given it in full measure and now I am endeavoring to go ahead with the work of His Glorious Vineyard in India. Let those who hate and find fault with me – remember that verily He is able to raise the lowest to the highest degree of honor – and to bring the highest to the lowest degree of abasement! – But God knows I want only glory, praise and everlasting good for every one – even those who spend the valuable time of these heavenly days speaking against me!

My refuge is 'Abdu'l-Bahá! My strength is 'Abdu'l-Bahá! My stronghold is 'Abdu'l-Bahá! Who can prevail against me while I am faithful to Him – trying my best to do His Will? Again "Let those who think they stand take heed lest they fall." The tests of God are <u>very great</u>!

Suppose I had done all of the terrible things – which people say I have done – and <u>He</u> forgives me? Should they not rejoice over the good fortune of a sinner – instead of soiling their tongues by re-iterating his sins? – Oh, Lysa – when will the people begin to <u>practice</u> the teachings? Are they so saintly and free from sins – that they can afford to breathe the sins of anyone? Your love for me was only tested once more – May and Juliet and Mariam also went through the fire of trial on my unworthy account. God bless you all and keep you safe in the arms of His Great Love – and may my poor life be acceptable in His Path, for your redemption! There is in my heart naught save love and good wishes for every soul upon the earth. Especially for you, and dear good John D. – You have heard I presume that Dr. Fareed is married to a very beautiful rich young lady from Chicago – who accepted the teachings? They are at present on the Nile.

Edward is here with me – I asked 'Abdu'l-Bahá to send him with me to India – as He said a man was necessary to be with me.

Mrs. Stannard is here also, we are working together. Give my regards to John D. I hope you will soon marry and be <u>happy</u> ever after!

More another time.

My loving regards to Mrs. Goodall and Mrs. Cooper and all Friends

Please write again soon

As ever

Your faithful

Lua

Lua wrote from Bombay on March 5, 1914, to Annetta Woodward that the rosary beads she had sent for Unis, her god-child, were still in the possession of the friend who had been instructed to mail them and had then lost the address. She asks that a blue tassel be put on the beads to match the turquoise she was enclosing for the child. Lua asks for news of family and friends and of the progress of the Cause, and sends greetings to the friends in Washington DC.

March 5, 1914   29 Forbes St
                                       Bombay
                                       India
                                       c/o Bahá'í Hall

Dearest Natekeh

It was only now that I have found out my beads (rosary) did not reach Unis and I am sending another string exactly like those, – blessed by the Master. I was in a great hurry and gave the package with address on separate paper to be mailed by one of the friends who now notifies me the address got lost and the beads remain in his possession. Please put a blue tassel on these beads to match the little turquoise I am enclosing in this letter for my little God-Child. I am very sorry for the delay and can't imagine what you have been thinking of me as I wrote the beads would soon be there &. Well, at last I fulfill my promise & shall do so in every case if I live. I have not been well in India, the climate is very bad, and does not agree with me! I am working hard just the same notwithstanding physical weakness. Please do write to me – I love you very much and would so like one of your nice long letters.

Kiss my little Unis for me and wish her every happiness Do tell Mrs. Haney I want to hear from her too. I am giving public lectures and teaching in private every day. Please, now do forgive this delay and write me soon. All about the progress of the Cause in Washington. I trust all of the believers are united together and that they are doing very good work! Please remember me kindly to all of them. Especially dear "Fern" Ambrose. I hear my sister Hebe has a baby-boy! What a joy for them! Have you seen it, or them recently. I know Baltimore is some little distance but I thought you might have been over there for a week as you used to go often. If you have seen Hebe do write me about her and the baby, as you <u>see</u> them!

Ursie wrote me a day or two after the baby came, since then I have heard nothing from any of them!

Please give my loving greetings to Fred and your Brother. I hope he is in a better condition by now.

With greetings and loving remembrances – In His Name
    Yours as ever
        Lua

It was the hope of the friends, especially of Lua and Edward, that 'Abdu'l-Bahá would travel again, this time visiting India, Persia, and other neighboring countries. As we have seen, the Master had apparently authorized them to write to the Bahá'ís in North America and Europe that contributions would be accepted for this purpose. There was always a worry when collecting funds that were destined for 'Abdu'l-Bahá that some spiritual reason would arise which would mean that He would not accept them. A letter from Edward written March 7, 1914, shows this concern. The letter must have been considered important enough for a copy to be made for the Getsinger files, for the letter is clearly labelled "copy" and written in Lua's handwriting.

Dear Friends:–
Your letter just received and answer at once. Regarding the money for 'Abdu'l-Bahá's trip to India, it is just this: Mrs. Stannard, Lua and I were told that we had permission to write to U.S. friends that contributions would be accepted for His <u>next</u>

journey – (Persia, etc) and they would be accepted. We have written.

Second: Contributions made in Paris before going to England and U. S. were <u>not</u> refused.

Third: If any American contributions have been refused for the above purpose, there was some reason – perhaps there was not the right spirit manifested, or too much trying to be the first, foremost, or some personal aim etc.

Fourth: The only question is that of doing it in the right way. The more quiet, the more assured of being accepted, the more publicity, the more certain of refusal.

Fifth: On acct. of the stir it would cause in Haifa about the many money orders etc. coming, if <u>many</u> people sent letters individually, it is not wise that this be done.

But the better to have it collected and personally brought to 'Abdu'l-Bahá or if not possible sent in so few lump sums as possible. The Temple is not as important as the work of the One who is the Founder of the Temple,

        Yours,
         In His Name
         E. C. Getsinger

On March 10, 1914, Edward wrote from Bombay to Joseph Hannen, "For God's sake Joseph stop that notice!!" The hope of the friends in India, including Edward and Lua, that the Master could visit that country, might be in vain if the travel fund drew publicity within the Bahá'í community. It now looked as if the Master could not come until September as the monsoons were due. Edward writes, "The work here is progressing well considering it is India."

                         Bombay Mch 10/14

             9

My Dear Bro Joseph.
Just a line as the mail boat goes soon. Yours at hand. and the proof sheets of the Persian Am. Articles coming in hand. Am sending some my articles in Native paper. Mr. Powell writes me about Esperanto's getting up fund also that a report on appeal

is to be published in the Esp. Journal. and Star of West. For God's sake Joseph stop that notice!! It will ruin everything. If a single thing goes into print the fund will be returned. This must be the quietest thing the Bahá'ís ever did. Just by letter, no print, no reports – nothing in print or the enemies will make capital out of it.

Let it be a few of love offerings and not limited in any way. Send it "to be used as 'Abdu'l-Bahá sees fit". I know whereof I speak. Any other way runs poor chances. I doubt wisdom of Esperanto move, but it's been done – so cant do anything – but stop all print. Those that are giving large sums, are knocking this plan on the Q.T. but unless you both make a fatal mistake, you will win out.

Dont seem possible that He can now come before Sept. as the monsoon is soon on.

Work here is progressing well considering it is India.

Regard to all friends.

Yours in haste

E. C. Getsinger

Edward reported that "our work is beginning to count, and are getting some believers from good class" in a letter to Joseph Hannen written from Bombay on March 12, 1914. The first Hindu believer, Vakil, had left the day before for the first pilgrimage to 'Abdu'l-Bahá. The new believer was making this visit even though he might be disowned by his family and made an outcast.

Mch 12/14
Bombay

9

Dear Bro Joseph! –

Enclosed find envelopes, and to this address 'Abdu'l-Bahá has directed, that all Bombay matters be sent, and no more to Janesheed Kahadad, as things have been stuck away, and none but he had use of them. Assembly here progressing fine: Our work is beginning to count, and are getting some believers from good class. Janes [sic][95] are becoming interested now. Hot seas. is on and we may have to go to the hills for a while.

Greetings to all the friends. Vakil has turned over all Ahmed's letters so we all enjoying them. He and 10 others left for Haifa yesterday. He is the first <u>Hindu</u> believer to visit 'Abdu'l-Bahá. A fine spirit and this visit may cost him dearly, as it may disown him and outcaste him. We were in Sura several days and made a good opening there. Please tell Mason about the change for Assembly address.

> Very truly yours,
> E.C. Getsinger

Edward lectured in Calcutta on March 28, 1914, on the subject of "A Message to the Sons of Mazda". The complete text of the talk is preserved in *Star of the West*.[96]

Meanwhile, Lua brought Elizabeth Nourse up to date with the news:

> Bombay, India
> March 19, 1914

My beloved "Menita",
Your letter rec'd and was so very glad to hear from you again. I am pleased to know that you are sending some money to the Master. I hope you sent it <u>direct to Him</u> and to no one else. I am afraid a blunder has been made for I hear from Wash. that a Miss Barnitz is getting up a subscription to send the Master here! Dr. G. wrote her about the matter and I did <u>not know it</u>. I feel quite certain 'Abdu'l-Bahá will not accept <u>any money</u> raised in this manner! It was only intended that a few who could would do so from their <u>hearts</u> and for the sake of India (were to contribute) [written along the side of the letter]. I have heard that the matter was placed before a committee in Wash. and objections were raised and <u>opposition</u> manifested! Of course this would be in <u>America</u> over <u>anything</u>! And I knew it – thus I wrote only to you & Mrs. Haney in confidence. Well, it may turn out all right. I hear Mrs. Parsons sent $100.00 to Miss Barnitz to start with – as it seems <u>she</u> wrote Mrs. P <u>before</u> you had time to send my letter to you, to her regarding the matter. Oh if only Dr. G. had just kept out of it! – But it may be the Beloved will accept it – and then it will be all right! Oh dear me – how India needs Him only God can know! And may God in His Mercy send Him here soon.

Mrs. Stannard is doing very splendid work in Calcutta lecturing and writing on the Cause. She is very selfless and a truly devoted servant to 'Abdu'l-Bahá! She has means of her own so that she can go about from place to place! The distances are very great here and the R.R. travelling very expensive! The Master said Bombay was the Center of India so I am staying here and trying to establish a <u>spiritual</u> <u>Center</u> here! Many people are becoming interested and we hope to soon set India on fire with the Message of Bahá'u'lláh! One meets a new religion (or rather a new phase of an old religion) and a new language every time one turns around. It makes the teaching very difficult and calls for the greatest amount of patience: The Jains a sect of Hindooism – furnish the most fertile soil for a universal religion of any people I have met here. Mrs. Stannard writes that the people she has met are all very religious and naturally philosophic – but <u>ortho-dox</u>. They listen and <u>mentally</u> agree – but go on in their own way when it comes to practice! Theosophy has rec'd a great set back in India on account of Mrs. Besant's trying to foist on the Society the "Great World Teacher" in the Person of a small Hindoo lad – whom she is educating at Oxford![97] The lad's father objects to having his son posed in such a position and has sued Mrs. Besant for the custody of his son. It is a dreadful mess – and it has been in the courts and newspapers so much that everybody is disgusted. People are deserting the Theosophical ranks by hundreds! What temerity for a human being to select the Great World Teacher – as if God had gone to sleep or was no longer able to judge Who and What the World needs. He sent His Great Messenger Bahá'u'lláh – and also the Great World teacher 'Abdu'l-Bahá – over half a century ago! – The Theosophists are awakening here and there to the realization of it too!

In time all will know!

How I would love to see and talk with you today! My heart just longs for you and Phil! Is he still praying for me? Tell him not to forget how much and often he must pray for "Aunt Lua".

A letter just rec'd from Mr. Hannen says "Mrs. Boyle told me confidentially that $2000.00 had been raised in Philadelphia and Atlantic City. – I hope you sent your contribution straight to the Beloved. And I hope they will send the money as fast as they collect it and not wait until a large sum is collected! Mr. Hannen also writes that they are <u>not</u> making it a wide-spread subscription, and I am very glad.

Please remember me most lovingly to all the Believers in your little nest. I think so often of the last visit I paid to you. I have not had any clothes made since! Now all at once everything has gone to pieces! I must have something made very soon or make my "Skindoo" like the "Hindoo". – I am teaching and working like a beaver day and night. Next week we hope to have a big public lecture in Bombay!

I am hunting some beads for you! The India beads are not so nice as those in Egypt. – Please do write me often! Much love to dear Mrs. Harper. And all others – Specially Phil! Catharine Boise, Marie and her tall handsome brother!

Please darling pray for
> Your unworthy
> "Little Mother"
> Lua

Lua wrote to Miss Alma E.E. Albertson about this time.[98] The first page of the letter is missing but Lua speaks about her health at unusual length and explains points important for Bahá'ís to understand.

Yes, I was ill in Haifa, and suffered but it was good for me, as it helped purify my soul so I could better appreciate my visit to that Holy Place! "My calamity is my providence" & I have not been well at all here – the climate of Bombay is very bad as it is warm and damp and full of malaria. But weak and sick as I have been I have done a good deal of work. Two days before I arrived in Bombay my temperature was 103½ degrees – so you may understand I began my work here physically handicapped! I did not recover from that fever for four weeks. And when I finally did throw it off I was very weak and anemic. I am not myself yet but am much better than I was. Oh yes "Nursie" dear I remember how you felt when I left the hospital and all of it! It was a piece of bad management from which I am still suffering! I did not realize it at the time – nor for a little while after – but I know now it was a shock from which I have not yet recovered. Had not Dr. Slater cared for me I would not have been able to stand the journey to Egypt! Oh, how I love those two dear souls! My heart swells with gratitude when I think of them! Please give them my most loving greetings and tell them I should so love to hear from them sometimes. I am so glad things are getting better in Chicago! Oh may the children of the Covenant of God be united and love each other as they should! May His Glorious Lights illumine them and gather them together in "radiant acquiescence" to know and do His Holy Will.

Dear, the Sun of Bahá'u'lláh has not set, nor will it set for thousands of years to come – but that Sun now shines through the "Center of the Covenant" 'Abdu'l-Bahá – and to Him all must turn! Mr. Remey's article in the Star of the West "Let the New follow the New" – explains it very wonderfully well, I think – Any further knowledge on the subject can be found in the "Tablet of the Branch"! Oh why do the people pay attention to what <u>other people say</u>! Why do they not follow what 'Abdu'l-Bahá and Bahá'u'lláh say! How many times has 'Abdu'l-Bahá said this is the Dawn of the Day of God – whose Manifestation was Bahá'u'-'lláh! The same Sun shines through both the Father and the Son and you can not separate the Light – ! Today is the Day of God – in which the Sun first appeared through the Báb – then Bahá'u'-'lláh – and now 'Abdu'l-Bahá. <u>We</u> come in the time of the "Covenant" and not the time of the Father – thus we must turn to the "Covenant" and to no one else – for the reason that we are still upon the <u>Earth</u> and <u>so is He</u>! – Praise be to God! Therefore He is the "Point" the <u>Center</u> the source of all good – all knowledge all Light all understanding – Everything!

Do you not remember <u>what</u> I was told in my dream? Don't be disturbed by any of these things, and if you want new light and help call upon God in the Name of the Covenant – Thus "Ya 'Abdu'l-Bahá Mar Keza Mesook" translated means, "Oh 'Abdu'l-Bahá Center of the Covenant". Please give this to no one but Mrs. Slater and Ella Greenleaf. Others might think I am giving a <u>new</u> Greatest Name! which is not so – I am only telling you to call upon God and Bahá'u'lláh <u>through</u> the Center appointed by Him! Do you <u>see</u> the point? Oh Nursie dear – do love everybody in my place – on my behalf! Do you know there is no feeling of anything but love in my heart for <u>all</u>! [underlined three times] and most of all for those who hurt me, and were <u>not</u> my friends! I see all of their double-facedness – as <u>faithfulness</u> to <u>Him</u>, – and love them for it! If they are faithful to Him, and I am faithful to

216

Him, in time we shall all meet upon "the Emerald Hill of Faithfulness" in the perfect Love of full understanding; and for that time I can well afford to wait for you see I was not unfaithful either to Him, or them – Nor did I wrongly accuse anybody!

God bless us all and keep together in His Fold!

In regard to Haifa, had you written me that you would go I might have arranged your expenses for Mrs. P may have been very glad to have taken you with her! However it may be best as it is. I was so anxious to have you with dear Rouha for your own sake – as well as hers. – Time will tell whether the wedding of which you speak is for the best or not! Let us hope it is! And that both of them will ever deserve and enjoy the good pleasure of 'Abdu'l-Bahá! – Gladys is a sweet spiritual child of God and I hope she has chosen wisely. And well. Her parents were with her and all parties were consulted as according to Katab-el-Akdas! – Do write me soon – Oh if the friends knew the encouragement of their loving words more would write me. I know Edward is well and happy. Sends greetings to all. My love to Emma Lundberg, Mrs. True, Ella Greenleaf, Dr Zia, May and Fanny Lesch and all – dear Betty Herrick included. Go and see Lottie Pratt when you can – and give her oceans of love from me! I really love her very sincerely and tenderly!

Never mind the Master Doctor's scolding – it was not his best self – remember that and be very patient! How is Charlie G– ? Please tell Ella and Mr. G to write to me. Ever your devoted sister friend

Lua

Mrs. Stannard is in Calcutta doing good work for the Cause. She is very capable and works & sacrifices continually! I want you to know this! Do you ever hear of the Milburns?
Answer soon. I wish you were here with me!

In April Lua travelled to Jhalarapatan at the invitation of the Maharajah of Jhalawar. Her account of this journey may be found in the next chapter. Returning to Bombay in the last week of April, she found bad news. The collection of money to send 'Abdu'l-Bahá to India had gone awry, as both Lua and Edward had feared it would.

Bombay Apr. 24th,14

My beloved Menita,

I have just returned from a visit to one of the Prince Rulers in India where I remained thirteen days his guest. I delivered one public lecture and talked to many people. And am invited to return in the autumn. My heart is broken over a letter from Acca today from Sohrab which contains the following "I am so sorry that the cat got [out] of the bag! The Master has given up the idea of going to India for the present; because some 'busybodies' wrote from America that a number of the Friends are collecting a fund for his travelling expenses. He sent a cable that he is not going, and told me to write to return the money to the contributors and also told me to let you know that I cannot come to India now. This same mistake was made when the fund was collected for his expenses to America. Before it was sent Him they behaved so badly that the Master refused to accept a penny of it etc." – Oh darling, I wrote you that I was afraid as soon as it became public and anything like a <u>collection</u> was made He would refuse it. I wrote you first that I felt only four or five persons should be consulted etc. as I felt sure He would refuse otherwise. There are some who are determined not one penny shall be <u>given for anything save the Temple</u>. Now that He has commanded the money returned to contributors you have <u>your</u> amount back! Oh, if you had only sent it <u>direct</u> – then it would have been accepted! It is such a pity that He cannot come – for no one else can possibly do for India what He can! It is cruel to raise the hopes of the people, and then disappoint them. You see it is impossible for the people here to go to Him on account of the Caste which does not permit them to leave India, and besides the <u>mass</u> are too poor anyway – I feel simply heartbroken – for it need not have been if someone had not meddled! Send Him your contribution anyway and beg Him to accept it – if not for India for the Cause, as He shall see fit: –

I have been invited by the Prince of Jhalawar to go to Cashmir for May and June – where he will present me to the King of Cashmir who is the Greatest Ruler in India, next of course to Viceroy. His State is very large and very beautiful and he is very wealthy! I am waiting now for orders from the Master! It is a long journey from Bombay. Please kiss my own dear Phil for me and give my love to all the "other children". Write to me soon. With

218

loving greetings to all the Friends especially Mrs. Harper whose smiling face I never forget and for all the others Alláh-u-Abhá. – How I would love to see and talk with you today!! Oh! Oh! I am just most "bustin!"

Your own "Mother"

Lua.

Lua wrote to Mrs. Parsons on May 15, 1914, about 'Abdu'l-Bahá's decision.

Bombay, India
May 15, 1914

My dearest "Noor",

Until you receive a better appellation I shall continue to use the above beautiful name of Light! Your dear letter has given me much hope. I am so glad to hear from you, and to receive the book which will be such a help to me. I am very sorry to hear from the Beloved Master that He will not require the contributions from America and has returned the same. I was afraid – when I heard it had been made a <u>public</u> collection it would be so. <u>My</u> idea was that only a few who could and would be glad to should be asked to contribute – and that each one should send his or her contribution <u>direct</u> to Him "without letting the left hand know what the right hand was doing"! But Mr. Getsinger wrote without my knowledge to Miss Barnitz and this other plan was formed which has ended as I felt sure (when I heard it) it would. Oh if the American Bahá'ís only knew India's need of 'Abdu'l-Bahá they would all pray that He would come quickly. I have sent Mrs. Haney an account of a recent visit I paid to one of the Maharajahs of India, requesting her to make and send you a copy. There you will see how I have succeeded with Hindoos and Muhammadans. Yes, on the trip out here – the Hindoo, the Mussulman and a Greek Catholic all became friends so that they correspond with each other up to date! The power of the Spirit is wonderful in its uniting force. I have been asked by the Maharajah of Jhalawar to visit Kashmir, where he will introduce me to the King and Court of that earthly paradise! The Maharajah of Jhalawar is a great friend of 'Abdu'l-Bahá! Yesterday a cable came from the Beloved telling me to "Go Kashmir" – It is a long journey four days by rail and three days by Caravan! I shall start as soon as possible! My wardrobe is not fit for a King's Court – but I shall rely upon the garments of the Spirit to cover all defects!

I went to Poona May 6th where I delivered two lectures to very large audiences – some estimated the gathering as two thousand – but surely there were fifteen hundred present. They were very appreciative and have [invited] me to come again. I hope to be able to leave for Kashmir June 1st – and shall go to Poona in the meantime if possible – Am so glad you like "Lady Lotta Pratt". I do not hear from her often either. She loves her friends but does not write many letters. She was so kind and good to me! Do go to the Beloved – with all of your family if possible and may the choicest blessings be yours! Please dearest write me when ever you can, you cannot imagine how I appreciate a line from you or any of my real friends. A tablet from the Divine All Glorious One – assures me of success in India – How grateful how thankful am I for His Mercy. With kind remembrances to Mr. Parsons & Jeffrey Boy – I am as ever

Your devoted Lua

Edward wrote to Joseph Hannen on May 17, 1914, that literature from the Christian viewpoint was useless in India, so the leaflets supplied by Chicago could not be used. The rainy season was on and all work was at a standstill. They were awaiting instructions. The fund for 'Abdu'l-Bahá's journey to India was still on Edward's mind.

May 17, 1914
Bombay

9

Dear Bro Joseph!-

Yours of the May 12 at hand. We are receiving Ahmed's Diary from Vakil, so that matter is now OK. In regard the literature from Mr. Boyle – all such as was in Washington and from a Christian standpoint are useless here, hence I dont see why bother about them. Mrs. G. also thinks the same – we cant use the leaflets etc. of which we got a supply from Chicago.

The damage seems to have been done by the Esperanto plan

to contribute, but the Temple Executive committee has made that as an excuse to not endorse etc: But I think the same will yet in <u>some</u> <u>way</u> be acceptable though the present intent of the money may have to be changed.

The rainy season is on and all work is at standstill and are awaiting instructions. With kindest regards to all the friends – Yours in <u>His</u> Service

Am writing with a fan in one hand hence brevity and scribble
    E. C. Getsinger

XV

We must now retrace our steps to the early months of 1914. On March 21, Lua began to write her journal, recounting from memory what had happened since their arrival in late 1913. She kept this "Indian journal" until June 30, 1914. It is reproduced here in its entirety.

The scope and number of her activities is astounding. In her letter to Agnes Parsons in May 1914, quoted in the previous chapter, Lua describes the large audiences who attended her lectures in Poona and her exuberation at 'Abdu'l-Bahá's instructions to visit the Rajah of Jhalawar in Kashmir – as well as her views on having nothing suitable to wear: "It is a long journey, four days by rail and three days by Caravan! I shall start as soon as possible! My wardrobe is not fit for a King's Court – but I shall rely upon the garments of the Spirit to cover all defects!"

Lua had already visited the Maharajah of Jhalawar in early April. In many ways this visit was one of the high points of her Indian journey, but it was only years later that an account was printed in *Star of the West*.[99] Her journal recounts the visit in detail.

March 21st, 1914
Bombay India
According to the Bahá'í calendar this is the New Year Day!

I therefore begin my journal on this day! Notwithstanding the fact that I said I would keep it all along. I trust I shall be forgiven for having waited until this auspicious day before beginning to chronicle the events occurring in my very busy, if seemingly useless life! We all say too much and <u>do</u> too little and this proves that <u>impulse</u> is exercised at the expense of truth and reason. I fully expected to be able to write something every day in this book – after reaching India – but upon my arrival Dec. 4th, 1913 I found myself to be quite ill, and very uninteresting – Thus I refrained from afflicting my friends – In thinking back to Christmas I may just state that to one born and raised in New York – Christmas in Bombay was a very droll experience! Early in the morning the friends came bringing garlands of flowers and "English" plum pudding! (The kind that is made and shipped all over the world in tin cans.) Later more Friends came bringing more garlands and English Fruit cake with some very delicious fruits & later still, some more Friends bringing more flowers, fruit and more plum pudding – until at sunset the number of fruit cakes and puddings had reached the mystic limit of seven – 7 – ! The sun shone warm all day, the temperature being 80 (degrees) – and the half-naked men, and often wholly naked children on the street – The strange music in native quarters, the swarms of flies and clouds of dust all formed a weird contrast to our old fashioned New England Christmas – with its snow, sleighbells, Christmas trees, Santa Claus and turkey dinners! –

January 1st, 1914 – came and went much after the manner of the Christmas only with <u>less</u> plum pudding! – I felt very far away somehow and was glad when the Holidays were over.

Jan. 15th, 1914
Finds me in Surat where I am lecturing on the Bahá'í Teachings. No one has ever talked on the subject before in Surat. Mr. N.K. Vakil for some time a Bahá'í lives here as does Dr. D.J. Edal Behram who met 'Abdu'l-Bahá in London 1911 – and to whom I have explained the Cause in detail since I am a guest in his house and am lecturing at his request before the Theosophical Society of which he is a member. Through him I have met Judge and Mrs. Advani! Took dinner several times with them there meeting some very interesting people Mrs. [?] Ali Akbar of Bombay – Mr. Dubash and Mr. Yusufali of Baroda, a barrister and close associate of His Highness the Gaikwad of Baroda.[100] Through the kindness of Mrs. Advani (one of the most spiritually beautiful characters I have met in India) I addressed a meeting of ladies one afternoon, on the subject of <u>unity</u> of <u>religions</u>! All were apparently pleased, but I afterwards learned that most of them said "We know our own religion and why trouble about

another one!" – During my stay in Surat I was much surprised to find a policeman following me everywhere. And at last he called at Dr. Behram's house making careful and minute enquiries as to where I had come from, for what purpose was I in India and particularly in Surat – I answered all of his questions very simply and truthfully, which he promptly wrote down for the purpose of showing the Dist. Collector Mr. F.G.H. Anderson. It seems political schemes have been carried on and nourished under the cloak of religion in India and much harm has been done by those who wish to rebel against the Government – by preaching their seditious doctrines under the guise of religion, much stress having been laid upon <u>universal</u> <u>brotherhood</u> etc. Thus when I began teaching the Bahá'í precepts – I was at once a "suspicious" person! This came about too from the fact that I had recently been in California where the Young Hindoos headed by Hyar Dayl have "hatched schemes" to try to bring about a revolution in India![101] Had the British official Mr. Anderson known how I had talked several times to the Young Hindoos in California against Hyar Dahl and his policies he would have congratulated me instead of regarding me with suspicion. I was a friend and not a foe! This he did not know and therefore made it impossible for me to deliver any more lectures in Surat! As to Hyar Dhal (and all like him) he has only hurt instead of helped India! The methods employed by him are not from this century! There is to be revolution in India as well as every other country – but it is the revolution of the Spirit through the power of God's Holy Word. I am returning to Bombay tomorrow having been here just one week!

Feb. 1st, 1914

Dear me – two weeks more have passed in which I have been so busy talking that I could find no time to write. We have been delivering lectures in Bombay to large and interested audience upon the Bahá'í Movement – its rise and progress! Mrs. J.S. Stannard and myself held a "partnership" lecture at the Brahmo Samaj Hall which was attended by about three hundred people! The people of India love to listen to lectures – but very little impression is made upon their minds by public talks! One must meet them again and again and overcome their object[ion]s through kindness more than philosophical reasoning – for when it comes to philosophy – they are Masters in it. They have been born in philosophy and brought up on it!

What the whole of India needs is a spiritual baptism! We read the Gospel of Buddha and the Bhagavad-Gita finding them full of the utterances of Truth – but the followers of the same have become like the Christians with the Gospel, and the Jews with the Bible – followers in name only: They do not know the spiritual significance of the words they read – then they run after doctrines, dogmas and creeds. And are full of prejudices, superstitions and animosity! The many "castes" of the country make things very <u>difficult</u> when it comes to spiritual teachings! And the many different languages but add thereunto! In no country in the world does one so feel the necessity of a universal religion and a universal language – as in India! May the good God hasten the day when <u>both</u> shall be realized!

Feb. 15th

More lectures and many private talks with individuals who have become interested but we all feel that the work is very slowly progressing. God may be doing much however while we are standing still! Mrs. Stannard is leaving for Madras. How I shall miss her! But India is a very large country and there are very few Bahá'ís and fewer Bahá'í teachers! So she is going there and then on to Calcutta. She is a beautiful soul and so intelligent. Our loss is some one's gain so we bid her "goodbye" and God speed.

Feb. 19th

Surat again! Dr. Edal Behram met Mr. Getsinger and myself at the station and we are now in his very comfortable bungalow by the river where we enjoy the cool breezes wafted through the shady garden surrounding his house. We are to be received by the Nawab of Sachin this afternoon at 5 o'clock. He is a Mohammadan Prince, and I hope will become interested in the teachings of Bahá'u'lláh.

8:30 p.m.

Well, we have visited the Prince of Sachin, His Highness the Nawab who rec'd us very graciously indeed and talked to us for some time! He had never heard of the Bahá'í Movement so it was going back to the "Beginning of things" in his case! He is a freemason – and seems to think the brotherhood of that organization very good and sufficient if all men would become masons! When I asked him "What about the women?" he had to smile 'ere he answered "We will take care of them, if they will let us!" Then I pointed out the fact that the majority of men these days could not pay the fees necessary to become Masons – and besides a truth that had to be kept so secret was not one upon which the vast body of humanity could thrive! As the great Founders of the different religions had always declared God's Truth publically [sic] so that all who would might benefit therefrom. I gave him some literature which he promised to read and told him about 'Abdu'l-Bahá! He listened very attentively then said – "I would like to see Him. Will He come to India?" I replied "I hope so!" Then we took our departure. I have rec'd one or two letters from him since. He is a young man only twenty-eight – and the world is alluring him in many ways at present. He may see its evanescence soon – for he seems very sincere.

Feb. 20th
Called upon the Collector of the Dist. today and "had it out with him"! I think Mr. Anderson has a little clearer understanding of the Bahá'í Movement now and if he is just he will never associate it with Hyar Dayl and revolution again.

Feb. 21st
Spoke before the Theosophical Society this afternoon. My subject was the "Divinity of God's Messengers". – Of course everything resolves itself into a talk on Bahá'u'lláh and His teachings – no matter what the subject may be! I don't know what I said in the hour and a quarter allotted me – but they all seemed pleased when I had finished – so much so that they requested me to speak the next evening which I could not accept on account of another engagement.

Mr. Getsinger has spent these three days past in studying the Gathas and teachings of Zoroaster – from Max Muller's translations, a very good set of which is owned by Dr. Edal Behram. He is making copious notes and expects to write an article on the subject. It is very ancient lore and very hard to decipher. I do not envy him his task!

Feb. 22, 1914
Returned to Bombay!

March lst

Have been ill ever since. Fever: – and fever-blisters upon my face and hands have made me most uncomfortable. But then, much can be said against the climate of Bombay: – When one considers the number of deaths weekly from plague, smallpox and typhoid – a little fever now and then with accompanying "blisters" – is not so bad but that it might be worse! – so I think I will forgo all mention of the climate of Bombay – and mention its beautiful beach where I often go at sunset just opposite church gate station to watch the Parsees at their evening devotions upon the sands. It is one of the world's beautiful sights! No temple or church in any land under the sun can compare with this vast temple of sky and sea lighted by the ever changing colors of the sun as it sinks into the ocean – made by itself to look like liquid gold! Often too, the silver crescent of the new moon is discernable [sic] hanging low near the horizon which is sure to be soon followed by the appearance of the Evening Star in its wake! I have seen the setting sun, the new moon and the Evening Star all at the same time, against a background of such brilliant color – as would defy the powers of the greatest artists to describe! I felt like worshipping the "Great Artist" who made it all – like the Parsees do – and I could understand why they build no churches when I saw them worshipping in this greatest of all temples – "not made with hands!" Our ancestors all worshipped in the open out "under the blue" – if they worshipped at all – for churches and temples are modern when compared to the life of man upon this planet! And I for one think it's what the Great Architect intended when He made the High Arch and studded the same with the sun moon and stars! You may think me pagan or heathen – but I never want to see a church again! – When I saw the Temple of the Palms in Egypt I thought it ideal – but it's nothing in comparison to the Beach of Bombay! [Here Lua makes a note in her journal: *This does not mean the Mashruqel Ashkar which when completed will not be a Temple so much as it will be a monument of Unity among the Bahá'ís! As its purpose is not one of worship only! May the great day of its completion soon be witnessed by all!]

March 10, 1914

Still working under the difficulties of miserable health! But thank God – working just the same! Now there are people of different religions coming nearly every evening. It is very interesting to see them together. Some Hindoos say – "Goodbye" immediately when Mohammadans come in; but others who are more liberal and broad-minded stay and enter into discussions – which I sometimes break up – by serving tea! I have to do it for they become heated, and that leads to bad feelings – and I find that tea brings everything down to a normal temperature very soon! At first the Hindoos refused my tea – but the Mohammadans praised it so much – and took occasion to laugh at them for depriving themselves so often until they too – took it – just to be "good sports" – I think in the beginning but now to be sociable and because they like it! The Jains – one of the oldest religious sects in India – have become interested in the Bahá'í Movement and invited me on two occasions to speak before their "Brother-hood" which I did much to my own and their <u>seeming</u> satisfaction!

The task of uniting people of different religions is not so simple as it sounds! Age old prejudices do not disappear in a moment – even when the people have recognized them to be so disastrous to progress peace and civilization. They are deeply ingrained in the very reality of a person and must be gradually and patiently uprooted and replaced with something better! And oh the Patience it requires! Dear me – a Bahá'í teacher needs must be a <u>real</u> saint to do this most difficult work successfully! On this 10th day of March Mr. N.R. Vakil the first Hindoo to become a Bahá'í left for Acca – Haifa – with Sey'd Mustafa[102] to visit 'Abdu'l-Bahá. It required much courage on his part to take this step for it means the giving up everything and being willing to become an "outcaste"! He is very brave however, and said "I would rather be an 'outcaste' in India and in the Kingdom of Bahá'u'lláh and I am going!" No member of his family knew he had gone – until he was one day out at sea; then they received his letters which he mailed as he boarded the steamer! His brother came the next day to see us and enquired for his address which we gave him. He did not seem much disturbed over his departure but he said "I fear our father will be greatly dis-pleased!" Jesus Christ said "He who forsaketh not father and mother cannot be my disciple!" Dear, good brave Vakil – has surely followed his Master (A.B.) in this respect and may all blessings be his!

From Mar. 10th until the 20th I was busy teaching individuals and talking to many privately – giving no public lecture. On the afternoon of the 20th I rec'd a letter from his Highness the Maharajah of Jhalawar asking me to visit him and to please state the time I could come. I answered by telegram that I would come immediately leaving Bombay Mar. 31st.

After which the next day was spent in getting ready – everything was "hustle and bustle" as we were obliged also to move from the apartment we had been occupying to another place. In some mysterious way I took a very bad cold which added considerably to the confusion as I could scarcely speak aloud. Some dear Parsee women Bahá'ís came and finally things got "packed up" and I was ready to start.

Now thus far I have written my journal backwards and from memory! Really I am going to do better hereafter and try to write up to date!

I am going to record in detail my visit to Jhalawar under the heading of

What constitutes a Prince?

It was His Holiness, 'Abdu'l-Bahá who first mentioned to me in Ramleh, Egypt in July 1913 – His Highness the Maharajah Rana of Jhalawar and as I am now travelling in India, I thought a visit to His state might afford me some new experiences, as well as opportunities to meet with India's most enlightened class, consequently I wrote, stating the source of my information concerning him and expressed a desire to meet him should it please him to grant my request!

My letter brought a courteous reply to the effect that I would be rec'd. with "pleasure" and further stated that His Highness had had the pleasure of meeting 'Abdu'l-Bahá while travelling in England (1911).

Therefore I left Bombay Mar. 31st arriving at Shri Chhatrapur [sic] April 1st at about seven o'clock in the evening.[103] The ride from Baroda had been long and tiresome on account of the dust and heat coupled with the miles and miles of level uninteresting plains parched barren and brown! I was travelling with a Parsee girl companion who was familiar with several of the many languages spoken by the people of India and I found her company invaluable, for otherwise I could not have made myself understood, besides my cold had temporarily robbed me of my voice so had I been able to speak the language I was unable to make myself heard. We were thankful to reach the little railroad station at last, which terminated our journey – and to find a very fine modern automobile awaiting us. Our baggage secured we were soon ensconced inside and flying swiftly along the remarkable smooth hard country roads. There was a new moon giving just enough light to make the shadows weird and ghostly as we sped along through little stretches of leafless trees and underbrush. The stars were shining in myriads and the evening air became cool and balmy, which was most refreshing after the intense heat of the day. Now and then some tall graceful palms would loom up in the distance, wave their branches by the assistance of the breeze and be lost to view. Across the plains we could hear the cry of foxes, and the deep baying of hounds.

The distance from the R.R. Station to Jhalarapatan is some sixteen or eighteen miles; and knowing this I had settled back among the comfortable cushions to thoroughly give myself up to the quiet enjoyment of all the mysteries of an Indian night, – when my little companion in a voice full of consternation suddenly broke out with "Oh Khanum, (Lady) we have [been] riding ever so long without even seeing a house! Do you think these men (chauffeur and footman) are carrying us off to some place from which we will never be able to return?" Now, Mehrie had never travelled; and I suppose the pale moonlight, the mysterious shadows and the quiet whispers of the night, all made their impression upon her too – but her impression was vastly different from mine! I had some little trouble, owing to my hoarseness and the hum of the machine to make her understand that everything was all right and to assure her that we were not being carried off to the wilds!

I do not believe she was quite satisfied however until the lights of Jhalarapatan were discernible in the distance and she was evidently relieved when we were safely deposited in a very comfortable bungalow, one of the Guest houses belonging to His Highness.

One of the servants handed me a letter which proved to be an invitation from His Highness to dine with him that evening at 8:15 – It was already far past the hour but as a carriage was waiting to carry me to the Kathi (summer house occupied by H.H.) I felt I should go and hastily arranging my toilet departed – much to the dubiousness of Mehrie who did not like the idea of [my going] off alone in the night again to some other – perhaps far away place! Arriving – the Private Sect'y of H.H. Dhabhai Shadilal BA LLD was standing on the varandah [sic] to welcome and conduct me to the dining room where I was presented to His Highness and seated at once without further ado or introduction to his other guests!

I was seated next to H.H. with Major Condon on my left who began talking with me immediately as though he had always known me; this surprised me a little for we Americans are apt to find English people a bit "stand-offish". I learned eventually that the Major is Irish and perhaps after all this may have accounted for his geniality!

Anyway I was happy to feel the entire lack of conventionality! Most Americans are unaccustomed to the conventions surrounding Kings and Princes which may or may not be a very good thing – I was greatly pleased to find myself like one of a happy group of friends. But I soon discovered the secret of this to be the remarkable personality of H.H. himself. He is a man of perhaps thirty-five or eight years of age possessing a temperament difficult to describe in as much as he is at once both very dignified and extremely simple; His face is calm and placid, and at the same time very mobile and expressive of a tender sympathy which might well adorn the countenance of a good pure woman; followed immediately by expressions of such forceful courage and unswerving will as might become the character of an ideal man!

His bearing is both majestic and genial while at all times and on all occasions he is most courteously kind to everybody, even his servants whose loyal obedience to him is something to be remarked; as it is entirely free from the spirit of servility, and absolutely characteristic of a spontaneous desire to serve through loving devotion! His lavish hospitality was dispensed on every hand. His guests were provided with such viand and wines as could not fail to satisfy the most epicurean; and with cigars and cigarettes please the most fastidious; though he himself never drinks anything stronger than coffee and has never even tried to smoke in his life!

He is a man of discernment, wide travels and erudition. In all India it would be difficult I think to find a Prince more practically utopian, or more sincerely concerned about the advancement and education of the people over which he rules. His state is by no means the largest one in India but according to its possibilities – it is certainly one of the most progressive! By the charm of his altogether pleasing personality, and the force of patient example, he is slowly but surely overcoming the age old and time worn prejudices and superstitions of his people, replacing them with tolerance, liberality and broad-mindedness – along ideal lines of moral, ethical and scientific education.

He is devoting much time and money to the building of schools and libraries, and has established co-education in his state. When he became the chief of Jhalawar sixteen years ago there were only four schools – now there are fifty, with applications for more. He is very wisely turning most of his attention to the youth – both male and female, fully awakened to the fact, that the future good of his province lies hidden in their hands, and more especially in the hands of the mothers of the coming generations. He is erecting a beautiful new school for girls in Jhalarapatan, which I understand is to be perfectly equipped that they may be taught all practical things of life as well as to become familiar with science and literature!

On the second day of my visit (Apr. 3rd) H.H. asked me if I would like to visit the different places in his state near his abode, and upon signifying a desire to do so, he appointed one of his officers to accompany me the following morning at 8:30. The carriage arrived at 8:15 and as I was ready I did not wait, thinking the officer might meet us outside! We had driven perhaps five miles and were looking over the ruins of an interesting old temple, built perhaps twelve or fifteen centuries ago when a very intelligent looking and extremely well-mannered gentleman came up quite out of breath saying "Pardon me – but I was not late in keeping my appointment, I was at your place and service exactly at the hour set by His Highness and I have followed you on my wheel. I hope my service may be acceptable to you!"

This was my first meeting with Mr. Ratilal M. Antani BA and Magistrate of Jhalawar.

When I saw his card I felt sorry that one whose calling rend[er]s time so very valuable should have been sent to conduct me through bazaars, temples, schools, etc! Upon expressing something of this sort – he very politely but not without a certain note of pride – quietly replied "My highest duty as well as my greatest pleasure is to obey the slightest wish of His Highness – our Maharajah!"

The pleasure was evident in his smiling face, – and the duty, one felt instinctively to be a task of love!–

The four following mornings were devoted to show my companion and myself about. We visited the hospital, a new building where we were most cordially welcomed by Asst. Surgeon Dr. D.K. Marn LM&S and Dr. K.R. Rao an Indian lady physician! One interesting case was that of a woman whose husband in a rage had cut off her nose and upper lips! But the hospital staff had made a new nose and lip for her from the skin of her forehead and sides of her face. As we stood looking at her she suddenly raised her hands and said something to Mr. Antani, the magistrate, which he explained was a curse upon him for having sent her back to her husband when she was before him in court, which had proved so unfortunate a decision for her!

From there we visited the jail, where we were most graciously received by the Warden, Mustafa Hussain Riza who personally conducted us through the entire institution! And a more ideal jail could not be found! I was struck immediately with its spaciousness and cleanliness. Sunshine and fresh air permeating every nook and corner!

The cells were all 10x12 ft, with high ceilings and immaculately clean! The building is so constructed that all the cells open into a court or patio, therefore the inmates can look out upon flowers and green grass.

We were passing among the rug-makers, when one man, spinning cotton – suddenly fell upon his knees before Mr. Antani the magistrate who had sentenced him, begging that he should do something that he might remain in the prison, as his time had expired – saying "I am being taught useful things, I like my work and desire that I be retained here as I have nothing and no place to go when released – let me stay and work – and learn."

I was then told that H.H. is endeavoring to institute a system of education and practical labor among the prisoners so that upon expiration of their terms they go out morally benefitted possessed of some trade or craft wherewith they can earn a livelihood and become useful citizens. H.H. regards all forms of criminology as disease and is therefore introducing methods which will transform punishment into progress, – adversity into advancement and meanness into manliness!

Another interesting incident in connexion with the jail must here be cited. One evening three of four days previous to my departure H.H. turned to me suddenly and said – "I am visiting jail tomorrow morning; I have some questions to put to a prisoner. Would you care to accompany me, or is one visit sufficient?" I accepted the invitation with eagerness and the following morning at 7:30 o'clock His Highness appeared at the door of the Guest House, in his private carriage attended by two footmen and two mounted guards. I was all ready thus no time was lost; the jail is not far from the house we occupied, hence we were soon inside its huge iron doors, being welcomed by the astonished warden, who had no intimation that His Highness was to pay a visit that early in the morning! We were walking towards the prisoners when I noticed that the Maharajah was entirely unarmed – even his walking stick he had left with a footman at the entrance, and unattended save by myself. The warden was following some little distance behind us – while the keepers who had assembled in the courtyard remained in line like soldiers at attention, but unarmed so far as I could see. His Highness walked among the prisoners and talked with them as a kind father might talk to wayward children, listening with kindness and patience to their complaints which were few, and speaking encouraging words which brought the light of hope in their faces. With one prisoner he spoke at length; the man was weeping and evidently most contrite. As I could not understand the language in which he spoke H.H. explained that the prisoner before us had been the leader in a plot to injure and dethrone him. "I feel very sorry for him," he continued, "for his grievance was against me personally, and his crime was committed entirely through ignorance! The administration compels me to punish and keep

234

him here – otherwise" but here he turned quickly away not however before I caught the expression of compassionate regret which had overspread his countenance. Next we went to the printing and book-binding department: On top of one of the presses was an old man sixty-five or eight years of age whose face was seamed and bore marks of suffering. At a word from H.H. he came down and knelt at his feet. The machinery was making so much noise, that his voice could scarcely be heard, thus H.H. ordered him out into the courtyard, where in the friendly shade of one of the buildings he began talking to the man who had again fallen upon his knees, and whom he commanded to arise. All of the prisoners wear about their necks a stout cord from which is suspended a card bearing their names, crime and sentence. This man's sin was dacoity[104] and his sentence was twenty-four years, sixteen of which had elapsed: whether he had been guilty of some other misdemeanors that his sentence was such a long one I do not know. He stood before us then an old man with clasped hands, – quivering lips, drawn features and frightened eyes; broken in heart and spirit, a picture of human suffering and hopeless despair.

His Highness put to him some questions to which he replied in a nervous high keyed voice.

"Why did you do this deed?" said H.H. as he stood holding his card in his hand. "My Lord" replied the man "it was in 1898 that awful year of famine when I committed this offense and there were reasons why I felt I must do so!"

H.H. "Dacoity is a very bad thing! do you feel you have suffered sufficiently now, not to do anything against the law again?"

Prisoner – "Oh my Lord I am an old man now and my days are nearly spent. I desire that the end of my life should be marked with some good actions!"

H.H. "Tell me what do you most desire?"

Prisoner:– "I desire freedom my Lord – that I may not die in jail."

H.H. "<u>Then you are free!</u>" As these words were spoken the poor man stood for a moment as though stunned! Then slowly through the gloom of that twisted pitiful face a light began to dawn! It was the light of hope rekindled in a heart so long despondent that a few seconds were required ere it leaped into flame and transformed his entire being! With a great heart-bursting sob, he threw himself once more in the dust before his Prince and the continuation of his sobs was the only sound which broke the tense silence that had fallen over us!

Never shall I forget the scene!

The Maharajah seemed suddenly like a great tree whose goodly thick-leaved branches were swaying in the heavenly breeze of divine compassion, casting cool shadows of protection over all of us! –

I felt it distinctly! and curiously enough, I also felt a great kinship with the man upon the ground! Suddenly the tears rushed to my eyes and a great cry welled up in my heart that the "Prince of Princes" might one day say to me "You are free! Free from the prison of self! – Arise!" –

"Arise" said His Highness to the man, "Go, and have your chains removed!"

All were so astounded that no one moved, until the warden wonderingly asked "Are his chains to be removed?"

"Yes" he replied "that is what we are waiting for!" I may insert here that this was an unusual proceeding – for prisoners were seldom released save on the birthday of the Maharajah, or as a mark of thanksgiving on the part of H.H. over the safe return from a long journey, or on the recovery from an illness on the part of some member of his the royal family.

Then a man came and cut off the iron bands which had encased his ankles for sixteen years and his chains fell to the ground! Again my heart cried out to the "King of Kings" that the chains of desire and selfishness might likewise be stricken from me, that I could walk free from fetters, as he now walked back to His Highness, smiling in gratitude. He told the man to gather his belongings and come to the palace; – after which we departed! I was informed that evening that the man had been received by His Highness and given new clothes, food, money, re-instated in his caste – (He is a Rajput the same as H.H.) and assigned some labor on a small farm near the palace of the Maharajah!

Surely man most resembles God when he bestows generosity and exercises mercy! I asked H.H. if it were not a source of great joy to be able to do such deeds? "Yes" he replied very simply "and I hope I may never exercise my power for harm to any soul."

236

Would that all people to whom power is given should think likewise; we would have a different kind of a world to live in, very shortly! One very pleasant morning was spent in visiting the High School which I found very well equipped in every way to facilitate the understanding and advancement of the pupils; among whom were some very bright and intelligent minds. Every pupil is given the same opportunity whether he be of high class or low. This is due also to His Highness who regards and is endeavoring to reward capacity – more than caste. After visiting the different class rooms –

The principal, Babu Indrasen BA, by religious faith a Jain; the Second Master, Ram Haram BA, a Brahman; Third Master, Pandit Govardhan Lal BA, a theist; Professor of Sciences Pandit Liladhar Sharma, an Agnostic; Prof. of Oriental languages Mahammad Sadiq, a Musselman. Balmantras S. Busari, Pub. Librarian and Mr. Ratilal Antani, Magistrate, two more Brahmans but of different sects and caste and myself a Christian-Bahá'í all repaired to the Head Master's office, where we sat around his table and discussed Religion from these various standpoints for an hour or more in the most friendly manner imaginable. I found all of these gentlemen not only very intelligent, but extremely broad-minded and liberal! And when we think that half a century ago, such a meeting would have been impossible, we are justified in feeling that the veil of racial prejudices and religious differences, is slowly but surely vanishing; and we can but feel encouraged in our belief that one Great Universal Religion will soon unite human souls – so that the Fatherhood of God, and the Brotherhood of man, will be an evident reality and no longer a mere vision of dreamers and poets!

This little impromptu gathering and its import was talked of in the town, and that evening the Minister and Uncle of His Highness – the Maharajah Balbhadra Singh, called to see me. It was near the dinner hour so we could speak only a short time; but it was long enough for me to recognize in him a sincere spiritual soul, as well as a man of learning. He called again the following morning with several other gentleman and we discussed at length spiritual Teachers and teachings, which terminated with a request that I should meet at his home that afternoon other citizens of Jhalarapatan and speak to them on the subject of "God's Messengers to the World" which included a historical sketch of the Rise and Progress of the Bahá'í Movement. Between seventy-five and a hundred people were present, and all together it was a very pleasant affair, marked by genuine hospitality and kind appreciation. I expected to leave the next day April 8th for Lucknow, to attend and address a religious convention held there from the 10th to the 14th of April. But the following morning my little companion was quite ill, which resulted in my having to cancel my engagement and remain five days more the guest of His Highness in Jhalarapatan. I regretted the cause of my stay but I must confess I was not sorry to be longer detained in the midst of these highly good people. I was made to feel very much at home and more than welcome. His Highness very kindly sent his own private physician Dr. Ramlal to attend my companion, under whose skill and care she soon began to improve. One who did not know to the contrary might have thought her to be his only patient, as he called twice each day and spent much time over his investigation into the Cause of her illness, the correction of which will prove of everlasting benefit to her.

When he pronounced her able to travel, I asked for his bill. He thanked me very graciously and said, "You are the guest of His Highness whose servant I am therefore, there is no bill, as I have only been fulfilling a duty!" And by no means whatsoever, could I induce him to accept any remuneration for his most effective services. Imagine, too, my surprise when the servants who had been sent to care for us in the Guest House also refused to accept "tips" – saying "We are not allowed to accept anything from guests. – His Highness pays us for our services, which we trust you have found competent and satisfactory." One servant who had waited on us at breakfast and lunch came to me the night before our departure and said "Please I would like to ask a favor from you as a remembrance!" "Yes, what is it?" I asked thinking perhaps he had changed his mind regarding the "tip".

"I would like your permission" he replied, "to call my little daughter American Begum (Lady) so that whenever we speak her name it shall serve as a reminder of your visit!" To say the least I was deeply touched!–

Among guests who came after my arrival were the Prince, Princess and young Prince de Broglie [sic] of Paris – old friends of the Maharajah. They had been to India before, travelling extensively throughout the country – tiger-shooting and panther hunting in which they seemed to find much delight. The Princess is a very "good shot" I was told. She declared she found their expeditions into the jungles after "big game" great sport and very exhilarating! Never having fired a gun in my life, or hunted anything other than the various kinds of autumn nuts found in the forests of "little old New York State" I could neither understand nor enter into her enthusiasm. Her son had travelled throughout America, therefore we found much in common to talk about. He is very well read and interested in spiritual subjects – thus we had several interesting conversations.

April 13th was the date set by His Highness for his departure en suite for Kashmir where he had decided to spend the summer months thus Apr. 12th was our farewell dinner and meeting with him and others whom we had come to so know and respect that the thought of saying "Goodbye" was not at all a pleasant one. The dinner table was beautifully decorated in green and white; the shaded candles casting a glow of warm pink over all. After partaking of a sumptuous repast – we repaired to the salon where an entertainment including native dances, music & songs had been provided. The costumes of the dancers were remarkable! Some thirty or forty yards of silk heavily embroidered with gold and silver were gathered into short skirts, reaching half way below the knees; a blouse of thin material also embroidered and cobwebby. Sarees thrown over their heads, falling in graceful folds around the entire figure completed the costumes barring the many bracelets, bangles and rings which adorned their bare arms, legs, fingers and toes!

It was my first experience in listening to native music and songs, all of which impressed me as strange, uncanny and mysteriously sad! It was music without harmony; which called forth peculiar emotions: It reminded me of the desert, and roused within me somewhat "The mood of divine discontent".

Its spell was subtle, but never the less compelling; – it made me yearn for the infinite impossible, and long for the throbbing silence which follows inconsequent exquisite sound!

I leave all descriptions of the terpsichorean art, as executed by the indigenous dancers of India, to those whose powers of portrayal are greater than mine; for I assure you any attempt on my part, in that direction would simply be a confession of my inability as knowing how, either to begin or end it! At a gesture from H.H. the music ceased and after much bowing and saluting, the musicians and dancers noiselessly withdrew –

Almost immediately a servant appeared bearing a silver tray, upon which was a cut glass bottle of exquisitely delicate perfume, and decoration, made from spun gold ribbon woven into a four-sided braid, from which hung a heart-shaped insignia made of padded green silk – embroidered with tiny gold beads and surrounded by a short thick silver fringe. Then began a most beautiful little ceremony of leave-taking. His Highness took the perfume and poured a few drops into the outstretched palm of each guest, after which each head was bowed that he might garland our necks with his decoration and amulet of heartfelt good wishes – "to speed each parting guest" – and this was his silent "goodbye".

———

Next morning Apr 13th, 1914. His Highness left for the North amid the touching farewells of His people and the firing of guns!

We spent the day "packing up" and preparing for the journey back to Bombay. Mehrie was feeling much better and happy over the prospect of soon being "at home" with her family!

Apr 14th 7.30 a.m. the motor came to take us to the station Shri Chhatrapur and the ride of sixteen miles in the early morning was most enjoyable. The thermometer had registered at noon the day previous 101 (degrees) – so we were very glad not to go later as all indications were the heat of the day would be equal to that of yesterday! There was a cool breeze, and the birds were singing joyously as we rode along. We saw numbers of monkeys by the roadside and sitting on stumps of trees looking very wise and solemn like. Many beautiful peacocks too were seen here and there. Their feathers shining so gloriously in the sun – making a strange contrast with the monkeys – their neighbors in the jungle! The jungles of India are wonderful! I feel often that I would love to live in the heart of one for a long time and just quietly observe the inmates therein – snakes and all the living creeping creatures found there, in such vast hordes!

One hears curious tales from those who have penetrated deeply into the jungles: There is a charm about them which "calls" one like the desert! But then, the "voice of silence" is full

240

of a subtle music – all its own – which is inexplicable! Once heard, it can never be forgotten – for it is akin to the soul and reality of man! I do not wonder that such men as Thoreau sought and still seek the wilds! What is there in the world of commercialism for a soul like his to commune with? Man like that who waits for the "great hour" to strike? "To him who waits, the stars are friends – The restless ocean the azure sky – All things in nature, speak and prophecy – To him who waits!"

Apr. 15th
We arrived at eight o'clock this a.m. very tired, hot and dirty. Javanmard had arisen to meet us though he lives far from the Station, while we found Mr. Getsinger still reposing in the arms of Morpheus! Javanmard is one of the Bahá'ís of Bombay and is a very good man. Very kind and self-sacrificing! His entire life is one of service to the Cause and his devotion to 'Abdu'l-Bahá is remarkable! All of the Bahá'ís here have been most kind and thoughtful. They begged 'Abdu'l-Bahá to allow us to be their guests while in Bombay – and they have done everything in their power to make us welcome and comfortable. We are now in an apartment only across the road from Calaba Station and upon my arrival, I find everything – even to an electric fan has been provided for our comfort. May God bless these good faithful souls, who for the sake of His Love, shower such kindness upon these, the least and most unworthy of His Servants! – May all blessings descend upon those who are faithful to the "Center of the Covenant".

———

April 22nd
Really, I have been too busy writing letters to Acca and America to write in this book. This Book is becoming like an "accusing conscience" to me, every time I see it I am reminded of my promise to Mrs. Nourse to write in it, all that happens!

Much has happened which I cannot write and much has happened which is not worth writing and the rest is what is herein recorded! It all seems trivial and worthless to me but I must keep my promise and write something that occurs in this daily routine of letters also from His Highness the Raja of Jhalawar [who] invites me to Kashmir! Upon this earth 'tis said – Kashmir is a bit of heavenly paradise! I haven't any money with which to undertake the long journey of seven days from Bombay; – have written 'Abdu'l-Bahá and shall wait for His decision! Dear me – what a difficulty this money question is! And no one can work even in the Cause of God these days without it. Mrs. Stannard could have accomplished so much more if she had had a little assistance. She has an income and from it she does everything herself but as it is a limited one of course her work is limited accordingly. But I have <u>nothing</u> – no income – yet I am expected to work and travel just the same. Well, I have 'Abdu'l-Bahá, and He is not only income, but <u>banker</u> and <u>bank</u> as well! Whatever He says I will do for He will make it possible!

This going to Kashmir presents a wonderful opportunity for service, as the Maharajah of Jhalawar will be there & has kindly offered to introduce me to H.H. the Amir of Kashmir who is a Hindoo but most of His people are Mohammadans. What a splendid thing to unite the Mohammadans & Hindoos! This is one of the dreams of His Highness of Jhalawar! If they were <u>united</u> India would be theirs in a day, and no foreign power could possibly hold it! But at present they fly at each others throats upon the slightest provocation! This question regarding "Unity of Races" – and Religions – presents very serious aspects in India which the Western mind cannot conceive at all! If the Bahá'ís were awake to the necessity of the same, they would never, especially in America, raise such a question as that now being agitated in Washington, D.C. "The colored question!" – The Washington Bahá'ís have a wonderful opportunity to set an example for the world if they but would! As yet however they are asleep and "Unity of Races" is still to most of them – but <u>three</u> words in the English language – which sound well in public speeches! "Selfishness" of course and wanting "to have my way" – is at the bottom of the condition in Washington otherwise the teachings and commands (Read I Corinthians III – 3. <u>That's the reason why</u>![105]) of 'Abdu'l-Bahá on <u>that</u> <u>point</u> would have been effective – long ago! It is a case where fools must learn by experience I suppose! That <u>expensive</u> school which seems always to be full!

April 25th
Rec'd a letter from Poona inviting me to speak there May 7th before the Summer Conference held yearly in that city. My subject is "The Unity of Religions."

I like this subject for it enables me to approach the Bahá'í Movement from so many standpoints that when I really come to the point I have so many defenses thrown up all around that the Bahá'í position is impregnable! Indisputable – and undeniable! I have secured a very good copy of the Gospel of Buddha (Paul Carus' translation) and am deeply interested in making a thorough study of the same!

Buddha had a "Peter" in the disciple of Shariputra who tried to walk on the water and who fell in – for lack of faith – same as did Peter who started to go to Jesus. Buddha said to Shariputra "Great is thy faith, but take heed that it be well-grounded!" Buddha also revealed the ineffable name "Amitabha" meaning endowed with boundless light from Amita – infinite, immeasurable – and Abha, ray of Light, Splendor Glorious; bliss of Illumination! The invocation of the all-saving name "Amitabha Buddha" is still a favorite tenet in the Lotus or Pure Land of Buddhism. That Holy Blessed One said in answer to Ananda (His St. John) who asked "Who shall teach us when thou art gone?" "I am not the first Buddha who came upon earth, nor shall I be the last. In due time another Buddha will arise in the world, a Holy One, a supremely enlightened One, endowed with wisdom in conduct, auspicious, knowing the Universe, an incomparable leader of men, a Master of Angels and Mortals. He will reveal to you the same eternal truth which I have taught you. He will preach His religion, glorious in its origin, glorious at the climax and glorious at the goal, in the Spirit and in the letter. He will proclaim a religious life, wholly perfect and pure; such as I now proclaim. His disciples will number many thousands while mine numbered many hundreds!"

Ananda then asks; "How shall we know Him?" And the Blessed One said: "He will be known as Maitreya which means "full of kindness": "or He whose name is Kindness!" – Were it not for the thousands of disciples we might say such a One was Jesus! The Buddhists are looking for Him now to come. And Mrs. Besant says He has come, and is Chrisna Murta [sic; see note 97] – whom she is educating at Oxford England! We cannot see how a "Supremely enlightened One" would or could be in need of Oxford or any other institution of learning! If He is in need of the education of men How then can He be the Educator of man? No. The Lord Maitreya promised by Buddha will be inspired with all knowledge by God; and will be in no need of any university training. For He will come to train and instruct not to be trained and instructed! How very similar are the teachings of Jesus Christ to those of Buddha who came 600 years before Him! This only goes to prove that Truth is eternal and changeless! I love Buddha! And I love Jesus; and in the world of immeasurable Light I believe they love each other – I feel it!

May lst. 1914
Am preparing to go to Poona. It is not a long journey from Bombay therefore my preparations will take little time – besides I am only to stay a few days. Doulet – Mehrie's sister goes with me this time as Mehrie is not yet well! I have been reading more of the Gospel of Buddha and find the following on the subject of "Oneness" – "The eternal verities which dominate the cosmic order are spiritual; and spirit develops through organisms and comprehension. Originally, all things were made from one essence; yet all things are different according to the forms which they assume (or organize & through which they manifest) under different circumstances and states. As they are formed so they act, and as they act so they are! It is as though a Potter made different vessels out of the same clay. Some contain sugar, some rice, some milk, some water, some curds and whey, and others still are vessels of impurity! There is no diversity in the clay used. The diversity of the pots is only due to the molding hands of the Potter who shapes them for the various uses circumstances may require! All things originated from one essence (substance) and they are developing according to one law. (evolution) As all are from one substance, and there is but one law – hence, there is but one truth not two or three!"

"Oneness in its true significance, means that God alone should be realized as the One Power which animates and dominates all things, which are but manifestations of Its energy!" Bahá'u'lláh. How similar are these teachings! Though Buddha lived 2367 years before Bahá'u'lláh! But it proves that "Truth is one!"

May 6th
Poona! I was so surprised to find hills and mts. a short distance out of Bombay! And oh how refreshing the air! It was like drink-

ing champagne after the close moist atmosphere of Bombay! The mts. are interesting though not very high! It was 7 p.m. when we arrived, and were met at the station by Sohrab, Kai Khusroe's son who at present is the proprietor of the Rajmahal Hotel! And Judge Khendawalla who will preside at my lecture tomorrow evening. I am told the lecture will be held out in the open compound and will be mostly composed of students. Every year at this time Poona has a course of lectures. Spent a very pleasant evening with the family of Kai Khusroe whose wife is a sister of the Kai Khusroe who sacrificed his life for Sidney Sprague.[106] It was a joy to meet this whole family! They are very well educated and interesting especially Bebe and Mehraban! I slept so well for it is several degrees cooler than Bombay and such a clear atmosphere. I am writing this before retiring for I fell asleep in my chair while the others were talking and chanting and they let me sleep on until nearly midnight! I am glad to be here and wish Edward had come too; he would enjoy the change – but he dislikes these rail-way journeys in India! Well, they are not very comfortable and not at all clean! One encounters many minute creatures in the cushions whose acquaintance are not at all desirable!

May 7th. 8 a.m.
A visitor so early in the morning? Yes, Mr. Chiplunker from Bombay who made all the arrangements for the lecture tonight. I could have slept longer but it was not to be as Bebe appeared directly with a tray containing coffee which served to dispel the charms of Morpheus and I was soon dressed and down to see my caller whom I had met many times in Bombay and who expects soon to go to America to finish his studies along physocological [sic] lines. He is very earnest and thinks "to solve the problem" there – but the problem he is working on has the "answer" only in the teachings of Bahá'u'lláh. This he must learn from experience! He is young, so there may be time! But what a pity he must waste so much time to no avail. I have told him this – but he is one of those who must "see for himself" admitting the while that Bahá'u'lláh is great and glorious – only there may be a "short-cut". How humanity ever tried "to climb up some other way!" The sun is very hot, and it is real tropical weather – but then I am in India, what else could there be!

245

P.M. 5 o'clock – Looks very much like rain, and I am to speak at 6.30! I had a remarkable dream last night in which I found myself in the open country in a very large house with no idea to whom it belonged or how I got there! Going from a spacious veranda into an immense room I saw a very venerable man of great dignity – dressed in the uniform of a General – though I was unfamiliar with the dress – (i.e. to what nation it belonged). His face though very grave was extremely kind. I begged pardon for intruding but asked where I was, to whom the house belonged, and how I came to be there? To which he smiled and said,

"It is my house and you are simply here with me; it is perfectly all right and you need not be troubled I will see that you are comfortable!"

"But" I replied "How did I get here?" Again he smiled and answered, "You are here with me."

"Am I a prisoner?" I asked

"Oh no" he answered "you are free!" Then I felt I must not take up his time, as he seemed to have much to do – so I went back to the veranda – which was very high from the ground. I found a soldier pacing back and forth, carrying a rifle. Going to the railing I leaned over and looked down to find that the distance to the ground was at least two stories – and yet it seemed like the entrance to the house. As I raised my eyes from the ground I saw coming at quite a distance a soldier who was walking slowly, with seeming difficulty – waving now and then above his head a white flag! The soldier pacing back and forth also saw him and raised his rifle! "Stop" I called out sharply – "don't shoot – he carries a white flag! He is coming to ask for something!"

"Yes," he answered "You are right," and then we stood side by side watching him, and saw at the same time many more soldiers coming on behind him – but at quite a distance. They all seemed very weary and advanced slowly, almost painfully for they wavered and halted many times! When he had advanced within "hailing" distance I said to the soldier, "Ask him what he wants?"

"You ask him," he answered; with that I leaned over the rail of the balcony and putting my hands to my mouth shouted "What do you want?"

246

"We want bread," came the reply, "We are starving!" These words affected me very deeply and turning to the soldier I said "Bring me some bread that I may feed them!"

"I cannot" he said "without permission from the general!"

"Go bring me the bread," I commanded. "I will be responsible to the general." As He turned to go for the bread – the soldier carrying the white flag cried out "Either give us bread or in mercy shoot us all – for we are too weak to fight – we cannot engage in battle in this condition – for we are dying from hunger!" The soldier returned with a few loaves of bread which I threw down to them and they fell upon them like hungry wolves, making the most pitiful noises. I was heartbroken at the sight and realization of their sufferings! Then without leave or license I rushed into the large room where I had found the general to see him seated at a table surrounded by officers, all of whom <u>directed</u> by him, were studying and contemplating maps which were spread out before them. I was instantly aware that they were planning some kind of an attack. Thus without hesitation I went up to the general's side and said, "Oh please do not plan for a battle for they are all dying from starvation, they have sent an envoy who is outside with some others and they beg either to be mercifully killed or given bread!" By this time I was weeping, but continued to plead for them; the general was gravely listening and most of the officers had risen to their feet. Then the general arose and turning to me said "Don't be so agitated – I am just – have no fear! Be calm! Do not weep!" Then he took me in his arms as though I were a child and still went on comforting me.

"But", I pleaded, "Do come & see them!" and taking his hand I started for the door – he came with me and together we went to the side of the veranda and looked down upon a vast multitude of soldiers who had by this time assembled below! The expression of infinite pity of tender compassion which overspread his countenance as he saw them in their weakness, wretchedness and helplessness – is indescribable! He stood very still and just gazed down upon them with the glance of Divine Love! All of the officers had followed us and were looking on also – a great silence fell over everything! Everyone seemed to be alive only with feeling – which was too deep and painful for words. Then the general suddenly leaned forward – and shouted with all the force of his powerful being – "You shall have bread! You shall have bread!" The relief which instantly came to me was so great that I awoke – to find it was just dawn and out in the garden somewhere, a bird began to sing ever so sweetly its morning matin!

8 P.M. It rained in torrents! The meeting place for the lecture was a large compound which accommodates at least two thousand people. The Chairman had made the introduction speech, making the vast audience somewhat acquainted with "Mrs. Getsinger of America" – and her mission in India when I arose to speak. Perhaps twenty minutes had passed and I was just "warming up" when the first great drops began to fall – I continued a bit dampened but not cooled – (at least in ardor) when the clouds just seemed to open and <u>pour</u> <u>out</u> their contents! In a moment everybody was wet through. Umbrellas went up – and I <u>went</u> <u>on</u> until the chairman arose; and after whispering to me, "Will you stay and speak in a hall tomorrow night?" to which I said "with pleasure" – He announced that I would continue & finish my address the next evening in the Brahmo Somaj Hall – and dismissed the crowd!

We were laughing like a crowd of happy children in the first rain of the season, the coming of which was hailed with delight for its appearance insures full harvests and dispels fears of famine! Several people said, "Your coming has blessed us with the rain – and we are thankful!" Everywhere half clothed men and naked children stood in the streets revelling in the downpour! I didn't dislike it myself and I was drenched! The earth and trees just drank it up – and then emitted the fragrance of gratitude! I was invited to take dinner with Mrs. Sarabjee – the converted Christian Parsee – for whom Helen Gould built a large and beautiful school in Poona over which Mrs. S. presides as Principal. She bundled me into her carriage and just carried me off wet clothes & all, to her house where I was soon made very comfortable! It continued to rain for an hour or more, and then the clouds all scattered leaving the sky blue & clear, studded with brilliant stars – and a half moon. We had an excellent dinner and talked on Bahá'ísm until 11.30 when Mehraban, son of Kai Kusroe, came for me and I returned to the Hotel, feeling I had had a most enjoyable evening – with a most pleasant and charmingly interesting lady. She is such a good Christian, that in reality she is a Bahá'í! Her whole life has been a sacrifice for others! –

May 8th 1914
It has been delightfully cool all night and everything is clean & fresh after the rain! How one appreciates & realizes the workings of nature to be the blessings of God in a country like this. It is very touching to see these simple people raising their clasped hands in thanks for the downpour of last evening – which seems to have infused new life into everybody and everything. The birds are singing new and glorious songs, green things have sprung up during the night and the trees seem to be spreading out their branches differently this morning just to silently express their gratitude!

How good and perfect is God, and all of His actions! "Only man is vile!"

"All things of the world arise through <u>man</u> and are manifest in him, through whom they find life and development; but man is dependent for his (spiritual) existence upon the Sun of the Word of God!" says Bahá'u'lláh. Oh, if man could only <u>realize</u> this and become awake to his great responsibility he surely would cease to be "vile"! It is ignorance which makes men beasts – yea, lower than the brute creations! What a wonderful being God has made man – that "through <u>him</u>" everything below him, is to find life, and development; and yet the majority of human beings are ignorant of this mighty and divine birthright! Man has no excuse to offer either for <u>The</u> "<u>Word</u>" upon which he is dependent for existence has ever been made manifest by God – according to man's capacity to receive and understand it! God never tries to reap where He has not sown! And He never requires more than He, Himself has given!

10 o'clock P.M.
My audience in the hall tonight was as large as the one dispersed by the rain last night, and they seemed very appreciative. I spoke for one hour and fifteen minutes – after which the chairman spoke for twenty minutes most beautifully – fairly eulogizing Bahá'u'lláh and 'Abdu'l-Bahá with whose lives and teachings he was very thoroughly acquainted. He was a Parsee – but now a Theosophist unhampered by narrow mindedness and therefore

an earnest and sincere seeker after Truth. His remarks were a glad surprise for all Bahá'ís present and a very fitting climax for my "very ardent and zealous attempt" to show forth the "Unity of Religions". One gentleman came up to me – and after shaking my hand very warmly – and thanking me for my address – begged for some literature on the subject. I had none! But promised to send him some from Bombay! "Oh I am leaving tonight for Zanzibar" he said. "Give me your address in that place and I will send it there!" I replied. He was very grateful and when I refused any money for the same he said "If you keep up such talks "backed up" by free literature – your Cause is sure to spread – I hope to be able to interest the people of Zanzibar in it – when I know more myself." And thus, the Glad Tidings of the "Kingdom having Come" are being carried everywhere: even to the remote places of the Earth – and the islands of the Sea!

The need of Bahá'í literature of the <u>right</u> order is very necessary, and we have nothing. Mrs. Stannard is writing as much as she can but India is so vast that her excellent articles are like a drop of rain in a great parched desert! I am going back to Bombay tomorrow for we have heard that Vakil and Seyyed Mustafa are returning the 10th just two months exactly since they left for the Holy Land, and I am very anxious to hear their news and see them after their visit to the Beloved.

copy of a letter dated July 17th, 1914 from Dr. K.W. Jokhi

Dear Mrs. Getsinger,
Many thanks for your kindly remembering and sending me literature on the Bahá'í Movement.

I was on a tour so could not write earlier. I read the books carefully and am glad to say that one day the religion of the civilized world will be the religion of 'Abdu'l-Bahá. The principles, as well as the high ideals of unity and brotherhood which are imbibed from the pages of these pamphlets, are at present like a dream to the majority. I expect the Golden Day in the very near future when these ideals will be reality.

The success of this cause depends on our joint efforts. I shall be glad if you will kindly send some more literature which may further enlighten my soul. Wish to hear from you often.

Hoping for you, sound health and good cheer which will enable you to work more in the Bahá'í Movement

Yours brotherly –

Dr. K.W. Jokhi

This letter has been rec'd and I send copy to complete the story and outcome of my visit to Poona

May 9th

This morning I have had a very remarkable visit with an ex-judge in Poona who attended my lecture and became greatly interested in the Bahá'í Movement! He is very desirous of two things – first that I should return to Poona and deliver a lecture on "The World's Great Teachers" – or "The Great World-Teachers" whichever title I like best – (and I prefer the latter) and second that I allow him to paint my picture!

I am very willing to grant the first request but the second – never! My picture has been painted by Juliet and that is quite sufficient. What will anyone care for my picture – when all the world will soon be seeking a glimpse of the features of the Beautiful Beloved One that Heavenly Face of 'Abdu'l-Bahá! (May all the faces be its sacrifice!)

I wish I could leave a painting of myself as a personal remembrance executed on the canvas of "good deeds" by the brush of "ideal thoughts" made visible in the many colored oils of "sacrifice" and "servitude" in the Pathway of the Beloved One! Such a picture would be worthy of hanging in the gallery of the Memory of the "Friends of God"!

I discussed religions with the above named gentleman for some time. And although a Hindoo and believer in "caste" he was very quick to see the points to be gained from a universal religion and agreed that from no other standpoint could universal peace be possible on this Earth! But if people would only accept that which they see and do that which they know! The difficulty lies not in being unable to make people understand – it comes from not being able to inspire them to arise and do! To act! to live!! To be!!!

The educated class of India are very intellectual and very quick to mentally grasp anything! and when they have done so, the majority of them seem to think that they have reached the goal! When it comes to <u>practice</u> – they still cling with great tenacity to their own religious tenets and beliefs which they acknowledge themselves to be corrupt and full of foolish superstitions. It requires patience and a perseverance that is heavenly – to make <u>any</u> spiritual headway – especially among the Hindoos! The Vedantists and Brahmins are much more prepared and ready, while the Mohammadans really manifest spiritual capacity.

3 P.M.

It is nearly train-time and just now one of the Bahá'ís came with a basket of mangos, figs and grapes, asking that I accept them on behalf of Mr. Getsinger with best wishes etc. that they (the Bahá'ís) had hoped to see him also in Poona but were disappointed! I told them if the Tree of their Disappointment brought forth such excellent fruits he would be glad to disappoint them again I was sure! – They all went to the train & waited until it "pulled out" and then stood waving their kind "Goodbyes"!

May 10th (Sunday) Bombay

The ship has arrived bringing our good brothers Vakil and Sey'd Mustafa again safely back to the shores of their "Motherland" – India – the land of mystery and simplicity! How glad are we to welcome them! How their faces shine with the Light of the Love of the Beloved One – whose Glorious Presence they have but lately left. His Song is on their lips – His Light is in their eyes – His joy fills their hearts, and His Love radiates from their entire beings making us, oh so glad! Sey'd Mustafa brings me a blessed tablet which says "Be thou assured and tranquil! Do not worry over anything whatsoever. The divine mercies of Bahá'u-'lláh are vouchsafed thee and His Bounty in perfect confirmation will reach thee and the victory of the Kingdom is guaranteed thee! Be thou therefore assured and tranquil!" – These words are shafts of scintillating light emanating from the Orb of Divine Effulgence (The Center of the Covenant) and have brought such courage and hope! These blessed words were revealed in Haifa April 19th, 1914, and reach me May 10th! which makes it forever a memorable day! I shall now just look forward with patient expectation to the arrival of these confirmations which alone will enable me to do any work in the Great Vineyard of God! Were all the money in the world at my disposal I could do nothing without the assistance of these promised confirmations! So I am anticipating I am expecting I am praying I am <u>waiting</u> for the "assured" bestowal! "And when in silent awe we wait – and word and sign forbear; The hinges of the Golden Gate – Swing noiseless to our prayer." Thus shall I <u>pray</u> and <u>wait</u>!

———

What a wonderful change do we perceive in Vakil. He went from us a "child" and has returned in the full stature of a "<u>man</u>". Even his voice is changed. It is vibrant with the music of the spirit! Which proves that his ears caught the divine note when in the Presence of the "Great Organ" and his whole being has been attuned thereto! – Blessed is he! <u>How</u> blessed is he!!

When he left he only knew a few words of Persian – he returns speaking it fluently, and beautifully! He says he did not study he only spoke it – whatever he knew & and it just naturally came as a bird might fly and alight on the limb of a tree – so the words flew and alighted in his mind! Again – <u>blessed</u> is he! For this is <u>only</u> another manifestation of those <u>silent</u> <u>miracles</u> which are so often wrought in the Holy Presence of "The Mystery of God"!

One more thing regarding Vakil – He is a <u>soul</u>, now clad in the garments of a pure simplicity whose head is adorned with the crown of humility!

May 12th, 1914
A letter from Edith Sanderson! What an "age" since I rec'd a letter from her! And during that "age" how many changes have taken place! Her dear Mother – who was one of my best friends – has gone on the "long journey"! But in memory is she ever-present! Those who knew her well will never forget her! How vividly comes before my mind now – the many times she so kindly entertained me in her lovely home in Paris, #46 Avenue de Malakoff! Memory holds up the winsome picture of her dignified and pleasing personality as she presided at the head of her well-appointed dinner table – dispensing cordial hospital-ity with a grace which characterizes the "Grande dame" only; and she was <u>that</u> and to the "manor born"! Also – as she sat in a large chair in the softly lighted Library after dinner; the graceful folds

of her black silk gown dimly outlining her still beautiful figure, and off-setting the snow white hair – glistening like a silver crown on a moonlight night, above her lofty brow, and again in her own room reclining upon her "chaise-longue" surrounded by her favorite books and pictures, where we discussed the story that has many beginnings but no ending! Sincerity was one her strongest characteristics and therefore it was a joy to talk with her. And too she was very faithful to her friends. I shall never forget how she helped me once when all others were disagreeing with me. She turned suddenly toward me and said <u>very</u> quietly almost under her breath "Whatever you do – I shall always believe that your intentions are ever to do right!" She possessed keen insight and she seldom passed any judgements! She was broad minded, liberal and tenderly sympathetic without outward show of emotion. She was one to whom her friends could turn in time of trouble and feel sure of "finding her there"!

She didn't accept the Bahá'í Movement fully until she met 'Abdu'l-Bahá and His Great Surrender called forth <u>her</u> <u>surrender</u> which came spontaneously, sincerely, first mentally and then spiritually – which was so characteristic of her! The Magic of His Words captured first her mind and then the potency of their divine power stormed and captured the citadel of her heart and at last she too understood and loved Him! Now, the artistic home is broken up – and Edith is alone almost in the world. From Haifa she writes "Why be sad? When we detach ourselves from ourselves, the sadness that makes the heart so heavy will depart! There is another kind of sadness which is good to have; it puts us in deep sympathy with those who suffer and at the same time sets us free!" One who has suffered less than Edith Sanderson could never think and write such sentiments. They need no comment for they are the utterance of a soul that has gained <u>knowledge</u> by experience! Then she goes on "Here I am again in beautiful Haifa; – it is truly the Land of Peace!" With never a word of her great loss – although she knows how I loved her Mother and probably for <u>that</u> <u>very</u> <u>reason</u> refrains from mention of her name! Dear Edith may the peace of the "Land of Peace" ever be yours, also that <u>greater</u> <u>peace</u> which caused "beautiful Haifa" to be the "Land of Peace" past the understanding of all men!

May 15th, 1914

I am waiting very anxiously to know what I am to do about going to Kashmir as I have written about the same to the Master and He has cabled me to "go" but I have no means with which to make the journey. I am waiting for money to come from Ahmad Yazdi who sends 10 (pounds) per month from the fund he has on deposit supplied by dear Mrs. Goodall to the Beloved Master for our journey and expenses in India. It is now May and I have not yet rec'd the April Allowance! This makes everything very difficult for I cannot avail myself of the opportunities offered to spread the Cause – for in India like every other place the railroads will not carry passengers free of charge, and as by rail the journey from Bombay to Kashmir is eight days (or rather five days by rail and three days by "Longa") it is quite impossible for me to "walk". Well, I must <u>wait</u> that is all!

Mr. Getsinger has given three lectures before the Theosophical Society on his own theory of creation and evolution, at the conclusion of his talks, the President of the Society said, "His theories do not differ in the main from those taught by Mme Blavatski in the "secret doctrine", a book written by her many years ago. Therefore while all the "learned lecturer" had said was very interesting it was not new to the members of the Theosophical Society!" About ten days after his last talk I was invited to deliver a lecture on any subject I might choose! So I took the subject of "Evolution Through Involution" and then gave 'Abdu'l-Bahá's wonderful talk verbatim on that subject with the chart to illustrate it – and which is surely <u>entirely</u> <u>original</u>. But at the conclusion thereof the same gentleman said – "We are very grateful for this wonderful lesson furnished by the Great Teacher 'Abdu'l-Bahá; but in substance we have all that in our own Theosophical literature which has been contributed by our own President Mrs. Besant and while we are glad to hear the view points of others we feel no need of adopting them!" And so they go on living by their imaginations and superstitions so steeped in the same that they are not even able to distinguish the difference between Light and darkness! – Perhaps, when Mrs. Besant brings forth their "Lord Maitreya" their eyes may be opened; and I am sure they will have a rude awakening! At the present time Theory and Truth are the same to them. They put both in the same category and are "smugly" content with what they have!

255

May 20th

Still waiting to be able to go to Kashmir. A very beautiful letter came from H.H. of Jhalawar who is expecting me to come and has taken great pains to write me all about the journey: at just what places I must stop and change – the things necessary & &. What a pity that I cannot start! Still there is in my inability to do so a wonderful lesson to be learned and I must learn it – I want to go – 'Abdu'l-Bahá has cabled "Go Kashmir" and yet I cannot go! The believers here have offered to pay my expenses, but 'Abdu'l-Bahá's instructions when I left Port Said were these: "When you want to take a journey if the believers offer to buy your ticket – you must say "no, I will get it myself with my own money! I have money &" – So I have – but it is in Port Said and therefore quite useless when it comes to buying a ticket in Bombay! But, at least I am privileged to prove to them – that all the women who come to India from America are not like two with whom they have had some previous experiences; and who not only allowed them to pay their travelling expenses but took all the money they could get, by one pretext and another besides. So my having to wait is not in vain, after all! No matter, if I am inconvenienced – I hope they will have a little better opinion of American women thereby, and in time forget all about the others, who acted in such a way as to make us all feel heartily ashamed! "One sows and another reaps" declared St. Paul. I must confess the reaping of their sowing has come at a most inauspicious time – but if I can only "gather it" in such a manner as to make another similar sowing impossible, I shall be both repaid and extremely pleased!

We are reading now the marvellous words spoken by 'Abdu'l-Bahá in praise of Mirza Abul Fazle [Mírzá Abu'l-Faḍl].[107] How blessed is he to have lived and died in the days of The Covenant! But to have lived as he lived that his death becomes the occasion for such remarks, such eulogy on the part of the Beloved One of the Universe – is that which causes us to wonder! We all knew and loved him; and the American Bahá'ís are especially indebted to him for laying the first solid foundation of the Cause of Bahá'u'lláh in America – but none of us knew him as he was to be known now (or then) none of us loved him as he deserved to be loved – because none of us realized that an "Angel of Heaven" had come to dwell in our midst. It is only since he has winged his flight to his own native abode that our eyes have been opened by the magic of 'Abdu'l-Bahá's words in his behalf and lo! we behold <u>what</u> manner of man was he! Alas! Mankind are so! They cannot appreciate the beauty – until the rose has ceased to bloom. They cannot miss the music until the sweet voiced bird has flown! But there was <u>one</u> (and that one still is) who knew, loved, and appreciated him <u>then</u> as now – who was then – and ever will be – his best Friend! And through the words of his best Friend – we all know him and love and appreciate him as we should and will ever continue to do – throughout all the worlds of the worlds! For the words of his <u>Friend</u> are immortal and day by day their full significance will more forcibly dawn upon us! – Oh to be able – to live – to do, to act, to be – and to die – as he, Mirza Abul Fazle did! But alas, alas – such power is granted to but very few – and those few are heavenly souls – "the angels of God!" On one fact we can all rejoice – we have the opportunity of making his best Friend <u>our</u> Friend – and this is no small thing! So let us try at least to follow in His footsteps to emulate his noble example, to walk in his lonely pathway of severance through this dim country of the world, imbibing the full perfections of his lofty character – and who knows, we too, may someday arrive at the supreme goal – <u>The Feet of His Friend!</u>

May 30th
Today in America they are decorating the graves of the soldiers and recounting their many deeds of valor upon the battle fields where they shed their blood for a <u>word</u> "patriotism" and for their flag – the stars & stripes – "the flower-flag of the Nations."

So it was once – "the flower flag" among all the flags but that was long ago when the country was new – and men were fighting for principle for the right to worship God – <u>who</u> in those days they really loved – and upon whom they called in their helpless-ness & distress – until He heard and answered them – and delivered them from the hands of their oppressors – But today the "Flower Flag of the Nations" is that Snow White Flag – devoid of all stripes and stars – which 'Abdu'l-Bahá has unfurled and put into the hands of His Standard Bearers to carry and wave throughout the countries of Earth – which under its shelter-ing folds will one day become the "United Kingdoms of <u>God's</u> Country", the world. 'Abdu'l-Bahá's soldiers are marching

257

throughout the length and breath of all the lands today raising their voices in proclaiming the Kingdom of Peace and Righteousness as <u>having</u> <u>come</u>; and they are fighting and waging warfare (the warfare of love; of bloodless battle) to plant its fair banner on every soil and to unfurl its shining folds beneath the blue skies of every clime! May God help us <u>today</u> as we cry out in our distress. And may He hear and deliver us from the hands of the oppressors; the hands of ignorance which are ever raised in violence, hatred and bloodshed against the soldiers of peace, love and everlasting life! Many of 'Abdu'l-Bahá's soldiers also sleep in their graves today but there are none to decorate them, with flowers, save those, who – like them are willing to lay down life and sleep beside <u>them</u> for the sake of that wondrous Word of God – which shall soon cause all warfare to cease and be no more! – which shall change carnage into concord, battle into bliss and death into life, strewing all the graves of all soldiers with the blue forget-me-nots of His undying Love, and transforming the whole earth into the Paradise of God! That day is to come! The dawn of its fair morning is already crimsoning the sky! The Nightingale of Reality from the Rose Garden of Knowledge is now singing its marvellous matin which heralds its approach! Soon the dark night will flee before the piercing rays of its golden rising Sun and lo! <u>The</u> <u>Day of</u> <u>God!</u> –

June 5th

"Red rosy June"– Once more in the grand march of time, you have brought us your flowers! Flowers of Remembrance; of sweet memories of other rosy Junes which came and went all too swiftly – all too soon! And so too you will go! But while you are here let us catch your hands and dance with you along the Highway of life – until we must relinquish you for another partner who shall come to claim his <u>waltz</u> – in the ballroom of Time! – But while you are here "let us dance and keep step with the stars" while we grasp at the fluttering garments of joy and try in our heart to know all Reality! The Reality of one of your roses – for instance which today are so beautiful and tomorrow are withered and gone! On Christmas Eve 1911 I was in California the Land of Sunshine & Roses! which bloom not in <u>June</u> but the whole year round! – A rap upon my door! A messenger boy bringing a large box of roses with no name simply the following "Messengers to

Lua" – But Messengers from whom? And <u>what</u> are the Messages? I thought, puzzled & wondered a good deal and finally just said "It is somebody's unique way of remembering me at Christmas!" But the other day I was reading in *Sabhana*, Tagore's[108] wonderful Book on "The realization of Life" the following –

"A flower has not only its function in nature, but has another great function to exercise the mind of man. And, what is this function? In nature its work is that of a servant who has to make his appearance at appointed times, but in the heart of man it comes like <u>a messenger from the King</u>! <u>Such</u> a Messenger is a flower from our Great Lover! Surrounded with the pomp and pageantry of worldliness, we still live in exile, while the insolent spirit of worldly prosperity tempts us with allurements and claims us for its bride. In the meantime a <u>flower</u> comes across with a message from the other shore and whispers in our ears 'I am come. He has sent me. I am a Messenger of the beautiful, the One whose soul is the bliss of love.' This island of isolation has been bridged over by Him, and he has not forgotten thee, and will rescue thee even now. He will draw thee unto Him and make thee His own. This illusion will not hold thee in thraldom forever." <u>Also</u> Flowers bring "love-letters to the heart, written in many coloured inks!" Ah, on that Christmas Eve could I have but read their messages aright – what a different day would the morrow have been? But thank God, their messages, though at the time not understood were fulfilled. For the "Great Lover" 'Abdu'l-Bahá did draw me across continents and seas – unto Himself again! After long months of weary waiting, loneliness and separation He sent a <u>cablegram</u> this time – which called me once more to His Holy Presence. And now this June time finds me far away from Him again, in India – still yearning to be near! But I have learned by being far, that nearness is of the Spirit! I now understand the <u>ways</u> of the Great Lover better and I hope I shall never again be unable to read His Message aright or fail to recognize His Messengers. About separation Tagore also writes: –

"When the singer has his inspiration he makes himself into two; he has within himself – his other self as the <u>hearer</u> and the outside audience is merely an extension of this other self of his. The lover seeks his own other self in his beloved. It is <u>his joy</u> that creates a separation, in order to realize through obstacles an-

259

other union!" So yet again may I attain His Meeting! The very difficulties and obstacles which assail me in separation are also Messengers from Him bringing me the joyous Messages of His Love and bidding me "wait and long and trust and yearn – and love and to <u>him</u> <u>be</u> <u>true</u> for the Morning of Meeting shall once more dawn and the night of separation will be forgotten in the blissful joy of divine union when soul shall respond to soul and spirit shall embrace spirit in a delirious intoxication of <u>meeting</u> in which parting can claim no portion and in which separation hath no share!" But when? and where? His Messengers of "parting" and "separation", now my comforters, whisper "When your longing reaches the full measure of His capacity for joy – <u>then</u> will He draw thee to Himself again! When you have walked upon the Highway of loneliness until you have reached the Garden of Severance <u>there</u> wilt thou find Him waiting with arms out-stretched to welcome thee."

As if to confirm the above written pages – a large bouquet of flowers has just been brought to me! Flowers of various kinds and colors – a symbol of beauty for each <u>messenger</u>. The Rose is the Messenger of the King! The snow-white camellia is the Messenger of Parting. The purple Flowers (which I have never seen before) the Messenger of Separation and the whole bouquet is a love-letter for my heart from the Greatest of Lovers! and the various messages have become the words of a wondrous song which my soul sings to the music of my heart beats as I dance with June! "I shall <u>meet</u> Him. I shall meet Him!" That Lover of mine – <u>again</u> "I shall <u>meet</u> him!"

June 6th

A telegram announces the coming of Hashmatu'llah, one of the Indian believers who is coming from Haifa. This young man has been attending college in England and was in London with Mirza Ali Akbar! He will arrive Friday the 12th. I wonder what news he will bring from the Beloved One! Surely he will be another Messenger!

June 11th

We were on the porch watching the approach of a storm when our brother Vakil suddenly appeared at our gate! How glad are we to see him – how welcome is he. Hashmat'ullah and he were school mates thus he has come from Surat to meet him and is going to the steamer early in the morning!

June 12th, 1914

Hashmatu'llah and Vakil have come bringing their glad "Good-mornings" and "Allaho'Abhas" and best of all Hashmatu'llah brings the "good news" of 'Abdu'l-Bahá's splendid health! When He is well all the world is well! Therefore are we all happy. He tells us also of the progress of the Cause in London; the splendid work done there by Mirza Ali Akbar, who is now in Haifa enjoying the "Well done! Good and faithful servant" vouchsafed him by the Beloved who never overlooks or fails to reward the services of His trusted ones! Mirza Ali Akbar has made an extensive search into all the Writings of Suhbi'Ezel [Ṣubḥ-i-Azal] in the British Museum – whose Cause Prof. E.G. Browne more or less espouses! Now when his treatise on the subject is complete we shall be able to compare first hand his words with those of Bahá'u'lláh and thus prove to every body how futile were his thoughts and how foolish his claims. In reading Browne's own words describing his meeting with both S.E.[109] and Bahá'u'lláh we are struck with the remarkable difference which strongly characterizes those interviews when perusing the account of his meeting with the former, we are aware that after difficulty he has encountered a man, whom in no way he describes as wonderful or even magnetic! He says he is dignified and humble and hospitable &. But when he meets Bahá'u'lláh his whole being undergoes a <u>shock</u> and he is forced to "involuntarily bow before One who is the object of a devotion and love that kings might envy and Emperors sigh for in vain!" The wonderful word-picture of Bahá'u'lláh in his introduction to the *Traveller's Narrative* has made Prof. Browne known and renowned throughout the civilized world! Before reading this book – which he has so ably translated – no one knew even of the existence of such a scholar outside of Cambridge in which worthy institution he is still the Prof. of Oriental languages – But now his name is a household word in the homes of Bahá'ís through all the countries where the Cause of Bahá'u'lláh has made him famous – yet he seems perfectly oblivious of the fact! If he lives long enough he will find out that this is his sole claim to any <u>greatness</u> whatsoever! And this greatness lies in the fact that he was describing the Greatest Characters the world has ever seen or known. Whatever he writes of Bahá'u'lláh and his teachings holds the attention and one reads at times with awe; – but of his efforts in connection with S.E. we admire his English and pass on – entirely unimpressed!

But, what a privilege <u>was</u> his – has been his – and yet is – his – if he could but see it!

June 13th

Hashmatu'lláh with us again this evening – Vakil gone! The long delayed monsoon broke over Bombay just as Mr. G., H.U. and myself returned from a walk on the Beach. And such a storm! Such lightning, such thunder! The whole heavens at times were one vast sheet of flames! Again a perfect net-work of livid spears of colored flashes, darting, shooting, hissing, striking and vanishing with deafening roars of thunder! For the first time however, since I had the terrible experience of a cyclone in the middle West – when I was dreadfully shocked by electricity – I was able to sit still and watch it! I started once or twice but I was glad to find the old fear and nameless dread were no longer with me. I enjoyed the aerial display of heavenly "fireworks" and wondered at the power which caused it all! The air has become twenty degrees cooler which guarantees the prospect of a good night's sleep for which I for one am most devoutly thankful! Oh, the <u>nights</u> since I have been in India during the long hours of which I have not been able to sleep makes me regard any prospect of being able to entice Morpheus to my couch as a great blessing indeed! Thus "Good night and come sleep – Gentle sleep that knits up the raveled sleeve of care!"

June 14th

Sun shines bright – too bright this morning! All the clouds have scattered and the heat is steady and intense – though there is a change in the air – it smells <u>cleaner</u>. Hashmatu'lláh came after lunch and invited me to go to Agra with him to attend his marriage June 28th and also to do some work in the Cause there. It seems the thing to do for thirty (pounds) have arrived yesterday from Ahmad Yazdi – paying up May, June & July (in advance) Agra is half way to Kashmir, and though (pounds) thirty is not sufficient for the journey after I have paid up all debts and

secured the things necessary for the undertaking I have consulted Mr. Getsinger and am going to Agra with the hopes of
being able to go on! Of course it means packing, going downtown
buying things for Mr. G. to eat (i.e. stocking up in canned goods
&) while I am gone, buying things for myself, and a general
hustling all round! And oh, it is so hot! The perspiration pours
out all over one's body at the least exertion – but a door has
opened for new service in a new field so I <u>must</u> do everything
necessary and go!

Monday June 15th
Up very early to try and pack before the sun becomes intolerable!
Went to bank with Edward and from there to different place to
procure things. In one store I am sure they thought we were just
married and were going to set up house-keeping. For we bought
corn, beans, peas, jellies, honey, biscuits and dried prunes, all
the things they had, or at least one & sometimes two of each
commodity! But, I did not know how long I would be away and
Mr. G. would be alone with the servant who cooks for and looks
after us! We returned a little after noon completely exhausted
by the heat and exertion. Nothing was so good as the electric fan
and ice-water after that. If one has never been in the Tropics the
word "heat" has little or no significance. I wonder daily, how the
people who are out in it from morn til eve ever survive! But it
is indigenous and I suppose that answers the question!

Tuesday June 16th
The cheering news (?) this morning which Edward brings me is
the temperature of Agra as recorded in the Bombay Chronicle,
"110 degrees all day yesterday with no signs of rain"! What an
outlook after all I have endured in the "melting pot" here! It is
enough to daunt the stout-hearted and I am not surprised at
Edward's not wanting to go (for he too was invited). He says he
has seen the record for days and it has only varied a degree or
so! Still I <u>must</u> go – for it is an opportunity to spread the Cause
in a new city where as yet no work has been done! It rains a little
and then the heat becomes indescribable for the whole earth
seems like a huge reservoir of steam in which we must swelter!
Never the less, the man has come for my trunk and I am off for

263

the depot! The believers and Edward were there to see us off and the long journey began on their "Goodbyes & best wishes".

Agra June 18th 1914

Here at last! So dirty, so saturated with the fine dust of the desert through which we passed so weary and worn out with the heat and lack of sleep that the bungalow which I am to occupy seems like a heavenly mansion and a refuge of restful peace! It is large and would be cool if there were any air in motion! It is about 9.30 P.M. we have bathed in cool water and had dinner which was all so highly seasoned with pepper that I felt as though infernal fires had been kindled in my stomach after eating it – but with the help of water (no ice) I managed it, and now everything is very still and quiet. I have been walking about in the yard for some time seriously contemplating climbing up on the roof to sleep for the house inside, lighted by kerosene lamps, is like unto Daniel's "fiery furnace": Dan. III-6. There is an old woman going in and out – she comes and talks to me in a language I have never heard before, while she chews "pan" – and looks like a "fire eater". Her lips, tongue and teeth are red and disgusting to look at! I haven't an idea what she wants or if she is trying to tell me "The story of her life". Hashmatu'llah and his beautiful sister Mahmouda are in the parlour talking together in another language, and I wouldn't disturb them for the world for well do I remember those precious hours I spent with my brother Will when he returned from school or from the war between America and Spain and I can understand their utter obliviousness of all other save themselves! And who would not be oblivious to everything and everybody if allowed an opportunity to talk with Mahmouda. Never have I seen so beautiful a woman in all the East. She looks like a slender girl, her figure is so petite and graceful yet she is the mother of two children! Her face is like a beautiful exquisite cameo, so finely cut is every feature and her eyes twin stars under the blue black clouds of her abundant hair shining with a softness and radiance which remind one of the land of dreams, in the distant far away, yet ever mysteriously near! Her voice like low sweet music comes to me now and then, like stray notes from some dear half forgotten song! But every tone is vibrant with love, – <u>love for her only brother</u> in fact her only real flesh and blood relative (as her

264

father, mother and sister are all gone)! How I appreciate the joy which swells her heart tonight as she talks with him again face to face after the long absence and separation! No! Not for all the world would I disturb them to find out what the old woman wants or for any <u>other</u> purpose! What would I not give to see and talk with my brother Will tonight? I look up into the clear sky, and search in vain for his dear, calm face among the stars! Oh, where is he now I wonder? 'Abdu'l-Bahá said when he went on his last long journey "He has but gone home!" and (secretly) "in some heavenly azure which needeth no sun for light; in the Court of the King's high pleasure He sits as His feast <u>tonight</u>! Sweet are the song and the story which echo through mansion above– Sweet is the King's great glory But sweetest is the Wine of His Love!" which so intoxicated him so that he could but "go home"! Oh my brother, I miss you as I have never missed in all the years since you went, but I would not call you from His feast <u>"tonight"</u> even to comfort me or soothe the sorrow which <u>your going</u> has caused my heart. I only ever miss you, but I am glad that you are <u>home safely home</u>!

June 22nd
Oh these days of "hell-fire"! Never have I experienced in my life, anywhere, such heat! The air is like the fiery blasts from a furnace and simply dries the blood in one's veins. I have had a peculiar singing in my ears all day, and last night did not sleep one hour for the suffocating atmosphere. I simply lay and fanned myself – when I was not walking in the compound, where I still fanned and fanned trying to be cool. It would not be difficult to convince me that the City of Agra is a department of the Nether regions – very near the "central boiling cauldron" – thereof too! How I shall get through today I cannot imagine. The sunlight is so bright and penetrating it hurts the eyes and makes one's head ache terribly! At least that is the effect it has on me. We are to have a gentleman and his wife to dinner tonight and I hope the meal will consist only of <u>ice</u>! Dear me, how I appreciate those little things which are in just common daily usage in America, and even in Bombay. Never until now have I know the real value of ice-water!

5 P.M.: It is <u>just unbearable</u> but I must bear it – <u>smilingly too</u>! A carriage was sent to take me to visit the marvellous "Taj Mahal" and I went hoping the drive in the gardens would prove a little cooler than the interior of the house but my hopes were vain! We have just rec'd a note from the gentleman who was to dine with us that his wife has <u>collapsed</u> from the heat & therefore they will not come. I am giddy, and feel every moment as though I should fall – therefore am glad I will not have to make any extra exertions.

Later: The gentleman came without his wife, who had regained consciousness and he hoped would be all right! We sat in the compound and tried to talk but it was impossible so we gave it up and the gentleman has returned to his home! From the <u>depths</u> of my soul I pray for rain!

Morning June 23rd

My prayer was heard and answered! About midnight a strong wind began to blow filling the air with dust which fell everywhere and covered everything! We were nearly smothered when it began to thunder and lighten and <u>then</u> came the rain! – Oh, how thankful I was! I ran out in my nightgown and got drenched in it. Every organ of my body was grateful, and I just could not help exclaiming "Oh, the kindness of God!" It is still raining and the birds are so happy that they are singing as they fly about dipping into every little puddle! Truly God is good to all of us! and now I know too, the real value of rain!

June 26th

It was cooler for one day & night – during which I <u>slept</u>! But it is now burning hot again and this afternoon I am to meet the "learned" members of the Muslim Library of Agra! Hashmat'ullah put a little notice in the paper of my being their guest and a Bahá'í teacher who invited any one who desired to call etc. I hope we shall be able to discuss the Bahá'í Movement to advantage!

7.30 P.M. The delegation of "learned gentlemen" have come and gone. They came at three o'clock and have just left. They were fourteen in number and their leader said the first thing – "We are militant Mohammadans and have come to disagree with you!" I looked on all of them, and said, "Well that will not be such a difficult matter! You are <u>fourteen</u> and I am <u>one</u> – from appearances you cannot only disagree but be victorious as well! Sit down please and be as comfortable as your Agra climate will allow – and let us hear your grievances if you have any!" They smiled and seated themselves! "Disagreement is not one of my strong points," I continued, "for the Religion I believe in and am teaching is a religion of love, agreement, unity and peace! And calls for much moral courage on the part of each soul who would practice it!" Then I gave a historical account of the Movement – the essentials of its teachings and of the lives of its Founders! To which all listened attentively. Then they asked the difference between a Manifestation and a Prophet – to which I answered that the Manifestation Bahá'u'lláh while not differing in some respects from the Prophets came in this day as a fulfiller of all Prophets who had preceded him. He claimed to be the Promised One of all therefore He was something plus a prophet. This led to discussions and difficulties of course, which were explained and either accepted or rejected! In the midst of the conversation one man – who had said nothing up to that time suddenly asked "How would you like a piece of pork?" "Thanks," I answered "I would not care for any on such a hot day; – but pray tell what has a 'piece of pork' to do with Bahá'u'lláh's being or not being a Prophet of God! If you wish to know whether or not He advocated eating pork – why not ask your question to the point and I will answer that he did not though his teachings plainly point to the truth uttered by Jesus – i.e. 'That which goeth into the mouth defileth not a man – but that which proceedeth from the mouth defileth him!'" They decided the question was out of place, and arose saying "We will come again tomorrow."

June 27th

3 P.M. The "learned" members of the Library have again appeared and we engaged in the discussion of the Religion of Bahá'u'lláh. It soon became evident to both Hashmatu'lláh and myself that they were not "truth seekers". They were only anxious to prove Mohammed the "Seal of the Prophets" and establish the fact that Islam is the only true religion & and all the world must be Islam. Then I asked if "Islam" did not mean "submission to God" to which they said "Yes, of course!" Then said I, "You argue against yourselves when you reject Bahá'u'lláh who was the essence of submission to God's Will – also that He

had taught us 'submission' as well as to accept Mohammed as a prophet and Messenger of God! Therefore you are your own worst enemies as well as enemies to Islam!" This called forth such expression as "Madame, this is no argument; and no answer to our criticisms &" "Well," I replied, "go and read the teachings of Bahá'u'lláh – they will do you no harm and will certainly add to your knowledge", and they all shook hands thanked me, & left. But the article which appeared in the newspaper afterwards!? Well, let it here be unmentioned! They wrote as they liked without regard even to the <u>Person</u> under discussion.

June 27th, 1914

A telegram from Mr. Getsinger announced "Maharaj Jhalawar left Kashmir letter from him here". Thus all possibility of my going now is at an end! A great opportunity to serve the Cause has passed unseized. Well, I tried my best but it was not in my hands! Perhaps God, for some wise reason did not wish it, after all!

June 28th

Today everything is "hurry and scurry" over the wedding preparations of Hashmatu'llah which is to take place at 2 P.M. Later. The ceremony has been performed and the bride has been carried in a "palakin" to the house of the bride-groom! It was a remarkable procession through the streets, the bridegroom heading the same riding a horse. I rode in a carriage just behind the "palakin" of the bride with several gentlemen to whom I delivered the Bahá'í Message as we slowly drove along. Arriving we congratulated "Bride & Groom" and departed for our several separate places!

June 29th

I am leaving for Bombay tonight after a most pleasant visit with many noble souls, different members of Hashmatu'llah's family, among whom his beautiful sister and charming bride have left an everlasting imprint upon my memory and heart! The "Goodbyes" will soon be spoken and I shall be on the train again covering the distance between here and Bombay which is only a small portion of the journey through the jungle of human existence which every soul must take alone – as alone as I am now!

June 30th 1914

6 *A.M.* Finds me at Ajmer after a sleepless, suffocating night on the train, where the grilling heat made my head ache to the point of non-endurance! This last June day will be spent on the road to Ammedabad where I shall arrive if all goes well at 8.30 p.m. and tomorrow morning I shall be in Bombay. This last day of the month brings me to the last page of this book upon which I must also write farewell to it and say "Goodbye" to June and many hopes, which the events of this month have shattered! At midnight July will be knocking upon the door of Time and I wonder whether with her the world will dance and be glad or weep and be sad? Thus my dear friend and "spiritual child" Mrs. Nourse, I finish this "record" on the road, having reached a station where I stop for a short time to start on again if it be the Will of the Great Conductor.

Lua Moore Getsinger

XVI

The disappointments and "shattering of hopes" which Lua mentioned in her diary entry for June 30, 1914, are not recounted in her letter of May 22, 1914 written from Bombay to Juliet Thompson, nor in her letter to Elizabeth Nourse of June 12th, while she was still waiting for the money to arrive that would enable her to go to Kashmir. It was only on June 27th that she heard of the Maharajah's departure which rendered her visit impossible. We know she was bitterly disappointed not to be able to go: "A great opportunity to serve the Cause has passed unseized. Well, I tried my best but it was not in my hands!" One might also speculate that Lua's disappointment had to do with Edward's unwillingness to accompany her on her journeys, despite the invitations he had received; in fact, Edward was soon to leave her. Perhaps, too, she had a foreboding that she would never return to the United States. "Julie – how I would love to talk with you – and your dear Mother for just a little while but somehow I feel I shall never see either of you again in this world and I have no hopes of seeing you in any other world for I am not good enough."

My dearest Juliet
Your very welcome letter reached me this morning and I reply at once for today is mail day. I have been working all I could – spreading the Cause here and there notwithstanding the terrible heat. And until one has been to India one does not understand what heat means! – I am not strong physically – but I am better than when I first came to this country. Dear Julie – how I would love to talk with you – and your dear Mother for just a little while but somehow I feel I shall never see either of you again in this world and I have no hopes of seeing you in any other world for

I am not good enough. Mrs. Stannard is certainly doing very splendid work – she is such an enlightened soul! I am glad you love her so much! She deserves it. I am happy to know your mother is a confessed believer. Bless her darling heart! Kiss her for me! – No dear, I have not heard of _____ being here <u>now</u> – but, I hear plenty of her <u>having been here</u>. We are having to live down her <u>bad</u> deeds! – for she said she was a Bahá'í. Glad to know Mrs. Krug is so spiritual and loving.

Dearest, if I have ever done anything to make you happy I am so thankful, and I hope you will ever remember that action and forget all my shortcomings and faults. I long that your life should be full of joy, & this will come I know with obedience to 'Abdu'l-Bahá, our Beloved. – When you write to May again give her my love. – I have written her several times but have not heard from her. How I love her, & oh how I long that she too should <u>always</u> (throughout eternity) be happy! Glad to know the Cause is progressing in New York – May you all, be ever so greatly blessed! Goodbye my Julie – I love you with all my heart.

Your unworthy.
Lua
Pray for the spread of the Cause in India!
May 22, 1914 Bombay

Lua wrote to Joseph Hannen requesting a copy of a translation and reporting that nearly five thousand people had died of the plague.

Dear Bahá'í Brother:-
I wrote you a long letter some time ago requesting a copy of a translation which Ahmad Sohrab says is with you. Did you receive my letter, and if you did will you please try to send me the Master's words?

It is very warm in India everywhere now and we are suffering from the heat. In one week 4,885 people died of plague – the week ending May 23rd – and many of them were in Bombay. I have never experienced such terrific heat in any place. We are working when it is possible. Mr. Getsinger is well and I am better than when I first came to this country. Please remember me to Pauline and all members of your family. Wishing for you and yours every blessing and the eternal good pleasure of the "Center of the Covenant" 'Abdu'l-Bahá –

     I am yours in His Service
       Lua M. Getsinger,
Bombay India
18 Churchgate St.
c/o Javanmard
May 29th, 1914

The terrible heat continued to hinder work for the Cause. Lua wrote to her Bahá'í "friend and sister" Pauline Hannen that "for the past three weeks I am here just existing as that is about all one can do". She mentioned that she would give a lecture to the Theosophical Society, at their invitation, on June 11. Lua planned to proclaim "The Center of the Covenant" as the Great World Teacher. This would be in opposition to Mrs. Besant who was educating Khrishnamurti at Oxford for that position, as we have heard before. Lua refers again to the matter of the money which had been collected for the Master's journey to India. "Any matter which is founded upon disunion these days, is bound in time to fail!" Lua wrote.

My dear little Sister

Many thanks for your letter and the enclosures. The particular thing I wanted is not here. It was some words spoken to me by 'Abdu'l-Bahá (Nov. 16, 1913) regarding an editor in Calcutta which Ahmad writes was incorporated in his diary! I am very glad to hear from you again and all of your news is acceptable! So Carl is a man! Grown up? Where is my Paul? I suppose I shall be having newspaper clippings of him too from some part of the world before I realize is he no longer a little boy! It is most trying now in India on account of the extremely hot weather. Bombay is like a huge Turkish bath. Only by the aid of electric fans can one become either cool or dry! I have been out of the city to other places giving public lectures – but for the past three weeks I am here just existing as that is about all one can do. I am lecturing again before the Theosophical Society June 11th by request of Society and shall declare the Center of the Covenant to them as the Great World-Teacher instead of Mrs. Besant's boy who is being <u>educated</u> in Oxford. At what time in the history of religions was a Messenger of God in need of a college education? If the World Teacher for the 20th Century must first be educated at Oxford, then <u>Oxford</u> is the place for all of us – so we can receive our knowledge <u>first</u> hand!

I know the Rev. Mr. Vail very well! I spoke in his church a year ago last March and had several interviews with him in Chicago. He is a truly illumined and beautiful soul! Your attitude towards Mrs. Allen I think the right one! If she is doing anything not pleasing or acceptable to 'Abdu'l-Bahá – it will all fail – but if He accepts her efforts there she will be successful and do beautiful work. She wants to serve & let alone she will find out any mistakes she is making. All are being terribly tested these days everywhere! Some are tested and do not <u>know</u> it – they will awaken and find that much they thought, said, and did <u>was</u> <u>wrong</u> – and let us hope they will be wise enough to desist along such lines in the future! If so, then the lesson has not been in vain! You ask me to pray for you, my dear little sister I am more in need of your prayers than you are of mine, however, I hope the desire of your heart to serve more in the Master's Vineyard will be granted you and all of your services will be very acceptable unto Him! We have heard <u>direct</u> from the Master that the money is to be returned to the contributors. I am very sorry that Miss Barnitz made it a public matter – as this was not intended! – for the experience of raising money in <u>that</u> <u>way</u> had been encountered some two years ago – and it met the same <u>verdict</u> from 'Abdu'l-Bahá. Mr. Getsinger wrote her and I suppose she thought it was right – though why both of them did not remember the other time – I don't know! It's over now, and in future perhaps some people will learn not to meddle in things which do not concern them. Mrs. Stannard's idea was entirely different and it would have been carried out so as not to offend any one. Anyone with the least bit of wisdom would have known better than to have gone <u>ahead</u> when it met with <u>opposition</u> the first time it was presented to the Committee – which I understand it did! Any matter which is founded upon disunion these days <u>is</u> <u>bound</u> <u>in</u> <u>time</u> <u>to</u> <u>fail</u>! 'Abdu'l-Bahá has sent a beautiful tablet to India recently regarding His Coming and what is necessary on the part of India <u>herself</u> to make His Appearance here possible!

– He is powerful to do whatsoever he wishes; and is not in need of America or the money from any of her <u>disunited</u> Bahá'ís!

I send Bahá'í greetings to all members of your household and hope you are all very well and very happy. Remember me for what little good I have been able to do and forget all of my many imperfections.

With best wishes for you spiritual success
    I am as ever
    Your unworthy friend & sister
      Lua M. Getsinger
June 5th, 1914

Lua was still expecting to be able to go to Kashmir to meet the Rajah when she wrote to Elizabeth Nourse a week later. "As soon as I can, I shall <u>obey</u>!"

> 18 Churchgate St.
> c/o Javaumard
> Bombay
> India
> June 12th

My dearest Menita

Yours of May 18 arrived this A.M. the mail leaves tonight so I have but a short time in which to write you. I sent a long account of my visit to an Indian Prince to Mrs. Haney asking her to send you a type-written copy! Have you rec'd it yet?

I am so sorry to hear about Mr. T's death – but not surprised. You remember I told you one day I did not think he would live long. I saw it in his face! Just a passing something – which I had seen in my brother's face several months previous to his death! Give my love to Mrs. Tompkins, and tell her he is not dead but <u>living</u> in a better world! Remember me lovingly to Mrs. Harper too! I will pray for her! There is now no hope of 'Abdu'l-Bahá coming to India! It is so very warm here that really Bombay is one huge Turkish Bath in which no one can either get dry or cool! Several of the Believers here have died, – <u>two</u> within ten days of <u>plague</u>. I know the majority of American Bahá'ís do not want me to be "happy or carefree" – but if they could only realize the effect of such thoughts on the Cause they would think differently. Today we do not simply <u>hurt</u> individuals by our words and thoughts – we hurt the <u>World</u>! – How I love my Phil's poetry – tell him it is a <u>smile</u> of his which has travelled all the way across lands and seas to <u>me</u>! I will write something for him soon. He must be ever so good to his Mother while I am gone!

I too wish you could have "Master Dr. Pratt" look the children over! Boise would be so much stronger I know. Darling Menita I love you tenderly devotedly, wherever I am "in the wide wide world!" I too so often wish I might see and talk with you! You are on the farm now I suppose and I do hope you are all "rosy-red apples" and very happy. I have not been able to go to Kashmir yet on account of not having money enough although a cable came from 'Abdu'l-Bahá telling me to go! As soon as I can, I shall <u>obey</u>! We only have $50.00 per month for two people to live on! The Bahá'ís furnish our lodging place but the rest I furnish from what Mrs. Goodall sends! Oh this working in the Cause with no means is very trying! – In India one sees hundreds of people daily half naked – and nightly sleeping on the ground with no other place to lay their heads! So going about like disciples of old with nothing – is not at all effective here. They need help, and often times a cup of tea preaches the Truth better than the most eloquent words to these people!

> With much love to all
> Your unworthy "Mother"
> <u>Lua</u>

At last, in July, Lua shared with her friends some of her sorrow that Edward had left her. No letter to Elizabeth Nourse seems to have survived from this time. To her dear friend Juliet Thompson she wrote that she wanted to continue her Bahá'í service but found that poverty was keeping her from activity; she no longer had clothes fit to wear on the street. 'Abdu'l-Bahá had given Edward permission to leave and come to Haifa and in order to pay his passage, the couple had to borrow money from the committee. Lua was worried about where she would live: "I am staying in a place rented by the Believers until Sept. 1st after which time I shall not have even a <u>place</u> to lay my head!"

Bombay July 21, 1914

My own Julie:-

Thanks for your dear letter which has just reached me and which finds me "alone in the rain" in India! Edward did not wish to remain here any longer for many reasons – and one was that our means are so limited that people could not travel and work upon the amount monthly at our disposal – thus he asked permission to leave and the Master granted it by a cablegram. He left for Haifa July 15. You have written of your financial condition, now listen to mine. I have less than one English pound – and am in debt £13, – (thirteen English pounds) to the Committee here – for we had to borrow <u>this</u> amount to pay Edward's journey to Haifa – and I have no clothes fit to wear on the street! I am staying in a place rented by the Believers until Sept 1<u>st</u> after which time I shall not have even a <u>place</u> to lay my head! I cannot accept any money from the believers – (and they have most kindly offered it – but now I am the one privileged to <u>live down</u> the effect _____ and _____ made – who took all they could get from everyone! It is telling too slowly but the strain is terrific! So many doors have opened for me to go and lecture – I have rec'd invitations to ever so many places, but cannot stir one step on account of <u>having no means!</u> – Thus here I am now alone and without anything! But Julie I do not care! To myself <u>nothing</u> matters any more. I am only sorry that the work suffers! Yet it will be <u>done</u> – if <u>not by me</u> – by someone <u>better fitted</u> to do it! The time is fast approaching when only the <u>worthy</u> will be allowed the privilege of working! God is testing His Servants now as never before – but it is sure He <u>sits</u> by the crucible as He faces the flames. When we have become so pure as to reflect the image of His own Face – He will remove us from the Fire and not till <u>then</u> for the days are now come when "the Assayers of Existence, in the portico of the Presence of the Worshipped One ('Abdu'l-Bahá) shall accept naught but pure virtue and shall admit naught except pure deeds". So rejoice Julie, that you are found worthy to be put into the crucible, this final "melting pot" of trial! Trust in Him who is very near thee – <u>nearer</u> than He has ever been before! When you can rejoice in poverty as you would in wealth it will cease to exist – for it has only come to teach you the lesson that neither wealth nor poverty – in <u>themselves</u> are anything – one always succeeds the other, and the one is only useful when rightly used – and the other is absolutely a non-existent thing as the appearance of wealth its opposite completely annihilates it! Thus dear, for the time – just accept it and be calm, it will all pass – and soon be but a little shadow of the night on the face of a fair morning! In one of the Upanishads it is said: – "Only those of tranquil mind, and none else, can attain abiding joy, by realizing within their own souls the Being who manifests one essence in a multiplicity of forms." And Bahá'u'lláh says, –

"Turn thy sight unto thyself that thou mays't find me standing within thee, powerful, mighty, and supreme!"[110] And this is true, that it is impossible to turn our sights – unto ourselves as long as they are occupied with things outside ourselves! I believe with Rabindranath Tagore that "Through all the diversities of the world the One in us is threading its course towards the One in all; that is its nature and its joy." Hence the use & necessity of oneness and unity! Again in the Upanishads – "This deity who is manifesting Himself in the activities of the universe always dwells in the heart of man as the supreme soul. Those who realize Him through the immediate perception of the heart attain immortality!" – But the realization must be through the heart and not the head. Hence the absolute necessity of being calm! As it is said "Be still – and know that – I am God!" So dearest Julie, do not be troubled over anything, be calm and still and the perfect realization of that Being now on Earth in human form known as 'Abdu'l-Bahá will be granted thee in thy heart of hearts – and at that time thou wilt know thyself richer than all the queens of the earth! In regard to what you have written about meeting me and "touching the hem of my garment in the other world! – I have no hopes, even of attaining the other world – if by that you refer to the Glorious Kingdom of Abha over which 'Abdu'l-Bahá will reign throughout eternities of eternity! I have never done anything to merit such a blessing and I never expect to be able to bring forth a service which will be acceptable enough to gain for me a passport into His Holy Presence! The one virtue I possess (and before Him that may not even be a virtue) is – I love Him enough to be willing to die even spiritually for His dear sake! I can say now as did Kurrat'ul'Ayne [Ṭáhirih] for she said: – "The thralls of yearning Love constrain, in bonds of pain and calamity, these broken-hearted lovers of Thine to yield their lives – in zeal for Thee." – And with what wholehearted zeal did she yield up her life (which she counted less than nothing) to her Beloved! – and being <u>women</u> we must not fall below the standard of her example – even if we <u>are</u> <u>unable</u> to rise above it!

Regarding the Kinneys I rejoice that they are so angelic in showing you such kindness, May the eternal good pleasure of 'Abdu'l-Bahá be their reward for <u>any</u> <u>kindness</u> they bestow upon you and your dear mother– ! In reference to their being my "true friends" – now – and "speaking of me beautifully, showing the greatest fondness and love for me – This is from <u>their</u> goodness undoubtedly – but their love or hatred – their praise or their blame is the same to me <u>now</u>. For the reason that I did nothing <u>to them</u> to incur their hatred when they hated me – and I have done nothing to them now – that they should again love me! However I wish for them and theirs all the blessings of this world and the worlds to come, may each succeeding day – as the days go by her kind remembrances of one who is all unworthy of being remembered.

From one whom you knew as

<u>Lua</u>

After Edward Getsinger left Lua in India, Lua remained at her post, trying to continue her work as soon as the rains subsided. In later letters, one sees that Edward's leaving plunged her into illness which lasted all through September. She wrote Joseph Hannen on August 17, 1914 requesting six copies of the little booklet *Bahá'í Principles*. The letter on file has Hannen's usual typed note about when it had been received and answered.

Aug. 27th, 1914 (rec'd and ansd. 10/3/14)

My dear Brother Joseph,
Could you manage to send me 6 copies of the Little Booklet "Bahá'í Principles" published some time ago by the Occident Orient Society? They are so very useful and I need them very much.

I am becoming very busy again since the rains are subsiding. My sincere greetings to all the Friends.

I hope you are all well and in perfect unity now. I am confident that power was given you to fulfill your new task in Washington. Greetings to Pauline

      Your sister in the
         Service of the Covenant
         Lua M. Getsinger

Lua wrote to Joseph Hannen again in October requesting the printing and sending of a thousand copies of the "Love Letter" of 'Abdu'l-Bahá[111] with the "laughing" portrait of the Master as a frontispiece. Dr. Edal Behram would defray all expenses. It was in this letter she wrote of the illness mentioned above, saying that she had been the guest and patient of Dr. Behram since September 1 and was now without fever for the past two weeks.

                    Surat (India) Oct. 16, 1914

Allaho'Abha

My dear spiritual bro.

I wrote to you some weeks ago requesting the sending of "Bahá'í Principles" – as yet have received no reply. I am writing now at the request of Dr. Edal Behram, of Surat, the Lamp of whose being was lighted by the "Hand of Power" in London, 1911, and who is a highly spiritual soul. He wishes very much to have a thousand copies of the "Love Letter" of 'Abdu'l-Bahá with the "laughing" picture of the Master taken by Mrs. Cabatt (Mrs. Parson's friend) printed for distribution in India. Have the picture reproduced either in black and white or the chocolate color of original, on the first page, then the printing to follow. He wishes it done very nicely and will defray all expenses. Will you please see to it as soon as possible, and let us know immediately the cost, so the money can be sent on to you. Mrs. Parsons can get the negative if necessary, for picture. You cannot know the good this will do now in India. Since the war came, our work has been laid on new lines, and we are going ahead on recent new instructions from the Beloved. At first we all thought we must give up the field, but as usual He has opened other doors, and we are going on!

I have been ill ever since Mr. G. left, with fever and nervous exhaustion; but now I am on the "high road" to new health. I have been in Dr. Behram's home since Sept. 1st, his patient; but for two weeks the fever has left and I am now gaining in every way.

A new Confirmation, accompanied by new energy, has come, and all that the Master promised and intended from our visit to India is vouchsafed, and will soon be fulfilled. The fires of test and trial have been enkindled, and in them, we have been tried with the result that His Word will be established and His Work accomplished. A marvellous phenomenon has occurred in the outward world. A most wonderful and brilliant Star appears every afternoon between 5 and 5:40 on the North-western horizon, visible to the naked eye, before sunset and none of the astronomers can either name or account for it! It sets blood-red at 8:30, growing during its stay ever bigger and brighter! The people were at first filled with fear, thinking a German aeroplane was coming, but as the Heavenly Messenger appears day after day, in the same place, their fear has given way and the Joy of Glad-Tidings and Good News is replacing it!

It is wonderful, and every day we watch for it and all of us pray for the Appearance of India's Real Star of Spiritual Guidance soon to arrive upon her shores! In the Inner World, the Bahá'ís know the significance of the Star, and we are all praising and thanking God. Our hearts are filled to overflowing with His Love and Mercy and we are serving in all humility before the grandeur of His Majestic Presence. We know that only in appearance is "Calamity" – "Fire and Vengeance" – in reality it is "Light and Mercy"![112] We ask you and all the Friends to pray for us. Mrs. Stannard also was obliged to go to the hills for a rest and recuperation. She left Calcutta Sept. 20 but will be ready for service the last of October, the same as this most unworthy servant, and then both of us will start out again, to proclaim the Glad-Tidings of the Kingdom.

I am so glad you are going to help out on the literature question by sending some for a circulating Library of Bahá'í Books. Both Mrs. Stannard and myself have put books into the hands of as many as possible, but India is so vast and her need so great that so far it has been like a few drops of water to a great and parched desert. Through His Highness the Maharajah of Jhalawar, I was enabled to place a fine assortment of our literature in the Public Library in Jhalarapatan, besides putting many translations of the Hidden Words into the hands of those who only read and understand Hindustani. We are sending a report of Dr. Edal Behram's work in Surat to the STAR OF THE WEST, and from it you will see the Power of the Center of the Covenant in India! When I left Port Said a year ago, I received a certain sum of money from His Blessed Hands which was to be expended in His Name though he did not so stipulate, only he said whenever you can give to the poor something. I then and there set aside that amount to be given to the poor in His Holy Name. On my first visit to Surat in January, 1914, a portion of that sum was given in His Name to Dr. Edal Behram, who out of his own earnings had rented and opened a home for the infirm and destitute of Surat. I went with him to visit this place, and those poor people – poor beyond the comprehension of the people in America – sent their appeal to my heart, which resulted in 'Abdu'l-Bahá's donation. The receipt for the sum given was sent to him and he was pleased, and his good-pleasure acted like magic, for money began to pour in, which enabled the good, kind-hearted Dr. Behram to purchase the house and remodel it (the repairs are still going on) which will afford accommodations to all who in future apply. Thus is the Power of the Beloved One made manifest, and thus does His divine Magic transform misery into Mercy, helplessness and homelessness into an Asylum of Shelter and protection,

Please convey most wonderful Abha greetings to all the friends and Beloved of God in Washington and Chicago, and please do pray for us, Mrs. Stannard and your humble sister, as we go on with the work of the Vineyard under the most trying circumstances in this far-away place – which you cannot realize in neutral America!

May the blessing of 'Abdu'l-Bahá be upon the Assemblies in those cities, and may each and every member thereof be the recipient of His everlasting Good-pleasure and divine Bounty. With love to Pauline and your entire family, I am, as ever,

Your sister-servant in the Service of the
Center of the Covenant
Lua Moore-Getsinger

P. S.

Please send this letter to Dr. Bagdadi. To him and his dear sweet bride we all send greetings. L.M.G.

Lua's warm concern and love for her friends continued and she wrote to Louise Bosch in October. She again mentioned the five special souls of her heart's deepest love: Louise Bosch, May Maxwell, Mariam Haney, Juliet Thompson and Mary Lucas. Her letter states that she had been ill most of the month of September, losing twenty-eight pounds. This letter shows a significant spiritual growth and development as she shares some of her pain with one of her dearest friends.

<u>Allaho'Abha</u>   Surat, India
                                                    Oct. 28. 1914

My dear Lysa

I am sure I am the last and therefore I hope the "best" to con-gratulate you upon your marriage to John D. You know that saying "The last is the best!" – Thus may my congratulation prove the "best" for it is – I assure you – a vehicle only to carry the sincere and humble prayers of my heart for a long life of double blessedness. How many times I have thought of you and been glad to know you are "mistress of a mansion" on a hillside in far away Golden California. May you both be ever so happy and as a reward of good pure and useful lives – become the recipients of a gift which will ever enable you to distinguish the <u>real</u> from appearance and "to know all voices from the King!" – I am in appearance very far away from your home on the hillside but in reality I am <u>there</u> <u>with</u> <u>you</u>! I can see you gathering your fruits and know you are very well-content with what you have. I am not yet an <u>entirely</u> severed soul but I am walking on <u>that</u> road & have progressed far enough so I can see both to the right and left with an unobstructed vision. But <u>what</u> I have had to suffer to attain it! However I am very thankful for it all, for it has taught me to know that <u>praise</u> and <u>blame</u> emanating from <u>people</u> both equal – x+0=0! They blame today, they praise tomorrow, and the next day blame again – and what does it all amount to? Years ago 'Abdu'l-Bahá said to me once suddenly apropos of nothing – "When you reach the place where praise and blame are the same to you – you may know then you have advanced and God is favoring you!"

But Oh Lysa – the pain of reaching that place has been

terrible and will continue to be until every last least little bit of my <u>human</u> <u>self</u> is <u>dead</u>. But thank God it is dying slowly – but nevertheless <u>surely</u> dying! Edward as you may have heard has returned to America! He did not like India and has gone to Washington. – You will know some day – dear Lysa – many things and I wish I might see <u>you</u> now to tell you the <u>truth</u> [here underlined four times] of some things. However Truth needs no telling – it becomes evident! – All one needs to do is to <u>wait</u> and endure the tests of God! I am infinitely grateful to be here – though we are surrounded on all sides with difficulties the like of which I have never before encountered! But I see the sun shining at "the end of the road" – so I push on – and am learning to not even <u>look</u> <u>back</u> along the way over which I have journeyed! The <u>whole</u> past – is but an incident in a day's march along the "Highway of Severance from all else save God!" Each morning is a new life – a new creation, a grand <u>opportunity</u> for <u>progression</u>! So <u>on</u> looking ever <u>ahead</u> – we <u>must</u> go! –

One thing has never changed however – and that is my love for you – May – Mariam and Mary and also Juliet. I may never hear from you or see you again in this world but I <u>know</u> that throughout eternity I shall love you no matter if you all <u>hate</u> me in time – for I have had it all explained to me how <u>that</u> love in my heart for you is a reflection of His Love – No matter how distorted and imperfect the reflection – on account of the <u>imperfect</u> <u>mirror</u> of my soul yet the reflection <u>is</u> <u>His</u>! [underlined three times] and therefore time – space – praise blame – height or depth – heaven or hell – <u>nothing</u> <u>can</u> affect it! – When all others have been tried – and if you are in any or all disappointed you can say with certainty "<u>Lua</u> <u>loves</u> <u>me</u>!" Oh Lysa – believe it – only that love is real and to be relied upon – which asks <u>nothing</u> not even recognition – in return! And such is the Love of the Beloved – and that is why – through "thick and thin" – in sickness or health – in weal and in woe – we <u>cling</u> to Him. Even when He <u>slays</u> – still we trust! – When He censures – yet we <u>praise</u> Him!

People may call us mad! But blessed is such madness; it makes of the worldly wise those "little children" who find their way into the Kingdom!" – Let me but be God's <u>fool</u> – and the <u>treasures</u> of the knowledge of <u>men</u> – shall never be touched by my (mental) hands – nor desired by my soul!

In this strangest of strange lands – I am learning wonderful lessons – the very existence of which I never dreamed! The following was told me this morning – by oh well – you would not believe me if I told you and it does not matter <u>who</u> said it – this is what <u>was</u> <u>said</u>!

"As fishes playing in a pond covered over with reeds and scum cannot be seen from outside, so God plays invisibly in the heart of man!" And do you know dearest, it is for this very reason that man ever fails to see Him! Man ever looks to the "<u>reeds</u>" which make up his body – and the "scum" which arises from the impure thoughts of his mind – and is utterly unconscious of the "fish" swimming in the pure waters of his soul! – Bahá'u'lláh says for this reason I know, "Turn thy sight unto Thyself that thou mayest find Me standing within thee – powerful – mighty and supreme!" And when the sight is <u>thus</u> <u>turned</u> <u>to</u> <u>the</u> <u>self</u> <u>for</u> <u>the</u> <u>purpose</u> <u>of</u> <u>seeing</u> <u>God</u> – the <u>self</u> is no longer seen and He stands revealed in the calm clear depths of that which was, is, and ever shall be <u>His</u> <u>own</u>! We do not belong to ourselves – we are <u>His</u> – good or bad – and "He doeth whatsoever He <u>willeth</u> until whomsoever He <u>wishes</u> – by <u>merely</u> saying-&– -!– (The Logos!) But – tell me, are you and yours well, happy & content? – I can of course answer my question by saying in just so far as you are obeying the commands of God – you are <u>really</u> well, happy and content! – But, I want to hear if you wish to tell me – and spend the time to write one so unworthy of both your time and thoughts!

If it would interest you I might tell you that physically I have been quite ill for the entire month of Sept. but am now much better though I have not regained the twenty-eight pounds of flesh I lost. But that's nothing! I am well in soul and have less to carry about physically in this extremely hot climate. It is nearly the <u>1st of</u> Nov. (my birthday) and the temperature is 96 degrees in a secluded spot – which means it is about 102 degrees in the sun! The heat is <u>withering</u> I can assure you just as the torrential rains of July and August were wasting and debilitating. But I have lived through both "sun and shower" and will probably pull on for sometime yet – and if I don't – happy day which witnesses my release from the case of body in a gloomy world! I love to serve and like to live for <u>that</u> purpose – but whenever I have outlived my usefulness I hope I will be allowed free passage very soon! And I would "put out to sea" without even the stipulations of "sunset and evening star" – the "one clear call for me" – would be all that I should ask or require! I have not heard from May since I left America. When you write her will you tell her that I love her more than ever – and am so glad she has such a good husband, such a lovely home and blessed child! I seem to see her <u>always</u> surrounded with these blessings – the gifts of 'Abdu'l-Bahá and I am so glad for her <u>that</u> <u>they</u> <u>are</u> <u>hers</u>! May she realize – and of course she does – their value! Remember me to her and say "When you think of Lua – <u>pray</u> for her – don't trouble or bother to write, she understands and wishes for you now, as always, a life crowned with supernal joy!" When you see Mr. Dunn remember me to him – and to Mrs. Davis, and to all the <u>others</u> – whether they love me or hate me – believe me true or believe me false it makes no difference – and I send <u>them</u> my love and best wishes in

      <u>His</u> Name who is the "Center of <u>The Covenant</u>"
         Yours as ever
         In humble service
            Lua Moore Getsinger
#29 Forbes Street
Bombay, India

As usual, it was to Elizabeth Nourse that Lua unburdened her heart. The first pages of this letter are missing, but it is clear that it must have been written near the end of October. Despite her evident anxiety about what Edward will be saying about her in America, she seems to be in good spirits and is planning her future services in India. At the same time, she feels alone, and casts a longing eye towards her friend's more settled life: "How fortunate you are to have the "Kiddies" and a home to keep them in! Count your blessings when you feel discouraged, and think of me wandering over highways and under hedges with no place to call my own! But really dear I am learning wonderful lessons. . ."

. . . Well I am surprised how that Mouse's tale got mixed up with this letter. Where was I? – Oh yes. – I do hope you will stay as long as you can in the wild woods and enjoy every minute of it! I wish I were with you sleeping on the porch listening to the mysterious whispers of the night! But alas! How far away I am – where there are no cool woods or <u>cool</u> anything save way up in the mountains where I have not been, and have no prospects of "going"! Since Mr. Getsinger left for America I have not felt well – was not well when he left. The lst of Sept. I came to Surat at Dr. Behram's invitation for I was then quite ill – I suffered from fever & a nervous collapse – and for four weeks was just good for nothing! I had lost flesh on the trip to Agra – on account of the very intense heat – and continued to lose until twenty-eight pounds just took leave of my bones and I looked like a shadow! I have gained three pounds – and am much stronger now. After the war broke out 'Abdu'l-Bahá sent word that I should travel and teach – so I am soon leaving for another part of India – don't know yet just <u>where</u>. Will write you always! Oh dear heart – if you knew how your letters help me you would write oftener! I am alone here – in a strange and very lonely land! Suffering? Not now – <u>that</u> is passed! I have at last attained a partial if not yet complete severance! (Only for <u>you</u> – When Mr. G left – it was the last human tie to break – and <u>he</u> broke it ruthlessly! – I love him – not with the clinging human affection whose only fruit is <u>pain</u> but with another kind of love which lifts my soul above both bitterness and blame and makes me to wait the fullness of time which will perfect his spiritual evolution – and give to me – all that of him which is <u>mine</u> to have. If I could see you I would tell you what I cannot write! Only this – Menita – I trust you to know the <u>Truth</u> when you hear <u>any</u> <u>story</u> regarding your "Little Mother". If you are in doubt be frank enough to write me, and as I fear God and the displeasure of 'Abdu'l-Bahá – I will tell you everything truly as it <u>was</u> <u>and</u> <u>is</u>! He may not see you – but if he does – I ask you only defer judgement until <u>you</u> <u>know</u> <u>both</u> sides.)

The Bahá'í work has all changed character more or less – since war was declared! We cannot give public lectures as freely as before, and during these days of such weakness and shattered nerves I have only been teaching Dr. Behram and his son – the fundamentals and great principles of the Bahá'í Faith and writing articles. One will come out next month and one in December. One article is entitled "The Lovers of God" and the other "The Desired One of the Nations". I will send them both to you – when they come out. – I do not know how much longer I shall be here – it looked very much at one time as though I should have to leave immediately as the police and political agents were suspicious on account of my German name – but it was all made plain that I am an American and Mr. G. also American <u>born</u>. "What's in a name?" The whole world knows that Bahá'ís are people of Peace – and faithful to the Government they are under. But dear me – even Bahá'ís must abhor the deeds of the Germans. And clearly we cannot love aggression and injustice – even if we are neutral! I am glad the American people are praying for <u>peace</u>. I wish good President Wilson would ask them to all pray <u>weekly</u>! I never knew I loved the English so much until now – but I do and I can't help wishing them success for I am convinced they are in the right – and are fighting for <u>principle</u>.

These are days foretold by Christ and the other <u>Messengers of God</u> including Bahá'u'lláh and 'Abdu'l-Bahá and we cannot expect anything but struggles and trials – for some time – perhaps three years to come. We have heard that the Panama Exposition 1915 in San Francisco has been abandoned. Is it true? How disappointed the Californians must be after all their expenditure & trouble for the past two years! – I hope the "Records" have reached you by this time and that you will see the significance of a dream which I had in Poona and wrote therein. Glad you & the "Kiddies" liked the visit to the Prince. I wrote Mrs. Haney to <u>give</u> you a copy but it is in the "Records" so it doesn't matter.

I shall be glad to have the tablet you mention and also to get any other Bahá'í News. Please remember me to the little group in Atlantic City – and do try to get people to attend the meetings and then conduct them according to Mr. Hannen's recent tablet! – Be patient with the questions & realize that a soul must be <u>taught</u> the same as a child in school – little by little!

Do pray for me and please do write me as often as you can. How fortunate you are to have the "Kiddies" and a home to keep them in! Count your blessings when you feel discouraged, and think of me wandering over highways and under hedges with no place to call my own! But really dear I am learning wonderful lessons – I know what Christ meant when He said "All that the Father hath is mine!" We are all in <u>reality</u> very rich – We only think we are poor. How could it be otherwise when Bahá'u'lláh said "I have <u>created</u> you rich – why do you make yourselves poor?" – Then, even though we have no place and nothing – we only need to <u>think how</u> we were created – and we find that we are all Princes and Princesses – living in a land of plenty! The trouble is we do <u>not</u> <u>think</u> often enough! For as we <u>think</u> so we are!

It will be almost Christmas when this reaches you and I wish you would spend it in your nest in the woods. How the children would enjoy it! The woods in winter are just as interesting as in Summer and to some much more so! It would be a new and novel experience for all of you!

God knows where I will be <u>then</u> – but wherever I am – my heart will be sending you best wishes for a Merry time! There has appeared on the North-Western horizon of India – a most wonderful bright and luminous Star – which is visible at 5:30 P. M. <u>before</u> sunset. Many people thought it a German aero-plane and were terrified the first nights at its appearance! The astronomers can neither name nor account for it. Some say its a good sign and some say its bad – but good or bad – its marvelously beautiful. I call it 'Abdu'l-Bahá's star – and am trying to believe it a Herald of His Coming to India. Be that as it may and as God shall decree – the Star has a great attraction for me. I go out every night to look for it and watch it nearly every moment until it sits blood red in the sunset line at about 8:30 P. M. So many people are watching it that I feel it a great point of concentration in the Sky. Only it means so much more to me than to most people, I am sure. I hope you tell Phil my messages on the Evening Star – for they are always addressed to him – with love to you and all the other members of the family thrown in – on any extra beams of light which I find handy! I truly must stop now or the mail will refuse this letter. Be very weary of <u>Mice's</u> <u>tales</u> – and tell Phil I hope he will learn a wonder story from his <u>Hop-toads</u> and write it to me! I could just on writing forever – I love you all so much – but really I must stop after sending my love to Mrs. Merriharper and all the other dear good Friends. Send me "a round robin" for Christmas – or New Year's if you can and there is time!

> With most devoted love from
> Your very own "Little Mother"
> <u>Lua</u>

Sorry to send such a scratched up looking copy – but it is "<u>first copy</u>" and I am too busy to re-copy. So you must pardon me.

Am sending under separate cover a book which shows Dr. Behram's Bahá'í Work.

Joseph Hannen wrote to Lua in December that her order was being attended to. The copyright for the smiling picture of the Master had been obtained and the leaflet would soon be sent. He hoped she had received the booklets.

— 9 —

Please note new
Post box number

Post Office Box 1319
Washington, D. C.
December 7, 1914

Mrs. Lua M. Getsinger,
18 Churchgate Street, c/o Javanmard,
Bombay, India.

Dear Bahá'í Sister:-
Your valued favor of the 16th October came duly to hand. I am, as always, most happy to hear from you, and in this instance it affords me much pleasure to know that I may be of some little service.

As to your request for copies of the BAHAI PRINCIPLES booklet: This was received and answered on October 3rd last, and I hope you got the books safely. If not, the shipment will be duplicated, or in any event more can be supplied on request.

Concerning the issuance of the "Letter of Love", which Dr. Behram desires to get out with the "Smiling Photograph" of 'Abdu'l-Bahá: I at once took this matter up with Mrs. Parsons, as the first requisite was to obtain permission for the use of the photograph, which is copyrighted. This I have been able to arrange, and I write to-day to say that the publication will be arranged at the earliest possible moment. There will be some little delay, incident to the approaching Holiday Season; but this will be wholly in the interest of producing a better piece of workmanship. I shall keep you posted as to developments. Bahá'í love from us all.

Faithfully yours
[Joseph Hannen]

XVII

Lua left India on November 17, 1914, sailing from Bombay exactly one year to the day after sailing from Port Said to India. She arrived in Syria on December 3, 1914. The Holy Family was in "the hills of Galilee" as Lua put it and she joined them, spending time in the village of Abu Sinan. She wrote to Mrs. Goodall on January 1, 1915.

Allaho'Abha!

Abou Sinan Syrie Jan. 1st, 1915.
"A Happy New Year" to Everybody

Dear Bahá'í friend and Believer
I am glad to write you of the very good health of the Beloved Master and family at the above mentioned place of safety in which I found them on my arrival Dec. 3rd. I had been quite ill in India for some weeks and upon my return to Bombay Nov. 2nd I consulted the American Consul who advised me to leave India partly on account of my German name and partly because he considered it very ill advised for me to lecture and speak any more upon the Bahá'í Movement. As you may imagine everything was in turmoil and confusion after war was declared. Mr. Getsinger left just before (July 15th) or otherwise, he might have been hustled off to prison with all the other Germans who were similarly treated. I left Nov. 17 and was so happy to find all of the Holy Household well. I am as you may imagine most thankful to see them all again after a year's absence.

I hope to go out and serve in the Cause again as soon as I am well and able financially to do so. The money you so kindly sent (200 pounds) is exhausted and if you should wish to assist me further in teaching in the Cause you may send whatever your heart prompts you to send for said purpose to the Beloved – c/o Ahmad Yazdi P. Said. I know not at this writing if I am to return to America or go to some other place, but wherever He sends me I shall be glad and happy to go for these are the days when service in the Cause is more than necessary. Poor war-stricken world – the evil days have come upon us and now we must minister to the wounded – the <u>spiritual-wounded</u> as best we can! – I know you are all doing all you can and may the Holy Spirit confirm and assist you – and all the Friends. The Master spends most of His time in Acca where He is the Light and Hope of all the troubled people who without him would be in the depths of despair indeed! – I close sending you greeting and asking your prayers – that I may be assisted in further serving in the Vineyard of God.

Yours in the Covenant
Lua M. G——

All members of the
family send you and Ella
most loving Greetings

A note written on the back of an old invitation to the West Englewood Unity Feast in June 1912 reached Elizabeth Nourse from Abu Sinan:

Abou Sinan
Syria Jan. 11, 191[5]

Dear Menita:
Here I am all safe & sound in the Highlands of Galilee with Master and family who are all well and happy. The Master spends most of His time in Acca comforting and caring for the poor and hopeless. He is so wonderful and inspiring these dark days! So far all is quiet here! I am much better than when I left India thanks to the quiet and cool climate of Syria. Send much love to my Phil and all of you. All send you loving Greetings. As ever, Your Lua.

Lua wrote more poetically to Mrs. Goodall's daughter, Ella, later in the month after a visit to Bahjí, where Bahá'u'lláh is laid to rest.

Abou Sinan, Syria
Jan. 26th. 1915

Dear Ella:-

On Jan. 23rd the Holy Leaves, Zeah, Tooba, and Monevar Khanum and myself left here for the Bahaji to visit the Sacred Tomb of Bahá'u'lláh, as I had not been able to perform this Sacred privilege since my arrival Dec. 3rd. and besides we all felt it very important at this time to repair to that High Court of Appeals and pray for the Believers all over the world. The Beloved and Rouha Khanum have been in Haifa for the past two weeks as there were very many things which demanded the Master's personal attention and supervision. We covered the distance between here and the Bahaji in two hours and a half riding upon donkeys and walking, arriving just before sunset. The day was perfect! Bright sunshine, blue sky, soft spring-like breezes bearing to us now and again the fragrances of wild flowers dotting the green grass and edging the pathways beneath our feet. The Mountains of Carmel and Lebanon, and the silver green olive orchards skirting the lowlands, making a fantastically beautiful background for it all, lending majesty and that mysterious silence which is so fitting and necessary for such a pilgrimage. The formerly arid desert outlying the Bahaji, – under Nature's soft caressing hand, lay transformed before us into gardens of marvellous beauty, carpeted with green velvet, richly embroidered with anemonies, narcissus and white orchids all growing in wild and abundant profusion. As we dismounted, I stood still looking with rev[er]ential awe upon the indescribable splendor spread out before me and tried to imagine it once a barren region waiting to be blessed by the Magic Presence, which forty-seven years ago, transmuted it into rolling plains of such weird and wondrous beauty as now held me spell-bound, but I could not; – it seemed to me then, it had been always, and would always be the most beautiful spot on earth! As I paused drinking its wonder and delight a red-crested yellow-breasted black-winged bird flew over my head and alighting in a rose-tree just outside the window of the Holy Tomb poured forth a melodious vesper-song which served as a most suitable requiem to the dying day, and for the loved. . .

Lua's letters mention only briefly the visit of Edward

293

Getsinger to the Holy Land in the early days of 1915 and nowhere does she hint that their parting was to be permanent. When he visited the Master after leaving India in July 1914, Edward had seen the suffering of the people of Syria which apparently touched him deeply. An article describing this which he hoped to have published is quoted below.

HAIFA, SYRIA

The entire population of Syria is in a state of lamentation. Turkey is mobilizing, and all men between the ages of twenty and forty-five are called to the colors, or rather forced to go to the front. Hardly six months have passed since the soldiers of the Balkan Army returned here, and now they must again join their regiments. But this time every available man is taken, by force if necessary, or he must pay $170.00 in gold, which will respite him for six months only. But all the banks are closed, and refuse to pay one dollar, thus even such are unable to buy themselves out of service. But the Turkish officer knows how to get gold from banks. He takes checks from the prominent recruits, takes them to the bank and demands gold, and always gets it; otherwise another prisoner is added to the jail on some pretext or other.

Food of all kinds has doubled in price, and within two months there will be a famine in Syria. The Government has confiscated eighty per cent of all food stuffs in sight both for man and beast, is taking sheep by the thousands, and for this pays no money whatever, simply giving a receipt for the same payable after the way, but that means never.

The officers have taken all bread winners, leaving the women and children without means of support, and in some cases with a meager supply of food stored for winter use. Even in these cases the soldiers have broken into the very homes of the bereft and taken this small store. The merchants have had their shops cleared of stores and been given a receipt, which means bankruptcy. All horses and wagons are taken. These and all other confiscated stuffs are sent to Damascus, where about 100,000 men recruits are stationed and being drilled daily for nine hours. There the men enter shops and help themselves to whatever they wish.

The farming section everywhere is devoid of men, and their women and children are hastening to the villages and cities for protection from the marauding bands of Bedouins who are making night raids upon the defenseless homes. Thus the cities are being crowded and no food for anyone, nor money with which to purchase it at famine prices. Beyrout, Haiffa and Acca are thus contributing to Damascus, while Jaffa and surrounding villages send to Gaza, where also another multitude is being concentrated and drilled daily.

The Turkish officer is relentless, and war time to him is simply "booty-time". For example, a merchant in Beyrout complained to the Commanding Chief about his subordinates breaking into his shop and taking three hundred bags of rice. He was promptly put behind the bars for his pains. A few days later, a subordinate in Haiffa took a fine Arabian mare from a wealthy native. The owner remonstrated and finally offered to compromise by delivering two horses and taking back his mare. The offer was accepted. When he came with his two horses, these were also confiscated. He went to Beyrout to complain to the Commander, and after a few minutes' interview was put into jail, where he met his friend the rice merchant. Later both were released upon paying a heavy fine in gold. This at once prevented others from taking their grievances "higher up".

The poor women, weeping with their children, sit for hours at the doors of the well-to-do, begging for bread, and this is rapidly becoming a luxury. A few ships are arriving at these ports now where formerly ten to fifty arrived weekly. Any food stuffs entering the port is confiscated. The little money that was in circulation outside of the closed banks is rapidly being concentrated into the government chest by the men who buy off their services. During the Balkan War, at the end of one year the conditions were not as bad as they are now, at the end of one month. The winter is fast approaching, and God help the poor.

The entire population is divided into two camps – against Germany, or against France. Besides the Germans who have colonized here, the French have acquired a considerable influence through their schools, conducted by the Friars and Sisters, and this has created a feeling for France through a tie of language. Consequently, aside from the German and Greek element, the entire Christian population is with France, and the

295

entire native or Arabic and Turkish population with Germany.

During the first ten days, there were numerous scuffles in the cafes between Christian and Moslem sympathizers, during which time cheers rent the air, but soon the Christians found it best to repress their enthusiasm. It is not at all difficult to foresee what might happen should Germany be defeated; and such a possible riot was rapidly smoldering into flame because the French and English were daily sending in to Syria false news of their successes and Germany's defeat. A final uprising against the Christians was only averted by the fact that Germany had a direct cable communication with its colonies through Constantinople, and which was closed to the French. Thus news of Germany's advance and success came through, and this allayed the fire of Moslem fanaticism.

Daily these natives crowd about the bulletin boards before the German banks and Consulates to read the news as translated into Arabic. And the next day the French news comes by wireless to Port Said from Italy and thence by Egyptian cable into Syria, and is found to be completely contradictory. But confidence has been lost in them, even by the sympathizers of France, because they had to admit the advance of the Germans into France and towards Paris; and when even French dispatches admitted the removal of the seat of government from Paris to Bordeaux, that crushed all friendly hope for France in this section.

The English connection with the war in these parts is hardly considered. The speculation is mostly in regard to what is Turkey going to do, and when? Generally it is considered that Turkey will only attempt to defend the Dardanelles against Russia; again, that it will assist Austria against Russia, or that it will march to the Balkans at the opportune time. But one thing is certain, and that is that the Turkish Army is a reserve force for Germany just as soon as she has settled matters in a definite form in the West and can turn her main force eastward into Russia – then the Turkish Army will be found on the march. And should Italy attempt to advance into Albania, then too Turkey would protest. The Moslem rank and file talk much about their possible advance into Egypt, to help the Arabs wrest Egypt from the grasp of the English. But in such a case, the Arabs of the interior of Egypt and Africa must first be consulted. Since Egyptian postal authorities do not permit any newspapers to leave Egypt, the people of Syria are in ignorance as to what is happening in those parts. All suspicious looking letters into Syria are first opened by the Egyptian postal authorities. The only outside news that enters besides cable news is Italian newspapers from Naples via Italian steamers that still ply these ports. The newspapers in a measure confirm the German cabled war news, although such news is nearly ten days old upon arrival.

The degree of oppression of the people by the government has been such as to make even the Moslem a rebel at heart, and any Power landing troops in Syria at this time would be welcomed with open arms.

Such a great contrast is observed between the spirits of soldiers of different nations going to the front. The Turkish recruits invariably curse their government openly; the Frenchmen in these parts are not hastening home but say they will remain here until a French steamer is sent for them; the Austrians, among which are many Jews, show an eager spirit to get to the front, but nothing compared to the Germans, who are simply beside themselves to get to the fray. I have seen incidents that caused me to marvel. The special train that carried recruits of these nations to Aleppo and from thence to a near seaport, had left Haiffa. Next morning there arrived twelve belated Germans. They refused to wait four days for the next special, but hired a small sailboat, into which they crowded and sailed for Beyrout, where rail facilities were more available.

On these trains were the sulky Turk and Arab, the serious looking Jew, the eager Austrian, but the German bars description. With war songs, songs of party, songs of victory, every kind of song, he gradually infects the rest with a spirit that commanders sigh for.

One officer told me, with a rather melancholy mien, that if the Turkish soldier only had that German spirit, they would be invincible. That confidence individually possessed by the German soldier forecasts half the battle won.

At Aleppo, a German Army Surgeon examines every man. A few are found incapable of the long march to seaport and are turned back. These actually curse their luck though having left wife and babies behind but a few hours before. These are told to report again for duty within a specified time, which melts the frown into a smile. From Aleppo, these recruits work their way into Turkey, then Austria and Germany, as the case requires. But I am told by a Turkish officer that the Turkish soldier protests against going to the front, not because of his disloyalty to his government but because of the terrible hardships they must endure on account of the poverty of the Turkish Treasury. While at the front the last time, they had one square meal every three days; the rest of the time they were on half rations and were advised to pull up their belt tightly. But, he said, "when fighting begins, their anger is turned on the enemy, and they fight as well as any other."

These painful sights and his humanitarian feelings moved Edward to attempt to collect a fund to be used to feed the poor in Haifa and other places in Syria. Correspondence shows that he thought food would be of more value than money and he tried hard to make arrangements that would not endanger 'Abdu'l-Bahá or the Bahá'ís in the Holy Land. By the Fall of 1914 he had a plan, but evidently questions were being raised as to whether it had the approval of 'Abdu'l-Bahá.

> 2626 University Place, NW
> Washington, D. C.
> October 22, 1914
> ALLAHO ABHA!

Mrs. Corinne True
  Chicago, Ill.

My dear Sister in El Abha:-
I have been consulting with different Friends in various cities regarding a relief fund for the people of Haifa. In order to avoid misunderstanding I did not intend to consult by mail, consequently waited until the plan was sufficiently endorsed and changed to satisfy all, before sending it out to other cities. The great need and distress together with the Master's anxiety for the poor were apparent when I left Haifa, and they must be apparent to all of us here, that it seemed the height of folly for me to ask for <u>a Tablet granting me permission to</u> inform the friends in America that the poor of Haifa were in need.

298

The Master's words to me, herein quoted, were deemed sufficient at the time and ought be sufficient for the Friends everywhere in order that they arise to the emergency. In the various cities this servant has <u>only consulted</u> as to a <u>plan for relief</u>. It is not necessarily a Bahá'í matter, for 'Abdu'l-Bahá is assisting the people of all races and religions – over 300 stranger refugees, women and children, are looking to the Father of the Poor for food and shelter.

One plan for all to follow seems better than five or six various methods by that many different cities. The plan adopted for general direction is inclosed. I have <u>asked</u> for no money, <u>received</u> not one penny, and don't <u>expect</u> to handle any of the money, nor am I one of the treasurers. I simply am the <u>messenger</u> to speak of the great need. It is for you in Chicago and other places to answer the call. With that my connection ceases. By November fourth English and Egyptian Banks will be open again for business, so that the fund can reach Haifa by way of Port Said. But that is a matter for the general treasurer to have charge of. He has not yet been selected, but since the Goodalls are by this time in Dublin in consultation over this and other matters, there the matter may be decided.

In New York some of the Friends demurred, because <u>I had no Tablet</u>, but is it possible that a Believer must have <u>a Tablet when only heralding the needs</u> of the STARVING? Had I known about the conditions here I certainly should have come prepared, but I thought the Master's conversation as quoted herein was deemed enough by me.

As the Goodalls will no doubt return to Chicago, you will know more from them. I could not come to Chicago hence am sending my message by mail. It will have to be accepted for what is intended, and not as per the vicious attack some of the self-important who warn the Friends against disobeying a <u>letter</u> of the law and then swallow a whole alphabet. I do not understand why I or the plan should be attacked, when I am only <u>asking for succor for the poor</u>. Can anything be more disgraceful? Have some Bahá'ís come to this?

I made a proposition to Roy Wilhelm, to Mr. Mills, and also to Mrs. Parsons that we send a cablegram to 'Abdu'l-Bahá to confirm my message, but all of them thought that it would defeat the very object desired; so the matter stands for the Goodalls and

Mrs. Parsons and Mr. Fred Lunt to take up. In the meantime the Friends are getting subscriptions so as to lose no time.

I lay this matter before you to do with as you see fit in Chicago. This is only for the one fund and is not expected to be continued. As soon as this fund is sent that ends this particular effort. I make this plain so that you will know that it is not intended to interfere with the Temple Contributions.

> Very truly yours,
> In His Service,
> E. C. Getsinger

Each subscriber to the Haiffa Relief Fund is called upon to donate his or her contribution in the spirit of the following supplication:-

O God of Names!

Thy Mercy is limitless and Thy Patience without end. Thy Bounties are beyond the comprehension of the creatures, and Thy gifts are shrouded in mystery to the unseeing. We acknowledge our humility before Thee, and our nothingness. Thou hast entrusted us with the dross of the earth and made us stewards in Thy Household. All we possess is Thine and at Thy command. Therefore, O Lord! accept from Thy stewards such as we have to offer, for such use as in Thy wisdom Thou seest fit to make of it, for the Cause, for the Friends, for the needy, for the servants, in short – for the Cause of God!

For Thou, 'Abdu'l-Bahá art not in need of anything save the Supreme One, and art independent of all the creatures of God.

But, 'Abdu'l-Bahá, to whom shall these stewards turn in the service of their stewardship if not to Thee? How shall our possessions be wisely applied if not by Thy direction: so, we beseech Thee, to accept from these stewards of God their offering, that Thy hand might wisely apply to the needs of the Cause and its Friends.

> E. G.

The collection of the fund brought many difficulties. On October 14, 1914, Mrs. Florian Krug sent a cable to the Master, "Getsinger collecting money, claiming you will dispose of it for relief around of you. Do you sanction?

Cable me instructions. Krug." An answer was received on the following Tuesday, "Krug Wilhelm, 104 Wall Street, New York. Positively I do not accept money. Abbas."

Edward made the following statement dated October 24:

It has just come to my notice through a rumor that a maid-servant of God in New York City took it upon herself contrary to advice, to cable 'Abdu'l-Bahá relative to Relief Fund. It is stated by Friends here that she received a reply several days ago to effect "Not acceptable". If this is true, I have not yet been so informed. The R. R. and telegraph in Haifa are in possession of the Army Officers. Any such funds coming to their knowledge would no doubt cause the Believers to be "squeezed" to the limit, until they themselves had most of the fund. Anyway, secret opposition developed in New York City and the matter best be dropped. Perhaps some few Friends can find comfort in the defeat of relief for the refugees in Haifa. E. C. Getsinger

Despite this word from 'Abdu'l-Bahá and his own state-ment, Edward went on with the Haifa Relief Fund which meant so much to him. In the process he endured criticism from the Bahá'ís and felt attacked. To his perception, ambitious others wished to have the control of the project in their own hands. A cable to Mrs. A. J. Parsons dated October 23, 1914 states:

Confidential word from New York says Kinneys cabled Haifa week ago and reply came will not be accepted. Our fears were realized understand officialism I now suggest quite [quiet] work outside Chicago New York and have you send quietly what is now subscribed past five days suffered great depression the reason now clear.

C. Getsinger

In a letter to Mrs. Cooper dated November 11, 1914 Ed-ward recounts his meeting with Harlan Ober and Ali-Kuli Khan where the formation of a committee made up of "level business men" was discussed. Edward writes:

Money might be transmitted to Mirza Jalol – since the transmission of money to 'Abdu'l-Bahá, <u>personally</u>, in face of the Krug cable and His words to me, is a <u>greater</u> violation than this servant is accused of when using the word "messenger" only. This cable must not be lost sight of. Secrecy must be observed all around from the press also.

Having come from them, I still maintain that <u>food</u> is the necessity, <u>not money</u>, especially since war in Turkey is declared. The State Department and Red Cross will no doubt give their offices for safe delivery, by <u>any</u> <u>means</u> that the Committee can devise. That bridge cannot be crossed until we reach it, as daily developments arise to which all plans must be finally adjusted.

Writing again to Mrs. Cooper on November 12, Edward conveys his doubts as to the wisdom of involving the American Consul or American war ships, as had been suggested by some of the Friends who were apparently carrying out their own plan and had decided that gold was needed by 'Abdu'l-Bahá, not food. "<u>American</u> Consul's <u>messenger</u> and a <u>warship</u> <u>delivery</u> to <u>Him</u>, [underlined twice] would no doubt cause Him to be compelled <u>to refuse all</u>, for safety sake, though the people starve around Him." The thought that Edward would go to Haifa himself must have been under discussion as he writes, "A final decision as to whether this servant is to go or not, will permit me to plan for my immediate future."

Finally, Edward set forth with several hundred English pounds worth of gold worn in a belt about his waist. 'Abdu'l-Bahá refused to accept the money and Edward's frustration at the misfiring of his mission to relieve the human suffering in Haifa, for which he had fought hard and worked diligently, was great. On the way to Haifa, Edward wrote to Joseph Hannen from Alexandria.

Alexandria Jan 10/15

Dear Bro Joseph and Friends:-
Arrived at Port Said 18th and had to come here to get steamer for Haifa, where I will be on the 25th. Briefly: – no mail has gone

into Haifa to Master, such as was in hands of Ahmed Yazdi, for two months. No word came out to him either.

Finally he selected a very old Believer, whose age was above suspicion as well as military requirements and sent him to Haifa 2 weeks ago, to reconnoiter. He got through allright. Then came back and took what mail he could pad himself with and left again for Haifa. He has not returned yet. He also took some contributions sent by individuals so that the sum sent all told is augmented considerable.

I am taking with me all I can pad myself with, and also taking in a belt something heavier, which, if the ship foundered, would make a life preserver useless for me.

All are well in Haifa. Persian friends also sent special messenger to Haifa from Teheran.

I desire to explain to friends in Washington, that when I left there, I did not know I was going to Haifa, merely had an idea, which was not a matter to give out under the circumstances. But as I had given out, when I arrived from India and Haifa, that from all that 'Abdu'l-Bahá said to me, I would be returning in 10-12 weeks, the friends ought to have been informed, in case they desired to send letters.

The General Treas. Mr. Randall, and those he consulted found it quite necessary to send messenger, the wisdom of which is confirmed at this end.

How long the aged messenger will escape detection remains to be seen. Mail from U.S. and other countries sent to Yazdi or Port Said, are opened under Martial Law, sealed and delivered. The only way to get mail to Haifa would perhaps be to mark plainly "Via Italian Mail Steamer". Then it remains on board until Haifa, as that line of ships and Greek, are the only ones going there, and will do so long as Italy is neutral, and from observation I would say that even Italy and Roumania are after something, which if they <u>do not get</u>, will perhaps enter the fray.

As long as these ships go to Haifa, food is quite normal there, but of course money is most needed there at all times at present.

It seems that 'Abdu'l-Bahá refrains from writing letters, as do all Friends in Haifa, in order to be free from suspicion for should the Turks lose in war with Egypt, the populace will rise up in riotous rebellion. So it seems, that for the present the friends refrain from writing all save urgent matters. Plainly written and understood cablegrams get through, slowly.

One in Egypt can <u>feel</u> the suspicion he is under, when moving about as a tourist. On the ship previous to mine, at Gibraltar, where all are held up and everybody questioned, they took off 8 men suspected as Germans. On my ship there were 12 Germans and Austrians in disguise as Swiss, etc. and all got through. It was wonderful, how, for 12 days these men went about – knew each other, yet gave no outward sign. Some had come from Venezuela, waiting in N.Y.C. for months, eager to go to the front, and were as matter of fact as if they were first going home for a visit. Whereas on ship from Naples, I met an English business-man going to India and for 4 days he talked war, and all the time he showed that he, as well as his people, were scared to death of losing and of German invasion. I wonder if that shadow is casting forth a coming event? Also, he stated time and time again, that England must be mistress of the sea in order to be master of commerce. Just business at the bottom of the war from that quarter. Thus the fruit of the Christian dispensation has been merely commerce and its accompanying civilization, and now the Christian Adam – Kings are fighting over the commercial apple.

If I remember right, John the Deciple [sic], in a vision, ate something which was sweet in his mouth and became bitter in his stomach. This may be the case with this apple jam, which every nation is ashamed to acknowledge as their own make.

I trust the Washington Assembly will continue to be a united assembly and work out the fundamental form of Central Comm. of secretaries. Though as individuals we may differ as to the best means to an end, yet any <u>constructive</u> measure which on the face of it, tends toward unity ought receive the support of the Bahá'í hearts and Spirit, as long as a useful purpose is attained, whereas such as see fit to oppose a generally accepted plan, it is best to let them alone and this in that same spirit. Anyway, can it be true that 75 or more Friends are in the wrong who see the wisdom of a thing or measure, and view a tablet in a certain way, are ready to unite on that basis for unity, and have one or two differ and oppose – yet both feel sincerely in the right. Can the 75 be wrongly guided? and only the two receive the true way? and not follow some of our friends, nor follow certain favored principles espoused by Bahá'u'lláh. Because, even these principles – each and every one, only stand as a part or whole, in the end according to the wishes of the House of Justice, and Bahá'u'lláh to this House the only unalterable point of Unity. Then why do we in Washington find a basis of disunity on the changeable and alterable principles, and lose sight of the Everlasting Basis of Unity.

God needs no one to defend Him, nor any one of his 29 principles. He is sufficient to rectify any mistake or deviation we might make. But dear Bahá'ís, are we, one or more, capable of rectifying a mistake we might make, when we mislead our "followers" of an iota into an error, and this error breeds discord? Can we undo our wrong to them or to ourselves? To the Cause? How dangerous it is to be one who has a following on an idea!

It is better to let our ideas, interpretations, stand for principle, etc. die unheard of, than to have to face a possible labor of undoing what we deemed was right, and yet was wrong. Can 50 friends see the same thing in the wrong way, and only 2 see it right and yet all call upon His Name in the same spirit, plus or minus ego? That is the crux – to be humble before the Lord and endeavor to penetrate His Will and subdue our own. No easy matter indeed and that is why God is more patient than his creatures.

I will try and get some news to you from Haifa, if it is possible to slip "one over the Turk".

Bahá'í Greetings to all.
E.C. Getsinger

And again, it is as certain as fate, that any person, white or colored, who is attracted to the Cause for any other reason than that a manifestation of God has come to his or her soul – to the souls of the world past and present – will ere long show the sign of his attraction where the principle which attracted them is jeopardized to their mind. Be that principle any one of the 29 for which Bahá'í revelation stands, there are just 29 doors of exit for such friends to leave the Cause by, who are attracted by anything save the Light of God itself, and not its colored rays. We must be followers of Bahá'u'lláh obedient to the Center of the Covenant, though he ostensibly contradict himself.

The Master received Edward lovingly, despite the refusal

of the gold, and continued His teaching and counsel. Edward later stated that he also consulted the Master at this time about his marriage. He recorded the Master's words to him during these days (January 26-February 5 1915) to share with the Bahá'ís; they were printed in *Star of the West* the following June.[113] Among 'Abdu'l-Bahá's counsels were the following:

The ones in real authority are known by their humility and self-sacrifice and show no attitude of superiority over the friends.

Some time ago a Tablet was written stating that none are appointed to any authority to do anything but to serve the Cause as true servants of the friends – and for this no Tablet is necessary: such service when true and unselfish, requires no announcement, nor following, nor written document.

Let the servant be known by his deed, by his Life! To be approved of GOD alone should be one's aim.

When GOD calls a soul to a high station, it is because that soul has capacity for that station as a gift of GOD, and because that soul has supplicated to be taken into His service. No envies, jealousies, calumnies, slanders, plots nor schemes, will ever move GOD to remove a soul from its intended place, for by the grace of GOD, such actions on the part of the people are the test of the servant, testing his strength, forbearance, endurance and sincerity under adversity. At the same time those who show forth envies, jealousies, etc. toward a servant, are depriving themselves of their own stations, and not another of his, for they prove by their own acts that they are not only unworthy of being called to any station awaiting them, but also prove that they cannot withstand the very first test – that of rejoicing over the success of their neighbor, at which GOD rejoices. Only by such a sincere joy can the gift of GOD descend unto a pure heart.

En y closes the door of Bounty, and jealousy prevents one from ever attaining to the Kingdom of Abha.

No! Before GOD! No one can deprive another of his rightful station, that can only be lost by one's unwillingness or failure to do the WILL of God, or by seeking to use the Cause of GOD for one's own gratification or ambition.

No one save a severed soul or a sincere heart finds response from GOD. By assisting in the success of another servant in the Cause does one in reality lay the foundation for one's own success and aspirations.

Ambitions are an abomination before the Lord.

How regrettable! Some even use the affairs of the Cause and its activities as a means of revenge on account of some personal spite, or fancied injury, interfering with the work of another, or seeking its failure. Such only destroy their own success, did they know the truth.

———

The more one is severed from the world, from desires, from human affairs and conditions, the more impervious does one become to the tests of GOD. Tests are a means by which a soul is measured as to its fitness, and proven out by its own acts. GOD knows its fitness beforehand, and also its unpreparedness, but man, with an ego, would not believe himself unfit unless proof were given him. Consequently, his susceptibility to evil is proven to him when he falls into the tests, and the tests are continued until the soul realizes its own unfitness, then remorse and regret tend to root out the weakness.

The same test comes again in greater degree, until it is shown that a former weakness has become a strength, and the power to overcome evil has been established.

———

Blessed are they who are the means of making unity among the friends, and pity on those who IN THE RIGHT OR WRONG are the cause of discord. For instance: when one is in the right in a case in dispute, and his minority prevents him from establishing this rightful matter, instead of agitating the subject, if he will humbly submit to sacrifice his position for the sake of unity and peace, GOD will accept that sacrifice and ere long the rightful matter will be established without any further dispute, by the Divine assistance; whereas without such sacrifice and submissiveness great harm might ensue.

The friends must be prepared to efface themselves at all times. Seeking the approval of men is many times the cause of imperiling the approval of GOD.

———

The worst enemies of the Cause are in the Cause and mention the Name of GOD. We need not fear the enemies on the outside for such can be easily dealt with. But the enemies who call themselves friends and who persistently violate every fundamental law of love and unity, are difficult to be dealt with in this day, for the mercy of GOD is still great. But ere long this merciful door will be closed and such enemies will be attacked with a madness.

Even though 'Abdu'l-Bahá had not accepted the money raised for the Haifa Relief Fund, Edward still hoped to get it through to Haifa through the good offices of Mrs. Stannard in Egypt. On returning exhausted to Washington, leaving the gold behind, he was outraged when the Bahá'ís demanded receipts for the disposition of their contributions. The Relief Fund was such a sore point to Edward that he was still writing indignantly about it two years later, and his letters during this period indicate a lack of balance. This may have been the final blow which determined Edward to sever all ties with Lua. Throughout the first half of 1915 he was considering filing for divorce, although Lua does not seem to have known this.

She continued to live as a guest of 'Abdu'l-Bahá's family after their return from Abu Sinan. A lead article in *Star of the West* by Elinore Hiscock, titled "Latest news of 'Abdu'l-Bahá", and written on May 13, 1915 states: "The holy family and Lua Getsinger have been staying in a village two hours inland from Acca, but now they are all returning to Haifa . . ."

In May Lua wrote to her old friend Agnes Parsons as she normally did. She tells of her activities in the Holy Household and indicates that she remained a guest of 'Abdu'l-Bahá's family because, the "Friends" being unfriendly towards her,[114] Edward did not wish her to return with him to America. Lua writes as though she does not consider their parting as being a rupture of the marriage, or in any way different from what had gone before.

Haifa, Syria
May 10th, 1915

My dear "Noor",

It is a long time since I have either heard from you or written to you; if you replied to my last letter from India yours did not reach me. I left there Nov. 17th (just one year exactly from the day we sailed for Bombay from Port Said) and arrived here Dec. 3rd. – I found all of the family in the "hills of Galilee" where we remained until two or three days ago when we returned to beautiful Haifa and are now comfortably settled in the Home of the Beloved. I am very happy and thankful to be here – although when Mr. Getsinger came in January the Master greatly desired me to return to America with him; but he said the "Friends" were not <u>friendly</u> toward me and was much opposed to my going – thus I remain "the guest of God in the Holy Land". And if they are unfriendly – their unfriendliness has proved a great blessing to me for which I am more than grateful! I was ill in India for two months after he left there for Syria and America, and was very weak, thin and weary upon my arrival here, thus was not sorry to remain longer in this heavenly place, under the Sheltering Love of "the Knower of Hearts"! Regarding each and all in my Native Land – I wish for them, all success, joy, peace and prosperity, and pray that divine confirmations may descend upon their hearts and heads consecutively and unceasingly. I love them, and their attitude toward me is acceptable whether it be amicable or the reverse. I have, thank God – walked long enough and far enough on "the Highway of Severance" to know that both the love and the hatred of <u>human</u> beings – are only good or bad according to the reception they find in our hearts – and should be regarded only as something to sacrifice for the sake of the "Love of God".

One day, about three months ago the Beloved suddenly asked me <u>in English</u> – "What do you want?" and my answer was – "The Love of God!" and thanks be to His Mercy – I received it – I hope to such an extent that I can but wish well and good for all and especially the "Friends". The letter you wrote Mr. G – Dec. 24th requesting him to return to you after reading the same to the Beloved is in my possession and will be sent to you when possi-

309

ble. We all felt very sorry that he should have come all the long way to bring the gift of the "Friends" only to be sent back with it; – but you see dear he had been told not to do it when he was here in the summer, and besides there was a divided opinion about the matter – thus the <u>refusal</u> was a love lesson in obedience for all. I can still but wish he had brought a few pounds of rice instead of that "which proved such hard food for Midas" in days gone by. He had difficulty in getting in and out of Syria with it – but fortunately all ended well – and we trust he reached America safely and returned it as directed – We have not heard from him since he left Naples Feb. 10th.

The news from California in the "State of the West" (Dec. and Jan. nos.) made us all very happy! I hope you were able to attend the Convention. What a splendid program they had! I hope to go out and serve again somewhere when possible, and I am a little stronger physically! The entire devotion of oneself to the Service of the Covenant of God is the only thing worth considering now! And oh, how the world needs spiritual severed souls to shed the light of Guidance – especially at this time! May I be found worthy! The time has passed these months so pleasantly and swiftly: while in Abou Sinan I assisted a young Persian Physician – who graduated from the American College in Beyrouth last year – in performing several operations by giving the anaesthetic for him. Several were operations on the eyes – and how much I recalled with gratitude the kindness of Dr. Wilmer in allowing me to attend his clinics in Washington, for I was enabled thereby to render real assistance. Please remember me to him when you see him, and tell him that some poor souls have received a benefit through his kindness to me. – I can give you the good news of the health and well-being of all here and the Beloved in particular. Thanks be to dear good God. You are often mentioned with sincere love and ever remembered! Turn always <u>to</u> <u>the</u> <u>Spirit</u>; you will be rightly guided when you listen to no other voices save "The Voice of the True One"! – You have been greatly blessed and are under the direction of "Him Who guideth Whomsoever He wisheth".

Will you please give my most loving greetings to Mr. and dear Mrs. Haney! How beloved and acceptable they are in the Holy Court of the Covenant! They have His Good Pleasure and what more could two souls desire.

My sincere greetings to Mr. Parsons, Royall and Jeffrey "Boy"
and much love accompanied by prayers, and best of best wishes
for your own dear kind self – As ever yours

>Devotedly
>Lua

Ahmad Sohrab sends remembrances and greetings

>In His Name!

In June, Lua wrote to Mrs. Goodall. Her letter vividly
recounts some of the difficulties that were being endured
during the war. She mentions the bombardment which did
little damage, though one person was killed. She enlists the
generous Mrs. Goodall's sympathy toward a youth left
without funds and needing education. Munavvar Khánum
added a postscript emphasizing Lua's request for funds to
send the boy to the Syrian Protestant College in Beirut.

>June 11th, 1915
>Haifa, Syria

My dear Bahá'í friend,
I am glad to be able to write you that, although we have had an
actual introduction to the manoeuver of war everybody is safe
and well. The bombardment was confined to a certain locality
and therefore the destruction was limited. One person only,
killed and thank God no wounded. It was terrifying while it
lasted – but all is serene and calm again. I have written you and
Ella several times do not know if you have rec'd my letters or not!
All communication is cut off now save with [those sent] via
America! We are wondering why none of you write us? You can
address your letters direct to Haifa c/o Mirza Mousin. Send them
open for they pass via Constantinople and must go under censorship. But please do write us and tell us the good news. We do not
want to hear anything bad for we have plenty of that kind here.
It may interest you to know that a dire famine stares the people
in the face for a year to come, on account of the locusts which
have come in such vast swarms as to darken the sun and still they
come! Everything has been consumed save a few wheat fields and
we are praying that they may remain unmolested otherwise there
will be no bread even for a single soul.

I have not heard from Mr. G– since his return to America – hope he reached there safely. One of the old believers died recently leaving six children. One is a boy twelve years old the only hope of the family for their future. And without an education he will not be able to do anything for them either! Do you think it would be possible for the Friends there to gather $150 per year to send this boy to the American School in Beyrouth for four years? The money could be deposited in a bank in America and we will write the President of the school to that effect and they will accept the boy as a pupil. You can not know what a blessing and help this would be for this stricken family whose sole support for the future depends upon this boy's ability to take care of them. Please will you ask the Friends if they can do this good deed and let us know as soon as possible if it is acceptable.

I wish I could write you in detail about many things but it is impossible now. Pray for the safety and well-being of our Beloved and family – for whom I hope to sacrifice everything even life if necessary.

Give my love to Georgie & Mr. Ralston and with greetings to all the Friends

I am as ever

Yours in the Faith

Lua

On July 18, 1915 Ahmad Sohrab wrote in a letter to Howard and Edward Struven: "Our dear mother Lua lives with the holy family at the foot of the mountains and is very happy." But her time in Paradise was coming to an end, for in August the war situation became so serious as to put 'Abdu'l-Bahá in danger once more, and he advised her to leave with other Americans on an American cruiser specially sent to take foreign nationals away from Syria. Lua wrote a long report "for the Bahá'í Friends" which she sent to Joseph Hannen who copied it and sent it out. Describing what she had witnessed in the Holy Land during those months of the First World War, Lua provides a moving pen-picture of 'Abdu'l-Bahá.

To Mr. Joseph H. Hannen.

For the Bahá'í Friends,

Returning from India I arrived in Haifa Dec. 3rd, 1914, going direct to Abou Senan, a little village high up in the hills of Galilee, where 'Abdu'l-Bahá, His family and followers then resided and where we remained until after the Feast of Rizwan in the springtime when everybody returned to Haifa and their own homes once more, assured by the kind consideration manifested by the commanders of the French battle ships that no harm was to befall the inhabitants of the small Syrian coast towns at their hands, which subsequent bombardments proved to be a fact, for they were always localized and news sent on shore before the firing began, warning people away from the place designated for destruction; thus no lives were lost, with the one exception of a poor man who was too near a particular spot upon which an aeroplane dropped a bomb. Nevertheless, the bombardments were terrifying though of short duration. It was wonderful to see the Master at such times sitting unmoved, watching from the window, as I beheld him on two occasions; His marvellous Face wearing the expression of one who knew and knows what needs must be and all the reasons why, calmly awaiting a pre-destined end which may include the Supreme Sacrifice of Himself.

During the first bombardment which destroyed the railroad bridge near Acca He was sitting thus. I was standing near Him gazing intently upon His countenance, trying to read and understand all that it expressed, when He turned and said with quiet determination, "I must go at once to Acca. My place is there before the cannons striking such terror to the hearts of the people now fleeing away in all directions. They are afraid, I must gather them. They are helpless and hopeless. I must rescue and assure them." And before the firing ceased He was ready to start out on this divine errand of the Good Shepherd; gathering the affrighted scattered flock from the hillsides and plains as He went along comforting, soothing and leading them back to the shelter of their own forsaken homes. As I stood watching Him descend the little hill upon which the house is situated, to mount His donkey waiting on the rocky path below – I thought my heart would break with longing to go with Him. – Then the knowledge that I too was a stray lamb which He had rescued from terrors worse than these was swiftly borne upon my consciousness, making me realize that His work is one which He <u>alone</u> can <u>do</u>. And I could only turn away to pray that all others might be likewise housed under the canopy of His Mercy in the heavenly sheepfold of His neverending Love.

During the last days of January and the first of Feb. the Beloved was in great danger; several nights he kept sleepless watch preparing Himself and certain members of the Household for what seemed inevitable. This news reached Abou Senan late one afternoon and the remaining members of the family there then shared the weary vigils of fearful anxiety. I was called to Haifa to make some statements concerning the matter, and when informed by the Master of all that was pending I could but marvel at His gentleness in dealing with its source, His patient fortitude, and His kindness to all concerned. Three of the Holy Leaves were in Haifa – having gone there with me. A telegram came, and the Master sent us all in great haste back to Abou Senan, Mirza Jalal and Mirza Mousin accompanying us. None of us knew the contents of the telegram nor its portents. He remained with Ahmad Sohrab in Haifa to meet alone what He alone knew might befall Him. In a few days it was reported in Acca that He was to be arrested and sent to Damascus. The friends and inhabitants of that place as well as Abou Senan were plunged into consternation and despair. Never shall I forget Bahaya Khanum (the Master's sister), when it was told to her. She received it as one accustomed to hard blows throughout a lifetime only could receive it! Her sweet, calm face paled a little, then she smiled bravely; walked quietly to the window beside which He always sat when there, and seating herself, looked out toward the Holy Tomb of Bahá'u'lláh just discernible in the distance. Thoughtful, silent, but still smiling, she slowly bowed her head in such evident submission to whatever Fate might decree, that we could not restrain our tears. Then she arose, saying very gently "Do not cry – until now God has always protected Him. Let us trust in God," and went out softly closing the door. Some hours after, at sunset, I found her standing alone on the balcony still looking out in mute appeal across the plains toward the Holy Tomb. Stealing quietly to her side, she slipped her arm around me without removing her gaze, and thus we stood together, Saint and Sinner, calling upon God's Great Name in the unison of a silence that vibrated to the pressing need and responded to the urge of Love in both our hearts.

The next morning 'Abdu'l-Bahá went to Acca where He remained a short time, quieting, helping and reassuring the people; then, without sending any word he came to Abou Senan! Oh, how we rejoiced to see Him! His smiling face, His clear, consoling voice, His loving solicitude dawned all suddenly like a glowing Sun in the midst of our darkness, dispelling for the moment our fears and setting our troubled hearts at rest. Two days after this I was called into His Presence with Monevvar Khanum, when He said: "I wish to tell you some things today which you may write after, and never throughout all the rest of the days of your life forget". Then He spoke for nearly an hour, and among other things said: "I have been in great danger and am still like one sitting under a suspended sword which may fall at a moments notice! For myself I do not care, and am ready for any sacrifice and yearn for the cup of martyrdom – but I am thinking of those whom I must leave, their helplessness when I am gone so cries out to me before I go that for their sakes I hope to be spared yet a little while. Still, I am prepared – and I now prepare you for a day will come when I shall go suddenly from the midst of all and you will see me no more. In the meantime re-read Mirza Abul Fazl's book and the Acts of the Apostles. I pray that you may be severed from all else save God and attain that which I desire for you!" I finished reading "The Acts" before sleeping that night and early the next morning told Him. He was sitting at the time in the middle of the room, His back to a window through which the newly-risen sun bathed His whole figure in golden glory, transforming His snowy hair, hanging about His neck upon His shoulders into a background of pure white light, against which I beheld His Face as "The Ancient of Days" and saw in it what I had never seen before! "You have read 'The Acts'?" He asked, looking searchingly at me, "And are you ready now to walk in the footsteps of the Disciples of Christ?" I only knelt at His feet and kissed the hem of His Garment, while the love for Him in my heart whispered to His Heart my reply.

The next day He left us as unexpectedly as He came, returning to Acca, Haifa. Gradually things settled down after that; the days came and went and weeks rolled by, bringing the Spring and with it the locusts which robbed the Summer of everything save the hot, white glare of the sun and the endless blue of a cloudless sky. Cut off from all the rest of the world we waited throughout the long days which disclosed such misery and woe on all sides, for news from the "Friends" in America, the only country from which any of us could expect to hear, but none came. About the middle of August reports filtered through from Constantinople that America was about to declare war on Germany.-

April 29, 1915, the following was revealed in Acca, which I recorded at the time: –

After relating a very amusing incident which He had just witnessed regarding some dogs quarreling over a bone down in the yard, and being dispersed by the vigorous kicks of a sleepy, stupid looking donkey standing in the sun over against a wall, 'Abdu'l-Bahá said: "The nations of Europe are like those dogs, and Turkey is like the bone over which they will quarrel. A great war will take place in the West, over a very small cause, which will eventually involve the whole of Europe in strife. Great bloodshed and loss of life will ensure; cries and lamentations will be raised on all sides. Great changes will take place; boundary lines will be removed; some countries that are now kingdoms will become Republics and some Republics will become Monarchies, and many surprising events will come to pass!" "Will America be included?" asked an American Bahá'í present. "No", replied the Master, "She will have internal troubles at that time, and her position across the seas will protect her and be a means of keeping her out of the conflict. She will come forward as a Peace Maker! You should be very thankful for this!"– Having brought the above to the Master's attention, I supplicated for America with all my heart, that though the Bahá'ís there may not have done as they should by way of obeying His Commands and instructions, to yet grant America the fulfillment of this promise. At first He answered hopefully, but when the subject was brought up again His reply caused us to be both grieved and troubled. Several days later we heard that an American cruiser was coming direct to Haifa to take away any Americans wishing to leave and the Jews who had gathered in great numbers from the interior and were waiting to be rescued. The Master then said to me "Now is the time for you to go – for should America declare war I would no longer be able to protect you in my house – besides,

316

I desire you to go and give news to the Friends in Egypt, India and France and then return to America and spread the Cause." August 27th we heard that the ship would arrive the 29th and all passengers were to embark at Haifa and be landed on the Island of Crete! When told this the Master said, laughing, "See – you are going to the very place where St. Paul went. Are you ready to walk in his footsteps?" I replied that I was ready to try and hoped that I might leave the Island without being ship-wrecked, but even so, I would still do my best! Mirza Haydar Ali, "The Angel" said "Begin teaching as soon as you get on board and tell them all about the Covenant, which will ensure your safety and enable you to go everywhere!" – The Master had been prepared for some days to go to Tiberias, but in the evening of Aug. 28th He said: "I wish to go to Nazareth to see the place where Jesus was brought up, where he declared in the Synagogue 'No prophet is accepted in His own Country!' I want to walk in His footsteps. – I want to sacrifice myself for all of the Beloved of God! I long to drink the cup which Jesus drank for the sake of Bahá'u'lláh, that His truth may be known, and His path made plain to all people!"

News had reached Haifa that day that the Military Governor of Syria had hung twelve men in Beyrouth and had sent word that he was coming to hang three more at the gate of Acca, as many more in Haifa, and was then on the way to Nazareth. The inhabitants of both Acca and Haifa were terrified. Government officials were hurrying away, business men were closing their shops and going home with pale faces.

Ahmad Sohrab had been informed by the Beloved in Febru-ary of a dire threat this same man had made regarding Himself, which is recorded in detail in his diary and which I had read in May; but the Master had made no reference to or mention of any of these things while conversing with us the evening previous. Early in the morning August 29th the Master called me and we drank tea together, after which He gave me some final instruc-tions regarding future service in the Cause and told me some things to strengthen and encourage me, for I was heartbroken at the thought of leaving Him and His household, surrounded as they are by such difficulties and trying ordeals, yet I wanted to obey Him and go, <u>smiling</u>, as he wished! About ten o'clock he came hurriedly into my room asking "Are you all ready to go?"

"Yes", I answered, "I am ready!" "We are both travellers today", he continued, "for I am going just now to Nazareth!" Imagine my feelings if you can, when I heard Him say this, for I knew He was going to face a foe vested with all material power to do whatsoever he chooses, which fact recalled His words of the night before, revealing in them an appalling significance. Almost immediately He called the inmates of the household into His Presence, and when all had assembled in the large hall He spoke a few words of loving farewell, ending with "Good bye!" "Good bye all!" and went into the vestibule where Bahaya Khanum and the members of His family, including myself, were gathered. He took His sister in His arms and kissing her on both cheeks, held her off, looked one long half moment into her face, and kissed her again; then, with her head drooping like a broken flower upon His shoulder, He looked intensely at all of us, standing in tearful silence around Him, threw back His head, raised His eyes, smiled and went out. Crowding in the doorway, we watched Him descend the steps, walk majestically down to the gate, where the carriage was waiting, and without once looking back, drove away. It had all happened so quickly that Ahmad Sohrab and the Friends had not time to come down from the Pilgrim's House on the Mountain to see Him and receive His farewell benediction.

We went back into the house which had instantly become so desolate and just stood or sat like dumb stricken creatures gazing in mute anxiety at the pale sorrowful features of the Greatest Holy Leaf, who sat by the window and looked with dry eyes at the Master's empty seat down in the Garden, previously devastated by the locusts and whose barrenness now added to the gloom settling like a pall throughout the house. I crossed the room and sat beside her; she quietly took my hand without turning her head and continued to look out of the window as if searching for a very vital part of herself, which had suddenly forsaken her! It seemed to me ages long gone and ages yet to be, came and met in the anxious and awful silence imposed upon us, until the entire past and future were merged into a pulsating present, which throbbed only with pain; pain which would eventually find its way in every soul upon the earth as it had already found ours and over which it held inexorable sway! Munira Khanum – the Mother – suddenly cried out "Oh God have mercy upon us!" And as if to answer her anguished appeal Khanum turned to her while the "brave smile" struggled with her trembling lips, and said, almost in a whisper, "At such times God has always protected Him, perhaps He will be merciful to us and save Him yet again! The world does not deserve it, but as He is the Heart of all existence God in His Mercy may spare Him that our spirits fail not entirely before Him, or our souls cease to be!"

Two hours after that the ship came and I too said "Good bye" and went away, only to return and remain one more night under the shelter of that lonely roof, lonely because its Shelterer had gone! The captain of the Cruiser had sent word through the American Consul who had been out to the ship that he would come ashore the next morning at which time I should embark. Thus shortly after sunrise August 30th, I said "Au revoir," this time and not "Good bye" by request of the Master's Sister, and departed, accompanied to the gate of the Custom House by Shogie Effendi, Ahmad Sohrab and Mirza AzizUllah Khan Bahadur. I passed through attended by our Consul and was introduced to the Captain who immediately took me and my belongings on the ship's launch, which was waiting, after which we steamed out into the harbor, boarded the Cruiser and sailed away. As I stood by the rail to catch a last glimpse of Haifa and Mt. Carmel now fading into the misty distance, the Master's words in Abou Senan came like a lightning flash across my mind. They had been literally fulfilled! He had gone suddenly from our midst and I was going and would see Him no more! –

It was terrible to leave thus without knowing the outcome of His journey to Nazareth, but I trust before this reaches you you will have heard from Ahmad Sohrab (who promised to write immediately to America) of His safe return to Haifa or of His sojourn in Tiberias.

XVIII

A crisis was now about to break, through Edward filing for divorce. Lua had been a target of envy and rumor for many years, the latter possibly caused by the jealousy of her own husband. Gossip had made her out to be a "Magdalene" and one who was not firm in the Covenant. This latter charge was accentuated after Fareed's defection. The fact that they had travelled long months together had linked their names. It is not an uncommon practice for angry husbands to accuse their wives of infidelity and Edward was no exception.[115] He wrote to Agnes Parsons on July 29, 1915 explaining his actions in bringing formal charges of infidelity with Dr. Fareed and another Bahá'í. The letter is quoted in part below:

I wrote you last that I intended to take a serious step before the month closed, but was not permitted to procrastinate any longer, as the urging within me was too strong, so much so, that I went two days later to Wash. and applied for divorce. We were unable it seems to avoid publicity entirely, as only the "Star" gave a short notice. Later in Sept. when the matter comes up, we hope to avoid any mention.

I had decided not to write to any one about this, our own private affair, but as no doubt you will be besieged by the friends of Lua's and mine, it may be well for you to know a few facts in order that less gossip be indulged in and which you might be able to allay.

There is no cause for the Friends to bestir themselves in this matter, for, it has been talked over finally between us, and agreed to end this running sore on our lives in the two words, but it is not agreeable to either of us, that necessity of the law compel me to sue in the Dist. of Columbia. As you know, I have been living in Va. for 3 months in order to get a residence, but found that I could not get a legal residence nor legal divorce. Then I went to Pa. and was doing the same thing, when suddenly out of a clear sky, I was powerfully informed in spirit to go at once to Wash and begin proceedings.

This was the 4th prompting I have had in 7 months, and dared not put off any longer, as I hated to do so, in fact did not want a divorce.

We have been married just 19 years and it is nine (9) years since Lua met _____, and from that time, 9 years, she has not been a wife to me – refused on pretext that she had no love for me, and that such association should be based on love. I agreed to that argument, but tried to win her by kindness, patience etc. this she admits in her own hand writing. But no avail. I was not her "affinity" and she kept on trying to find hers in every one save me and God.

. . . I had 3 dreams in succession within 2 months, to go ahead, but delayed. Then the mission to Haifa with fund came up, and I did not want to go to Haifa with the fund, for the reason that I was continually being prompted to begin proceedings, and not delay.

At Haifa I found Lua, and she was 10 miles in the country. After 3 days she came, and with Ahmed A. B. sent her to my hotel, Ahmed as witness, to ask if reconciliation was possible. I said positively no! Ahmed took my decision to A. B. and he only said, "Very well, then I will have to plan for Lua otherwise!" When A. B. saw me, he repeated what he said before in August and again to avoid publicity as far as possible. I returned to the U. S. and said not a word to any one, save Mrs. Barnitz – just a hint, because I was in her house, and she may not want the matter to be housed there. I went to Va. quietly, but to no avail – I had to go to D. C. to get proceedings. Lua could have perhaps avoided some of the stigma had she not violated the admonitions of A. B. i. e. for her to not write about me or my friends to any one, to cease in other words, her persecution of me and friends, which has been her habit for years, casting aspersions on my character and upon any lady with whom I have ever been seen or even spoken to, including the whole Barnitz household.

. . . Also, it will come out before the court, that during past 8 – 9 years, I have suffered from contractions of the spine in lumbar region, because I had no wife. I did not know why I had these contractions and pain, until I met a Dr. Jacobs of Kansas City on ship coming home last trip. He studied in Vienna Hospital and was driven out by war. He examined me, and told me the cause and the theory of medicine covering it. Gave me medicine and with help of hydrocine I have since been very much better.

Lua has yet something to acquire in spirit. She must overcome as the rest of us have to overcome. A. B. has a plan for her and this tie is an obstacle to the plan. I can not figure it out any other way. Besides this ulcerous fact must be healed – for sake of both of us. The Cause will stand – never mind the Cause. Kings and oppressors have not swerved it, how can we two worms do anything to harm it . . .

I trust this statement will help in adjusting matters in your mind. And I ask neither blame for Lua nor exoneration for myself – just these facts.

E. Getsinger

Lua left Haifa on August 30, 1915, bearing the following Tablet from 'Abdu'l-Bahá.

Haifa, August 27, 1915

To the beloved of God in America – on them be glory and bounty!

The maid-servant of God, Lua, was a long time occupied in India in spreading the fragrances of the love of God. She is now ready to return to the regions of America. Show her every consideration. She is firm in the Covenant of love. In reality she worked vigorously during her sojourn in India, and she is worthy of love.

(Signed) 'Abdu'l-Bahá Abbas

The American cruiser *Des Moines* took her to the island of Crete and then to Port Said, Egypt, where she arrived, exhausted, on the 14th of September. Her first letter from Port Said was written to her dear friend, Louise Bosch, expressing her spiritual aspirations and love for 'Abdu'l-Bahá most eloquently. Lua felt that He was the hope of the world. It is apparent from this letter that she did not yet know of the bolt that was about to fall.

Grand Hotel de la Poste
J. Albrand, Propr.
Port Said Sept. 15, 1915

My beloved Lysa.

Yours dated Dec. 22nd 1914 reached me today here, or rather I reached it for I have just arrived from my eight months' sojourn in Haifa with the Beloved and family! Oh, only God knows how I appreciate the privilege of having been there during that time! And after my year in India I was so physically exhausted when I arrived that I could scarcely stand – but one glimpse of the Beloved's Face, and one word from His divine lips dissipated everything! My sufferings and trials were transmuted into happiness & joys – and the remembrance of the agonies endured all obliterated! So that now in response to what you have written I can only reply Thank God I was found worthy to be sent to India and tried by the purgative fires which she always enkindles for those who cross her borders. She is a Motherland & receives into her arms all the souls whom God wishes to remould and purify. 'Abdu'l-Bahá knew my need as well as hers when He sent me there! And I thank Him for His Mercy to one of His most unworthy Servants. My experiences in India are beyond description but they are all pearls of great price! I entered the Path of Complete Severance from all else save God – there, and now I am walking onward knowing my destined end and way – having one aim, one object before me – "The Center of the Covenant" – who has "blazed the trail" that I may herald and proclaim His high and holy mission and unfurl the Standard of His Cause! – When I left Haifa on one of our American gunboats it was to go forth once more into the world to do His work and obey His commands. I left Him well – and all members of the family the same.

He is as ever the Heart and the hope of the people about Him. He faces His enemies and cannons alike fearlessly! He inspires courage and radiates Love. He sends forth His heavenly blessings and divine assistance on the wings of prayers during the silent watches of the night – when the angels descend to share His vigils, and carry His spiritual messages to all parts of the earth and back to the Great White Throne! Blessed is the ear that can hear; Blessed is the eye that is opened and can See! – The sufferings in Syria are beyond any mortal's telling! There is no fruit or vegetables – everything was eaten by the locusts just as all was nicely grown and nearly ripe. Hundreds are dying from starvation while diseases of all kinds stalk abroad to waste and kill. Men young, old, lame, halt and blind are being sent to the front bare-footed – half naked – hungry – sick – downhearted and hopeless – a vast army of misery whose battle cry is "God let us die" – whose standard is <u>oppression</u> and whose commanders are tyrants deceived by the Great Arch Deceiver! Oh the horrors, the woes, the suffering, the helplessness and distress – God, help me to forget them – and ever remember the calm, patient, majestic Face and figure of the Master who saw – and still sees it all – who faced all situations with a fortitude and courage that was and is sublime! He goes about simply doing good, and ministering to a people whose sole comfort He is – smiling, encouraging, feeding, liberating, and <u>waiting</u> – waiting as one who knows that it all needs must be – for an end ordained by God. The hands on the clock of time are pointing out the great Hour which soon shall strike and then the shackles and chains shall fall. Humanity will awaken from her manacled and barbarous state into a new resurrection – a new realization! She will be taken down from the iron Cross of Crucifixion, arise from the grave of her former self and ascend into the heavens of <u>Man</u> the Image and likeness of her God – upon whose all glorious name she will unitedly call – and then He will answer – "These are my people!"

My dear Lysa, my spiritual child and friend, for you, May, Mariam, Mary Lucas and Juliet I would be only too glad to sacrifice my soul and save you from all suffering – by suffering for you! I only hope I may be found worthy to teach you by <u>living</u> the true life of a Bahá'í in the midst of all trials. Pray for me, and know that I shall ever keep on trying – no matter what happens – to serve Him – the Beloved – the Center of the Covenant – who is the Knower and Keeper of my soul! My love to Mrs. Davis, Mr. Wilson, John D. and all the Friends. I shall write soon all about my experiences in and about Haifa! – Thank God the Beloved is well and with us. He is all there is (in) life or death. He is the Divine <u>all</u> <u>glorious</u> <u>Reality</u> Thanks for your beautiful letter & your sincere love for this most unworthy of all Servants. In His name, Lua

From Port Said Lua wrote a touching letter to Zeenat

324

Baghdádí on September 20, 1915. This letter was published in *Star of the West* the following month.[116] In the letter she describes the suffering in Syria due to the locust plague and then writes this, which was crossed out by the typist, "I know there are many in America who expected to see me crushed and it may disappoint some of them to know that with everything I am not even discouraged – let alone not being 'downhearted'." The next sentence is not deleted. "I am sent forth again to 'Herald The Covenant' by Its Holy Center, and I shall do it with His divine assistance better and more powerfully than I have ever done." The following is again deleted, "Those who expected me to do otherwise did not stop to consider my firm faith in the 'Covenant of Love' when they denounced me and continue to denounce – neither did they take into their contemplation His Great Mercy and Forgiveness! I sought shelter in Him who standeth to Judge every soul in these day – and 'who judgeth not from the sight of the eyes or the hearing of the ears but who judgeth in righteousness and Truth'. When He sent me to India nearly two years ago – He called me to the 'lofty summit of unchanging purpose!' I answered His Call – It may be now He has chosen me to attain that incomparable station – Time, and my work will tell!"

The following is the letter as printed in *Star of the West:*

Port Said, Egypt
Sept. 20 1915

Mrs. Bagdadi, Chicago.
Dear Zeenat Khanum:
I promised your brother, who came to see me on board our American Cruiser, Des Moines, August 30th, which took me and many hundreds of refugees from Haifa, that I would write you as soon as possible after reaching some destination from which it would be possible to get mail through to you. I arrived in Port Said, September 14th, so tired and exhausted that I could do nothing but talk to the friends who have been so long without

news of 'Abdu'l-Bahá! Praise be to God! when I left he was in good health though surrounded by difficulties and dangers which I am powerless to describe.

What he has not done for Syria! "The army of God," as 'Abdu'l-Bahá named the locusts – which came in such clouds as to darken the sun – completed the difficulties by way of misery, starvation and death. Such suffering as was manifest on all sides can scarcely be believed. People were coming day and night begging and weeping at his gate. He became the sole comfort and hope of the people whether they are believers or unbelievers!

Your mother and family were well and your mother especially was so wishing and longing to hear from you. There is no reason why you cannot write direct to Haifa as long as America is neutral and you do not write about war matters. The Bahá'ís in America could have been writing all this time <u>direct</u> to Haifa; but they have sent everything to Port Said which was cut off from Turkey a year ago. 'Abdu'l-Bahá said, <u>now</u> the friends should not address him – as he did not wish to trouble them – and <u>perhaps their letters would not reach him</u>; but that anyone could write Mirza Ahmad Sohrab or other friends in Haifa, so long as America is not in the conflict. Thus please Zeenat, do write to your mother and family; but write in English or Arabic. No news had come from Fatima Khanum for a long time and I am sorry to say that nothing had been heard from any of Dr. Zia's people for some time . . .

I am enclosing a photograph of a tablet to the American Bahá'ís which was revealed August 27th, and which I got through the custom house with the assistance of the American Consul at Haifa. Please ask Dr. Zia to translate it to Mrs. True and then give it to the STAR OF THE WEST. I do not just yet know when I shall reach America as I have some work to do in France first. I am writing an account of my last months with 'Abdu'l-Bahá and family to Mr. Hannen which will probably be sent to all centers . . .

I am sent forth again to "herald The Covenant" by <u>its holy Center</u>, and I shall do it with his divine assistance better and more powerfully than I have ever done . . .

Please say to all the friends that I love them all, and I am ready to meet them in the spirit of the Center of Gods' holy Covenant which is naught save pure, spiritual divine love! I wish everybody success in the service of His Great Cause, and ask them to pray for me – the least and most unworthy of all His faithful servants. . .

With the most sincere Bahá'í greetings to you and your husband, I am as always,

Yours in the service and love of 'Abdu'l-Bahá
(signed) Lua

She wrote vividly to Joseph Hannen about the situation in the Holy Land. Her letter to him from Port Said, Egypt, was also published in *Star of the West*.[117]

Port Said, Egypt
Sept. 21, 1915

Mr. Joseph H. Hannen, Washington, D. C.
My dear Bahá'í friend:

I arrived here a week ago from the Island of Crete, having left Haifa on our American cruiser, <u>Des Moines</u>, which brought away from Haifa two hundred and ninety refugees and myself. I was ready to leave the middle of June on the U.S.S. <u>Tennessee</u>, but as some of the students in Beyrouth succeeded in getting away, 'Abdu'l-Bahá decided that I should stay until later. When the news filtered through of the possibility of America declaring war, and our gunboat came to the very port of Haifa, he said: "Now is the time for you to go and give news to the friends in Egypt, Europe and America. It is a long time that they are without any word, and I desire to send you to them, after which you are to go and teach." Then he wrote a tablet to the friends in America, gave me my instructions, and I left. I shall send a photographic copy of the tablet on the next mail, with a short account of the last few days in Haifa, which were stirring and moving ones for everybody.

'Abdu'l-Bahá was well, though surrounded with the greatest dangers and difficulties when I left. He left Haifa for Nazareth at noon, August 29th, and I sailed the next morning, August 30th . . . He has been encompassed by difficulties on all sides for months, and more especially since the locusts came and de-

327

stroyed everything, which has caused hundreds to suffer and die from starvation. We were absolutely without news from any quarter for months and greatly wondered why no one from America wrote, as it was the only neutral country from which news could come. And now that must cease also, as far as addressing 'Abdu'l-Bahá is concerned; but I do hope you will try and write Mirza Ahmad Sohrab, if only post cards. Letters via Constantinople must all pass the censorship, remember, so no word about war, politics or prophecies!

We passed through three bombardments, which were all localized, therefore no lives were lost. What the people are to do there this winter, only God knows. The cold rains will be an added misery to their already manifold woes. It was wonderful to witness the calm majesty of 'Abdu'l-Bahá as he went about among the people, whose only hope and help he is!. . .

I shall come to America as soon as possible, though I have work to do elsewhere first. I enclose you a translation of the tablet above-mentioned, and will send photographic copy of the original next mail. I send the French translation, made in Haifa by Shougi Effendi, 'Abdu'l-Bahá's grandson; also the English. Please let the friends see them. I have had such a fatiguing journey, and feel so very exhausted physically that I cannot write more at present; beside I only just have time to catch the mail, which closes at midnight. Please give my most sincere greetings to all in the service, and love of the Covenant of God, especially your dear wife, Mrs. Haney and Mrs. Parsons. 'Abdu'l-Bahá said: "Tell everyone now is the time to teach and spread the Cause!" The friends in Cairo and here are all well, and send greetings to all in Washington.

O these days of trial and test! The whole world has been flung into the melting pot. Each individual soul must be put into the crucible and "tried as gold is tried and refined as silver is refined". The Center of the Covenant now sitteth as the Refiner, and it is he who judgeth the purity, capacity and station of every servant. He is the divine assayer who accepts and rejects. He alone knows the hearts, and in him only can one find justice and truth. He is the judge of the high court in the supreme concourse, who renders judgements in righteousness and stations the souls of his sincere worshippers! In this day all must be sure that he is the <u>Center</u> from which every <u>living</u> soul is sent forth, and to which every faithful and sincere one must turn!

More later. As ever, yours faithfully,

In the Center of the Covenant

(signed) Lua

It was about this time that the news of Edward's divorce proceedings reached her. Lua was deeply hurt by Edward's charges and expressed her anguish in letters to Agnes Parsons and Elizabeth Nourse. She also took action to defend herself against the rumors that she was not firm in the Covenant by sending a photograph of 'Abdu'l-Bahá's Tablet of August 27th to her correspondents; as we have seen above, she asked for it to be published in *Star of the West*. But even in the midst of distress at Edward's accusation, Lua was concerned about the dearth of correspondence reaching the Master from America, and also about Mrs. Stannard and Agnes Parsons, who had been put into an awkward position as a result of the continuing story of the Haifa Relief Fund.

Port Said

September 25, 1915

My dear Bahá'í "Noor"

We arrived here Sept. 14 via the Island of Crete. News came through from Constantinople of the possibility of America's declaring war on Germany about Aug. 15th. On the 24th the American consul sent word that our gunboat the Des Moines was coming to Haifa to take away all Americans and refugees. The Beloved then said, "The time has come now for you to go – for should America declare war it would be impossible for you to remain in our house – beside you might be sent as a prisoner to Orfa". I was ready to leave on June on the U.S.S. "Tennessee" but as the students from Beyrouth left at that time it was decided almost at the last moment that I remain which was fortunate for everybody has been without news of Him here in Egypt and India ever since. I hope the American friends have been receiving recent letters from Ahmad S– They could have been writing direct to Haifa all this time – We had been entirely without news for months as everybody was writing to Port Said which had been cut off from Turkey ever since England declared war nearly a year ago – on that country. I wonder no one seemed to think of this and send letters direct – The Master had sent word that Ahmad Yazdi was not to send any more letters by any one from Egypt – but He did not say that the American Friends could not write about the Cause direct – providing no mention was made of the war or prophecies of Bahá'u'lláh regarding the same. Three weeks or more before I left one day a postal was received from Mrs. Gibbons in New York addressed to the Master – congratulating Him on His birthday May 23rd. It brought tears to all eyes! Such a pathetic little postal it was – I had written several people before that asking them why they did not write? That day the Master told me to "Write Mrs. Haney that the time is passed to address anything to me!" He remarked, "Their letters may not reach me and I do not want them to trouble to write when I may not receive them." This made us all feel very sad – for He had been talking so much about His departure from this world that we feared He meant <u>that</u>, for He remarked again after a pause "they may write Ahmad Sohrab or others here". I did not put this in Mrs. H's letter as clearly as I am now writing it to you – for I did not want to agitate her feelings – or cause others through her then to become excited. But things have occurred there since which made another situation and also made these words more clear to all of us. About this, I cannot even now write you. I can only say that when I left the Master had gone to face His worst foe and had bade us all "goodbye" as though none would see Him again. I hope you have rec'd news from Ahmad S. that it passed and He is still safe & well in Tiberias or has returned to Haifa. I was obliged to leave in a few hours after His departure so I am ignorant of the final outcome. Ahmad S– said he would write to America as soon as they heard of His safety or return to Haifa.

I wrote you in April I think, telling you of Mr. G's difficulties in getting in and out of Haifa with the American gold which the Beloved told him to take back to America. He sent Mrs. Stannard £180 ($900) so she tells me – from Naples to be sent to the Master or members of the family without letting them know where it came from – This amount is in her hands! She feels she cannot force it upon the Master after He has rejected it or spend it for other charitable purposes (as has been recently suggested) without the knowledge and consent of the Contributors. Knowing you had largely contributed to the sum he brought – I thought I would write this to you! It is impossible to send it to the Master who I am quite sure would not accept it if He knew it was the same money which He told Mr. G. to return. Mrs. Stannard suggested that I take it for my expenses when I first arrived, as I am without means to go further at present – but I told her knowing the circumstances – as I do – I could not accept one penny of it beside I have no permission from either the Master or Contributors to do so. Mr. G offered me £5 (25.00) of it in Haifa after the Master had refused it – but I told him I could not accept what the Master refused and told the Beloved afterwards who said I had done right. I wrote Mrs. Haney that the sum had been put back and I hoped Mr. G had done nothing else with it – meaning that I hoped he had done exactly as he had been told to do with it – for he had written me from Naples – "A word to the wise is sufficient I have found through Mrs. Stannard a way into the wisdom of the Master", which made me think that perhaps he had left it with her which proves to be the case. Mr. G has misunderstood this statement of mine and accuses me to Mrs. S. of implying that he might use the money himself – which was not intended! I do not remember exactly <u>how</u> I worded it to Mrs. Haney but I know what I meant. For when we talked about the money after he had said "Goodbye" to the Beloved I begged him to do as the Master had told him to do with it. I am aware since my arrival in Egypt only of his recent proceedings against me! – He knows that his <u>motives</u> in doing as he has do not yet appear on the surface but in time all will be revealed. All the defense I have to make to you or the Bahá'í World I send enclosed in the Tablet "To the Beloved of God to America"! – The photograph is from the original in the Master's own handwriting. So far as the Cause or those in it are concerned the great Defender of the Faith and the Faithful heard my Cause, tried my case – and rendered His judgement!

Two years and a half ago Lua Getsinger was called by cablegram from America to the Presence of 'Abdu'l-Bahá in Ramleh,

Egypt – her heart and soul with all their secret faults, imperfections and sins were voluntarily laid bare before Him. She had been bitterly deceived and was forgiven and "Called" "to the lofty summit of unchanging purpose" then sent to India to work in and serve the Cause. Mr. Getsinger <u>knew</u> all this and he also <u>knew</u> – and <u>knows</u> – that she has never seen that "violator" with whom he accuses her since he left California in 1912 – and has never had any communication with him since 'Abdu'l-Bahá told her certain things in Egypt 1913 – regarding him <u>which she did not know before</u> and that she has never even sympathized with him or his since he and his family were declared "Deniers and Breakers of the Covenant" by the Master in 1914 –

Yet, it has remained for a Son of Germany in the great "Day of the Covenant" to accuse her whom He hath forgiven – to debase her whom He hath uplifted and to defame her whom He hath defended! – Even had she been a Magdalene – <u>who is he</u> to stone her <u>after</u> her Lord and the one whom he acknowledges as his Lord had forgiven, trusted and sent her out to herald His name? – In the days of Christ all went out ashamed – <u>before</u> Jesus said "Neither do I condemn thee"! His judgement will be found in Persian Hidden Words no. 44 – What he has approved will prove him – "With what judgement he has judged – he shall be judged" because he has sought to set aside the judgement of the Covenant of God – who standeth to judge <u>every soul</u> in this day!

Dearest Noor – I have only this to say to you – I am neither daunted or discouraged by anything – I shall go about my Master's business and declare the Covenant as I have ever done hoping for greater results of my endeavors – for I answered His <u>Call</u> when I went to India and He has "chosen" me to attain, and sends me to America where my work will reveal any new capacity I may possess and station me in His Kingdom. I know I shall come as a test to many – who have long ago consigned my soul to hell and who rejoice in all that is said against me. They did not take into consideration my firm faith in and unchangeable love for the Center of the Covenant – nor His Great Mercy – when they denounced – and continue to denounce me. They did not know that during my first visit to His Holy Presence eighteen years ago the following tablet was revealed and written by his own blessed Hand for me.

(He is God)

The Presence of the Hon. Lua Getsinger – 46th from the year of Dawning – Oh thou shining and spiritual Gem.

Gladtidings to thee from the Generosity of thy Lord. Be happy on account of the Gifts of thy Lord which shall soon surround thee, <u>and</u> <u>thou</u> <u>art</u> <u>confirmed</u> <u>in</u> <u>The</u> <u>Covenant</u>"

(Signed)

'Abdu'l-Bahá Abbas

At the time none of us knew the teaching of Bahá'u'lláh concerning the Covenant – but He knew the future – and my needs & in His Mercy confirmed me! – Does anyone think that they can shake one whom <u>He</u> <u>has</u> <u>made</u> <u>firm</u> – Does anyone imagine they can cause <u>to</u> <u>fall</u> – one whom He has established? Let them try as they have tried! Let them hate, accuse and curse – Let them reject and stone if they like now – but let them beware <u>how</u> they judge! This letter is not for publication and is in no sense intended for a vindication – it is a strict statement of <u>simple</u> <u>facts</u> – which I desire you to share with Mr. and Mrs. Haney and Mr. and Mrs. Hannen – I have asked, begged (and requested others to do so on my behalf) for severance from all else save God – for many years – He is now answering me! I rejoice and thank Him. I long for suffering until I am purged from all else save His Holy Spirit and then may I sacrifice my life in His Path made so narrow and perfect by the Feet of His Beloved His Son – His Covenant through whom I have learned the fear of God – which has liberated me from the fear of <u>any</u> <u>man</u>!

Please excuse this badly written epistle. I am so tired and exhausted nervously – from recent experiences and journeys from Haifa to Crete and from there on a small Greek vessel here that I really cannot do better. I have been ill in bed since my arrival too but spiritually I am, thank God, well refreshed and ready for any exigency!

When I departed from Haifa the Beloved was well though encompassed with difficulties and dangers such as cannot be described. He sent His divine Love to all. I and others supplicated that America be protected and not drawn into the war! At first He answered as though she would not enter the conflict – but after a few days when the subject was again mentioned He said – "We must be submissive now to what ever happens!" – I said "I know we do not deserve that you should supplicate for her when the Bahá'ís there have all fallen so far short of obedience to your commands – but please forgive us and still protect America under the mighty wings of your prayers for the sake of God's Holy Name!" And He only very sadly answered "If God wishes; I am submissive to His Will!"

God bless you and yours. May <u>His</u> <u>Spirit</u> guide and give you ineffable peace and joy.

As ever yours in the Covenant
Lua

Port Said Egypt
Sept. 26, 1915

My beloved Menita:-

Yours of July – found me here when I arrived Sept. 14. Via Island of Crete to which place I was taken on board our American Cruiser the "Des Moines" sailing from Haifa Aug. 30th from there I came to Egypt on a small Greek vessel reaching P. Said as above stated. I was very tired mentally, and physically exhausted from recent experiences and long journeys. I was so glad to hear from you again. I wonder if you have rec'd my recent letters from Haifa? I wrote Phil also from there. You or anybody could have written me, Ahmad S– or the Beloved direct to Haifa any time as the way has not been closed to America which was really the only neutral country from which news could come! Shortly before I left the Beloved said – ["]Write them now that I do not want to trouble them to write me for the letters may not reach me – but they may write to Ahmad Sorab". Oh dearest I cannot tell you of those last days for I cannot bear to think of them. The Beloved was surrounded by so many difficulties and dangers and spoke to us so much about His departure from this world! He said some of the Believers must arise like the disciples of Christ and do the work! They must be prepared to suffer and endure any trial.

Oh dear heart what troubles are coming to this sorrow laden world. There is no escape I am afraid for the planet itself. Save through the Greatest of all Sacrifices! May God protect the Heart of Existence – and thereby save the earth <u>itself</u> from destruction. I supplicated for America that she go not to war and at first He said that she would not – but afterwards He said "we must be submissive to God now – in everything". I said "I know the Bahá'ís have not obeyed you as we should have done but please ask God to have Mercy upon us – let us try again." Again He answered only "we must be submissive!" It made me feel that America will have <u>a very</u> narrow escape if she can even avoid the conflict now! – I still hope and pray! Dear Heart I was already to leave the Beloved in June on the "S S Tennessee" but it was decided that I remain almost at the last moment – Then He said to me "You may go to Mrs. Nourse until you hear from Mrs. Goodall and communicate with me" – I was expecting to get money from Mrs. G here (you know the Master told her to pay my expenses) and I wrote her sometime ago that I was to be sent out to work again – there is none here yet for me – thus I am obliged to wait until I hear from her. Dearest I shall come to you when I get to America again you may be sure – I long to see you and tell everything I cannot write. The Master told us to read the Acts of the Apostles so much – And was it not strange when I finally left Him I had to go to <u>Crete</u> the Island where St. Paul went (Acts 27 – 2 – 7) – I told the Master and He said "I send you now to walk in the footsteps of the Apostles" – I hope I may accomplish as much as St. Paul did. I am not one bit discouraged – though I know since coming here all Mr. G. has lately done against me. I rejoice! I am free from all else save God which enables me to better serve His Great Covenant! I hope now to accomplish more then ever in His Vineyard. Pray for me. My way is hard – the path is narrow – but my spirit is light and I fear <u>no man</u> for I have learned the <u>fear</u> <u>of</u> <u>God</u>! I am sending an account of my stay – the last of it in Haifa to Mr. Hannen – soon. – I enclose you photograph of Tablet to the Beloved of God in America and translation – it was revealed Aug. 27th. and is in the Masters own handwriting. How Merciful He is to me. How He saves and protects me under all circumstances and oh, how I love Him! I adore Him as never before – Oh Menita He is the Ancient of Days – the Center of the Covenant through which every blessing come[s] to everyone. I am ill in bed for the past two days – so please excuse this scrawl – When I last saw the Beloved – He was going away to face His foes – He bade us all "Good by" and left very suddenly. I left in a few hours after He did and do not know the outcome. Hope something has come from Ahmad S– since to America who said he would write as soon as anything was known – He did not go with Him –

Give my love to all and especially Phil whose messages I still receive from the Evening Star

Love to you dearest child of my soul.

      Your own "Little Mother"

        Lua

Cable address

Lua c/o Yazdi Port Said

The same day, September 26, 1915, Lua wrote to "My dear Spiritual Sister," disclosed in a postscript as Louise Waite, poet, singer and writer of songs. In this letter Lua said that the Tablet from 'Abdu'l-Bahá she was enclosing would be a test to Mrs. T. [True]. Lua added a postscript saying that Mrs. Goodall was also placed as a "mother"[118] on the Pacific Coast, as was Mrs. Krug in New York and Mrs. Parsons in Washington DC. Lua mentioned that the "mothers" were assigned "henchmen" and helpers. Dr. Zia was told to assist Mrs. True in Chicago.

                    Port Said Sept. 26, 1915

My dear Spiritual Sister

Thanks for your kind inquiries regarding me in Mrs. S. [probably Mrs. Stannard's] Letter. I had arrived but a few days before your letter came. I remained nine months in Acca in the home of the Beloved and now as I look back upon them it seems but nine days – so quickly did they pass. We were enveloped in difficulties and dangers and surrounded by misery, wretchedness and woe beyond mortal telling! Yet the Master was calm, majestic and <u>the Master</u> at all times. I saw Him sitting by the window one day watching a bombardment – perfectly unmoved, with an expression upon His Face which I can never forget! It was as though He knew what needs must be the reasons why – and the results for which He calmly waits. He <u>knows</u> – therefore He <u>always smiles</u>. One evening after singing one of your songs – He spoke of you – asking "Do you think her poetries very beautiful?" "Yes very beautiful – very beautiful!" And I somehow felt you would

336

write better and more beautifully after that & your recent poems which Mrs. S. has shared with me prove it! Dear Singer of Songs – let nothing discourage you! Look up to the "Center" and receive the great baptism of God through His Covenant which He ever faithfully keeps with His people. All the world may be unfaithful – but God is True. You are remembered and often spoken of in the Land of Desire. The children sing your heartfelt songs in the Presence of the Glorious Beloved. What more can you desire? He loves you! What does it matter if all the rest of creation hate you? I want to tell you something here regarding Mrs. T. [True] – I think without doubt she was told to be a "mother" to the Believers in Chicago and I believe Dr Zia translated for her! Now these two years and a half have revealed her capacity for the High Place to which she was "<u>called</u>" not "<u>chosen</u>" – She must give an account of herself first and the performance of her stewardship – before she can be "chosen" to maintain her position and <u>stationed</u> in it. She has persecuted me even while I was a member of the Master's household – and written that I am a Nazik.[119] But dear, I did not mind. I trusted in my Lord and God – who knows all hearts – and who revealed the enclosed Tablet for the American Believers Aug. 27th – This will be a <u>test</u> for her and all who expect me to be <u>crushed</u> and discouraged – especially now after Mr. G's recent proceedings. But I am not! I shall go ahead just the same Trusting in the Center of the Covenant – relying upon Him – believing in Him and clinging to the Hem of His Garment! And I would tell you to do the same and pray for Mrs. T. "Blessed are you for you are persecuted!" I copy the tablet mentioned. The original is in the Master's handwriting & I have sent photographs of the same to America already. . .

This will come as a test to many and especially Mr. G. who has done what he has done – for reasons which the future will disclose. That is, however, between him and his God!

The Beloved and family were well when I left, – though in a most grave and serious condition on account of famine and the tolls of war.

I must close. Sending you all love and greetings in

The Name of the Covenant

I am yours faithfully

Lua

P. S. I may just add here that Mrs. Goodall was also placed as a "mother" on the Pacific Coast. Mrs. Krug in New York and Mrs. Parsons in Washington. I think these are all the women who were especially called at that time. They were given henchmen & helpers and I believe Dr. Zia was told to assist Mrs. T[rue] in Chicago and Mr. Remey was to perform like services for Mrs. P[arsons] in Washington. The Kinneys and Mrs. Krug were to work together – in New York. The Ralstons and Mrs. Cooper were to assist Mrs. Goodall on the Coast.

The Great Hour is soon to strike. The Great Curtain will soon be lifted which will reveal all <u>as it is and not as it seems to be</u>! "Wait!" <u>Waite</u> is your name. Louise, – Waite
LMG
Learn to wait patiently and do pray – <u>pray for me too.</u>

The letter below, probably written to Joseph Hannen, is in the Parsons files in the U.S. National Bahá'í Archives.

Port Said
Sept. 30 1915

My dear Bahá'í Friend.
Enclosed please find the photograph of the Tablet the translation of which I sent you a week or more ago. I had hoped to send you by this mail an account of my stay in Haifa which is written but which I will not send for another week hoping in the meantime to be able to get some news through our American Cruisers which have recently visited Syrian shores to bring away more refugees – I may be obliged to return to Cairo tomorrow for a few days after which I hope to leave for France, and from there go to America. I have been obliged to rest quietly here for a week as I was so exhausted by the journey and many experiences during the last few weeks in Haifa. I wrote a long letter to Mrs. Parsons last mail which I requested her to share with you and Pauline. Please remember its contents are <u>not</u> for the public. I have been staying with Mrs. Stannard here for the past two weeks and I am fully informed of many things of which some may deem me ignorant. I am sorry that Mr. G. has so forgotten some things that he felt he could do as he has done – but that is for him to answer to his God. I do not know when I shall arrive in America – but when I do then perhaps I may be better understood by you

and a few others. I send loving Bahá'í greetings to all the friends. I trust you are all working to advance the Cause for this is the only thing which can contribute to the Master's happiness in this world.

May His Good Pleasure ever be your priceless treasure – and the assistance of all those who believe Him to be the Center of the Covenant.

Faithfully yours,
In His Name
Lua M. G.

The Bahá'í institutions responded to Lua with immediate support. Three weeks later on October 16 an entire issue of *Star of the West* [120] was devoted to news from Lua and to the subject of the Covenant. Extracts from her letters to Zeenat Baghdádí and Joseph Hannen were printed under the title, "Tell Everyone Now is the Time to Teach and Spread the Cause!" 'Abdu'l-Bahá's Tablet to Lua of August 27th was reproduced no less than three times, once in the original Persian – the photograph Lua had sent. The issue ended with the following comments by the editors:

In the light of the foregoing, further comment on our part is unnecessary. "Peace be upon those who follow guidance."

It is evident that those who are favored with a written word of approval from 'Abdu'l-Bahá should receive every consideration. Lua Getsinger has been thus favored; "she is worthy of love."

                                            Cairo, Egypt
My beloved Menita,
Your cablegram brought a flood of joy to my heart. How kind of you to send it to me just at the time when I am here alone not knowing what my fate is to be, i.e. whether money will be sent so I can go to America or not. I know now it will be a test for those who have believed Mr. G. to know what the Master has written the American Bahá'ís regarding me for he has shamefully gone ahead maturing his own plans for over three years – using me for his "blame-timber". Now, his own deeds will betray him

– for he has put me aside and I can no longer screen him. He has perjured himself – to accomplish what he has done – and the results will fall on his own head. All will know soon his reasons for the same which are and have been other than what he makes apparent. I am sorry for him – because the Master has told me what the end would be. Oh, it is all too bad, but it is done and I must bear it the best I can. I am not discouraged for I know it is the last of the "Dark Night" for my soul! The light of the real dawn is already breaking for me and how thankful I am to the Good God! You will never know what your cable did for my heart! – God bless you for it – a hundred times! I long to see you and tell you the many things which I have stored in my heart since I saw you last! The two "Records" had to be left in Haifa at last as I could not take them through the customs – but they are safe and are being kept by Rouha Khanum for you! I think the question regarding your land on Mt. Carmel has been fully understood and settled at last. It is yours and a beautiful spot! May you sometime see it and find it more beautiful than a "Garden of Dreams." Oh dearest Heart – do pray now for your far away "Little Mother" that she may see you soon – for I am not to remain long in America even if I succeed in getting there, and oh, I do so wish to see you again before I take another and perhaps last long journey. The Master so wished me to do some work in entirely new places there before calling me to go somewhere else. I told Him the prophets have all been without honor in their own countries. What can I expect for myself in America?

It is hardest of all to become a test to the "Friends" – And that I am and have been! Dear I am enclosing you a copy of the first tablet I ever rec'd from the Master's hand – and in fact it was the first tablet ever written to an American. I had paid the visit to Acca and returned to Haifa when this was forwarded to me. I did not know its deep significance then but the years since have taught me. Does anyone think they can make unstable or unfaithful, that which He has established and confirmed? If so then they have yet to find all such thoughts vain and futile! He knew what the future had in store for me and I did not! He confirmed me then and therefore made my soul a rock to resist the storms of denunciations and accusations which have so often encircled it! But my faith has never wavered! My Love has never ceased and I am His – as He is more than mine!

340

Tell dear Phil that the evening star is very bright here on the desert where the sky is always blue. And every night it gives me his message and takes mine to him. Does he receive it? Also tell him the twinkling star beams of our heavenly messenger have deposited three lovely topazes in my hand for him. It is a wonderful story but true – all for Phil. Does he not remember seeing the sunlight dance across the sea, while I was in India and become like little topazes? They were on their way to him then – but as I came here they just danced right to me for fear they might become lost if they tried to find him all by themselves! I wonder if you are in the woodland or by the seaside now? I love to think of you all in the little woodland nest with the creepy things and birds. I know Phil loves it! Poor Patsy! I am so sorry he died. I hope you will find another to take and fill his place! Give my love to dear Mrs. Harper and all the "Friends". I think of and pray for them especially "Merry Harper" – I have recently written a couple of articles for the "San Francisco Bulletin" which you might like and am going to send another about Egypt and conditions here. Life is very interesting but intensely sad everywhere. I go often to see the wounded soldiers and speak to them of the Cause. Oh it is awful to behold those who have returned from the Dardenelles – yet they are all cheerful and full of a calm courage that spells determined success. "Yes", they say – "It was hell – but we hope to return and fight again!" Poor Turkey is awakening to the fact that she has been deceived and is suffering bitterly. The gloom is awful there!

We have heard no word since I left Haifa from the Beloved! I sent Mr. Hannen a full account of my sojourn in His Presence and asked him to surely send you a copy. – Tell my own Phil to pray hard for Aunt Lua now for she needs it very much. I am not well – have never recovered entirely from my illness in India – beside I suffered so much mentally there! It is over however and I shall be all right.

With love to all
    Your "Little Mother" Lua

On November 25, 1915, Lua wrote to Mrs. Parsons thanking her for her letter of October 27th and enclosing some teachings from 'Abdu'l-Bahá on "Justice & Mercy". Her attitude to those who have hurt her is forgiving, and she is

341

concerned that Edward's good motives in wishing to help in the war relief should not be misunderstood, lest he be further wounded.

Cairo, Egypt
Nov 25, 1915

My dear Noor.

Yours of Oct. 27th rec'd. and I thank you very much for the same. Was glad to read what Mrs. True wrote you, for she was in quite another attitude toward me not so very long ago. – However, I realized then that she really thought I was not firm so forgave her, & prayed for her while in the Holy Presence. So far as I am concerned, there is absolutely no one among the Friends for whom I entertain anything save love and the very best of wishes no matter what they have said or done – for well I know that all things will be known as they are and each soul must stand for what he or she really is! This is the Day of God – in which truth will become paramount; – We need only to wait and be patient, God in time will reveal and make clear every matter. In regard to the "fund" – No one – even the Beloved who knows all things – including the motives back of every act, ever said that the "offering" was sent in any other Spirit than the spirit of "perfect love" – and all that I wrote you regarding the same was not intended for any other "interpretation" but was a simple statement of facts. However, if there is any partisan feelings and the showing of my letter to those with whom I asked you to share it – would in any manner augment such feelings, I am glad & thankful you do not send it to them. I do not desire to become a further test to anyone, and like you wish to have nothing to do with partisanship. I do not think however the Krug telegram was "the cause of the main difficulty"! The difficulty lay in the fact that the originator of the "Relief Fund" had been told not to engage himself in collecting money for anything & and it was a love lesson to teach him obedience to the Word of the Beloved, who said of him after he left – "He wished to help us – and did what he could but I had told him not to do so!" There was never any question as to the good intentions and motives, and we all felt very sorry as I wrote you, at the time. Of course there was lack of understanding and unity among the Friends which in itself was enough to make the whole thing unacceptable in the

"Court of Oneness" and it is indeed regrettable that upon such a project there could be no loving co-operation; all of which only proves that the Friends are still more desirous of having their own way in all matters – than they are anxious to promote union and harmony on the earth, or even to forget self long enough to do a great good to those who are in dire distress and need. God help us all and forgive us our many mistakes – Little by little we will learn – and if the doors of His Mercy are not closed before we awake to the reality – We may yet become united and Serve Him in love – based upon implicit obedience. He is now choosing His Jewels – which shall in the future constitute His Crown! And dear Bahá'í Noor – I ask God from the very depth of a contrite heart that you may be one of the most brilliant among them. All have been called – Now they will be tested and tried – until it will be known who among them are the "chosen". Those who can forgive and truly love the most – surely stand the best chance. – Yet others may attain!

I am sorry to learn of Royall's injury but dear, perhaps the loving Father has mercifully closed one of his eyes that the other may be opened "to the Holy Beauty of the Beloved"! Try to think so and I am sure it will help him. I sincerely trust Mr. Parsons is better and will come out of his trial with the deeper spiritual vision. All best wishes to Jeffrey Boy and his progress both spiritually and materially. I am enclosed you a little poem which has helped me to transmute "stumbling blocks into stepping-stones". I am waiting to hear from Mrs. Goodall and am ready to go to America as soon as the way opens for me! I am glad to be able to inform you that through our American Cruiser the "Des Moines" – which arrived in Alexandria a few days ago – I received news that the Beloved One is in Haifa and well. His enemy has been Mrs. ___ – severely punished – and thus will all be dealt with who seek to harm Him. I presume you have heard 'ere this from Ahmad Sohrab of His safe return from Nazareth. I went to Alexandria myself and know this is authentic. He was seen in Haifa and was still bearing all of the difficulties which surround Him with sublime fortitude which inspires all with hope. Oh may God in His Great Mercy spare Him yet to the world a little while until more of us realize Him as He is – "The Most Sacred Temple of Abha" as well as the Center of the Covenant. When we really know – then we will obey – if we love him!

And surely all of us need His guidance still for His is the word which can change the hearts of men – some at least – without which there can be no progress. Your letter was very helpful and I thank you for its frank loving spirit. I trust you will "see the Father's Face in all" – for then all will behold His Face in you. "For this is the sign of His chosen – that they must be <u>His</u> alone!" God bless and comfort you – confirm you and cause His Holy Spirit to constantly descend upon you, is the affectionate prayer of

> Yours faithfully
> In His Covenant
> Lua
> Port Said Egypt

XIX

Some time in October Lua travelled to Cairo, where she spent her last months among the Bahá'ís. During this time she fell ill with bronchitis and a painful bout of intercostal neuralgia, but she kept up her voluminous correspondence, writing to give news of 'Abdu'l-Bahá to those who were far away. A letter from her old friend Hashmatu'lláh to George Latimer, written from Ghatia Azam Khan (now Pakistan) on November 5th, says: "This week I had a letter from sister Lua from Cairo, telling us of the stirring times she passed through in Haifa . . . It is most heart-rending to hear that the people there have no money and no food."[121]

A letter to Martha Root on November 24th, from Muhammad Said Adham in Tanta, Egypt, tells how "Mrs. Getsinger went to Alexandria to inquire from the American S.S. that arrived from Syria, about the health and conditions of 'Abdu'l-Bahá and the friends there. She returned from Alexandria with the good news of his wellbeing and safety, as well as that of the friends."[122]

Despite her ill health, Lua continued her service till the very end. Elinore Hiscox, another Bahá'í teacher in Cairo at the time, wrote to Martha Root two weeks later, on December 5th: "Mrs. Getsinger is at present stopping in Cairo, so we are joining our forces in our work here and it is good to have her here and the young Bahá'ís are very glad to meet her and hear her speak."[123]

But illness took its toll. 'Abdu'l-Bahá, in a prayer revealed for her after her passing, described it thus: ". . . through the difficulties that she endured in Thy Path, her very flesh and bones were melted, diseases and sicknesses attacked her, her frail body failed her, her nerves and

345

muscles weakened their functions and her heart became the target of conflicting ailments."

A premonition of approaching death is expressed in Lua's last letter to Elizabeth Nourse, written eight weeks before her passing.

Cairo – March 7th 1916

My own beloved Menita:

Yours at hand just as I am recovering from a long siege of bronchitis and intercostal neuralgia which gave me such pain that at times I thought I had been to the war, and was wounded. I was confined to the house and most of the time to my bed, – for two months. Thus you may imagine with what joy I receive your dear letter and the tonic effect it has on me. I have been wishing and waiting to hear from you for a long time and at the same time wondering if you have received the letters I have sent you. You do not mention them, therefore I conclude they have not been received. I so often think of Phil and as it is nearly three years since I saw him – I imagine he must be stout and taller – but just as merry and sparkling as ever – perhaps more so. The evening star here is as brilliant as the moon is there and I speak to it about my Phil every night just after sunset – when the desert sands are reflecting the afterglow. Ask him please if all my Astral Messages reach him – from the wireless station of my heart? You will soon be leaving to the woods again to dwell with the trees, birds, and bees – and all the creepy-crawly things – that make the night so weirdly strange – and fascinating. April showers will soon be splashing down – and up will come the May blossoms – which will redden with June and deck the Ball-room of Time for the dance of the Summer days – whose warm breath we already feel in Egypt! How I have wished to be with you to talk with you and commune together – about so many things – which I cannot write. I am now in the desert – among the burning sands and you are in the Capital City of Our Beloved America – but our hearts across the lands and seas beat together in the unison of perfect understanding and love, which fact constitutes one of my greatest comforts! – In regard to the question of Mr. G – I have nothing to say – He is doing what he is doing not because I have injured him – but for a reason which he thinks is hidden only in his own heart. But there are two in the world – beside himself who know the truth and reality of all his actions. He is being tried and tested as everyone else is – And, I feel only pity and sorrow for him. But it is pity and sorrow of such a nature that I have not raised nor shall I raise my voice against him, even in self-defense. Let him do to me all he can do – And may the result of his doing be not too great for him in the End. He has a lesson to learn which I am sure cannot be taught to him in any other way – Therefore I leave him in the hands of the "Great Teacher" – who will – I know – prepare the final trial as it should be – to produce the best and most needed experiences for all concerned. I am very sorry for the others whom he has implicated because they have not injured him either. And the law which will be operative in the end after he has finished with the courts of our country – is the one concealed in the following – "We get back our mete as in measure. We cannot do wrong and feel right – We cannot give pain and gain pleasure – The Justice avenges each slight!" – Oh my dear one – I have no hope of returning now to you – the time is passed. I am very much afraid when I have learned my final lesson which the desert has to teach me – my footsteps will be turned in another direction – and years may pass ere we meet again – even if we ever should in this world. A voice is calling me – and I must obey! It is insistent of late! It comes from far, and when I arise to answer it will take me to a country whose shores my feet have not yet trod. The journey will be long and lonely – but it will be undertaken for the sake of the Beloved and the Glory of God's Holy Covenant.

I want to thank you once more for all of your kindness and love to me. The remembrance of the days we have spent together is always a retreat of joy for my soul, and how often does it seek its tender comfort to repose for an hour away from all the din and noise of the world. It is my "Heaven-Chamber".

Will you give my love to my Phil, and tell him never mind writing letters in a reply to mine – he may answer by his prayers for me. Kindest best wishes to Catharine Boise, Marie and her mother.

And now my own Menita – Goodbye – "Until the day dawns – and the shadows flee away" –

Your "Little Mother" in

The Beloved Covenant.

Lua

I send loving greetings to Marian Haney, Mrs. Woodward – and the "Merry Harper" whom I never forget. God bless you all!

Some of her last moments are chronicled in *Star of the West*.[124]

Further word comes from Cairo of the last days of the brave maid-servant of the kingdom, Mrs. Lua Getsinger. Mrs. Getsinger went to Cairo last autumn, hoping to leave soon for America, and carry 'Abdu'l-Bahá's message of light to the friends in the West. The friends in Cairo loved her devotedly and opened their homes to her. For a number of months she was at the home of Mirza Taki Esphaim, "'Abdu'l-Bahá's faithful steward in Cairo," where she suffered a long illness through the winter. He and his wife cared for their American sister most tenderly. "Before and after this illness," Miss Eleanor Hiscox writes, "though she never recovered her strength, Lua Getsinger went about with heroic will giving the Bahá'í teachings, her work being chiefly among the young men, as they are the only ones among the Egyptians who know English. All listened to her eagerly, and all were wonderfully uplifted and blessed by her inspiring words. The lives of some were completely transformed by her influence. Such was the power of the words of Bahá'u'lláh upon her lips."

In the early spring she went to Shoubra, a suburb of Cairo, to the house of another Bahá'í, who greatly desired that she should remain there for a while for the sake of her Bahá'í influence upon his wife and her family, formerly Christian. And she spent her time in giving them all lessons in English, of which they had some knowledge. They all loved her devotedly and treated her as their own sister. It was there her last days were passed. One night (it was the 2nd of May) she awoke with a severe pain in her heart. She called the family, who telephoned for a doctor. But before his arrival she passed into the other world after uttering three times, "Ya-Baha-el-Abha."

The grief and sorrow of all the Bahá'ís was very great, for all loved her as a devoted sister. One of the choicest sites was selected for her tomb. No expense was spared by the Bahá'í friends for their devoted sister, beloved by 'Abdu'l-Bahá, in the last acts which could be done for her. How they all loved her!

How they still weep when they speak of her!

Here our sister Lua lies buried in the same city with Mirza Abul Fazl. The prophetic words of 'Abdu'l-Bahá have come to pass, for Bahá'í pilgrims and friends already visit her grave with offerings of love and devotion.

In the last days of illness she hovered between the will to serve on earth and the longing to fly away into the glorious freedom of "the immensity of the kingdom." On April 12 she wrote to Miss Hiscox: "Little by little I am seeing all the reasons *why* many things are as they are and the lessons I have to learn thereby. I am sure until the last day of our lives we will be learning lessons, for this world is a *school*, from which we graduate only when we leave it. I shall be so glad when the last day comes, and the school is forever (so far as I am concerned) dismissed. His will, not mine, be done!"

The lessons of the earth-world she learned beautifully in those last days of illness and trial. As Miss Hiscox says, her suffering "had a purifying influence upon her and seemed to burn away all the dross and to leave her pure gold. She had only love and forgiveness for all." She saw that every experience had been for the best. Like an angel ready to enter the kingdom of light, she turned her face, "a few days before her departure," to the picture of the Center of the Covenant, which hung on the wall, and said, with tears in her eyes but with manifest firmness: "All I want to do is his will and to be severed from aught else save God."

'Abdu'l-Bahá did not hear the news of Lua's death until four months later, probably because of the difficulties in communications caused by the war. Ahmad Sohrab wrote to Joseph Hannen:

It was one afternoon of the month of September, 1916, when the Master was sojourning along the shore of the Sea of Galilee, that we received the sad news of the death of the beloved Lua. No one could believe it. When the Center of the Covenant heard about it he was deeply affected and felt more than any one of us her great loss. Since that day I have heard him more than a hundred times exclaiming with a moving voice: "What a loss! What a loss! What a loss!"[125]

Star of the West published the following account of Lua's life signed by the Editors,[126] much of it as described by Edward Getsinger. Perhaps Edward's heart softened toward Lua after her death, as his comments about her in eulogy are kind and appreciative.

Mrs. Lua Moore Getsinger

A cablegram from Cairo, Egypt brings sad news. It states that, "Lua Getsinger died of heart failure May first and was buried at Cairo."

Mrs. Getsinger was one of the first persons in America who realized that a Great Light was shining again from the horizon of the Holy Land. And for many years she has been a brilliant voice to proclaim the Glad Tidings.

She was married to Dr. Getsinger in 1896 and they were members of the first party from America who visited 'Abdu'l-Bahá in Acca. Dr. Getsinger tells of how, on this memorable visit, 'Abdu'l-Bahá seeing, with his spiritual vision, Lua Getsinger's capacity, stepped up to her and put something in her mouth. A little later he said to her: "I have given you the power to speak and loosened your tongue. 'Lua' in Persian means 'Flag' ['Liva' is the actual Persian word meaning 'Banner'] and you must be my flag and wave it in the East and the West." Then the glorious servant of God gave an exhortation, as Dr. Getsinger says: "into which he put such spiritual force and emphasis that it seemed as though the very walls trembled and we were hardly able to stand on our feet. 'Abdu'l-Bahá was declaring that the millennium had come and the Kingdom of God was to be established on earth. He wanted Lua thus to proclaim it everywhere in a loud voice."

This was the first of many visits she made to the home of light at Acca. Long and carefully did 'Abdu'l-Bahá in his great loving kindness tell her how to teach the Most Great Cause. She travelled far and wide in her teaching. She was often ill. In referring to one of these illnesses her husband tells how 'Abdu'l-Bahá said: "I told the angel of death to stay away."

'Abdu'l-Bahá entrusted to her many missions of trust and responsibility. For instance, when "Mozaffar-ed-Din Shah [Muẓaffari'd-Dín Sh̲áh], of Persia, visited Paris, 'Abdu'l-Bahá sent her with a petition asking the Shah to stop the martyrdoms of Bahá'ís in his kingdom, – which he promised to do." Her last great mission was to India.

To further quote Dr. Getsinger: "When 'Abdu'l-Bahá desired further to acquaint the Maharajah of Jalowar with the Bahá'í teachings he sent Lua from Bombay to this enlightened personage who received her most graciously. He had invited 'Abdu'l-Bahá to breakfast with him in London and is a staunch friend of the Bahá'í cause. The Maharajah continued to exchange letters with Lua. In all these journeys," her husband says, "she never spared herself. Time and again I have seen her in a state of utter exhaustion yet she would pull herself together by sheer will power in order to keep her appointments. To this perhaps many friends can testify who have had occasion to entertain her during the past ten years. She knew but little rest for 'Abdu'l-Bahá had said, 'Day and night thou must engage in spreading the message. Nothing else will avail thee.' She never lost sight of her Master's business. When once a complaint was made of Lua to 'Abdu'l-Bahá he turned to the person who had made it and with a benign smile, said: 'But she loves her Lord.' She was generous to a fault, depriving herself often that others might have. She had a rare vitalizing power in serving others. She spoke with ease and brilliance and feared no one in debate. Her gift from 'Abdu'l-Bahá made her confident and victorious."

She returned from her mission to India in January, 1915, spent seven [nine] months with 'Abdu'l-Bahá's family at Haifa and there sailed in trying times on an American warship to Cairo. But much of the time in Cairo she was ill with that illness that at last permitted her to ascend into the "city of light". Thus passed a brilliant maid-servant of God from the service of the earth world to that of the unseen Kingdom.

May Maxwell's moving tribute to Lua, quoted in the Preface this book, follows.

A TRIBUTE TO LUA GETSINGER

Montreal, Canada
May 25, 1916

"Lua has ascended to the Supreme Concourse" – those are the words I heard. For hours I have seen Lua, the woman, the child, all love and tenderness, dying far away – alone. Far from the land where she sowed the seed from the Atlantic to the Pacific – from the land where she arose like the dawning star heralding the light of Bahá'u'lláh in those days when the Occident lay frozen in the grasp of materialism – and far from all those who should have loved her and cherished her as a priceless gift from God. I could see her frail form, her lovely sensitive face, her pleading child's eyes. I could only hear the cry of her soul, her yearning for sacrifice in the Path of God. Without home, money, or any earthly hope or refuge – after her years of suffering, service and sacrifice she attained her supreme desire and lay, at last a martyr!

Then I saw no longer the bruised and broken reed trodden and crushed to earth, whose fragrance shall perfume all regions. I saw the victorious Lua, majestic in her death – the Lua who shall live through all ages – who shall shine from the horizon of eternity upon the world when all the veils which have hidden her today from mortal eyes have been burned away. As Kurat-ul-Ayn was the Trumpet of the Dawn in the Orient in the Day of Bahá'u-'lláh, so Lua Aurora shall wave forever and ever the Banner of the Dawn in the Day of the Covenant. Even as her age and generation knew her not, seeing only her mortal frailties – so future ages and cycles will love her – adore her – venerate her blessed name – and strive to walk in the path of her utter servitude, severance, and sacrifice. The passion of Divine love that consumed her heart shall light the hearts of mankind forever and forever.

Great and wonderful were her qualities – in her own person she bore the sins and weaknesses of us all. She broke the path through the untrod forest: like the grasshoppers, she cast her soul and body into the stream and perished making the bridge by which we cross: she was a Niobe all her days, washing our sins in her tears: she was burned to cauterize our wounds. 'Abdu'l-

352

Bahá said that when one soul should arise and become severed from all else save God, that soul would open the way for all to attain. I believe that the last time Lua left her Beloved 'Abdu'l-Bahá she died to all save God and took the "step of the soul" by which the spirit of truth and reality dawned in the Cause in America. In fulfillment of His Holy Words, the light broke forth in Boston in the autumn of 1915: its rays were reflected in some souls throughout America and other parts of the Occident so that at that time the believers began to enter on a new era of spiritual consciousness, and here and there the fire of Divine Love and the reality of unity became manifest. The outcome was the bursting into the realm of possibility – the building of the Mashriqu'l-Adhkár, the outer sign of the appearance of the inner spiritual temple.

Those who were present at the Holy Convention realized that the reality of the Cause of Bahá'u'lláh had at last appeared in America, and on that day when the Divine Outpourings reached their height, many realized that the Spiritual Temple had come into being. Is it possible that on that day Lua attained the utmost longing of her soul? That in the laying of that first stone the mystery of sacrifice became revealed and her death was the consummation of her life?

May Maxwell

A year after her passing, Mrs. Maxwell spoke of Lua at the National Convention; her address was published in *Star of the West*. This account was written by Martha Root.[127]

Memorial Service for Mrs. Lua Getsinger

On the last day of Rizwan, and the last day of the convention, as it was the first anniversary of the passing from this earth of Mrs. Lua Getsinger, a short memorial service was held for her. Mrs. May Maxwell spoke thus of the spiritual mother of so many souls in America: "Lua needs no eulogy from human beings. But whenever I think of her I remember something that 'Abdu'l-Bahá said about her to me, 'It is indeed the truth that Lua has guided many, many, many souls into the Kingdom.'

"I think – as the convention is disbanding and we are going forth to the really great work for which in this convention we have received such inspiration, that it has been like drinking from a fountain of living water, it is fitting that we speak of Lua. It has seemed that last year's convention was like a limpid pool that was still and calm and deep, reflecting the image of the Center of the Covenant, on that day when Lua gave up her life far away in the land of Egypt. I think many of us felt last year that the spiritual temple came into being on that day and at that convention. But this has been much more wonderful, because it has been like a surging sea, the tempestuous waves of power surging through this convention in all our hearts and souls; but the depths – those great depths of love – of wonderful love that we all feel for one another have remained untouched and undisturbed; and they are surely the basis of all that work we are going forth to do.

"And if we can attain to any part of the sacrifice and service of Lua, we shall do well, because I never knew her to refuse any call, no matter how weak, exhausted, or tired. She would always give up everything to serve. One day in Paris, at one moment's notice she gave up her trip to London and gave up her tickets to give the message to one man, because he wanted to hear it from Lua."

A silent prayer followed in memory of that one who was among the first to herald in America the new Kingdom of universal love and peace.

A last tribute to Lua Getsinger was written after her passing by her beloved Master, 'Abdu'l-Bahá. This Tablet was dated December 18, 1918, and did not reach America until February 1919. It was sent to Joseph Hannen and translated by Ahmad Sohrab, who describes it as "a Tablet of Visitation in her honor".[128]

Supplication
for the Attracted Maid servant of God, Lua Getsinger, who ascended to the Supreme Concourse.
Upon her be greeting and praise!

HE IS GOD!

O Lord! O Lord! Verily Thy maid servant who was attracted with the fragrances of Thy Holiness, enkindled with the fire of Thy love, the herald of Thy Name, the spreader of Thy Signs amongst Thy people, – ascended to Thee with humility and lowliness, trusting in Thee with all her heart, liberated from all worldly ties and attractions, hoping for Thy Universal Favor and Mercy, desiring to enter Thy Radiant Presence, supplicating Thy all-encircling bounty, and begging for the descent of Thy glorious Bestowal!

O Lord! Exalt her station, submerge her in the ocean of thy compassion and establish her in the midst of the Paradise of Immortality, – in the Universe of Lights, the Center of Beatific Mysteries.

Oh Lord! She believed in Thee, chanted Thy verses, turned her face toward Thee with all her heart; her spirit was rejoiced through Thy Glad Tidings and her soul was purified through the fire of Thy Love. Then amidst the concourse of humanity, she arose in the promotion of Thy Word, suffered every thirsty one to drink from the goblet of Thy Guidance and healed every sick one with the antidote of Thy Knowledge. In Thy Path she traveled to distant countries and remote regions and gave the good news of Thy Kingdom throughout vast and spacious continents – until through the difficulties that she endured in Thy Path, her very flesh and bones were melted, diseases and sicknesses attacked her, her frail body failed her, her nerves and muscles weakened her functions and her heart became the target of conflicting ailments. Then while hoping for the immortal life, the eternal existence, she abandoned this mortal, ephemeral world.

O Lord! Grant her a palace in the neighborhood of Thy Most Great Mercy, cause her to dwell in the gardens of Thy paradise, the Most High; illumine her countenance with the effulgence of Thy Good-pleasure, in the Kingdom of Thy Glory; usher her into the heaven of Thy meeting and suffer her to live everlastingly in the assemblage of transfiguration, whose refulgent Lights are shining upon the world of hearts and the realm of consciousness.

Verily thou art the Forgiver, verily Thou art the Pardoner and verily Thou art the Merciful of the Most Merciful!

(signed) 'Abdu'l-Bahá Abbas.

The following, taken from notes by Mrs. Hauser of Chicago, is the translation of the verse revealed by the Master to be engraved on Lua's gravestone:

Verily, verily, the maid-servant of God, Lua, while serving in the Path of God and being attracted to His Breaths, abandoned this world, soared towards the Supreme Concourse and attained to the countenance of her Lord in the Kingdom of Names.

Appendix

Talks by Lua Getsinger

Oh my Daughter – know that thou art a woman, whose words will have a great effect on the hearts of the people, and to whose words they will listen. Do not lose one single opportunity in this blessed time to talk to the people – be prepared on all occasions, and put forth all the efforts within thy power to deliver the message and do not look to thy comfort, or to what you shall eat or drink or wear – or to name, fame, renown, wealth, or even as to how you shall sleep, but look only to delivering the Truth with sincerity and true devotion sacrificing any and everything for the Cause! – And if you will do this – by God – you shall receive a confirmation – which you have never imagined – or conceived in your mind, and for this, I am the guarantee – and of it there is no doubt.

— 'Abdu'l-Bahá[129]

The following five talks (and one paper) given by Lua in the winter of 1911 and spring of 1912 were recorded stenographically at the time, and later copied and sent to individual believers. Many of these notes are to be found in the personal papers of those who were Bahá'ís in the first decades of the century and even beyond: people were still copying out Lua's words in the late 1930s.

They are valuable today not only in providing a precious record of Lua in action: giving us a taste of that eloquence, that informal and direct manner, and that warmth and devotion which were so attractive to those who heard her. They bear study not only for their content, but for historical reasons, because they contribute to our understanding of the ideas current in the Bahá'í community at the time. Lua, within the framework of the knowledge available to Bahá'ís of her time, was exceptionally well-informed and accurate in presenting those ideas. A growing understanding of Bahá'í concepts and the increase of accurate historical information in later years was fostered by the Guardian of the Faith, Shoghi Effendi, through his authoritative writings and translations, and afterwards by the Universal House of Justice, the supreme governing body of the Bahá'í Faith.

However, the informed reader will find that much of the content of Lua's talks is still valid today; while her insight and perception is unlikely to be surpassed.

The reader is also referred to Lua's talk on "Service" (April 1905) and her talk on her arrival in California in 1912 to proclaim the Covenant and the station of 'Abdu'l-Bahá as Center of the Covenant (July 19, 1912), which may be found on pp. 98 and 162 respectively of this book.

THE WORD OF GOD

—oOo—

Talk given by Mrs. Lua M. Getsinger
California Club Hall, San Francisco, California
Sunday evening, December 17, 1911
Stenographically reported by B.S. Straum

—oOo—

One time in Acca, when 'Abdu'l-Bahá was trying to make us understand the possibility of man more clearly knowing God, he used this chart.

(The chart is dark on one side, light on the other and consists of circles. At the top a circle labeled INFINITE ESSENCE – GOD. Next circle to the right and on the light side written "Highest possible attainment by man – the Prophets". Circles descending to the bottom circle which is half in the dark and half in the light labeled "Human Kingdom." Three circles on the left labeled (ascending) "Animal Kingdom", "Vegetable Kingdom", "Mineral Kingdom". From the large circle at the top

are rays going out labeled "Love, Life, Knowledge, Faith, Forgiveness, Justice, Mercy, Primal Will, Beauty, Power, Generosity, Munificence, Peace, Righteousness, Purity". The chart is circular in itself with words written upon the rays at the top "Word of God", along the side "Spirit", at the bottom "The Christ Holy Spirit", and to the left "Matter".)

Just a word of explanation regarding the chart itself.

He likened the Infinite Essence, the Incomprehensible, unto the sun, the substance of which we do not know save through the analyzation of the waves of light emanating therefrom.

The first Effulgence emanating from the Infinite Essence, is the Word of God, the Creator.

The rays of light emanating from the First Effulgence constitute the Holy Spirit, or the Christ.

The darkened half of the chart represents the world of matter, and the other half the world of Spirit, or the Heavenly Kingdom.

We have, then, the Illuminator, the Illumination, and that which is to be illuminated.

Taking it for granted that the statements made in mythic or God-given writings must be absolutely true, however anomalous or irreconcilable with the facts of modern science and the deductions of enlightened reason they may appear to the natural mind, we affirm that the sacred scriptures are true in their own domain – the soul. By the sacred scriptures we mean the Word of God, the revealed Word of God, considered apart from its setting of Man's interpretation, or interpretations of that Word. And, farther, that they are equally true in respect to physical science; that through them Deity speaks to men, who may thus learn, if their comprehension will allow them, the secret nature of things, whether pertaining to the life of earth or of the hereafter.

According to the sacred Scripture, we are told: "In the beginning was the Word, and the Word was with God, and the Word was God." But before this, there was no beginning, because that which existed before this beginning of the Word, and the manifestation thereof, <u>always</u> <u>was</u> the Infinite Essence, the Unknowable, Incomprehensible, Almighty God, for we are told that all that <u>is</u> is as a result of the Word, that by the Word were all things made that are made.

Then the Word becomes the power through which creation takes place, and the process of this Word producing creation is the science of Divinity, which embraces the hidden and mysterious principles of every science, sacred and secular, for it is the science of Divine action in the works of creation, the science of universal existence, both active and passive, and its original foundation is not speculation, deduction or theory, but the revealed Word of God through Prophets and Speakers whom He has selected, anointed and sent into the world.

The Bahá'í Reformation teaches that all things existing in this material world were originally spoken into existence through the power of this Word – God. As to how, or what was the process, we do not pretend to say we know. That belongs to the realm of the divine alchemy of the Almighty Creator, which he forever secretes from the knowledge of His created beings. But through this Word were all things made that are made. All things – the mineral kingdom, the animal kingdom and the kingdom of man – were spoken into existence, after which the law of evolution was declared and established, and through this law they maintain their existence.

What called for this lesson on the part of 'Abdu'l-Bahá was a question, and the question was, "What is soul?" In answer to this question, he instructed me how to draw this chart – not this one, but one from which this one was reproduced. And now I wish to use his words, to give you the lesson verbatim. He said:

"As to thy question concerning the soul, know thou, verily, soul is a term applied to numerous realities, according to the exigence of those realities in regard to development in the world of existence."

Let us take one attribute now emanating from the First Effulgence of the Sun of Truth, the Word, – the attribute of life – and let us evolve it through the different kingdoms, until we find it manifesting itself in the kingdom of man.

"In the mineral kingdom it is called latent force, silently working away for the disintegration of the substances of that kingdom."

This power of life, or soul, then, manifesting itself in the rocks, is latent force. That is the term applied to it in that kingdom.

"In the vegetable kingdom it is called virtue augmentative, or the power of growth, which attracts and absorbs the delicate materials of inorganic matter and transforms them to the condition of growth. Thus the inorganic substances found in the

360

mineral kingdom become growing vegetable life through the effect of the Word of God. This vegetable soul, or virtue augmentative, or power of growth, is a quality which is produced by the admixture of elements, and appears in accidental or contingent organisms of which contingency is an essential necessity or attribute.

"In the animal kingdom this same power, latent force, virtue augmentative, becomes sense perception or instinct. This term soul, as applied to the animal kingdom, is also a natural quality resulting from the mixture of the elements, and it appears from their mingling and combination, for it is a quality which results from the composition of bodies, organism, and is dispersed at their decomposition. From this we are to understand that the animal soul, or the sense perception, is not endowed with the capacity of attaining immortality, as the life force is dispersed at the decomposition of the animal tissues.

"All things, then, up to this point, or to the human kingdom, are contingent realities, and not divine realities. A contingent reality, which continues as it is, and is perpetuated by the fullness of existence, will suffer no corruption, and will thus become a divine reality, for the accidental reality is only distinguished from the pre-existent reality by its subjection to corruption, for transformation is an essential necessity to every contingent reality, and this is what the Mature Wisdom has deemed advisable. This is also proven by physical science.

"The term soul, which in its fourth application, or in the kingdom of man, is called rational being; soul, mind, has a potential existence before its appearance in human life. It is like unto the existence of a tree within the seed. The existence of a tree within the seed is potential, but, when the seed is sown and watered, the signs thereof – its roots and branches and all its different qualities – appear. Likewise, the rational soul has a potential existence before its appearance in the human body, and through the mixture of elements and a wonderful combination, according to the natural law of conception and birth, it appears in its identity and becomes an individuality."

Well, now, what is soul?

Life, manifesting in the mineral kingdom, is latent force; manifesting in the vegetable kingdom, it is the power of growth; the same life, in the animal kingdom, becomes sense perception;

and then as a human soul, it is endowed with certain attributes which will enable it to attain for itself that something by which it can become perpetuated and become a divine reality.

All beings, to this point, have not the capacity to receive it, and we can liken existence unto a tree, and call it the tree of existence. In the mineral kingdom we find the roots of the tree of existence. The vegetable kingdom produces the trunk and branches. The animal kingdom brings forth its leaves and blossoms. But only in the kingdom of man do we find its fruit, the heart of which contains that which can reproduce the tree, for in the heart we find the seed from which the original tree was produced.

"Be it known that to know the reality or essence of the soul of man is impossible, for, in order to know a thing, one must comprehend it, and since a thing cannot comprehend itself, therefore man cannot comprehend himself. To know oneself in substance or essence is absolutely impossible. As the comprehender cannot be the comprehended, man cannot know himself in reality or essence.

"In order to obtain any knowledge of the reality or soul of man, the student must study the manifestations, qualities, names and characteristics of man.

"This much can be stated, that the reality of man is a pure and unknown essence, a Divine depositary; that is, it is an emanation from the Light of the Ancient Entity – God. This Divine essence, or soul of man, because of its innate purity and its connection with the unseen and Ancient Entity, is old as regards time, but new as regards individuality. This connection is similar to that of the ray with the sun, or the effect to the Primal Cause. Otherwise, the thing that is generated, or the creature, has no connection with, or relation, individually, to the Generator and Creator.

"Therefore, since the reality or soul of man is a ray of light emanating from the Sun of the Word of God, it is capable of manifesting all the perfections of Being. It is then worthy to be the throne upon which may be established the manifestation of the Names, the Qualities and the Attributes of the Ancient Entity. Inasmuch as this entity is capable of expressing the great virtues of Being, and is the greatest and purest of all existing beings on earth, from its earliest rise in the human temple to its resurrection from the grave of the body, it can be likened to a mirror

362

which reveals the seen and the unseen, which possesses the virtues of the world and of the Kingdom.

"The difference which exists between the mirror and the pure essence of the elements is the same which exists between the animal and man. The mirror reveals the image, but it is not conscious of the act, while the reality or soul of man, the pure mirror of God, is conscious of the reflection and the fact that it is revealing. (The animals are not conscious. They possess not the attribute of consciousness.)

"The human soul is an essence spiritual in entity and material or physical in function. It is defined as essence because it is independent in itself, while the body is accidental and dependent upon the soul.

"The personality and activity of the body are due to the individuality of the soul. Thus the soul is the cause of the life of the body, and the body, with all its organs, is but the vehicle of its expression.

"Since that pure essence (the human soul), whose identity is unknown, possesses the virtues of the worlds of matter and of the Kingdom, it has two sides: First, the material and physical; second, the mental and spiritual, attributes not found as qualities of matter. It is the same reality, which is given different names according to the conditions wherein it becomes manifest. Because of its attachment to matter and to the phenomenal world – that is, when it governs the physical functions of the body – it is called the human soul. When it manifests itself as the thinker and comprehender of things, it is called the mind. When it soars in the atmosphere of God and travels in the spiritual worlds, it is designated as Spirit." (The School of the Prophets)

The soul of man, the great substance which is a ray of this light, or which is life manifested in the most perfect organism which has been formed upon this earth, possesses nine great attributes or qualities which distinguish it as an identity, separate it from all other creatures upon this earth, and we can say of these qualities that they are to the soul what the organs are to the body. They are: perception, memory, imagination, abstraction, reason, judgment, consciousness, mental taste and will.

By perception we mean that faculty or organ of the soul which sees, hears, feels, tastes.

Memory is that which records.

Imagination forms.

Abstraction classifies, is that faculty or organ which enables us to know the difference between materials, and the proper use to which those materials ought to be put.

Reason argues.

Judgment decides.

Consciousness knows.

Mental taste detects.

Will acts.

Upon this tree of existence anything not possessing these <u>nine</u> attributes falls short of possessing the ability to become immortal. All the creatures below the kingdom of man are devoid of these nine faculties. The animals possess <u>five</u>, or less, of these faculties, but any being who does not possess them all has not the capacity to attain immortality or eternal life.

We have now reached the dividing line + the human soul.

"This rational or human soul, when quickened through the breath of the Holy Spirit, is eternal, everlasting, divine, heavenly, and shall continue with the continuation of its Lord. Otherwise, it returns to the contingent reality or potential existence in the sphere of its oblivion, concealment or extinction. This station is the lowest degree in the world of contingent <u>life</u>."

Hear that sentence well. "This station is the lowest degree in the world of contingent <u>life</u>." There is no death, then, for the human soul. When once the ray of light, life, has become developed through the different kingdoms of matter until it enters the human organism, it is forever established. It cannot be annihilated. It only can go back to the lowest degree in the world of contingent <u>life</u>, because for it there is no death.

Then, the line which divides the station of man into two parts, the material and the spiritual, becomes the point of man's extremity and God's opportunity.

How?

I had a dear brother who became greatly agitated over this question, and he studied and gave the matter a great deal of thought. He was a medical student at the time, or had just graduated from the Medical College, and after giving it a great deal of thought he wrote me a letter one day. I am going to read you a portion of his letter, because it very ably explains the point how man is to escape from the world of matter into the world of spirit.

"I read one day a definition of eternal life given by Mr. Herbert Spencer which appealed to me very strongly for some reason. I thought over it and tried to see if it would hold.

"'Perfect correspondence with environment would be eternal life.'

"That looked true enough in this life, for a man lives just as long as he can correspond with environment, and when he ceases to do so he dies. But would this hold true of the soul?

"Christ said: 'This is eternal life, to know Thee, the only true God, and Jesus Christ whom Thou has sent.'

"That did not conflict with my friend's definition, for 'to know God' is to correspond with Him. Life, then, is correspondence, or the union of the organism with environment. Life is not in the organism by itself, for, without environment, it is not. The organism is only half of being; environment is its complement.

"This is true in the natural life. Now I looked to see if it were equally true of the spiritual life.

"The natural man cannot, according to our definition, live eternally, even though he has perfect correspondence with the natural environment, for to last eternally the environment must be eternal, while we know nature is not eternal – that is, creation is not – but is temporary. Therefore, a man, to live eternally, must become a new creature, must acquire a correspondence with an environment which in its nature is eternal.

"Now, as I was trying to prove the spiritual from the natural, I began to look for something analogous to this new birth, this change from natural to spiritual. It is surely according to natural law or order – this new birth; in fact, must be another step higher than the one that led up to it, as from the mineral to the plant, the plant to the animal, and so on. How, then, are these steps brought about? Is it not also a new birth in each instance? Is there not a new creation?

"The mineral, be it ever so refined, can never become a plant, because plant life is a higher life. The life principle of the mineral cannot correspond to the environment of the plant life.

"The principle of plant life must bend down and touch the mineral ere it can enter the higher life. In other words, it is transformed, or has acquired greater correspondence with environment, but it must needs have another birth to become a bird, for the bird life is still higher, and the plant cannot correspond with the environment of the bird life.

"We can easily see, therefore, that the evolution is due to a higher principle bending down to the kingdom below it and elevating that kingdom to its standing, but it cannot carry it beyond the point of its own correspondence. Therefore, man cannot of himself go higher than natural man. His correspondence is only with the natural world, therefore he has no life beyond the natural world. A new and higher principle must enter into him and establish a higher correspondence, or he ceases to be when he dies the natural death.

"Now to return to Christ's definition: 'This is eternal life, to know Thee, the only true God, and Jesus Christ whom Thou has sent.' It is not in the power of man to know God, for naturally he has no correspondence beyond the natural world. How, then, is he to acquire this correspondence? Just as the mineral acquired its higher life, and that was when it was touched by the higher principle.

"Is this not Christ's teaching also? He said: 'The Father and I are one' – or the same principle. And again He said: 'I came that ye might have life.'

"From a spiritual standpoint, the natural man is dead, as the tree is dead from man's standpoint. But the God principle bends down, and touches man, and he acquires a new life, is a new creature, has a correspondence with a new environment, and, as this environment is eternal, the man born of the spirit is eternal, even according to science, as long as he maintains his correspondence.

"We have now the capacity for eternal life, but, as no organism can live out of environment, neither can the soul.

"The natural environment of the soul is God, and cut off from it the soul dies as surely as the body dies when cut off from its environment or food.

"Thus the only life of the soul is attained through communion with God by means of <u>prayer</u>."

You can readily see now how man as a human being, at this point, is indeed in grave extremity. He constitutes the highest organism in which and to which all life in kingdoms below him ascend and become involved. Through man, all things in this world rise and become manifest. But man is dependent for his evolution or ascension beyond the state of the human being upon the Word of God. This Word constitutes the natural environment of his soul, and without it he passes into the next state of existence dead – dead from the standpoint of the spiritually enlightened being. He lives – he exists.

When we reached this point with 'Abdu'l-Bahá I remember a lady said: "But what becomes of such souls? Will they always exist in the outer state, in the state of outward darkness?" He had referred us to some of the descriptions found in Revelation, describing the conditions of those souls who depart from this world untouched by the Spirit of God, unregenerated by the Word of God, who had not acquired a correspondence with the environment of the Word of God.

He replied by asking this question; "When you become enlightened upon this earth a little with the knowledge of God, when you have felt the touch of His Spirit upon your soul, and you have become the recipient of His mercy and His love, what do you wish to do first?"

She answered, "Of course I wish to tell others about it."

Then he said: "If in this world of matter, of ignorance and spiritual darkness, your first impulse is to communicate to others what little light you have received from coming in contact with the knowledge of God, what you have received from feeling His mercy and knowing a little bit of His love, how do you think you will feel when you have left this world entirely, which for the soul constitutes the glass through which we see but darkly? When you have ascended into the station or grade which you have attained for yourself in the next world, how will you feel toward those creatures who are below you?"

She replied: "If I had received light, and if I knew more than I did here, certainly I would be more anxious there to teach them."

He said, "That is exactly what will happen."

Those souls who have left this world unregenerated and unborn spiritually can be compared to those souls in this world born deprived of sight and hearing. What have we done for those souls in that condition? Have we not, through love and a greater and higher understanding, invented ways and means by which and through which they have come in contact with knowledge? Have we not institutions for the blind and deaf and dumb? If we know enough to do that here, and if we are impelled by the spirit

– the little amount of the spirit we possess – to do those good things to those who are deprived, shall we forget to be good when we get into the world of spirit?

So it resolves itself to this: that those who have received the spirit, who have felt its touch and have become regenerated by it, wholly or in part, ascend to the station in the next world which corresponds to their attainment. And, by the way, we shall have no more treasures than we lay up for ourselves while here. What constitute the treasures of the soul in the next world? That which enables the human creature to assume the title man.

Bahá'u'lláh says that the human soul is not called man because of wealth, adornment, education or environment. It ascends to that glorious station, the image of God, when as a soul it adorns itself with all the heavenly characteristics: love, life, knowledge, faith, forgiveness, justice, mercy, obedience to the Divine Will, beauty, power, generosity, munificence, peace, righteousness and purity.

If we have adorned ourselves in part, as souls, with these heavenly characteristics, we ascend only in part to the glorious stations prepared for the souls of God in the next or spiritual world.

If we have adorned ourselves completely and entirely, we ascend to the station of the highest possible attainment. The souls who have ascended to that station thus far are those who have <u>descended</u> from that station. Those souls are the Prophets and Messengers of God, who have come, through mercy on the part of God, to teach us how to adorn ourselves with those attributes and characteristics with which they are adorned.

Therefore, the station we shall occupy in the great hereafter depends upon ourselves.

Man, in his extremity, comes to the dividing line. There he meets or sees before him, the Primal Will of God. Just as the mineral had to sacrifice its own kingdom, the mineral, and become disintegrated before it could be taken into a higher environment, to form part of a higher life principle; just as the vegetable had to sacrifice its own kingdom, the vegetable, before it could become part of a higher life principle; and just as the animal must sacrifice itself and its kingdom before it can become part of the human kingdom of man; so must man sacrifice himself and the human kingdom. He must lay down on this altar of the Primal Will of God his human side, his human qualities, and adorn himself with the qualities of God, and must look up, in his extremity, and ask God to bestow upon him these attributes.

As a soul, and as souls, we are in need of food. We are in need of water and clothing. Here, at the altar of the Primal Will, we must ask first for the food which will sustain us as souls, for the water which will quench our thirst as souls, and for that garment which will screen us, protect us, from the inclement elements and forces all around us.

Therefore, first of all, we must ask for knowledge – that knowledge which constitutes food and makes us independent of all creatures, dependent only upon God. We must then ask and demand that faith in God which becomes the substance, the very essence, of all our hopes, and the evidence of this great unseen God – this great unseen Holy Spirit upon which our eternal existence depends.

Then we must ask for love, that love which will enable us to turn away from all else save God and be satisfied, that love which will enable us to go out and sacrifice even life itself for the Beloved – God – when we, as souls, have found Him.

Therefore, you can readily see from this chart that the Bahá'í teaching does not teach the doctrine or philosophy of reincarnation. We do not believe in the reincarnation of the human soul, because the human soul, when it has become touched with the Divine Spirit, is no longer human. It has left the world of the human. It has come forth in the full image and likeness of God, and when it has once extricated itself, through the mercy and love of God, from this dark world, why should it, to gain spiritual knowledge, go down again and put itself in this place where it might lose all it had attained, as the doctrine of reincarnation does not teach the soul retaining its memory. Some think they have recurrent memory, but there is a question. Imagination, that wonderful attribute of the soul which forms everything, plays us many false tricks. The reincarnation of the human soul is not a part of the Bahá'í teaching.

We believe in the incarnation of the Holy Spirit, for there is One which has incarnated itself many times upon this earth, that man may come in contact with the higher life principle, and be forever taken from the dark confines of matter into the realms of spirit.

"There is a law of involution as well as evolution, and there must be some point where forces meet and balance or find equilibrium.

"Human beings evolve, or ascend, and unfold into spiritual beings.

"The Holy Spirit involves, or descends.

"Humanity ascends, which is evolution.

"Spirit descends, which is involution, and finds embodiment in humanity.

"The Dove, or Holy Spirit, descended from on high to build its nest in the heart of Jesus that He, being lifted up, should draw all men unto Him.

"The fifth aspect of the soul is the soul of faith born from the Spirit of God. This is an irradiation from the Divine Spirit and traces and fragrances from the Supreme Holy Spirit. This is what assures eternal life for the human rational soul. This is that of which Christ said, 'That which is born of spirit is spirit.'

"We have also another aspect of soul, and that is the Holy Soul, the Holy Spirit, the Word of God manifested in the human temple, shining forth like the Sun of Truth to all horizons, and from which the penetration appears, the lights spread, the fragrances waft, the mentioning is raised, and the commands of God prevail."

Regarding the soul, after it has ascended into the other world, I wish to read to you what Bahá'u'lláh has revealed on this subject, or a quotation of what He has revealed:

"Concerning that which you asked about the Spirit, or the soul born of the Spirit, and its everlastingness after its ascension, know that it will ascend at the time of its departure until it enters the Presence of God in a form which, throughout all centuries, times, and throughout all circumstances and events of the world will remain unchanged, but will be everlasting as the perpetuity of the Kingdom of God, His Sovereignty, His Power and His Might, and from it will appear the traces of God, His Qualities, Providences and Favors."

The providences and favors are those things which the soul receives through the mercy, bounty and munificence of God.

"The Pen cannot move at the mentioning of this Station as it is in its Supremeness and Exaltation. The hand of the Divine Bounty will cause it to enter into a station that cannot be comprehended by expression, nor be explained by all the creatures of the existence."

'Abdu'l-Bahá likened our condition in this material world, in comparison with what the condition will be in the spiritual world, to that of a child while it is still in the matrix. As a child ready for birth, it possesses feet, hands, eyes, ears, nose and mouth, but in that little space, in that little dark world of the matrix, if it were endowed with consciousness, with speech, it might say: "Of what use are these hands? Why have I these eyes? For what purpose are these ears? And to what use shall I put these feet?" But when the time comes for it to leave the dark confines, the world of the matrix, and it comes forth into this great spacious world, it soon learns the use and purpose of the hands and feet, the eyes, ears, nose and the mouth, and it soon becomes conscious of the fact that were any of them missing or imperfect it would indeed be in a state of deprivation.

And so we, while we cannot comprehend what is this form which is spoken of, or what will constitute our vision, our hearing, our senses in that next state, we know that the substance or essence of the soul exists, that it will exist because it is a ray emanating from the Sun of the Word of God, and that owing to the nature of His bounty it will receive all that it can possibly take according to its capacity.

"Blessing be upon the spirit who departed from the body purified from the doubts and superstitions of the nations. Verily, it moves in the atmosphere of God's desire, and enters into the Supreme Paradise.

"All the angels of the Supreme paradise attend and surround it, and it will have fellowship with all the Prophets of God and His saints, and speak with them, and tell them what happened to it in the cause of God, the Lord of the Universe.

"Prophets and Messengers came only to guide the creatures to the straight path of God, and in order that people may be trained.

"Then, at the time of their ascension, with a perfect holiness and separation, and having been cut from the things of this world, they will repair to the Supreme Station."

The Supreme Station is that station prepared for those who have clothed themselves as souls entirely with these attributes, and, not only that, but they become Speakers of the Word itself.

"By the Self of God the rays of those spirits are the cause of the development of the people and the station of the nations. These are the leaven of the existence and the greatest causes of the Appearances of Divinity, and the works of the Universe. By them the clouds will shower and the plants of earth spring up; not one thing, of all the things, is existing without cause, reason and beginning.

"The greatest cause is that the Spirits were and are forever above us equal, and the difference between this earthly kingdom and the other is like the difference between the embryonic world and this world – though after the ascension it will enter in the Presence of God in a form suited for eternity and for the Kingdom."

In closing, I wish to read a quotation from Persia's greatest poet, Jalalu'd-dín Rumí, from his masterpiece, called the "Masnavi," and you will see that to all the wise souls this has not been a new thought.

The line on the chart called the arc of descent and ascent is as old as God. It is the way through which the soul is evolved and ascends.

He said:

EXTRACT FROM "THE MASNAVI" BY JALALU'D-DIN RUMI
(Translation by Prof. E. G. Browne)

"I died from the mineral and became a plant;
I died from the plant and reappeared in an animal;
I died from the animal and became a man;
Wherefore then should I fear? When did I grow less by dying?
Next time I shall die from the man
That I may grow the wings of the angels.
From the angel, too, must I seek advance;
'All things shall perish save His Face.'*
Once more shall I wing my way above the angels,
I shall become that which entereth not the imagination.
Then let me become naught, naught; for the harp-string
Crieth unto me 'Verily unto Him do we return!'"

*Koran XXVIII:88

Tuesday Afternoon, January 9, 1912
Bellevue Hotel, San Francisco, California
Stenographic notes by B.S. Straum

—oOo—

Mrs. Lua Moore Getsinger

—oOo—

(Introductory paragraph before my arrival)

No one has taken Jesus' place. He manifested forth the holy relationship of the Son to the Father, and showed the people of the world the way in which they could become characterized with the attributes of the Father, and thus become, through a rebirth, a regeneration of the Holy Spirit, sons of God.

Just now, in this Day, we declare the Father, not the Son, the same Christ Holy Spirit, re-manifest, but manifest in the station of the Father and not the Son. Therefore, you see it is not putting anybody in the place of the Son, in the place of Jesus Christ.

But if, in the beginning, God had a great plan by which He was to spiritualize the earth, by which all people on this earth were to know of Him and His ways, we must know what that plan is, and though it be altogether an entirely different thing from anything we have ever thought and conceived, if it be the plan of God there is no other way under the sun for any one than to follow that plan. And now, while it is a new and strange thing, from the point of geography and history, to contemplate the coming of One who represents to the people of the world at this Day, God made manifest, the Word again descended in the form of man, from far off Persia, yet we must not forget that God doeth whatsoever He wisheth, in whatsoever way He willeth, and when God gets ready to act He does not consult the wishes, the wants or the will of any of His created beings. He acts independently of His creatures.

He alone can make all things new. He alone can regenerate, by the power of His Holy Spirit, all peoples and things, not only upon this planet, but upon all the planets in existence.

And if this coming of Bahá'u'lláh in far off Persia be really the reappearance of the Christ Holy Spirit which was manifest 1900 years ago – and which Jesus at that time said would come again, and He went into the ways and into the signs of that second coming – why, we can do no better thing than to advance to it, with free minds and open hearts, and find in it that which it claims for itself. If in truth it be of <u>God</u>, nothing can destroy it. If it be <u>not</u> of God, it will die of itself. The more we investigate it, the sooner it will be over if it be <u>not</u> of God.

All these things which have appeared in this last half century – and we have had all the signs Jesus said should come preceding the coming of the great Day of the Lord during the presence of the Great One on the earth. We have had all the false Christs – perhaps not <u>all</u>, but we have had many. We have had false prophets, deceiving hundreds and hundreds of people. And for a time all has gone well. Everything they did seemed to prosper. But where are they now?

In Deuteronomy, when the people cried out to know the truth, and asked the question, "How shall we know the Prophet, or the One whom the Lord hath sent?" – for verily the Prophets of God are <u>men</u> – "How shall we know the Lord that sent the Prophet?" the answer was that when one arises on the part of <u>God</u> to deliver the message of <u>God</u> the things he shall speak shall come to pass, but when one arises of himself, presumptuously, and claims to be the prophet of the Lord, verily, the things he speaks shall <u>not</u> come to pass, and they need not be afraid, for he will surely die.

It does not mean <u>physically</u> die, but whatsoever he says shall die in the minds of the people through the things he proclaims not coming to pass.

Just think how many people have arisen in the past years! My husband kept count of the false Christs in America, and up to four years ago there were thirteen.

This is the Day in which Jesus said that "many false prophets shall rise, and shall deceive many". But, regarding the coming of the True One, He said that He shall come like a thief in the night, and only those who are watching shall know. He did not say <u>where</u> He would come, or <u>when</u> He would come, but He told <u>how</u> He would come.

I want you to contemplate a little now the coming of Bahá'u-'lláh, from the land of Nur (which produced Abraham), because when He arose and declared His divine mission all that province belonged to Him – the land of Nur. Nur is a Persian word, and it means "light". So from the land of Persia, from the Province of Light, there has appeared this great One who has proclaimed

Himself to be the Manifestation of God for the people of this Day and this Age.

I do not know whether Dr. Fareed has told you of the wonderful letters which He wrote to the kings of the world. All the kings on earth received a wonderful letter from Bahá'u'lláh between the years 1868 and 1870. And that you may have a fuller idea of what His divine Mission was and is, I want to read to you the letter which He sent to the Pope of Rome. It was Pope Pius IX. And after this I want Mr. Chase, who is one of the oldest Bahá'ís in America, to speak to you on what the Bahá'í Movement means to the people of the world to-day. . .

———

Stenographically reported by B.S. Straum

Tuesday Afternoon, January 16, 1912
Bellevue Hotel, San Francisco, California

—oOo—

Mrs. Lua Moore Getsinger (Following Mr. Thornton Chase)

—oOo—

Mr. Chase saying that it is impossible for a thinker to think a new thought, reminds me of something some one said to me last Sunday, – a gentleman who is very much interested in the revision of the different phases of religion now existing. He said:

"What do we need a new religion for? We have ten or twelve already. We do not need a new one."

I said: "I quite agree with you. We do not need another new religion, and the Bahá'í Movement has nothing of a new religion to offer. It simply offers religion, the truth and Word of God renewed to-day, to satisfy the time and the needs of the people spiritually."

So, in the Bahá'í Movement, you will find all of the teachings of the Christ reiterated, all of the teachings of Mohammed – the essential truths – reiterated. Also all the Buddha said, and so with all the great Prophets and Messengers who have appeared in the world, on the part of God, since time began of which we have any record.

One thing that it seems to me the people are failing to take into consideration in this Day is that great fact that when God created man and this world He must have devised a <u>plan</u> then, by which in time He would animate, spiritually, all people and things.

All of the Messengers who have appeared in the world on the part of God have pointed to the Great Day which was to come in this world, in which all the people of the world were to see the results of the <u>spiritual</u> life, the life which <u>God</u> has to give to His creatures, made manifest. Some of them speak of it as the Day of Peace, and some as the Day of God, Day of Resurrection, Day of Judgment. Anyway, it has been mentioned in one term or another as a far off, divine event that was coming, and to which all creation was moving as fast as it could move <u>spiritually</u>.

But that <u>that</u> time had not come twelve hundred years ago, when Jesus Christ appeared, He Himself proclaimed. He did not say in all His teachings, "I have come to establish on earth the kingdom of God." <u>His</u> divine mission was to <u>herald</u> that kingdom, and to explain what that kingdom was to be. And He likened that kingdom to many things, and He told what it would be as manifest in the hearts of the people and in the world, etc., but He never said, "I have come to <u>establish</u> it on the earth." But He did definitely point out that Another would come <u>after</u> Him who was to lead the people into all truth.

We do not take that to mean that One is to appear upon the earth and guide man into the understanding of <u>all</u> the truth that God has to give to the people of the world, because the truth of God is limitless, and though we live throughout eternity we will never come to the end of God's truth.

So this must mean something else. It must mean that One is to appear Who will guide us into the understanding of all the truth of God of which the world possesses any record.

And that one thing is the great focal point of the Bahá'í Movement: this wonderful guidance into <u>all</u> the truth of God of which we have any written record. And we even go beyond the written record, because the truth of God is being revealed to-day in every department of life. Science is bringing it to light. <u>All</u> the sciences are bringing the truth of God to light.

Why? Because the time that was prophesied from all time is achieved. That period of time, mentioned by Jesus and the other Messengers in different terms, as the "last days" and the "latter days," has appeared. We have lived up to it, and we are now in it, and the Day in which the Prophets have declared the Prince of Peace should appear upon the earth has dawned, and He has appeared.

I made this statement once before a lady in New York City who is quite well known in literary circles, and she said, "I do not approve of that at all." I was amazed to think that a created being of God could say, "I do not approve of anything which God might ordain," and it showed to me from a little individualistic standpoint the terrible amount of egotism that the world is afflicted with to-day.

God has made man so wonderfully, and He has endowed him with such perfection as a creature, that the use of these gifts and graces has put him in such a state that he not only not approves of what God does, but gets up to oppose it all over the world.

When God, the Almighty, desires to act, we have no record in religious or profane history, where He has ever taken into cognizance the approval of His people, for He doeth whatsoever He wishes, in whatsoever way He desireth, to whomsoever He pleaseth.

He is the Almighty, and in the beginning He had a plan – evidently He had one. All we know about Him, and all we know about the redemption of the world, and a higher state of spiritual understanding and divinity, come as a working out of this plan – this great plan – and all the Messengers who have appeared have declared that they have come because He has sent them to work out His plan and establish it in part, here and there, until now the whole foundation has been laid in the world, through the power of this Word of God which has been spoken through the different Mouthpieces Who have appeared from time to time. And now the world is ready for the great edifice itself, and the Great Architect must come now and building upon this foundation, the primal principles of truth, which has already been laid by His most trusted servants and His Son Who have preceded His coming.

It is the acme of wisdom on the part of every created being to concede such a thought as this, that He Who planned not only this little planet upon which we are existing, but the whole universe, must also have had a plan by which the creature was to be raised to a higher station than that of merely a human animal, by which everything was to attain to the limitations of its own perfection according to the organisms in which it manifests. And if that is true, the Great Architect will be able to make all sincere seekers after truth realize that His plan is the right plan.

Now, in this Day, when so many religions and religious systems exist, when so many cults and isms and lessons of truth abound, is that not a sign? Are they all not signs that the time is at hand?

All the signs which Christ mentioned in the 24th chapter of Matthew, it seems to me, have been fulfilled, even to the coming of the false prophets and the false Christs.

Some one might say right here, "How do we know Bahá'u'lláh is not a false Christ?"

He has made the claim definitely and authoritatively that He is another Manifestation of God, that again the Word of God is speaking. And in whosoever's mind such a question might arise, that mind has the right, the divine right, to such a question. And it behooves everybody to seek – not only to know that He has made this claim – to know not only all about it historically, but to seek spiritually to prove this claim, for Jesus said that in this Day many should appear showing forth great signs and wonders, and the very elect themselves would be deceived, if it were possible.

The "elect!" Who are they?

Those sincere souls who are seeking after God and His truth for the sake of God and truth alone, not for the sake of what God, as a great, powerful Being, might be able to bestow as a result of seeking Him, not for comfort, or joy, or happiness, which knowing the truth might give, but to know God just alone and to know the truth itself, because it is the right of every divine human soul on earth to know it.

Those who are going out to seek with such a spirit are the elect, and God would not be God if they could be deceived. His attribute of justice would vanish – it would be blotted out like a star in the sky – if those could be deceived. And they can not be deceived, and for this reason hundreds and thousands of people in this last half century have died, because they knew, and had proven beyond any question of doubt whatsoever, that Bahá'u-'lláh is to-day the Great Architect Who is going to build upon the foundation of His Word, which has descended in former centuries, the great edifice of truth, for upon that foundation is this day to be established His kingdom on earth as it is in heaven, His kingdom of righteousness and truth, on which all sincere seeking souls are to be ushered, through mercy on His part, through earnest efforts on their parts.

Well, now, if He has appeared and declared Himself, it behooves every one to know what is His plan, how we are to get into this state of happiness, of unity. And this is the key note of all His teaching, and we must all recognize the fact that God is one God, one Father, one Creator of us all, and that we are all now here, living in one home, members of one family, brothers and sisters.

We do not realize this. Very few people on earth realize this great truth, this great fact. If we did, we would have peace. We would not be talking about it so much. We would have it. It would be an established fact. It would just be.

The sun does not have to declare itself over and over as a shining luminous body. It is. And could humanity come into the understanding that God is one, that this earth, this whole planet, is a home for His creatures, and that we are all now members of His family, brothers and sisters, why peace would be. It is just a lack of realization on our part. But, in the hearts and minds of those wherein that realization has come and dwelt for any length of time, we have that condition, and that, to my mind, is one of the greatest proofs of the truth of the claim of Bahá'u'lláh.

He said: "I have come to bring peace on earth. I have come to make the people realize that this earth is one home. I have come to take away all the differences. I have come to unite the hearts of all My children." And He declares Himself to be the Father Whose kingdom and coming Christ promised, Whose kingdom and coming the Prophets foretold.

When we are told what it has done in the Orient, and what it is doing, we say: "That is very nice. The world needs it."

Many people take this attitude: "The world needs it. It is very good. But what has it to do with me?"

We should change that attitude at once, because we do not know whether it is good for the world or not until we have found out first if it is good for us. Then, of course, from an individual standpoint, we can understand it is good for the world, but not

379

until we have first found it is good for us. And when such statements as that are made they are made from the standpoint of
mentality, not from the standpoint of knowledge, not from the
standpoint of comprehending this great plan in any detail
whatsoever.

Every one of us is part of that great plan, and the plan will not
be perfect until it is worked out to the perfection of all its parts.

I have something to do in that great plan. The work that I
have to do is there to be done. If I fail to recognize the point, or
the fact, that that work is there for me to do, the opportunity will
be given me to do it, until it is absolutely proven to the great
Mind of God that I am not going to do it, that out of my little
individual egotism and conceit I think I can get along without
performing my part of the work that is necessary in His great
plan, and then another servant willing to do my work does it, and
the plan goes on, irrespective and regardless of me. It does not
make a bit of difference.

The great plan, in the end, will be worked out, only just that
little part designed for me is delayed a little while, but in the
great plan of God time is not taken into consideration very much,
for before the great Eye and Mind of God a thousand years is just
as the twinkling of an eye, and the work is done. There is all
eternity before me to regret having missed the opportunity to
do my part of the plan.

What is my part? To so prepare my own heart and soul,
through the knowledge of the Word of God, as to make myself
an entity, an individual stone, in the great temple of His truth
that constitutes His kingdom on earth to-day. His kingdom "on
earth as it is in heaven" will be a spiritual kingdom. In heaven
it is a spiritual kingdom, to be sure. On earth it will also be a
spiritual kingdom.

All these material things which stand in our way to-day, and
deter us in making the best use of the opportunity to fulfill and
work out our part of the plan, will also be transmuted and
changed, by the power of this great Word of God, until at last the
people will realize that all things material are but shadows, and
that whatever little reality they possess will be brought out, and
it will be so small, as compared to the great whole – the great
plan of God which is established in the heart of His people – that
we will just naturally turn away from them, and after a while we

will only think of material things as means to ends.

When we regard ourselves as creatures of God, and know that no two creatures are alike, the little bit of the work assigned to us becomes very important, because the <u>work</u> is an individual thing, too. Just that particular part assigned to me is different from the particular part assigned to you, and I am needed, really needed, in this great plan of God, to do just this particular work, to fulfill this particular part. If I do not do it, some one else with my same capability will be put in that place. It will be done.

It is a beautiful thought when we think we are necessary to God. And, in just so far as He created us different from some other creature, we are necessary to Him and to the fulfilling of His great plan. If we had not been, we would not be here what we are.

And then, looking at it in the other way, we see that we are not necessary after all, in the final analysis, because with <u>him</u> is the power to create as many like me as He chooses, until His great plan is completed. My little corner will not be neglected. The power of God will make some one else in my place who will do it much better than I. With no apparent effort, some one else will come and do it. Why? Because His Word never shall return unto Him void of result.

But how patient is God! Oh, how patient is God! All these years He gives us to do just a few little things. First of all, to turn to Him, the Great Helper, the Giver of Knowledge, the Giver of Love, the Giver of Faith, the Giver of all good Gifts, and just realize that He is the Helper, and Giver and Bestower of whatever we may need, or want, or desire, for the full completion and working out of His will.

How foolish an architect and builder would be if he called together all the people to build a house and did not supply them with materials. No matter how perfect his plan would be, if he did not have the material to carry out the minutest detail of his plan, it would be incomplete, it would not be finished. So, as we are parts of the great plan of God, we have only to turn to Him and get all the material necessary to build His great plan to its utmost perfection.

The only question is: "Do we want to? Do we <u>want</u> to?"

The question is not: "Does He want us to?"

It is: "Do <u>we</u> <u>want</u> to do it?" This question is for each one to answer to himself.

The Bahá'í teacher to-day can only tell the good news – the "glad tidings" as they call it in the East – that the Great Architect has appeared, the Father has come, the Prince of Peace is here, the plan is all made out perfect, ready for the builders, and invite you all to come and take your place according to your ability and talent and capacity, and work under His direction and guidance for the completion and fulfillment of His kingdom.

No one will be obliged to come. No one can hire another to do his work, because in this kingdom of God only those work who <u>love</u> to work. You cannot hire anybody to take your place. They must come as <u>servants</u> through <u>love</u>. And this love which makes one <u>want</u> to serve, which makes one <u>want</u> to do, is one of the great gifts He has to bestow upon any soul who will turn towards Him.

We are not to blame if, in the beginning, we do not love, because we cannot love without knowing, but when <u>knowledge</u> and <u>love</u> are both there for the asking, we <u>are</u> to blame if we do not <u>ask</u>. If we ask and do not receive from Him, Who alone has the power to give, then the responsibility is with Him, not upon us.

The trouble is not that we are not receiving from asking. The trouble is that we are not <u>asking</u> that He may give. Many things He gives <u>without</u> the asking.

I have given this message to hundreds of people who have never asked to hear it. I must say that very few who never asked to hear it have accepted it. It requires a peculiar thirst, on the part of the soul, to drink from the cup of God that will quench the thirst.

I find myself often praying: "O God——"

We have the water of His knowledge, but we cannot make the people drink. They will not drink it unless they are thirsty. Some drink when they are not thirsty, but it does them no good. It does them harm.

But we have so much faith in the Great Architect, in the Great Builder, that we know His Word will <u>create</u> the thirst, too, in time. And so, when there are but one or two, or a very few, it makes no difference to the servant in His kingdom, because we know that the Sun is going to burn so brightly, and it will become so hot that this desert of the world is going to be so devoid of the things that count as worth while, that the people will soon come into it by hundreds and cry out to know. All that is prophesied to happen in this time called the "latter days."

I thought, the other night, as I was attending one of those large meetings of Gypsy Smith: "O if I could only tell them all this Message, if I could only make them all hear that the Comforter, the Father, the Prince of Peace, Whose coming and kingdom Jesus prophesied, is here now, and that they are invited to come to Him, how happy I would be!" Then I thought: "No, I would not be, either, for what if no one of them believed it! What if none of them would come!"

'Abdu'l-Bahá said to me once: "If you should see thousands of people, millions of them, coming in one day into this Cause, you must not be astonished, and do not become too happy. And if, in one day, you should see thousands who did not come in, don't be sad, do not be sorrowful. Realize now it is the Cause of God, and it will live, and it will grow, and you have nothing to do but to do your little part in it."

What a great responsibility that takes off of one, to really and fully know that the great miracle of all the ages, the Word of God has again become manifest upon this earth, and is going on with that invisible but ever increasing power for the transformation and quickening of the whole planet, that all the people on it are some day to know the truth, from the least to the greatest, in every religion, among all the nations, amongst all the races, and that we have nothing as individuals to worry about except this: that we are to do our little individual part well, so that when the day is ended, and we go before the Great Architect and say what we have done, we receive His commendation. That is all. The Cause belongs to God. The kingdom is His, and it is here now.

One of the instructions of Jesus was this: "Seek ye first the kingdom of God, and his righteousness; and all these things shall be added unto you." (Matt. 6:33)

He did not say, "after you have found the kingdom." They are going to be added while you are seeking.

What is the trouble? We are not seeking. The world is not yet seeking "the kingdom of God and his righteousness," as it should be seeking; but the time will come, according to the prophecies, when all the world will seek it, and they will find it in a single day.

For ages and for ages we have been moving slowly along to this time, and there is an end to this time. This time, which brings together the close of the old dispensation and ushers in a new Day, has an end. There is no end to the world; there is no end to the earth; there is no end to creation. But there is an end to periods, and we are living in the end of a period of time, and it is not very much longer, according to the prophecies. And then, suddenly, all these seeds of the Words of God shall spring forth, as it were, in a single night, into blooms – into <u>bloom</u> – and the earth will become a paradise. "On earth as in heaven" the kingdom will be established and completed.

Well, what a blessing, what a great opportunity to come in and be a <u>builder</u>, be a <u>worker</u>, a <u>server</u>. That is the great foundation that is now extended to the people of this particular time, the time which began in 1844 and closes in 1917, according to prophecy. That is the time of the <u>greatest</u> servitude. That is the time when the creatures on this earth are to manifest forth their greatest love and their greatest faithfulness to God. Everybody will be in after that time, in a very short time, whether they love or not, for God is so bountiful, so merciful! But what a wonderful thing it is to realize we have a chance to help God do something.

Some one has said: "What is the difference between the Bahá'í Movement and Christianity?"

There is no difference at all. There is a great deal of difference as it is taught in the churches, as it is interpreted by <u>men</u> to-day – all the difference in the world. The difference is as great as from here to heaven, because Christianity, as <u>interpreted</u> to-day, is a very material thing. Christianity, as Christ taught it, was a pure spirit. It was just <u>truth</u>.

The Bahá'í Movement has gone back and takes every seeking soul back to those first principles of pure Christianity, and reiterates all the Christ pathway, step by step, until it comes to the end of what Jesus taught, and there you will find the great Guidepost – Bahá'u'lláh – standing to-day and saying: "I am the Comforter Whose coming He promised. I am the Spirit of Truth to lead you now further in the path of truth upon which humanity was not ready to walk nineteen hundred years ago."

The <u>path</u> was there. There is no doubt about that, because Jesus said: "I have yet many things to say unto you, but ye cannot bear them now." (John 16:12)

So the curtain was dropped at that point. The Veil of Might shut out the rest of the path, but now, through the power of the Word of God and the influence of the Divine Educators He has sent, all humanity has come to this point, and the Veil of Might has been raised. It has been torn asunder, and the Word has again descended in the form of man. The Holy Spirit that spoke through Jesus nineteen hundred years ago is again speaking, and the Light shines on the path. It is but a continuance of the path. That is all.

There is no difference between the Bahá'í path and the path of Jesus the Christ, – no difference – because it is the same Christ Holy Spirit, Light of God, emanating from the same great central Sun of Truth. This one shining pathway that goes clear around the world is one path. There are many Guideposts along the way, many heavenly Guideposts like Zoroaster, Moses, and Jesus, Buddha, Mohammed, now Bahá'u'lláh, but it is the <u>one</u> path, so there is no difference in it at all.

The Mohammedan will say: "What has Bahá'u'lláh to offer that Mohammed did not give us?"

Just where Mohammed stopped, He takes him on, on the same path. Just where Zoroaster stopped, He takes him along. So it is just a continuance of the path, or it is the path made perfect clear around the world. The circle is complete.

The circle of the shining path of God's truth is complete now around the whole earth. All the quarters of the globe have received their Messenger, their Teacher. All have had their instructions, and the last Great Teacher has come – nay, <u>more</u> than a Teacher. He is the Father, the King, the Prince of Peace.

Whether you who hear will accept and believe and advance, all depends upon how much you want to know God and His truth, not how you <u>think</u> you want to know it but how much you really and truly <u>want</u> to know it, for when one really and truly wants to know it he starts out and seeks until he finds, but when he only <u>thinks</u> he wants to know it he starts out and walks a little way, and then sometimes he goes back home, and sometimes he sits down and rests by the roadside. All these questions we have to answer for ourselves.

A Paper written by Mrs. Lua Getsinger, taken from Alfred W. Martin.

[This paper takes the form of notes. Ed.]

The Strings of the Heavenly Harp, each of which gives forth a peculiar note, while the harmonious blending of all produce a symphony of music.

Even as the seven primary colors of the prism when blended give us the ray of pure white light, so these seven great religions when blended created the pure white light of non-sectarian or universal religion.

> Zoroaster – Singer of God – Purity
> Lao-Tse – Philosopher of God – Reverence
> Moses – Interlocutor of God – Righteousness
> Buddha – Teacher – Renunciation
> Jesus – Son of God – Love
> Muhammad – Messenger of God – Submission
> Bahá'u'lláh – Fatherhood of God – Unity

. . . Each one of these six great religions by reason of the particular circumstances under which it came into the world and the particular type of evils against which it had to protect, sets forth a more-or-less one-sided ideal of life. Each sounds its dominant note – uplifts a side of life and makes development of that side, the main feature of its teaching, rather than development of all the possibilities of our human nature, in right relation and proper proportion – the physical and the intellectual, the emotional and the practical.

As an example, take Christianity, the religion with which we are most familiar. It is strongly representative of the feminine or emotional virtues, meekness, humility, resignation, compassion, self-abnegation, love; just as early Judaism in a large measure representative of the masculine virtues – justice, loyalty, fortitude, patriotism, power.

In His emphasis on self-abnegation, Jesus was led to attach small value to the pursuit of knowledge as a worldly object in life, and to look on the physical and intellectual life as a hindrance to the development of the spiritual life. But it is true that the very one-sidedness, this exclusive glorification of the gentler virtues was the secret of his success as a restorer of hope and faith to an empire sunk in despair and unbelief.

His message proved to be precisely what was then wanted and most needed. By uplifting the emotional side at the expense of the physical, intellectual and aesthetic, Jesus manifested a noble narrowness that saved the Roman world. But on the other hand this very one-sidedness makes it impossible to regard the ideal taught by Him as a complete note for the world today, etc.

The Universal Religion as taught by Bahá'u'lláh today becomes the heir of the historic religions inheriting the contribution of each to the formation of the complete ideal of human life, (No one contains it) for it is and must be nothing less than the harmonious development of all the possibilities of a many-sided nature, into one rounded life. Must be so, because the world has not been ready spiritually – it takes all of these and one more to make the ideal complete (and harmony).

Therefore Bahá'u'lláh testifies of all the others as being part of the great message of Unity and proves that were one missing, His Message would be imperfect and therefore unacceptable. As the beauty of the diamond does not shine from any one of its facets but is produced by all of them together, so it takes all of these seven great religious leaders with their separate messages combined in this great age to produce the beauty and excellency of the ideal life for humanity.

No one can conquer the other for a union is needed – under a new banner (a revival of faith) which proclaims that the only unity possible is not of system but of souls or <u>hearts</u>, made free first then united on the basis of God's Word, providing for the attainment of moral and spiritual truth by the method of religious freedom to the end that each human life may by understanding, be made richer, grander, greater, holier, more divine. As fast as man learns to value this freedom more than bondage to tradition or creed – to care more for truth than sectarian victory so fast will they accept the advent of Bahá'u'lláh whose universal Religion will lift them above all differences of color, class, and race, creed, doctrine, dogma tenet and sect – into that sublime religious brotherhood which has been the dream of the people of every age and every clime.

THE MASTER TONE

One Sunday morning in the far-off town of Basel, I sat in my window listening to the melodies of the bells. All the bells were chiming, and one mellow deep-toned tolling bell, swinging alone in its tall bell-tower, gave the master-tone to the clamoring strife of sound.

How their jangling voices wrangling in the air striving for the right of way! Yet in spite of it all, through the midst of it all, undisturbed by multidinous discords, even bringing them all into concord, came unfailingly to the ear the steady swing and sway of that calm mellow boom, which seemed to soothe the ruffled air, and from its own abundance lend grace and meaning to all that aerial disquietude, which else it had not had.

Such is the Master Soul as the mingling resonance of the one powerful bell resolved the conflict of sound into harmony, so one strong voice which rings with truth and holiness will overcome the discordant voices of sin and attune them all to the divine harmony.

———

Notes from Mrs. Getsinger's Talk
of June 13th, 1912

Zoroaster was the "Singer of God;" Lao-tze, the "Philosopher of God;" Moses, the "Interlocutor of God;" Buddha, the "Teacher of God;" Jesus, the "Son of God;" Mohammed, the "Messenger of God;" Bahá'u'lláh, the "Glory of God."

The "key-note" word which came through Zoroaster was Purity; Lao-tze, Reverence; Moses, Righteousness; Buddha, Renunciation; Jesus, Love; Mohammed, Submission; Bahá'u'lláh, Unity.

Why turn toward the East for prayer?

Every time a Manifestation has come, he has appointed a "Kiblah," or point, and they turn toward this point for the sake of unity. The sun rises in the east and as the sun is a symbol of God, so they turn to the East, because it is the dawning-point from which the sun rises. It is simply that all their faces shall be turned in the same direction. They used to turn to Jerusalem, but Mohammed appointed Medina, or Mecca. Now Bahá'u'lláh has said, "All turn your attention toward the East, wherever you are."

Bahá has said that one should pray three times each day. You know the Mohammedans pray five times daily, the Christians once. To unite them all and make it uniform, he said: "Pray three times each day – at sunrise, noon and sunset." Now the Bahá'ís all over the world (there are three million, according to 'Abdu'l-Bahá) are turning toward the East at the same time.

Is the ablution of the hands and face imperative?

It is not imperative; it is the symbol of washing your hands from the world, of cleansing your face from having turned toward anything else.

****

Choose any prayer you like. The Obligatory Prayer is to be used three times each day.

Are any original prayers used?

Yes; pray whatever your heart prompts. The prayers which have been revealed through Bahá'u'lláh are better than our prayers because he was the Manifestation of God and he knew the needs of all the souls. So the words which have descended through him are the food for all the creatures. There is not one phase of human existence left untouched. God, in his great mercy, has even instructed us how to pray and the very words to use! . . . If we knock at the door using God's own words, can he refuse to answer?

Has the meaning of the "B" and "H" in the name Bahá'u'lláh been given out?

No, the Surat-el-Hykel[Súriy-i-Haykal], which is not yet properly translated, explains the mystery of the Spirit of God manifesting itself in the human temple of man, and every organ of the human temple is addressed and a use assigned to it . . .

Do you think the time is ripe for us to know the meaning of all these letters?

The time is coming. The people are not yet in a condition to receive the spiritual significance, but when we arise and divest ourselves of material things, turning our hearts and souls to God through prayer, then the spiritual significance will be given us, because this is the Day of Revelation, the Day of God, when everything is to be made clear.

How can any human being let love take possession of the heart?

The first thing to know in this day is whether or not Bahá'u-'lláh is what he claimed to be. You know he said – "To all the denizens of the world, I am the Manifestation of God; I am the Christ, the Holy Spirit of God. I am the Father manifest. I am the Prince of peace; I am the Everlasting Father and the Almighty God." He [sent] this statement in his letters to all the kings of the various nations, making this claim. He either is that, or he is not that. There is no middle ground. No one can say, "He is a good man who has come to reform the world." He either is sent to this earth by God as the Manifestation, to unite all the people, or he is not. Now the first thing for any student of Truth is to absolutely settle it for himself, once and for all, whether he is or is not. If he is, then the next thing or next step is to know his Word and obey his Word. First you must investigate him, his life, his teachings; know what he taught. One can purchase books giving the historical part of his life.

Bahá'u'lláh said, "I have come into the world for the purpose of taking away three prejudices which have existed for centuries among the people of the world, to the extent of dividing them so that they go to war with each other. One prejudice is religious, one patriotic, one national. First these must be removed."

What a tremendous task it is to remove religious prejudices existing for centuries! He said, "I have come to take these differences away." Has he done this? We have now three million people in the world today who believe absolutely that he is the Manifestation of God. They are composed of Jews, Christians, Buddhists, Hindus, Mohammedans, Chinese and Japanese.

They have been turned by the word of Bahá'u'lláh to the contemplation of the word of God in their own Holy Books. They have all gone back to fundamentals and they find that, fundamentally, they all agree; and Bahá'u'lláh brings forth his word and says, "This is the Word of God today."

We have gotten away from the Word of God into the interpretation of the Word. For instance, in Acca, while 'Abdu'l-Bahá was still a prisoner, seventy pilgrims having journeyed to Acca for the express purpose of seeing 'Abdu'l-Bahá and investigating these teachings of Bahá'u'lláh, representing six religions and six nations, we were all there, and 'Abdu'l-Bahá said: "If you want proof of the teachings of Bahá'u'lláh, just look round at your-selves!"

Here were Jews, Mohammedans, Zoroastrians, Christians, Chinese, – from Russia, France, India, America, Persia, China – all seated there at this table and representing all these different nations, all these different religions, with all our different customs and manners, in a prison, and we had all gotten in through that gate and were seated in the house of Bahá'u'lláh, women and men together, all the customs of the Orient done away with! There we were, seated together, and 'Abdu'l-Bahá serving us! He said; "Bahá'u'lláh promised me that I should see the day when people of all nations would gather together in this city in pursuit of the knowledge of the Word of God which was revealed through him."

All our hearts were kindled through the realization of the promise Bahá'u'lláh fulfilled. One Mohammedan Judge sat across the table from Mr. Getsinger and he looked at him and me and the rest of us and said, "Fifty years ago I would have thrust my sword through your hearts before I would have yielded myself to sit at the table and eat with you; but today, through the power of the Word of God, as uttered by Bahá'u'lláh, I am such a changed being that I would let my own heart be thrust through to keep you from the slightest harm."

"What is this but the Spirit of God, to have wrought such a change in human beings that it makes this meeting possible?" We were all convinced. As 'Abdu'l-Bahá said that day, had we seventy been the only Bahá'ís in the world, we would have been sufficient to have proven Bahá'u'lláh to be a Messenger of God, because he had departed and none of us had ever seen him. We seventy represented three million in the world who were in the same state. So he has proven that his teaching does remove religious differences.

Does it remove racial differences?
Yes; because we were of all races. As to removing national and

patriotic differences, yes; because we would all rather have lived right there in Acca than to have gone back to our several countries . . .

A Manifestation speaks the same kind of words, but in those words there is a power which kindles the hearts of people and changes the character of human beings. There is a power hidden in those words. For instance, Bahá'u'lláh says, "You are all the leaves of one tree; you are all drops of one sea. Live together in unity." A special power is given to the words of Bahá'u'lláh.

The first thing is to consider his claim. He said, "I am the Manifestation of God." How are we to prove this? Through prayer only. It is impossible for me to convey my knowledge and absolute faith to you, because knowledge, faith and love are attributes of the Holy Spirit of God and no human being can bestow these upon another. If you want to know whether or not Bahá'u'lláh is the Manifestation of God, turn to God in prayer. Call upon him by any name you please, – any name, because God in essence is nameless, so call upon God by any name that you like and ask Him to give you faith in him and love for Him.

This knowledge of God is for every human soul; it is food, it is sustenance; without it the soul starves, becomes ill, and at last withers. Faith in God is for every human soul its water. It quenches its thirst and removes everything that causes agitation of the mind and spirit.

St. Paul gave the only definition of faith that is feasible. So many people think faith is a sort of belief in something. It is not so. Faith is the result of knowledge. Without knowledge you can have no faith. St. Paul said, "Faith is the evidence of things unseen and the substance of things hoped for."

God is unseen; you have no evidence of God; in your own soul you have no evidence. He is still an unseen Essence, an unseen Entity; but faith, but faith which comes to the human soul as a gift of God when asked for, gives you an evidence within your self which if all the people on earth should tell you "It is a lie; you are deceived," you would only become more firm. You would <u>know</u>, the same as you know the sun is the sun when you see it rising in the morning. So when you get within your soul one little atom of the faith of God, nothing can take it away. You have within you the undeniable evidence. Then all that you have hoped for comes to pass.

Faith gives you the substance of your hopes and the evidence of things unseen, and it is to the soul as water is to the body. It is the water of the soul. Then the soul needs protection and clothing, the same as the body, and the clothing of the soul, which will protect it from the inclemency of all the spiritual elements, is love for God. Love for God is a marvellous gift. Of all the precious jewels of the universe it is the pearl of greatest price. . . . You cannot force yourself to love a human being unless it comes in your heart. If it is impossible to force yourself to love a human being, whom you can see, how much more impossible is it to force yourself to love God, whom you cannot see! So you have to ask God for this gift too, and when the love of God is bestowed upon a soul it becomes for that soul its garment, which will protect it from everything save God.

Though everything is taken away from you, if you, as a soul, are clothed with the mantle of the Love of God, nothing can disturb or shake you.

Those who have given their lives in the Path of God have undoubtedly had to a great degree these gifts – Knowledge of God, Faith in God and Love for God. They took a young Persian man to kill him and told him to deny God. He said, "I cannot. I know that God is, and that Bahá'u'lláh is the Manifestation; I know it, the same as I know I am breathing. I could not deny my own existence while I am standing here." They said, "Say it with your lips." He said, "My lips would be cursed if for one instant they should deny the knowledge which has descended from God. I cannot use my lips in such a way." They said, "If you will deny Him and turn away from this Cause, you may have the most beautiful girl in the city for your bride." He said, "I already have a bride. My bride is the Love of God, and the only thing I ask is for you to do whatever you like with me so that I may go to God."

They brought fagots, pouring kerosene over them, and the young man stood there holding up his hands and singing the most wonderful song of praise, and he kept saying, "Oh my Beloved! At last the night of my marriage has come! At last I am to have my bride!" until the flames enveloped him and took him from sight. Did he not know beyond any question of doubt that Bahá'u'lláh was the Manifestation? Had he not in his heart the evidence and a love dearer than life itself?

There is a way to pray. We pray, but we do not receive because, Jesus said, we ask amiss. We ask but we do not believe we are heard. He said, "If ye pray, believe that whatsoever ye ask it shall be given you." That is the word of God, and in it there can be no changing, but it is because we pray amiss, we ask disbelieving, waiting for some miracle, waiting for something to happen outside of ordinary things around us, and every thing is made manifest through the surrounding existence.

Some people have wonderful spiritual illuminations, but usually it comes through the most ordinary channels. Prayers are answered through belief and through the most ordinary way. The answers come so simply and gently that we do not realize they have been heard, and sometimes they do not come at the time and in the manner we wanted, because we have asked for things we should not have asked for.

Jesus said: "Seek ye first the Kingdom of God and his righteousness and all other things shall be added unto you." We are not seeking righteousness of character, of spirit, of heart, but we are seeking those other things which we think are so important, and they are so unimportant that Jesus said – "Seek ye first the Kingdom of God and His Righteousness, and all these things shall be added unto you."

When God created man, He had first created this whole earth. He had inhabited the waters with fish, the air with fowl and had caused the trees to grow. He had deposited in the pockets of the earth rich ores, precious jewels, and then as the apex, the climax, He made man and gave to him as a free gift everything on this earth and gave him dominion over everything. But He said to man, "You give your <u>heart</u> to me."

Man does not appreciate the Giver of Gifts; he occupies himself with all these gifts. He says, I am going to have my share of them, not realizing that if he should turn to the Giver, these would come without struggles, sacrifices and trials, because these things are ephemeral. They do not last and do not bring happiness. It is only when the soul is fed from the table of the knowledge of God that he is satisfied.

Nothing but the love for God can afford protection to the soul. – Pray with sincerity, "Oh God, give me knowledge; Oh God! give me faith; Oh God! give me love!"

God has not heard you before because you have not prayed

right; you have not asked for the things that are going to benefit you eternally.

If Jesus Christ, Bahá'u'lláh and 'Abdu'l-Bahá prostrated themselves on the earth to pray to God, what should we do? Can we hope to get any knowledge in any other way? 'Abdu'l-Bahá can create in you the <u>desire</u>.

There is the prayer of aspiration and the prayer of supplication. Aspiration keeps us going on. In the *Seven Valleys*, written by Bahá'u'lláh, the first Valley is Search; then comes the Valley of Knowledge. Now you are just at the entrance of the second valley, but no one can take you in there but God. 'Abdu'l-Bahá can only create within you the desire to go. He can enkindle in your hearts the desire to go on, but you will have to pray. Turn your face to God and pray. No matter what you ask, it may not come just when you ask it. First ask for knowledge as to whether or not Bahá'u'lláh is the Manifestation for the people of this day. You must find out first whether or not He is the Manifestation of God. Of course it will be given you mentally. It is not belief; it is <u>Knowledge</u>. Why you have to go to God for it is because of the warning which Jesus Christ sounded for the people of this day – "In that day many shall come saying 'I am Christ, and many shall arise showing forth such signs and wonders as to deceive the very elect'". . . You must not believe that Bahá'u'lláh is the Manifestation of God because I say so; you must believe through positive knowledge which comes to you through God regarding that certain point.

Anyone can say, "I am a Manifestation of God." There are many people who have arisen and declared themselves to be Elijah, John the Baptist, Christ, etc. Bahá'u'lláh said, "I am the Father and I have come to establish upon this earth the Kingdom of God which Jesus, the Son of God, heralded." It is a wonderful statement, and it is either true or not true. There is no middle ground to take. He said, "I am that." You must be absolutely convinced that he <u>is</u> that. That will come to you through knowledge and study. Remember that it is not his life or the history of his life, but his <u>Word</u>. If his word is the word of God, nothing else is evidence but that word. If that Word does to the people of the earth what he said it would do, that is the <u>proof</u> that He is the Manifestation of God. He said, "I do not speak this Word. These are the Words of God." He told Napoleon [III], "Unless you arise and investigate this matter and take hold of this firm rope which is held out, your empire shall be taken from you, commotion shall seize your people and we see you among those after whom humiliation and death are hastening." This was sent to Napoleon in 1869, in 1870 his empire fell and humiliation and death awaited him.

Lua gave a talk in New York about the life of Bahá'u'lláh on the following day, June 14, 1912, the same day as 'Abdu'l-Bahá's meeting in Baltimore. Although it contained several historical errors (marked here by an asterisk*), it represents a good example of Lua's teaching methods. The life of Bahá'u'lláh was not well-known to the Bahá'ís at that time. Shoghi Effendi's authoritative history of the Bahá'í Faith, *God Passes By*, was not published until 1941.

Notes from Mrs. Getsinger's Talk
of June 14th, 1912
—***—

What is the meaning of "Latter Days?"

Jesus referred to a time to come as the "Latter Days;" Daniel referred to that time; Isaiah, all the prophets have referred to a period of time as the "Latter Days," the Day of Judgement, or the last hour, in various terminologies.

That time was ushered in upon the world in 1844, according to the dates given in the 12th chapter of Daniel. That time began in 1844 and it ends in 1917. It is a transitional period of time. It is the drawing together of the old dispensation of things and the ushering in of a new dispensation, a new Day of God. You remember Jesus saying that in the "Latter days" such and such things would happen, false Christs appear and false prophets come? But he said, "Beware that ye be not deceived; for all these are signs of the coming of the True One."

Today I wish to specially teach you regarding the coming of the Comforter as referred to in the 16th chapter of John, 16th verse, "And I will pray the Father, and he shall send you another Comforter, that he may abide with you forever; even the Spirit of Truth, whom the world cannot receive, because it seeth him not, neither Knoweth him; but ye know him, for he dwelleth with you."

(Mrs. G. also read from the 16th chapter of John.)

Jesus said, "Because I live, ye shall live also. At that day ye shall know that I am in the Father and ye in me and I in you." You know Jesus said constantly, all the time he was teaching, "I of myself speak nothing; the Father in me speaketh and through me the Father doeth all these works." The simile that I gave you the other day regarding the sun and the rays of light emanating therefrom – Jesus was a mirror in which were collected all the rays of light and from him reflected to the world. People could not see the source from which the rays of light came, but when they looked at him they saw this luminous being and when they heard him speak they heard these wonderful words. It was the voice of God, whom he called the Father, that was speaking in him and when the disciples would hear him speak and he said to them, "A little while and ye shall see me no more," they were confused and did not understand what he meant, and after he had spoken to them so much about the Father, Philip said to him, "Show us the Father, and it sufficeth us," Then Jesus seemed to have said (but <u>he</u> did not say – the voice of the Father – through Jesus, said) "Have I been so long time with you, Philip, and ye have not known me? He that hath seen me hath seen the Father."

The church has interpreted this to mean that Jesus and the Father are one and the same in entity and being, but they are not, because immediately after that <u>Jesus</u> said unto his disciples, "I go unto my father, and He is greater than I." That was Jesus, the Son of God, speaking; but when the Christ Holy Spirit spoke through Jesus, It said – "Have I been so long time with you and ye have not seen me?" Then he said unto them, "I will not leave you comfortless; I will come again." That Spirit, that Voice, which descended upon Jesus, the son of Mary, Christ, the Son of God, said, I will come again. I will send you another Comforter. I will not leave you comfortless. Then in the 16th chapter: "These things have I spoken unto you, that ye should not be offended. They shall put you out of the synagogues: yea, the time cometh that whosoever killeth you will think that he doeth God service. And these things will they do unto you because they have not known the Father, nor me."

Even the disciples were not realizing that the Holy Spirit, the Voice of God, was speaking to them through him and saying, "I am going now, but in a little while I will come again and be another Comforter for the people." Just think of the unenlightened spiritual condition of his disciples, who walked and talked with him and were taught by him for three years; yet when the crucial moment came, when the testing time came, Judas betrayed Him! Peter, James and John went with Him to the Garden of Gethsemane . . . and when Jesus returned from praying in the garden, he found them asleep. He wakened them and said, "Pray! for the time is at hand when the Son of Man is to be betrayed." Then he went back again and prayed, "Oh God! if it be thy will, let this cup pass from me!" He knew that the cup of his own being, the Cup of His Body, was the receptacle from which the world was drinking the Wine of the Spirit, of the Knowledge of God, and he knew that as soon as the cup was broken the world would not have any receptacle through which it could drink – there would be no vehicle. He was not afraid to die! His life had been one of turmoil, unrest and disease; but because he loved the people so much, he begged of God to let the cup of death pass from him and to let him stay there and serve them longer – not because he was afraid to die, as the church interprets it. But when the Voice of the Holy Spirit communed with him . . . He again went to the disciples and once more found them asleep, he then said, "Sleep on and take your rest." Then it was that Judas betrayed him.

The church has said that this Spirit of Truth which He promised came to the disciples after the death of Jesus Christ, at the time when they were all together in the Pentecostal Chamber and that they then received the Comforter. What did He say the Comforter should do when He came? "He will guide you unto all Truth." "He shall not speak of himself, but whatsoever he shall hear, that shall he speak, and he will show you the things to come." "He shall glorify me, for he shall receive of mine and show it unto you."

When they were assembled together in the chamber, according to the account of the Pentecostal Baptism given in Acts, they were all there, with the doors and the windows closed, when suddenly they heard a sound as of a mighty rushing wind and tongues of fire sat on each of them. Not one word was spoken, but they all received the spiritual baptism and were confirmed by the Power of the Holy Spirit to go out and deliver the Gospel of Christ to the people. But when the Holy Spirit came to them it did not show them nor guide them into the understanding of all the truth upon earth. It simply confirmed them to be in reality the disciples of Jesus Christ and to go out and deliver his Message, a part of which was this very verse; and they had to preach to the people that there was another Comforter coming.

"The angels of heaven know not the hour when the Son of Man shall come." That was known only to the Father; so they could not tell the people when this other Comforter was coming. It was only known to the Father. When the time was achieved to the end and that period was ushered in which had been foretold as the Latter Days (which occurred in 1844 with the appearance of the Báb, who preceded the appearance of Bahá'u'lláh), the world was made ready at that time for the advent of this Comforter, this Spirit of Truth whom Jesus Christ had promised, and for that reason the Báb announced the coming of One greater than himself. He said, "My service is only to tell the people of the world that the Great One is coming – the One foretold by all the prophets. He in whom the world will see God made Manifest will appear." And he said to his early disciples, "I do not know when he will come; but let us always have a place prepared for him." He did not appear during the lifetime of the Báb.

During the early part of the Mission of the Báb, he repeatedly said, "I shall sacrifice my life in the path of Him who is coming after me, and then He will appear." He delivered the Message to the people of the world in 1844 and was allowed to teach until 1850; but during those years he suffered imprisonment a great many times, was threatened and tortured; yet he went on teaching until 1850 when the government decided that the only way to stop the rise and spread of this pernicious doctrine was to kill the Báb who had announced this new message to the people. So after he had been confined for some time in the city of Tabriz, they took him out one morning in 1850 and suspended him by two ropes. They took his first disciple and using the body of the Báb as a cross, they placed the feet of his disciple over his shoulders, binding them together with a rope, and then called a regiment of soldiers and the government gave the order to fire upon them. When the smoke cleared away, the disciple lay upon the ground,* but the Báb was nowhere to be seen! Great consternation fell upon the soldiers and they said, "We have done a

terrible thing. This man must have been the Messenger of God."
But one of the guards stepped into a small guard house nearby
and found him kneeling upon the floor reading* as though
nothing had happened. He took him by the shoulders and
dragged him out, saying, "Here is the coward! He is hiding." He
said, "No, I am not a coward. My life is already given up, but I
have been left to give you a message!" So he spoke: "Hear the
Voice of God through Mohammed, the Prophet, who declared
that in the day when the Messenger should come, you would not
be able to hear his voice, and because of this you would rise and
kill him, and the noise of your hatred should resemble the noise
of a mortar. What is this that makes you kill me but hatred, for
what have I come to deliver to you but a message of love!"
Because of your hatred, you wish to kill me, and this noise that
is come from your guns is none other than the noise of your
hatred." Many of the soldiers threw their guns upon the ground
and refused to have anything more to do with it, saying, "He is
a man of God and it is a miracle that God has saved him." Then
the Báb said, "I am ready. Do anything to me that you like." So
they called a company of Armenian <u>Christian</u> soldiers,* and
these soldiers shot him to death.

When John the Baptist appeared, he had the honor and the
privilege of pointing out to his disciples whom he had taught.
When he saw Him, he said: "Behold the Lamb of God, whose
coming is preferred to me!" He showed them the One whom he
was talking about. But the Báb was teaching of some one whom
he had never seen, of whose earthly existence he knew nothing,*
because he had never seen him; but he knew and said, "He is
now upon the earth and He may appear at any time." Look at
his faith, and at that of his disciples! Hundreds had given up
their lives for their faith in his words. If the Manifestation had
not appeared, what would the world say today? – "Oh, he was a
man who had become obsessed by one idea!" – but which was not
true, for his words did come true, as directly after the martyrdom
of the Báb in Tabriz Bahá'u'lláh arose among the people. He was
born in 1817, and note that the transitional period spoken of as
the "Latter Days" closes in 1917 – just one hundred years exactly
from the birth of Bahá'u'lláh.

Bahá'u'lláh arose in Teheran and went out among the people.
His family was noted, being called the famous Nuri family, His

father being the Prime Minister.* Bahá'u'lláh traces his lineage directly back to Abraham. He is the direct descendant of Midian, the son of Abraham, through his third wife, Katurah.[130] He owned at this time the whole province of Nur.* He was a man of culture, but had never been to school, having had private tutors. He had no desire to take his father's place as Prime Minister (though they asked him to do so).* He simply said, "I am a believer in the teachings of the Báb."

They used to take the Bábís out in the public squares and accuse them of being Bábís, torturing them. Since 1844 until now, twenty thousand people have suffered martyrdom for the sake of this Truth.

Bahá'u'lláh boldly declared, "I am a Bábí", and upon hearing this, twelve very famous men, friends of his, likewise declared themselves followers; whereupon all thirteen were arrested* and chained together and put in a dungeon in the Teheran prison and the Government confiscated all their property.

Bahá'u'lláh's wife, sister* and son 'Abdu'l-Bahá escaped and were hidden for three days in a little stone hut, without a mouthful of water or a morsel of food. Then an old servant, Isfandiar crawled on his hands and knees through the grass until he found them and brought them water and food. The wife gave her gold and jeweled buttons to the servant to purchase bread for Bahá'u-'lláh.

Bahá'u'lláh was kept in prison for three months (together with twelve friends).* After the Government had to give up hope that they would die (from the hardships imposed upon them) they said, "We will kill them, but will save Bahá'u'lláh till the last." . . . And when at last they had killed them all* and the day came for Bahá'u'lláh to die, a most wonderful thing happened. The Ambassador of Russia,[131] who had been an old friend of Bahá'u-'lláh's . . . intervened, threatening vengeance, and succeeded in having his life spared. Bahá'u'lláh was then sent as an exile and prisoner to Turkey. He was released at the beginning of the winter in Persia and an edict was issued that anyone who wished to go into exile with him might do so. Seventy people voluntarily went with Him! They were allowed one dollar per month to live upon. They went through mountains infested with robbers and bandits, through snow and ice, but at last they arrived in Baghdad in safety – no one harmed but the child 'Abdu'l-Bahá, whose little feet had been frozen.

When they reached Baghdad, the Sultan said they must not teach, but must just live there; so the Governor gave them a place in which to live. After He had been in Baghdad for some time, the Governor of the city became so attracted that he was with Bahá'u'lláh day and night. He said, "What it is I do not know; but I love you and will do anything you ask me to." However the clergy made such trouble that finally the Governor said, "I do not know what to do." The whole city was in a turmoil . . . Bahá'u'lláh said, "Just let me go, and all I ask is that you will take care of my people (and see that they are not harmed)." He was then released and went away into the mountains, alone,* where He stayed for two years and no one heard from Him. After He had been there about two years, one day 'Abdu'l-Bahá said to His mother, "I cannot stand it longer – My Father must come!" and He began to weep, refusing to eat. Suddenly one night the door opened and Bahá'u'lláh came in, saying, "I have heard your weeping and prayers and I have come."*

Bahá'u'lláh then set out to the plain of Badasht and it was there, by the river Kebar, prophesied by Ezekiel, that He rose and declared Himself to be the Manifestation of God.* 'Abdu'l-Bahá had understood this before. He was the first to recognize Him as the Manifestation of God. Bahá'u'lláh was declared to the people in the most wonderful way by Kurat-ul-Ayn Who . . . seized a long stick and went out among the tents of the people, striking on their tents with the stick and reading in a loud voice the prophecy in the Koran and crying out – "I am the bugle!" until she reached Bahá'u'lláh's tent. Then she said, Oh my God, I know Thee, who thou art! There was a great tumult, and when the people saw this woman with <u>face</u> <u>uncovered</u> (and hair un-bound) . . . Bahá'u'lláh then arose and made it known to all that He was the Manifestation; but he said to Kurat-ul-Ayn, "Now you must go" (meaning, back to her tent).*[132]

After the martyrdom of Kurat-ul-Ayn Bahá'u'lláh lived in Baghdad[133] for some years and was then sent to Constantinople. On reaching Constantinople, after a three months' journey through the burning desert, they were put into the most fearful quarters. After a time, the Sultan of Turkey decided to send them to Adrianople, in Asia Minor. This is a very remote place. Here they remained five years, and again the Governor became a convert to Bahá'u'lláh. He allowed Him to write, and many wonderful books were written while He stayed there, and at this time were prepared the famous letters to the kings of the world.

From Adrianople the Sultan sent Bahá'u'lláh to Acca, in the midst of the desert, surrounded by walls 30 feet high and 15 feet thick. It was a penal colony, and the climate was such that it was said that even the birds flying over it, fell dead. Anyone sent to this prison lived only about three months. There was no water to drink but the sea-water filtered through the sands. Here they were confined in the Army Barracks, at the top of the highest building, in a room with a mud floor. They lived in this place for two years.

Note – It is worth the reader's while to read Isaiah 35th chapter in regard to Acca or the valley of Acca, and the great change which was to take place and did take place in the physical condition of the country after Bahá'u'lláh's exile to this penal colony.

Typed by F.J. Woodward,
July 1918

Notes and References

1. p. 181.
2. I am indebted to Robert H. Stockman for many of the historical details in this chapter. See his *The Bahá'í Faith in America*, vol. 1: *Origins 1892-1900* (Wilmette, Illinois: Bahá'í Publishing Trust, 1985), p. 90.
3. I am indebted to Richard Hollinger for generously sharing with me the results of his research.
4. W. Sears and R. Quigley, *The Flame* (Oxford: George Ronald, 1972), pp. 19-20. This quotation from Bahá'u'lláh came from the pen of E.G. Browne (see below, note 109).
5. Stockman, vol. 1, p. 30.
6. ibid. pp. 85, 93.
7. Sears and Quigley, p. 22.
8. Stockman, vol. 1, p. 90.
9. ibid.
10. ibid. p. 116.
11. One of nineteen Bahá'ís named by Shoghi Effendi as "Disciple of 'Abdu'l-Bahá", Mrs. Brittingham "became perhaps the most prominent woman Bahá'í lecturer, teacher, and writer in the West before 1912" (Stockman, vol. 1, p. 123). She was the author of *The Revelation of Baha-Ullah in a Sequence of Four Lessons* and compiled several booklets on the teachings, published by the Bahá'í Publishing Society. She heard about the new teachings from her sister-in-law, Charlotte Dixon, whose dramatic conversion is recounted in Stockman, vol. 1, pp. 118-119. Her account of Anton Haddad is found in Stockman, vol. 1, pp. 137-138.
12. O.Z. Whitehead, *Some Early Bahá'ís of the West* (Oxford: George Ronald, 1976), p. 15.
13. *Star of the West* (Chicago, 1910-1922, periodical. Reprinted Oxford: George Ronald, 1978) vol. 13, no. 7, p. 203.
14. Stockman, vol. 1, p. 151.

15. Lua was twenty-seven, if 1871 is correct as her date of birth.
16. Mary (Maryam) Thornburgh-Cropper, a Californian living in London, daughter of Mrs. Thornburgh, a friend of Mrs. Hearst. Mrs. Thornburgh-Cropper joined the pilgrimage party in Paris. She became one of the founder members of the British Bahá'í community.
17. May Bolles Maxwell's account of this first visit by Western pilgrims to 'Abdu'l-Bahá is given in *An Early Pilgrimage* (Oxford: George Ronald, 1969).
18. Stockman, vol. 1, pp. 144-145.
19. ibid. pp. 153-154.
20. Mírzá Muḥsin-i-Afnán, married to 'Abdu'l-Bahá's daughter Ṭúbá Khánum. Of 'Abdu'l-Bahá's four daughters, the two eldest were married at this time, while the two younger ones, Rúḥá and Munavvar, were still unmarried.
21. Mírzá Abu'l-Faḍl-i-Gulpáygání, Apostle of Bahá'u'lláh, Islamic scholar and foremost scholar of the Bahá'í Faith at the time; 'Abdu'l-Karím-i-Ṭihrání, a Persian Bahá'í who had settled in Cairo and had taught Kheiralla the Bahá'í Faith. Both were later sent to America by 'Abdu'l-Bahá to teach the believers there.
22. Stockman, vol. 1, p. 160.
23. ibid.
24. To a modern reader such sentences could convey erotic meaning, but on the contrary, tender phrases and loving words were used freely by women writing to each other in the nineteenth century. See C. Smith-Rosenberg, *Disorderly Conduct* (Oxford:Oxford University Press, 1985).
25. Stockman, vol. 1, p. 161.
26. Ḥájí Mírzá Ḥaydar-'Alí, *Stories from The Delight of Hearts* (Los Angeles: Kalimat Press, 1980), p. 126; on the subject generally see A. Taherzadeh, *The Covenant of Bahá'u'lláh* (Oxford: George Ronald, 1992), Chs.13-18.
27. Stockman, vol. 1, p. 162.
28. From a copy made in 1938 by C.B. Nourse, in the National Bahá'í Archives, Hawaii.
29. Mírzá Asadu'lláh-i-Iṣfahání (1826-1930), at the time "one of 'Abdu'l-Bahá's most trusted lieutenants". See R.H. Stockman, *The Bahá'í Faith in America*, vol. 2: *Early Expan-*

sion, 1900-1912 (Oxford: George Ronald, 1995), p. 36, and Ch.4. He later followed his son Ameen'Ullah Fareed in breaking the Covenant.

30. For a discussion of how the issue of reincarnation affected the American Bahá'í community see Stockman, vol. 2, pp. 32-33.

31. E.G. Browne, British orientalist. See note 109.

32. Ramona Allen Brown, *Memories of 'Abdu'l-Bahá: Recollections of the Early Days of the Bahá'í Faith in California* (Wilmette, Illinois: Bahá'í Publishing Trust, 1980), p. 11.

33. English believer converted by May Maxwell in Paris.

34. H.M.Balyuzi, *'Abdu'l-Bahá* (Oxford: George Ronald, 1971), p. 79.

35. ibid. p. 97.

36. H. Colby Ives, *Portals to Freedom* (Oxford: George Ronald, 1969), p. 85.

37. Balyuzi, p. 97.

38. Sybil Sanderson, an opera singer in Paris, sister of Edith Sanderson, one of the earliest American Bahá'ís in Paris. See *The Bahá'í World*, vol. XIII, pp. 889-890.

39. Balyuzi, p. 78. See also *The Bahá'í World*, vol. XII, pp. 679-681.

40. See *The Bahá'í World*, vol. V, pp. 414-417.

41. *Khátirat-i-Nuh-Sáliy-i-'Akká* (Memories of Nine Years in 'Akká), pp. 198-209. Written in 1942 (nearly forty years after the events described here) and published in Teheran, this is one of the prime historical sources for 'Abdu'l-Bahá's life in the first decade of the 20th century. No full English translation has yet been published, although excerpts by various translators are quoted in Bahá'í publications. This paraphrase is based on a translation by Siamak Zabihi.

42. 1872-1965. Born Mary Ida Parkhurst. 'Abdu'l-Bahá gave her the name Mariam, which she always used thereafter. For a memorial article of her life see *The Bahá'í World*, vol. XIV, pp. 343-346.

43. Mírzá 'Alí Muḥammad-i-Varqá and his son, Rúḥu'lláh.

44. *Star of the West*, vol. XV, p. 230.

45. "Thou knowest, O God, and art my witness that I have no desire in my heart save to attain Thy good pleasure, to be

confirmed in servitude unto Thee, to consecrate myself in Thy service, to labour in Thy great vineyard and to sacrifice all in Thy path. Thou art the All-Knowing and the All-Seeing. I have no wish save to turn my steps, in my love for Thee, towards the mountains and the deserts to loudly proclaim the advent of Thy Kingdom, and to raise Thy call amidst all men. O God! Open Thou the way for this helpless one, grant Thou the remedy to this ailing one and bestow Thy healing upon this afflicted one. With burning heart and tearful eyes I supplicate Thee at Thy Threshold.

"O God! I am prepared to endure any ordeal in Thy path and desire with all my heart and soul to meet any hardship.

"O God! Protect me from tests. Thou knowest full well that I have turned away from all things and freed myself of all thoughts. I have no occupation save mention of Thee and no aspiration save serving Thee." (Translated by the Research Department of the Universal House of Justice, Bahá'í World Centre; the Research Department also kindly points out that a slightly abbreviated form of this prayer is published in *Quickeners of Mankind: Pioneering in a World Community* (Thornhill: Bahá'í Canada Publications, 1980), p. 88). The original, held in the World Centre Archives department, is dated 1905, but Lua's own copy bears the date March 28, 1903.

46. American Bahá'í living in Paris and Washington, with whom Lua often stayed. She made several pilgrimages to the Holy Land, and appears in a photograph of a group of pilgrims in 1901, together with Sigurd Russell, a young boy in whose welfare she took a kindly interest.

47. Ethel Rosenberg was in the Holy Land from 21 April to 24 December that year, and witnessed the historic table talks of 'Abdu'l-Bahá with Miss Barney which were to become *Some Answered Questions,* while Laura Dreyfus-Barney stated some years later: ". . . it was on my third trip to 'Akká that I went with Miss Rosenberg and I stayed the winter of 1904." (Letter from Laura Dreyfus-Barney to Dr. Yúnis Khán, printed in his memoirs, p. 468.)

48. See Taherzadeh, *The Covenant,* pp. 232-233.

49. Helen Ellis Cole, a Bahá'í from New York, who had visited

the Holy Land on pilgrimage. Mrs. Cole died in 1906; see the Tablet of 'Abdu'l-Bahá quoted on p. 102.

50. These letters, written in French, have been kindly translated by Ingegerd Bischoff. Later Ridwania Yazdi and her two children Negaar and Tewfik did not stay loyal to the Guardian of the Faith. I am grateful to Negaar Yazdi Arnold for information about Mrs. Yazdi.

51. O.Z. Whitehead, *Some Bahá'ís to Remember* (Oxford: George Ronald, 1983) pp. 120-121.

52. See Stockman, vol. 2, pp. 258-270; facing p. 335.

53. *In His Presence: Visits to 'Abdu'l-Bahá, Memoirs of Roy Wilhelm, Stanwood Cobb and Genevieve L. Coy* (Los Angeles: Kalimát Press, 1989), p. 29.

54. See Stockman, vol. 2, pp. 284-286.

55. The information in the previous paragraphs about Elizabeth Nourse comes from tape recorded interviews with Catherine Nourse made by Gary Morrison in 1978, now in the National Bahá'í Archives, Hawaii. I am deeply grateful to Mr. Morrison for so generously sharing the results of his research.

56. Mírzá Muhammad-'Alí, half-brother of 'Abdu'l-Bahá and Arch-breaker of the Covenant of Bahá'u'lláh, who was trying to influence Western Bahá'ís.

57. Memorial articles in *The Bahá'í World* exist for four of them: Louise Bosch: vol. XII, pp. 705-707; Mariam Haney: vol. XIV, pp. 343-346; May Maxwell: vol. VIII, pp. 631-642; Juliet Thompson: vol. XIII, pp. 862-864. Mary Lucas's pilgrim notes were published in 1905 under the title *A Brief Account of My Visit to Acca* (Chicago: Bahai Publishing Society).

58. Together with Helen Goodall she was Lua's main financial support in her work for the Cause. She was one of those who were privileged to offer hospitality to 'Abdu'l-Bahá during his journey to the United States in 1912, and was also instrumental in organizing the first Amity Conventions for racial harmony. See *The Bahá'í World*, vol. V, pp. 410-414.

59. Vol. 1, no. 1 (Mar. 1910), p. 19.

60. Vol. 1, no. 2 (Apr. 9, 1910), p. 11.

61. Cable from Lua to Joseph Hannen in Washington DC dated March 23, 1910.

62. *Bahá'í News*, vol. 1, no. 2 (Apr. 9, 1910), pp. 12-13.
63. ibid. no. 7 (July 13, 1910), pp. 10, 15.
64. *Bahá'í News*, vol. 1, no. 16 (Dec. 31, 1910), p. 2.
65. *Star of the West*, vol. II, no. 14, pp. 13-14.
66. Lua obviously did not know that it was Fareed's illicit solication of funds that had estranged Mrs. Hearst. Mrs. Hearst always loved and admired 'Abdu'l-Bahá.
67. It is not clear which battle Lua is referring to here, but the incident is probably connected with the Mexican Civil War which ended in May 1911 with the capture of Ciudad Juarez by the revolutionary liberal leader Francisco Madero.
68. Tammaddun'ul-Mulk later made an attempt to divide the friends in Teheran. He was in London during 'Abdu'l-Bahá's first visit there in September, 1911.
69. Quoted by Lua in a letter to Purley M. Blake, February 23, 1900. It is not known if these were 'Abdu'l-Bahá's exact words, although Lua was usually careful to quote accurately.
70. Hyde Dunn, 1858-1941. He and his wife Clara were Australia's "spiritual conquerors".
71. *Star of the West*, vol. II, no. 16, p. 13.
72. Nathan Rutstein, *Corinne True* (Oxford: George Ronald, 1987), p. 102.
73. *Star of the West*, vol. III, no. 5, p. 3; the photograph appears in no. 6, p. 5.
74. Juliet Thompson *The Diary of Juliet Thompson* (Los Angeles: Kalimát Press, 1983), p. 287.
75. ibid. p. 295.
76. 'Abdu'l-Bahá, *The Promulgation of Universal Peace*, (Wilmette, Illinois: Bahá'í Publishing Trust, 2nd ed. 1982), pp. 172, 176.
77. Vol. V, no. 15 (Dec. 12, 1914), pp. 227-228. This is the same passage, with minor differences, as the one quoted by Lua in her talk of July 19th in San Francisco, given later in this chapter. A similar passage may also be found in a Tablet to Mason Remey, translated at Montclair a few days after the Master's statement in New York on June 19th (*Star of the West*, vol. III, no. 7 (July 13, 1912), pp. 16-17).

78. Thompson, *Diary*, pp. 311-312.
79. ibid. pp. 317-318.
80. ibid. p. 325. A photograph of the Unity Feast in Englewood with an account of 'Abdu'l-Bahá's address can be seen in *Star of the West*, Vol. III, no. 8.
81. *Hidden Words, Words of Wisdom and Communes* (Chicago: Bahá'í Publishing Society, 1905).
82. The stenographic notes give the following reference: "Talk given by 'Abdu'l-Bahá in New York City, Wednesday morning, June 19, 1912. Translated by Dr. Ameen U. Fareed. Notes taken by E. C. M. Revised by 'Abdu'l-Bahá and Dr. Fareed at Montclair, June 25, 1912." As previously noted, this passage was later printed in *Star of the West*, vol. 5, no. 15 (Dec. 12, 1914), pp. 227-228.
83. Mariam Haney, Lua's companion in Paris at the time of the petition to the S͟háh in 1902-3. See note 42 above.
84. Balyuzi, *'Abdu'l-Bahá*, p. 400.
85. *Star of the West*, vol. IV, no. 12, p. 208.
86. The prayer enclosed was the one revealed in Haifa on March 28, 1905, and can be read on pp. 71-72 of this book.
87. Azalís, the name used at the time to denote Covenant-breakers.
88. Isabel (Soraya) Fraser Chamberlain, see *The Bahá'í World*, vol. VIII, pp. 664-5. In the event she did not accompany the Getsingers to India, but while at Ramleh she showed 'Abdu'l-Bahá her compilation *Abdul Baha on Divine Philosophy*, published by The Tudor Press in 1918.
89. See *Bahai News*, vol. 1, no. 14 (Nov. 23, 1910), p. 6, report of Washington activites by Joseph Hannen, referring to Mrs. Nategha Woodward. Joseph Hannen's own son Carl bore the masculine version of this title, "Ná̤tíq" – Eloquent.
90. One of the "Disciples of 'Abdu'l-Bahá" named by Shoghi Effendi, Joseph Hannen and his wife Pauline (Knobloch) were members of the Washington Bahá'í community and especially active in developing the Bahá'í administration and in trying to overcome racial prejudice. They were among the first to hold racially mixed meetings in their house. See *The Bahá'í World*, vol. VIII, pp. 660-661.
91. Mrs. Jean Stannard had replaced Isabel Fraser as the

Getsingers' travelling companion. In *Star of the West*, vol. 5, no. 2, p. 19, 'Abdu'l-Bahá is reported as saying, "Mrs. Stannard has dedicated her life to the Cause. She knows neither rest not comfort. She does not sit tranquilly for one moment . . . She entertains no other idea save the service of the Kingdom and the promotion of the Cause. She is assisted by the Confirmations of God." See also vol. 5, no. 1, p. 5.

92. *Star of the West*, vol. 5, no. 2, pp. 22-23.

93. Ahmad Sohrab (Ahmad-i-Isfahání), who had studied in the United States and had returned to the Holy Land. Sections of his diary were published in issues of *Star of the West* at this time. He did not remain loyal to the Covenant during the time of the Guardian.

94. The first Hindu to become a Bahá'í. See S.H. Koreshi, "Narayenrao Rangnath (Shethji) Vakil, (B.A., LL.B), 1866-1943", in *The Bahá'í World*, vol. 9, pp. 637-8.

95. Jains, followers of Jainism.

96. *Star of the West*, vol. 5, no. 3, pp. 38-39 and 41-42.

97. Khrishnamurti, chosen as a young man in 1909 by Mrs. Annie Besant, President of the Theosophical Society, as the vehicle for the expected Messiah. The tenets of the Society were a belief in the brotherhood of man and the equality of all religions. Khrishnamurti later renounced Mrs. Besant's claims for him and severed ties with the Theosophical Society in 1929.

98. The letter on file has "April 15, 1915" written on it in another hand, but the date must be wrong, as the letter is written from Bombay and in April, 1915, Lua was in the Holy Land at Abu Sinan. The letter mentions Mrs. Stannard as being in Calcutta.

99. *Star of the West*, vol. XV, pp. 102-105. Lua had sent this account to Mariam Haney.

100. Baroda was known at this time as a progressive state under the rule of its Prince, the Gaikwad of Baroda.

101. During the long struggle for Indian independence from British colonial rule, a wide spectrum of action was advocated by the different political groups, ranging from non-violent civil disobedience to direct revolutionary action, as here.

102. Siyyid Muṣṭafáy-i-Rúmí: see *The Bahá'í World*, vol. X, pp. 517-520; A. Taherzadeh, *The Revelation of Bahá'u'lláh*, vol. 4, pp. 181-182.

103. Jhalawar and Jhalarapatan are over 600 kilometres north-east of Bombay, on the way to Delhi.

104. Gang robbery. A dacoit is a member of an Indian or Burmese armed robber band. The word comes from Hindi.

105. "for whereas there is among you envying, and strife, and divisions, are ye not carnal, and walk as men?" Another indication of Lua's thorough familiarity with her Bible. This is the passage 'Abdu'l-Bahá read to her in 1899 (see p. 34 of this book).

106. See Stockman, vol. 2, p. 263.

107. Mírzá Abu'l-Faḍl, Apostle of Bahá'u'lláh, who died in Cairo on 21 January 1914. Lua's words about him are prophetic, in view of what was to happen decades later, when her own remains and those of Mírzá Abu'l-Faḍl would be interred close together in the first Bahá'í cemetery in Cairo. In the words of the Guardian, the body of "the immortal Lua . . . [was] ceremoniously and reverently transferred by Egyptian brethren representing the local Bahá'í communities to the immediate vicinity of the grave of far-famed Abu'l-Faḍl in the newly established Bahá'í cemetery in Cairo" (Shoghi Effendi, cablegram January 7, 1943, in *Messages to America* (Wilmette: Bahá'í Publishing Committee, 1947), pp. 58-59).

108. Rabindranath Tagore, Indian poet and philosopher (1861-1941).

109. Mírzá Yaḥyá, Bahá'u'lláh's half-brother, called Ṣubḥ-i-Azal, who opposed Baha'u'llah. On E.G. Browne, the British orientalist who left the pen-picture of Baha'u'llah quoted here by Lua, see M. Momen, *Selections from the Writings of E.G. Browne on the Bábí and Bahá'í Religions* (Oxford: George Ronald, 1987).

110. Arabic Hidden Words, no. 13, an early translation.

111. Possibly the 1902 publication: *Letter of 'Love' from ABDUL-BAHA ABBAS to the 'beloved' in America* (Chicago: Bahai Publishing Society).

112. Lua is quoting from Bahá'u'lláh, Arabic Hidden Words, no. 51.

113. Vol. VI, no. 6 (June 24, 1915), p. 1.
114. This must allude to the continued gossip and innuendo which followed Lua's name.
115. Under Washington DC law, established in 1860, the only ground for absolute divorce was adultery. DC Code para. 964 et seq.; 31 Stat. 1189, c. 854 (DC Code 1929, T. 14, para. 61 et seq.). The causes for which divorce *a vinculo* could be granted included adultery committed during the marriage, habitual drunkenness for a period of three years, cruelty of treatment endangering life or health, and willful desertion and abandonment for uninterrupted space of two years. The grounds for divorce *a mensa et thoro* were drunkenness, cruelty or desertion. *Hatfield v. Hatfield* (1864) 6 DC 80. These provisions remained unmodified until 1935. *Tipping v Tipping*, 82 F.2d. 828, 829 (DC App. 1936).
116. Vol. VI, no. 12, October 16, 1915.
117. Vol. VII, no. 12.
118. The function of "mother of a community" was temporary, limited to a few, and is no longer practiced in the Bahá'í community today.
119. Refers to a name given to one who was a Covenant-breaker.
120. Vol. VI, no. 12 (Oct. 16, 1915), pp. 89-96.
121. *Star of the West*, vol. VI, no. 16 (Dec. 31, 1915), p. 128.
122. ibid. vol. VI, no. 18 (Feb. 7, 1916), p. 160.
123. ibid.
124. Vol. VII, no. 19 (Mar. 2, 1917), pp. 193-94.
125. *Star of the West*, Vol. IX, no. 19 (Mar. 2, 1919), p. 228.
126. Vol. VII, no. 4 (May 17, 1916), pp. 29-30.
127. Vol. VIII, no. 9 (Aug. 20, 1917), p. 117.
128. *Star of the West*, Vol. IX, no. 19 (Mar. 2, 1919), pp. 229-230.
129. Quoted by Lua in a letter to Purley M. Blake, February 23, 1900. See p. 36 above.
130. . . . "It is an especial blessing that from among the descendants of Abraham should have come all the Prophets of the children of Israel. This is a blessing that God has granted to this descent: to Moses from His father and mother, to Christ from His mother's line; also to

413

Muḥammad and the Báb, and to all the Prophets and the Holy Manifestations of Israel. The Blessed Beauty [Bahá'u-'lláh] is also a lineal descendant of Abraham, for Abraham had other sons besides Ishmael and Isaac who in those days migrated to the lands of Persia and Afghanistan, and the Blessed Beauty is one of their descendants." ('Abdu'l-Bahá, *Some Answered Questions* (Bahá'í Publishing Trust: Wilmette, Illinois), p. 213.)

131. A sister of Bahá'u'lláh, Nisá Khánum, was married to Mírzá Majíd-i-Áhí, a secretary of the Russian Legation.

132. Although events at the conference of Badasht in 1848 were dramatic, the announcement of the birth of the Bahá'í Revelation was not made at that time. Bahá'u'lláh Himself vividly recounts that when He lay chained in the fetid darkness of the Síyáh-Chál He became conscious of His Divine Mission. He was imprisoned there from late August, 1852 for four months.

133. The declaration of Bahá'u'lláh's mission took place on the eve of His departure from Baghdád. This period, April 21 through May 2, 1863, He spent in the Najíbíyyih Garden, subsequently designated by His followers as the Garden of Riḍván. This is the holiest and most significant of all Bahá'í festivals.

414

ABOUT THE AUTHOR

Velda Piff Metelmann is an American writer and photographer who lives in Denmark. An active Bahá'í for forty-five years, she discovered the feminist cause at the age of seventy, and has spent time each year since then travelling, meeting people and sharing ideas from the Bahá'í teachings about unlocking human potential. *Lua Getsinger* is her third book.